Gairloch Pier

Photo credits

Aberdeen & Grampian Tourist Board: p 33 top, p 33 centre, p 34 top, p 34 centre, p 34 bottom, p 35 top, p 35 centre, p 35 bottom, p 37 centre, p 160 bottom, p 251 bottom

Amanda Berry: p 39 bottom, p 192 bottom

Andy & Jenny Slater: p 46 top, p 46 centre, p 46 bottom, p 203 bottom, p 204 top, p 242 bottom, p 243 top

Argyll, the Isles, Loch Lomond & Trossachs Tourist Board: p 22 top, p 22 centre, p 22 bottom, p 23 centre, p 24 top, p 24 bottom, p 25 top, p 25 bottom, p 26 top, p 26 centre, p 26 bottom, p 165 centre, p 244 bottom

Ayrshire & Arran Tourist Board & Alister G Firth: p 11 centre, p 11 bottom, p 12 top, p 155 bottom

Bill Watt: p 245 centre

Burrell Collection: p 168 bottom

Colin Palmer - www.buyimage.co.uk - contact 01279 757917: p 29 top, p 31 centre, p 32 bottom left, p 44 centre, p 45 centre, p 48 bottom

© David Lyons / Alamy: p 32 bottom right

Drummond Castle: p 180 bottom

Dumfries & Galloway Tourist Board and Great Scot: p 9 bottom, p 10 top, p 10 bottom, p 10 centre, p 11 top, p 13 bottom, p 177 bottom, p 247 top

Edinburgh & Lothians Tourist Board, Gus Campbell, Harvey Wood, Douglas Corrance & Marius Alexander: p 18 centre, p 19 top, p 19 centre right, p 19 bottom, p 184 centre, p 238 centre

Greater Glasgow & the Clyde Valley Tourist Board: p 14 top, p 14 centre, p 15 top, p 15 centre right, p 15 centre left, p 15 bottom, p 17 centre, p 206 bottom

Helen Gordon: inside front cover

Hopetoun House: p 199 top

Iain Macdonald: p 45 top

John Gordon: p 23 bottom, p 45 bottom

Kingdom of Fife Tourist Board: p 27 centre, p 53 bottom, p 55 centre, p 179 centre, p 188 bottom

Lawrence Clark: p 51 top

Mellerstain Trust: p 217 top

Perthshire Tourist Board: p 29 centre, p 29 bottom, p 32 top, p 32 centre, p 52 centre, p 190 centre

Rosemary Macleod: p 18 top, p 196 centre, p 205 bottom, p 221 bottom, p 232 bottom, p 234 top, p 239 bottom

Scottish Borders Tourist Board: p 12 centre, p 12 bottom, p 13 top, p 13 centre, p 205 top, p 235 bottom, p 237 top

Shetland Islands Tourism: p 47 top, p 47 centre, p 224 centre

Sonia & Dave Dawkins: p 19 centre left, p 38 bottom, p 39 centre, p 40 top right, p 40 centre right, p 40 bottom, p 41 top right, p 41 top left, p 41 centre right, p 41 bottom, p 156 top, p 158 bottom, p 161, p 162 centre, p 169 top, p 174 centre, p 176 centre, p 185 bottom, p 189 bottom, p 191, p 194 bottom, p 195 top, p 198 bottom, p 201 bottom, p 202 bottom, p 212 top, p 213 bottom, p 214, p 219 centre, p 222 bottom, p 223 top, p 225, p 226 bottom, p 228 top, p 230 bottom, p 240 top, p 252 bottom, inside back cover

The Highlands of Scotland Tourist Board: p 38 top, p 38 centre, p 40 top left, p 40 centre left, p 41 centre left, p 43 centre, p 183 bottom, p 204 bottom

Published by Collins

An imprint of HarperCollins Publishers

77-85 Fulham Palace Road, Hammersmith, London W6 8JB

www.collins.co.uk

Copyright © HarperCollins Publishers Ltd 2007

Collins® is a registered trademark of HarperCollins Publishers Limited

Mapping generated from Collins Bartholomew digital databases

The grid on this map is the National Grid taken from the Ordnance Survey map with the permission of the Controller of Her Majesty's Stationery Office.

Printed in Thailand

ISBN 978 0 00 720635 3   Imp 001   TC12211 / BDR

e-mail: roadcheck@harpercollins.co.uk

Discovering
Scotland
Atlas & Guide

Contents

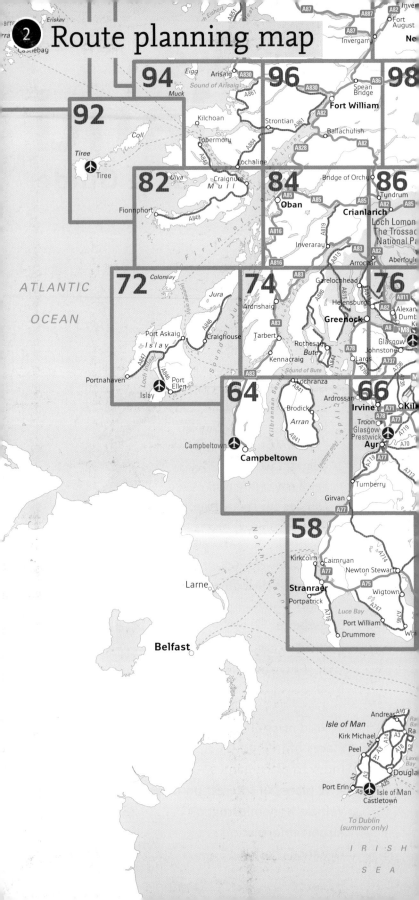

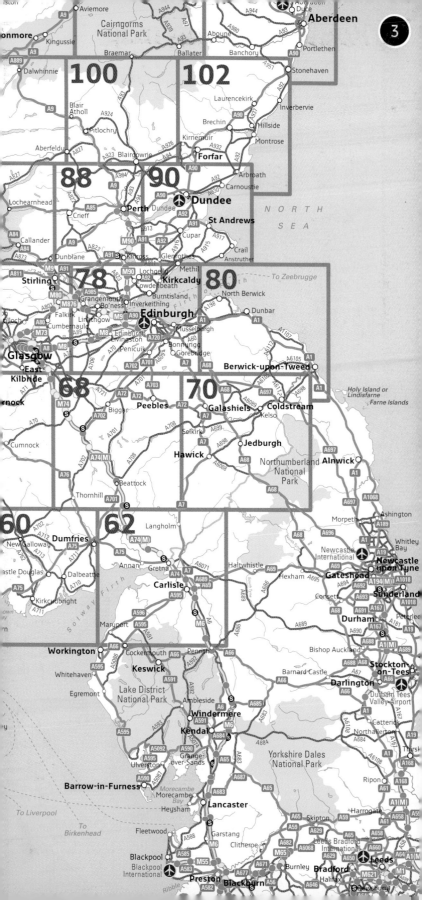

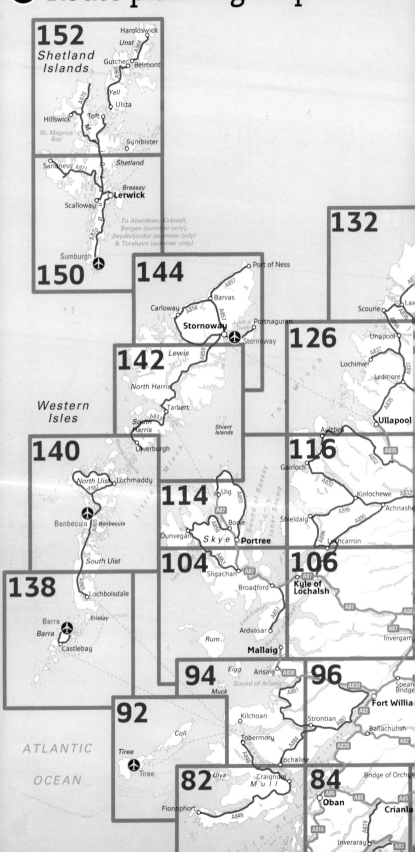

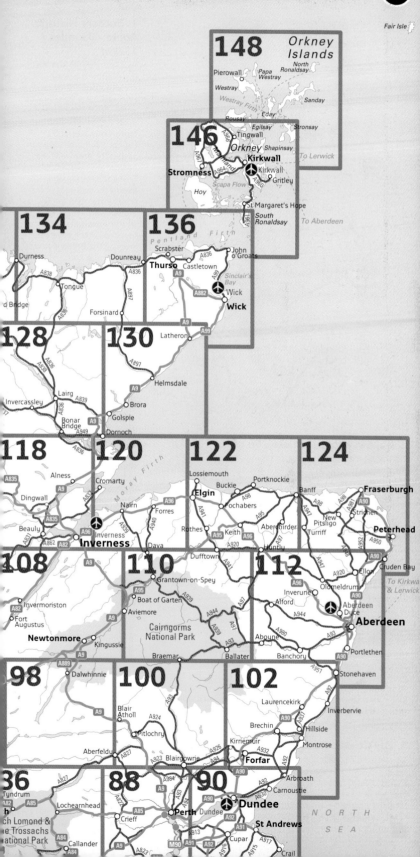

National Tourist Routes

1. Borders Historic Route - 95 miles / 152km

Forget the traffic and discover the dramatic scenery along the Borders Historic Route. Travelling in either direction between the great northern English city of Carlisle and Scotland's capital, Edinburgh, you can savour the area which has been at the heart of Scotland's history and culture for centuries and a major inspiration for Sir Walter Scott's romantic novels. Follow in the footsteps of the reivers by crossing the Border between England and Scotland at Scots Dyke and explore the royal burghs, woollen mills and market towns, historic houses and visitor centres of the Border counties. Here you'll be able to sample true hospitality, local goods, crafts and culture in an outstanding environment.

3. Clyde Valley Tourist Route - 42 miles / 67km

Turn off the M74 at Abington or Hamilton and follow the River Clyde through an area of contrasting landscapes, rich in historical interest. Attractions include the World Heritage village of New Lanark, the model industrial community founded by David Dale in the late 18th century. Also well worth a visit are the magnificently restored former hunting lodge of Chatelherault, near to Hamilton, the David Livingstone Centre at Blantyre or the cluster of fascinating museums around the market town of Biggar. If you want to try something more strenuous, you can take advantage of the extensive watersport facilities, theme park and nature trails at Strathclyde Country Park.

2. Galloway Tourist Route - 96 miles / 154km

This route, stretching from Gretna to Ayr, links the Robert Burns attractions in both Dumfries and Ayr. En route, it gives the visitor an introduction to the relatively unfamiliar countryside of the Galloway Forest Park and the industrial heritage of the Doon Valley. Seek out the Old Blacksmith's Shop at Gretna Green, the award-winning Robert Burns Centre and Bridge House Museum in Dumfries, or the Carsphain Heritage Centre. Enjoy the peace and tranquillity of colourful Threave Gardens, or ponder over the bloody history of Threave Castle, ancient stronghold of the "Black Douglas".

4. Forth Valley Tourist Route - 39 miles / 62km

This short route from Edinburgh to Stirling takes in the attractive old burgh of South Queensferry, which is dominated by the mighty Forth road and rail bridges. Nearby are Dalmeny House and the elegant Hopetoun House, one of Scotland's finest Adams' mansions. Alternatively, take a trip on the Union Canal from Ratho or delve in to the Lothians clay mining heritage. You can also visit the bustling town of Falkirk, with its own impressive mansion, Callender House and feat of 21st-century engineering, the Falkirk Wheel. Harking back to an earlier age, the Bo'ness and Kinneil Steam railway will feed your nostalgia with trips on its steam trains between Bo'ness and Birkhill.

5. Fife Coastal Route - 85 miles / 136km

Between the Firths of Forth and Tay lies the historic Kingdom of Fife. Best known is St Andrews, "Home of Golf" and seat of Scotland's oldest university. Just to the south of St Andrews are the picturesque villages of the East Neuk with their distinctive pantiled roofs and unspoilt beaches. More golden sands can be enjoyed at Burntisland and Aberdour. Less than 30 minutes from Scotland's modern capital is the country's ancient capital, Dunfermline, "The Westminster of the North" and final resting place of Robert the Bruce. Don't miss Deep Sea World at North Queensferry where the longest underwater safari will take you exploring far beneath the waves. Further west is 16th century Culross, an outstanding example of a 16th century town.

6. Argyll Coastal Route - 149 miles / 238km

From Tarbet on the bonny banks of Loch Lomond, climb steadily to a famous beauty spot that goes by the apt name of Rest and be Thankful. Descend to Inveraray and continue to follow the shores of Loch Fyne to Lochgilphead. Turning north, pass the lovely Crinan Canal and proceed to the bustling holiday town of Oban. Here there is an exceptionally fine view across the Firth of Lorn and the Sound of Mull to the Inner Hebrides. From Oban cross the impressive Connel Bridge and journey on up through Ballachulish to Fort William, which nestles at the foot of Ben Nevis.

7. Perthshire Tourist Route - 45 miles / 72km

Begins just north of Dunblane and takes you to Ballinluig near Pitlochry. A very attractive alternative to the main A9, the route runs through fertile, rolling farmland before arriving at the pleasant hillside town of Crieff. Thereafter, the lush, cultivated landscape changes dramatically and gives way to the rugged splendour of the Sma' Glen with its connections to Ossian and Bonnie Prince Charlie. Descend from here to the holiday centre of Aberfeldy and skirt the fast flowing River Tay on the A827, rejoining the A9 near Pitlochry.

8. Deeside Tourist Route - 107 miles / 171km

From the 'Fair City' of Perth all the way north to Aberdeen. The area around Blairgowrie has long been associated with soft-fruit-growing, and Blairgowrie itself is a popular touring base. Thereafter, the Highland landscape takes over as the route climbs 2182 feet (665 metres) on the A93, Britain's highest main road. Enjoy spectacular mountain views in every direction as you pass through Glen Shee before descending to Braemar. As you drive through Royal Deeside, you will pass Balmoral Castle, the summer residence of the Royal Family since the days of . Queen Victoria. Progress through the delightful villages of Ballater, Aboyne and Banchory before finally reaching Aberdeen, the Granite City.

9. Angus Coastal Route - 58 miles / 93km

Begins in the City of Discovery, Dundee, with its fascinating industrial heritage and maritime traditions and takes you north to Aberdeen, a stunning city of glittering granite. Along the way you will discover a spectacular coastline with picturesque seaside resorts - Broughty Ferry, Monifieth, Carnoustie, Arbroath, Montrose, Inverbervie, Stonehaven - as well as sandy beaches, championship golf courses, nature reserves, country parks and a fertile countryside reaching inland through the Mearns and the Vale of Strathmore to the scenic splendour of the Angus Glens and the Grampians.

10. Highland Tourist Route - 118 miles/189km

From Aberdeen to Inverness. On the way you can visit the Grampian Transport Museum at Alford. Continue through the lovely valley of Upper Donside and on up the heather-clad slopes of the Lecht to Tomintoul in the fringes of the Cairngorms. Here you will find yourself at the heart of whisky country. Take a guided tour round one of the many distilleries and your passengers can enjoy a complimentary 'wee dram' - which should set them up for the last lap through Grantown-on-Spey, a popular salmon-fishing centre and then on to the city of Inverness, the capital of the Highlands.

11. Moray Firth Route - 80 miles / 128km

A semi-circle around three of the most beautiful inlets on the east coast of Britain - the Beauly, Cromarty and Dornoch Firths - as it heads north from the City of Inverness into the heart of the northern Highlands. On the way you can enjoy wonderful scenery, seals and clan history at Foulis Ferry, salmon leaping at Shin Falls, whisky being made at Glen Ord and Highland wine at Moniack Castle. You can walk to the Fyrish monument folly, visit Beauly Priory or learn about the archaeology of the north at Ferrycroft, Lairg - or you can enjoy shopping for crafts and woollens in the towns and villages along the route.

12 . North & West Highlands Route - 140 miles / 225km

This route boasts some of the most magnificent scenery in Europe - wild mountains and lochs, foaming salmon rivers, rugged coastlines with mighty sea cliffs and secluded sandy bays, isolated crofts and large farms, small fishing villages and bustling towns. Starting at the thriving fishing village of Ullapool, the route winds its way north through magnificent mountain country as it makes for Durness in the north-west corner of Scotland. From Durness, the route heads east through gradually softening scenery to John o'Groats, taking you from one end of Scotland's north coast to the other.

North & West Highlands Route into Ullapool

Regions of Scotland

From the grassy hills of the Borders to the desolate Cuillin Ridge of Skye via the bustling streets of Glasgow, the landscape of Scotland is breathtaking in its variety.

Lonely glens, sparkling lochs and ever-changing skies give the land a character, which is reflected in the qualities of the Scottish people. Tough and self-reliant they have produced some of Britain's finest soldiers, its boldest explorers and most astute industrialists.

For general tourist information about Scotland the VisitScotland website is a good starting point. It's the official website of the tourist board and can be found at www.visitscotland.com. Alternatively contact VisitScotland on 0845 2255121 for help with planning your break and booking accommodation.

We have split Scotland into eight regions based upon the regions used by the tourist board. Read the following pages to get a flavour of the landscape and character of each region. For details of specific tourist attractions to visit use the directory located towards the back of this guide. Attractions are listed in alphabetical order and all have a map reference to link them to the map section.

South of Scotland

The Scottish Borders is an area of tranquil villages and textile towns, with a soft rolling landscape and a rugged coastline.

Visitors can enjoy a wide range of attractions, from craft workshops to magnificent historic houses and the great Border abbeys.

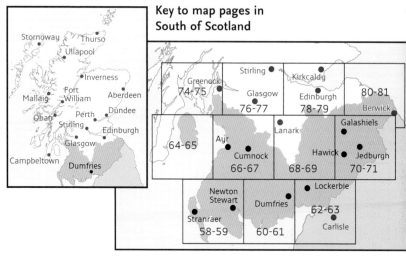

Key to map pages in South of Scotland

Tourist board regions for the South of Scotland:
Ayrshire & Arran www.ayrshire-arran.com
Dumfries & Galloway www.visitdumfriesandgalloway.co.uk
Scottish Borders www.scot-borders.co.uk

Gretna Green

Sited just across the border from England, Gretna Green is famed as the location of runaway marriages in former times. The tradition is explained at the Blacksmith's Shop centre, where marriage ceremonies are still performed at the anvil.

Dumfries & Galloway

The beautiful natural surroundings of Dumfries and Galloway – lochs and craggy hills, rugged cliffs and long sandy beaches, are ideal for fishing, golfing, walking and cycling. There is plenty to entertain the visitor, including birdwatching and a large number of beautiful gardens.

Galloway Forest Park

Located north of Newton Stewart in Dumfries & Galloway and covering around 300 square miles (770 sq km), Galloway Forest Park is Britains largest forest park. The Park contains some of the most natural ancient woodland in Scotland, dramatic scenery and an abundance of wildlife. It is a great place for bike riding as there are over 200 miles (320km) of cycle trails.

The Solway Coast

The Solway Firth is a shallow arm of the Irish Sea between the coasts of Cumbria in England and Dumfries & Galloway in Scotland. Fringed by tidal marshes, much of the coast is remote and a haven for bird-life. Follow the coast using the Solway Coast Heritage Trail, a 190 mile (306km) sign-posted route from Annan to the Mull of Galloway. Along the way are historic monuments, castles, abbeys and gardens as well as the pretty harbours of coastal towns and villages.

Rough Firth, an inlet of the Solway Firth

Midsteeple & fountain, Dumfries

Dumfries

Population 32,136. Known as the 'Queen of the South', Dumfries is a bustling town on the River Nith. It makes a good base to explore the hills, forests and streams of Nithsdale to the north and the cliff tops, nature reserves and sandy beaches of the Solway coast to the south. Robert Burns lived in the town from 1791 until his death in 1796 and there are several associated attractions to see including Burns House where he lived, the award-winning Robert Burns Centre and his family mausoleum in the graveyard at St Michaels Kirk.

Queen's Way

Queen's Way Tourist Route

Follow the A712 through the Galloway Hills from New Galloway at the head of Loch Ken south west to Newton Stewart. En route learn about forest wildlife at the Clatteringshaws Visitor Centre. Linked to the Queen's Way is the 10 mile (16km) Raider's Road, a forest drive from Mossdale north west to Clatteringshaws. It follows the route of a drove road once used by reivers to smuggle stolen cattle.

Newton Stewart

Population: 3673. The market town of Newton Stewart is a popular resort and fishing centre on the River Cree. It is a good base for a walking holiday in the Galloway Forest Park.

Glen Trool, Galloway Forest Park

The Rinns of Galloway

This 28 mile (45km) long anvil shaped peninsula is at the western end of the Solway coast. Stranraer (population: 11,348) is the main town and port for car ferry services to Northern Ireland. To the south west Portpatrick is a quieter resort.

The Mull of Galloway is Scotland's most southerly point.

Mull of Galloway

Ayrshire & Arran

This area offers all the contrasts of mainland and island life. The island of Arran has been a playground for generations of outdoor enthusiasts. It is easily reached by ferry from Ardrossan. On the mainland visitors can explore the area's industrial history, numerous golf courses and enjoy the heritage of Robert Burns, Scotland's most famous poet.

Ayrshire Golf

Prestwick Golf Club was the venue for the first British Open Championship in 1860 and Ayrshire has since become known as the 'home of the Open'. The area is now best known for the two prestigious championship courses at Troon and Turnberry although there are many other scenic links and parkland courses in the area to test all abilities.

Burns Cottage, Alloway

The Ayrshire Coast

Sailing is popular in the sheltered waters of the Firth of Clyde. There are marinas and sailing clubs at Troon, Ardrossan and Largs. Sea fishing is also popular with boat trips providing the opportunity to catch haddock, cod, conger and skate.

Robert Burns

Ayrshire is probably best known as the birthplace and early home of the world renowned poet Robert Burns. The life and works of Scotland's most famous bard are celebrated annually at Burns Night Suppers on 25th January. He was born into a poor background in the village of Alloway in 1759 and much of his life was spent in a struggle against poverty. Many of the places in 'Tam o'Shanter', such as Alloway Churchyard and the Brig o'Doon can be visited and there is a Burns Heritage Trail linking all sites with a connection to his life and works.

Isle of Arran

Often called 'Scotland in Miniature', the Isle of Arran offers a diversity of terrain and holiday experiences for the visitor. In the north the island is mountainous and unspoilt, peaking with Goat Fell at 2866ft (873m). The area offers a challenge to hillwalkers, climbers and cyclists. The milder south is more fertile and forested, with seaside resorts and impressive Bronze Age standing stone circles. The island is also known for its locally produced food and drink and the 'taste of Arran' includes cheeses, smoked fish, traditional ice cream and speciality ales from the Arran Brewery as well as whisky from Scotland's newest distillery.

Glen Sannox, Isle of Arran

12 South of Scotland

Irvine

Population: 32,988. Irvine was once the main port serving Glasgow until the 18th century when the Forth of Clyde was deepened and the Port of Glasgow developed. Since then it has fallen into decline and no longer operates as a commercial port. Designated one of five Scottish New Towns in 1966, Irvine is the only one which was developed around an existing town of substantial size.

Explore the country's maritime history, and in particular the story of Clydeside shipping, at the Scottish Maritime Museum.

Fishing at Irvine Beach

Berwickshire Coast

The east coast of the Borders region offers a range of scenery from the historic town and harbour of Eyemouth and the coves and small fishing villages of St Abbs, Burnmouth and Coldingham to the high cliffs and seabird colonies of St Abb's Head. Clear waters also make this a popular area for scuba divers.

Coldingham beach

Ayr

Population: 47,962. Ayr is the commercial and administrative centre of the area, as well as being the largest town on the Firth of Clyde coast. It has its origins around a castle built in 1197 by William I, of which there are no remains and was the site of the first Scottish Parliament in 1315 held by Robert the Bruce. Of strategic importance as a crossing point of the River Ayr, the 'Auld Brig' dates from 1470 and is still standing as is the 'New Brig', which was a replacement for the original 'New Brig' which was destroyed in floods in the 1870s. Ayr became a resort in the 19th century and continues to attract visitors to its long sandy beach, racecourse and numerous golf courses.

Cheviot Hills

Running across the northern part of the Northumberland National Park, the Cheviot Hills straddle the Scotland/England border and include vast areas of moorland, forest and sheep pasture. The four highest points are in England, the highest being The Cheviot at 2673ft (815m). Windy Gyle sits on the border and is the highest point of the range in Scotland at 2032ft (619m). The hardy breed of white faced Cheviot sheep originated here in the 14th century and is now found worldwide.

Cheviot Hills

Scott's View towards the Eildon Hills

Eildon Hills

South of Melrose are the three conspicuous peaks of the Eildon Hills. The middle peak rises to 1384ft (422m) and a way-marked route leads to the summit where a view indicator adds detail to the fine views available of the surrounding hills on a clear day.

Tweeddale

The Tweeddale valley runs north east, carrying the River Tweed from its source to the confluence with Lyne Water 3 miles (4km) west of Peebles. A roadside sign marks the place at Tweed's Well where the river starts its 97 mile (156 km) journey to the sea. The first part of that journey passes through a wide and peaceful glen to the pretty village of Tweedsmuir.

Fishing on the River Tweed

Border Towns

The peace and tranquility of the Borders that visitors find so attractive belies a turbulent past. There were times when Border people lived under constant threat of invasion and this history has left a legacy of castles, abbeys and great country houses to explore. Melrose, Jedburgh and Kelso are all abbey towns that are best explored on foot. Hawick (population 15,812), famous for knitwear and rugby, is the largest of the Border towns and is a frequent winner of national floral awards.

Kelso

Population: 5989. Kelso is an historic Borders market town, centred around a large Georgian square and attractively sited at the confluence of the Rivers Tweed and Teviot. West of the town, in parkland overlooking the Tweed, lies the impressive Castle of Floors.

Selkirk

Population: 5922. The ancient Royal Burgh of Selkirk was once a prosperous textile town. Many of the old stone woollen mills are no longer working, but there are a number of specialist tweed shops in the town. Selkirk also has a strong association with Sir Walter Scott which is explained at the Sir Walter Scott's courtroom in the town centre.

Peebles

Population: 7065. Peebles is a pleasant Borders town in an attractive setting on the banks of the River Tweed. It is surrounded by hills and is a popular area for walking and cycling. The 90 mile (145km) Tweed Cycleway from Biggar to Berwick-on-Tweed passes nearby.

Moffat

Population 2342. Moffat was fashionable as a spa town in the 18th century and is still popular as a touring base. Its wide High Street is home to the Moffat Ram, built in 1875 and now the centrepiece and symbol of the town. It sits on top of the sandstone Colvin Fountain which was restored to full working order in 2004. Local folklore has it that the sculptor, William Brodie, took his own life after casting the bronze ram without ears.

The Moffat Ram

14 Glasgow & the Clyde Valley

Glasgow is Scotland's largest city and the commercial and industrial capital of the west of Scotland. It is also one of Europe's great cultural destinations, with award-winning museums and galleries and a fine architectural heritage.

It is the UK's biggest retail centre outside London, with the top names in fashion and design as well as all the high street outlets. The Clyde Valley is a complete contrast, with dramatic ruined castles, industrial heritage and country parks.

Cora Linn Falls, Falls of Clyde

Lowther Hills

This range of hills between the valleys of the Rivers' Nith and Annan offer a wild landscape of tightly clustered peaks, the highest is Green Lowther at 2403ft (732m). The area once known as 'God's Treasure House' was famed for its silver, gold and lead deposits and many of the stones used in the Scottish crown jewels were mined here.

Biggar

This handsome old market town has a rich and varied history. The town received its Royal Charter in 1451 and still retains its medieval layout although most of the prominent buildings are Victorian. With many attractions in the town itself Biggar is also a good base for exploring the Scottish Lowlands.

River Clyde

The winding course of the River Clyde runs from the rolling hills of Lanarkshire through the towns and villages of the 'Garden Valley', through Glasgow and on to the sea via the Firth of Clyde. The Clyde became Glasgow's 'gateway to the Americas' when it was dredged, deepened and widened in the 18th century to make it navigable to the heart of the city. Glasgow consequently prospered and by the 19th century it was the greatest shipbuilding centre in the world.

Lanark

Standing high above the River Clyde the rooftops of the market town of Lanark are visible for miles around. The world's oldest surviving bell, cast in 1130, can be found in the Georgian church of St Nicholas. Just a mile south of the town is the village of New Lanark, a World Heritage Site, an early 19th century model of improved industrial communities.

Tourist board website for Glasgow & the Cylde Valley: www.seeglasgow.com

Key to map pages in Glasgow & the Clyde Valley

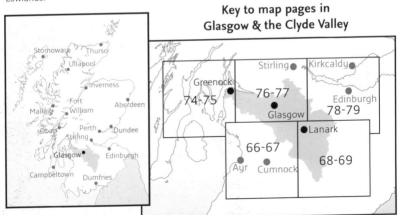

Clyde Coast

Charles Rennie Mackintosh

Architect, designer and artist Charles Rennie Mackintosh was born in Glasgow in 1868 and his quirky, linear and geometric designs can be seen all over the city. He studied at the Glasgow School of Art before winning a competition to design their new building which is now considered to be one of his finest works. The Lighthouse, which now houses the Mackintosh Interpretive Centre, the Scotland Street School and House for an Art Lover are all Mackintosh designs to be found around the city, although the House for an Art Lover was only built in 1996. Mackintosh was interested in all aspects of design. When working on the Willow Tea Rooms he designed everything from the building itself to the teaspoons and menu cards.

Clyde Auditorium, Scottish Exhibition & Conference Centre

Glasgow parks & gardens

Glasgow has over 70 public parks, many of them well worth a visit. Glasgow Green, the oldest public park in Britain, has a special place in the hearts of Glaswegians. In the west end, straddling the banks of the River Kelvin, the trees, slopes and statues of Kelvingrove Park are overlooked by the gothic towers of the University. On the south side of the city there is Pollok Park, home to the Burrell Collection.
The Botanic Gardens are to the west of the city and their 42 acres (17ha) are filled with natural attractions, including the celebrated Kibble Palace glasshouse with its fabulous tree ferns, exotic plants and white marble Victorian statues.

Firth of Clyde

15

The banks of the Clyde are scattered with remnants of the shipbuilding industry which once made this area a great industrial base. The first dock on the Clyde opened in Greenock in 1711. There are spectacular views across the Clyde from many of the small towns along the coast.

Paisley

This 12th century monastic settlement gave its name to the well known swirling teardrop or pine cone pattern called the Paisley Pattern after the town became the lead manufacturer of the imitation Kashmiri shawls which used the design.

Paisley Abbey

Architectural heritage

The architectural heritage of Glasgow is renowned worldwide. The city is home to some of Europe's finest Victorian architecture. Centuries of wealth and achievement have left a legacy of magnificent civic architecture, elegant residential crescents and an industrial heritage to be proud of.

University of Glasgow from Kelvingrove Park

City of Glasgow

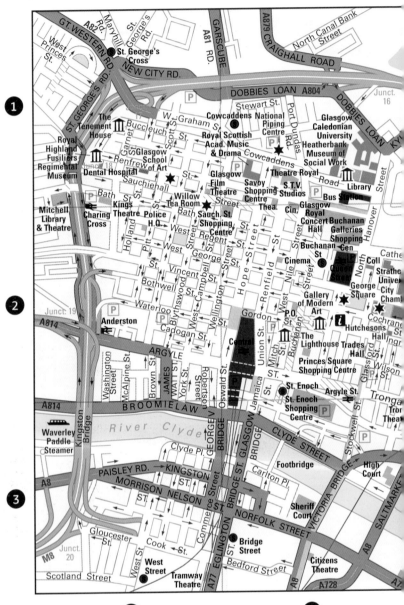

Population: 662,954. On the River Clyde 41 miles (66km) west of Edinburgh, Glasgow is Scotland's largest city. The city grew in importance from the 12th century, becoming a major industrial port during the industrial revolution. Following the decline of the shipbuilding industry in the 1930s Glasgow has restyled itself as a city of culture (European City of Culture 1990 and City of Architecture and Design 1999). Its many museums, galleries and fine buildings are testament to this. Scotland's largest tourist attraction, The Burrell Collection, has more than 8000 objects displayed in an award winning gallery in Pollok Country Park. The 'Oxford Street' of Glasgow is Sauchiehall Street which together with Buchanan Street, the Buchanan Galleries, Argyle Street, Princes Square and the St Enoch Centre form the main, mostly pedestrianised shopping area. The city has many theatres and concert halls where productions include opera, drama, pop, pantomime and musicals.

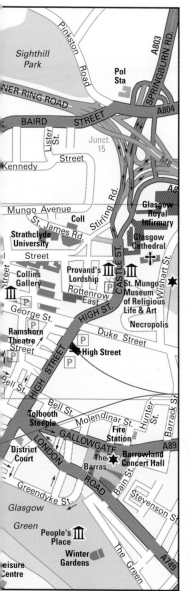

Useful information

Police
Strathclyde Police HQ
173 Pitt Street,
G2 4JS
0141 532 2000

Hospital A & E
Western Infirmary
Dumbarton Road,
G11 6NT
0141 211 2000

City centre Post Office
47 St. Vincent Street,
G2 5QX

Bus Station
Buchanan Bus Station
Killermont Street,
G2 3NP

Railway Stations
- Central Station
Gordon Street, G1 3SL
- Queen Street Station
North Hanover Street,
G1 2AF

Tourist Information Centre
11 George Square
G2 1DY
0141 204 4400

City website
www.glasgow.gov.uk

City Chambers

Edinburgh & Lothians

Edinburgh is one of the most attractive and historic cities in Europe. The city has preserved its heritage and embraced the new. It is a vibrant cultural, shopping and business centre with a huge amount to offer the visitor.

The castle dominates the city skyline while the tall buildings and narrow streets of the Old Town cluster along the slope stretching to the east of the crag. In striking contrast, and just five minutes walk away, is the Georgian elegance of the 18th century New Town. The broad streets here include Princes Street, the main shopping thoroughfare of the city.

Edinburgh Castle

Edinburgh's Royal Mile

Sloping gently from the castle to the Palace of Holyroodhouse the Royal Mile is a crowded, historic and romantic jumble of buildings. For a long time the Royal Mile was home to the poor and many of the old streets in which they lived remain today. It is now a fashionable area with many fine restored buildings and attractions.

Edinburgh Military Tattoo

Festivals

Edinburgh's annual festivals are acclaimed worldwide - the Edinburgh International Festival, the Festival Fringe, The Edinburgh Military Tattoo, the Edinburgh Hogmanay and the International Jazz and Blues, Film and Book Festivals present a wide range of events for the visitor.

Tourist board website for Edinburgh & Lothians: www.edinburgh.org

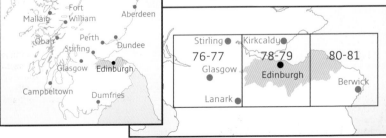

Key to map pages in Edinburgh & Lothians

Stirling ●	Kirkcaldy ●	
76-77	**78-79**	**80-81**
Glasgow ●	Edinburgh ●	
Lanark ●		Berwick ●

National collections

Edinburgh is the home of many of Scotland's national art and museum collections - the Scottish National Portrait Gallery, The National Gallery of Scotland and the Museum of Scotland.

Forth Rail Bridge

This remarkable cantilever structure is universally recognised as an engineering marvel. Its span of 1,710 feet (521m) is the largest of any railway bridge in Britain.

Firth of Forth

The estuary of the River Forth widens out into the sea between Fife Ness and North Berwick. At its narrowest point of one mile (2km) it is spanned by the Forth road and railway bridges.

Forth Rail Bridge

Musselburgh

Population: 20,630. This historic town on the outskirts of Edinburgh at the mouth of the River Esk was once an important trading and fishing port. It also has strong sporting connections with Scotland's oldest racecourse and golf course.

The Lothians

The Lothians surround Edinburgh with country houses and ruined castles and offer space for outdoor activities as well as a variety of nature and heritage-based attractions. Just south of Edinburgh in Midlothian is the medieval Rosslyn Chapel which has Gothic stone carvings and was featured in the Hollywood film 'The Da Vinci Code'.

North Berwick

Population: 5687. This small town on the Firth of Forth is one of Scotland's most popular seaside resorts. There are outstanding beaches and not far offshore the small basalt island of Bass Rock is the haunt of seabirds.

Bass Rock

Lammermuir Hills

The flat-topped hills of Lammermuir are popular with walkers and there is a network of ancient pathways in all directions. The summit of the Lammermuir range is Meikle Says Law at 1755ft (535m).

Pentland Hills

This range of grassy hills rises steeply from the southern fringe of Edinburgh and stretches 16 miles (26km) towards Carnwath in South Lanarkshire. The summit is Scald Law at 1898ft (579m). The area provides some delightful hill walking with splendid views towards Edinburgh and beyond to the Pentland Firth.

Paragliding in the Pentland Hills

City of Edinburgh

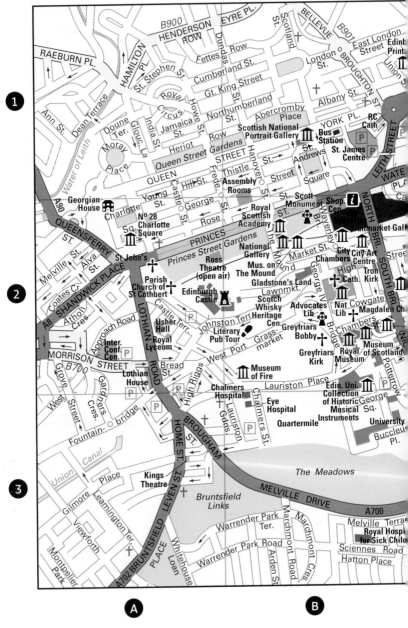

Royal Mile

Places of interest on the Royal Mile have
an index reference of D4

Population: 401,910. Scotland's historic capital is built on a range of rocky crags and extinct volcanoes. It is the administrative, financial and legal centre of Scotland. Its medieval castle, perched high on Castle Rock, was one of the main seats of the Royal Court. At the other end of the Royal Mile is the Palace of Holyroodhouse, the chief royal residence of Scotland.

Index to street names

Useful information

Police
Lothian and Borders Police
HQ Fettes Avenue, EH4 1RB
0131 311 3131

Hospital A & E
Royal Infirmary of Edinburgh
51 Little France Crescent,
Old Dalkeith Road,
EH16 4SA
0131 536 1000

Main Post Office
8–10 St. James Centre
EH1 3SR

Railway Station
Waverley Station
North Bridge EH1

Bus Station
St. Andrews Square
EH1 3DS

Tourist Information Centre
3 Princes Street
Edinburgh
EH2 2QP

City website
www.edinburgh.gov.uk

From the islands of Coll and Tiree, lying in the Hebridean Sea to the west, to the green slopes of the Ochil Hills east of Stirling, this area of Scotland straddles Highland and Lowland.

Peaceful glens, shapely peaks and clear blue lochs contrast vividly with the gentle hills and historic towns of the lowlands. Visit Stirling, which played a leading role in Scotland's past, or travel by ferry from Oban to the Isle of Mull, and on to Iona, cradle of Scottish Christianity.

West coast islands

The western coast is indented with inlets and lochs formed by glaciers thousands of years ago. The larger islands of Coll, Tiree, Mull, Colonsay, Jura and Islay each have their own character though all are part of the Inner Hebrides. Oban is the 'Gateway to the Isles' with ferries to many of the islands. Wildlife tours and cruises are on offer to experience the diverse natural wonders of the area.

St. Martin's Cross, Iona Abbey

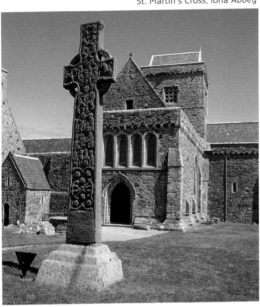

Mull & Iona

Mull is the second largest, and most accessible, island in the Hebrides. It can be a place for peace and relaxation, the venue for a sporting holiday or a wilderness for spotting wildlife. Inland the mountains reach their highest point of 3169 ft (966m) at the 'big mountain' Ben More, the only Munro in the Hebrides outside of Skye. Further west, one mile (2km) off the Ross of Mull, lies Iona, the birthplace of Christianity in Scotland and a centre of great religious importance for three millennia.

Stag on Jura

Colonsay

Colonsay lies 8 miles (13km) west of Jura in the Inner Hebrides. Its remoteness has contributed to the tranquillity and unspoilt natural beauty so attractive to visitors. Diverse wildlife includes seabirds, seals, otters and a colony of wild goats which have reputedly descended from Spanish stock on a shipwrecked Armada vessel. The rocky coastline is interspersed with sandy beaches, the most well known being the one mile (1.5km) long golden sands of Kiloran Bay.

Coll & Tiree

The low-lying islands of Coll and Tiree can be bleak and windswept, but the climate is mild and the islands hold the highest sunshine records for Scotland. Beaches are unspoilt and the Atlantic waves of Tiree are so popular with windsurfers that each October the island hosts the Tiree Wave Classic, a world championship windsurfing event. The islands are reached by ferries running from Oban.

Coll

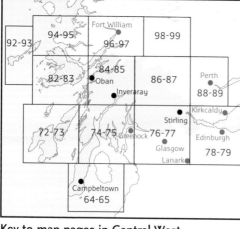

Key to map pages in Central West

Tourist board website for Central West Scotland: Argyll, The Isles, Loch Lomond, Stirling & The Trossachs
www.visitscottishheartlands.com

Kyles of Bute

Bute

An island of heather hills and flat farmland, Bute is separated from mainland Argyll by the narrow channel of the Kyles of Bute. The northern hills of Bute are most popular with walkers as they offer panoramic views. The island's capital is Rothesay which still has many remains of its Victorian heritage, including the fully functional Gents lavatories on the pier. Unfortunately the Ladies' do not have the same historical interest. It is known for its winter gardens and colourful promenade flower displays in summer.

Islay

The southernmost of the Inner Hebridean Islands, Islay has more hours of sunshine a year than anywhere else in Britain.

Tobermory

Population: 700. Built as a fishing village in the late 18th century, Tobermory is now the main town of Mull. Surrounded by wooded hills and with its brightly coloured buildings along the pier, it is an attractive place to visit or stay.

Tobermory, Mull

Islay whisky

The peaty taste of the single-malt Islay whiskies is both famous and distinctive. The southern distilleries – Laphroaig, Lagavulin and Ardbeg – use heavily peated malt to produce the strongest flavoured whiskies. The northern Islay whiskies are lighter flavoured. All eight of the island's distilleries conduct guided tours.

Port Righ, Mull of Kintyre

Kintyre

Connected by only a very narrow isthmus of land at Tarbert, the 40 mile (64km) long peninsula of Kintyre is almost an island. The often windswept west coast has many beautiful beaches such as Machrihanish and there are fine views across to the islands of Jura, Islay and Gigha. The narrow east coast road crosses river gorges through moorland and forest with views across Kilbrannan Sound to the mountains of Arran.

Mull of Kintyre

Follow the spectacular road down to the headland at the south west end of Kintyre. From the lighthouse it is only 12 miles (19km) across the water to Ireland. The Mull of Kintyre was popularised by the Paul McCartney & Denny Laine song in 1977.

Lorn

Bounded by Loch Awe, Loch Etive and the Firth of Lorn is the ancient district of Lorn. Loch Etive is a sea loch extending 18 miles (29km) from the foot of Glen Etive to the Firth of Lorn. It is known as one of Scotland's most beautiful lochs. A road bridge spans the loch near its mouth at Connel and beneath the bridge are the Falls of Lora, Europe's only seawater rapids. Loch Etive is fed by the 24 mile (39km) long Loch Awe, the longest freshwater loch in Scotland.

Campbeltown

Population: 5722. Set in a sheltered bay, Campbeltown is the chief town and port of Kintyre. The town was a prosperous fishing port in the 1800s. It was also once a major centre for whisky distilling although today Springbank is the only distillery remaining in production from a former total of 34 in the area.

Kilmartin Valley

This western coast glen is Scotland's richest prehistoric landscape. There are over 150 ancient sites including Bronze Age burial chambers, cup and ring marks, standing stones and sculptured stones. Visit the Kilmartin House Museum of Ancient Culture for an interpretation of their history.

Oban Harbour

Oban

Population: 8500. The bustling Victorian resort of Oban, the 'capital of the West Highlands', is Scotland's most popular west-coast holiday town. From this 'Gateway to the Isles' ferries depart for Barra, Coll, Colonsay, Islay, Kerrera, Lismore, Mull, South Uist and Tiree. It is an ideal base for exploring the mountains and glens inland. The calendar of Oban includes the start of the Scottish Islands Peaks Race, the West Highland Week yachting event and the Argyllshire Highland Gathering.

Dumbarton

Population: 21,962. At the confluence of the River Leven and the River Clyde, Dumbarton was once important as a centre for engineering and shipbuilding. The Cutty Sark was built here in 1869. An ancient castle overlooks the town.

Dunoon

Population: 9038. Sited on the Firth of Clyde, Dunoon is the main resort on the Cowal peninsula. There are ferry services to Gourock and pleasure cruises to enjoy the coastal scenery. Dunoon is also an ideal base for exploring the network of walking trails in the nearby Argyll Forest Park.

Helensburgh

Population: 15,852. On the northern shore of the Firth of Clyde is the Georgian town of Helensburgh. It was a favourite seaside resort for the people of Glasgow in the 18th century and is still a noted yachting centre with a popular promenade, pier and parks. The Waverley paddle steamer stops at Helensburgh on its route along the Firth of Clyde. The town is also the birthplace of J.L. Baird (1888 – 1946), the inventor of television.

Balmaha, Loch Lomond

Loch Lomond

Loch Lomond is Britain's largest stretch of inland water. It extends 24 miles (39 km) from Ardlui in the north, to Balloch in the south. Although generally narrow, the loch widens towards the south, where there are a number of wooded islands.

History & heritage

To the east are many sites of historical significance to Scotland, particularly during Scotland's struggle to retain independence. Stirling Castle is famous as a focus point of Scottish history but the region also holds associations with Rob Roy in the highland frontier country of the Trossachs and Robert the Bruce at the battle site of Bannockburn.

Callander

Population: 2622. Callander is the main tourist base for the Trossachs. The Rob Roy & Trossachs Visitor Centre explains the life of the notorious outlaw and folk hero, Robert MacGregor (1671–1734) who is famed for raiding rich Lowland properties to feed the Clan Gregor.

View from Stirling Castle

Stirling

Population: 30,515. This historic town sits on a volcanic rocky outcrop above the banks of the River Forth. The town grew up around the castle, and the original 16th century town walls are still visible today. There are many sites of interest within the town – the medieval castle, Cambuskenneth Abbey, Argyll's Lodging, Mar's Wark and Stirling Old Bridge. Stirling means 'Place of Strife' and it has been the site of many battles over the centuries. Two miles (3.2km) south of the town one of the most famous battles in Scottish history is explained at the Bannockburn Heritage Centre.

Central West Scotland

Falkirk

Population: 35,610. Falkirk once marked the northernmost frontier of the Roman Empire. Several sections of the Antonine Wall fortification are still visible in the town and the best of these is the ditch of Watling Lodge.

Breadalbane

The area of the Grampian Mountains between Glen Lyon and Strathearn is known as Breadalbane, meaning the 'high country of Scotland' in Gaelic. The powerful Falls of Dochart rush through the village of Killin, making it a popular centre for exploring the area.

Campsie Fells

The rolling hills of the Campsie Fells reach a height of 1896ft (578m) at Earl's Seat. The source of the River Carron is on the slopes of the fells 3 miles (4km) north of Lennoxtown. Walkers can follow the Campsie Fells Trail which links pretty villages such as Balfron, Kippen and Fintry.

Campsie Fells

Loch Katrine

The Trossachs

Aberfoyle is the southern gateway to the Trossachs. This breathtaking landscape of forested hills and lochs forms part of the Loch Lomond and The Trossachs National Park. It is home to a wide variety of wildlife incuding red deer, golden eagles and peregrine falcons. The Trossachs was the inspiration for Sir Walter Scott who wrote 'Lady of the Lake' in 1810 after spending time at the 8 mile (13km) long Loch Katrine. So popular was the poem that it resulted in an upsurge of tourism in the area. Cruises are available on the loch on the Victorian steamer SS Sir Walter Scott.

Ochil Hills

The rugged Ochil Hills range extends from Bridge of Allan eastwards to the flood plain of the Firth of Tay at Newburgh. The summit is Ben Cleuch at 2363ft (720m). Deposits of copper and silver associated with the geology of Devonian volcanic andesite have been mined at Bridge of Allen and Sterling Glen. To the south of the area between Alva and Tillicoultry is the Ochil Hills Woodland Park in the grounds of the former Alva House. There are woodland walks, a children's play area and picnic areas.

Paragliding in the Ochil Hills

Central East Scotland

Located just 80 miles (129 km) north of Edinburgh and Glasgow, this part of Scotland makes an ideal holiday destination.

Perthshire has mountains, lochs and castles, and opportunities for walking, golfing and fishing, as well as fine theatres, museums and restaurants. Angus and Dundee make a good touring base, with mountainous glens, rugged coastline, pleasant beaches and lots of things to see and do. The ancient Kingdom of Fife has plenty of character. The attractive East Neuk fishing villages nestle amongst the natural harbours of the coastline, and St Andrews is the location of the oldest university in Scotland, and, of course the home of golf.

Fife

The ancient Kingdom of Fife is bounded on three sides by the sea – the Firth of Tay to the north, the North Sea to the east and the Firth of Forth to the south. Although St Andrews is often the focus of attention for visitors there are other areas worth exploring. Rural north Fife is popular for walking, cycling and horse riding. Central Fife is dominated by the port and resort of Kirkcaldy and in the west is Culross, one of the best preserved examples of a Scottish burgh in the country.

Forth Rail Bridge

Pitlochry

Population : 2541. Sited on the banks of the River Tummel and surrounded by mountain scenery, the Victorian resort of Pitlochry makes a good base to stay. There is a visitor centre at the hydro-electric station on the edge of the town, and visitors can watch salmon leaping the fish ladder on their annual migration upstream.

Arbroath & Montrose

The historically important town of Arbroath (population: 23,474) grew up around its 12th century abbey to become an important fishing port. It is famed for the local delicacy of traditionally smoked haddock called 'smokies'. Further up the coast is the port of Montrose (population: 11,440), sited on the edge of a large tidal lagoon which is home to populations of geese, swans and waders.

Tourist board regions in Central East Scotland:
Angus & Dundee www.angusanddundee.co.uk
Kingdom of Fife www.standrews.com/fife
Perthshire www.perthshire.com

Key to map pages in Central East Scotland

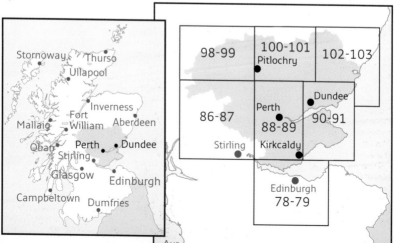

City of Perth

Population: 41,453. Sited on the River Tay 31 miles (50km) to the north of Edinburgh, this ancient cathedral city was Scotland's capital until the 15th century.

Perth is a busy market town and a centre for livestock trade. The compact city centre is easily walkable on foot and is home to many interesting attractions. To the north and south of the centre are the Inches, public parks with bloody histories that today offer more sedate activities. The gothic mansion of Scone Palace saw the crowning of 42 Kings of Scotland and is situated just two miles (3km) north of the city.

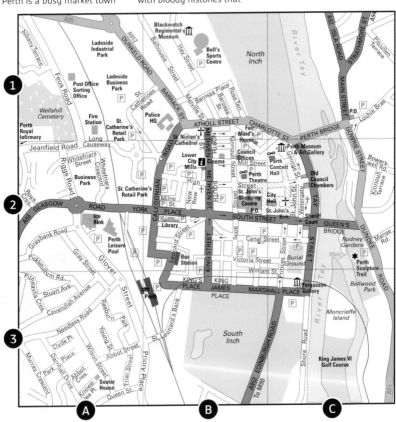

Index to street names

Useful information

Police
Tayside Police
Barrack Street,
PH1 5SF
01738 621141

Perth

Hospital A & E
Perth Royal Infirmary
Taymount Terrace,
PH1 1NX
01738 623311

City centre Post Office
109 South Street, PH2 8AF

Railway Station
Leonard Street, PH2 8HF

Bus Station
Leonard Street, PH2 8ET

Tourist Information Centre
Lower City Mills
West Mill Street
Perth
PH1 5QP
01738 450600

City website
www.pkc.gov.uk

Perth

Isle of May

The largest island in the Firth of Forth and site of the first permanently manned lighthouse beacon in Scotland. The island is now a National Nature Reserve and home to puffins, guillemots, razorbills and grey seals. Boats to the island can be caught from Anstruther and North Berwick.

St Andrews

Population: 11,136. This historic town stands on a rocky promontory. The University, founded in 1411, is the oldest in Scotland. The Royal and Ancient Golf Club, which is the ruling authority on golf, is also based in the town and visitors can learn about the history of the game at the British Golf Museum.

St. Andrews Castle

Loch Tay

This 15 mile (24km) long loch runs north east from Killin to Kenmore. In places it is over 500ft (150m) deep and over a mile across. The loch is noted for its salmon. Just to the north is Ben Lawers, Perthshire's highest mountain at 3984ft (1214m) and the ninth highest in the British Isles.

On the south shore above Acharn are the Falls of Acharn. The main waterfall can be viewed from the 'Hermits Cave' viewing area or a little longer walk takes the visitor to another platform from where the smaller falls can be observed.

Loch Tay

City of Dundee

Population: 158,981. Scotland's fourth largest city has a beautiful setting on the north bank of the Firth of Tay, 18 miles (29km) east of Perth. The

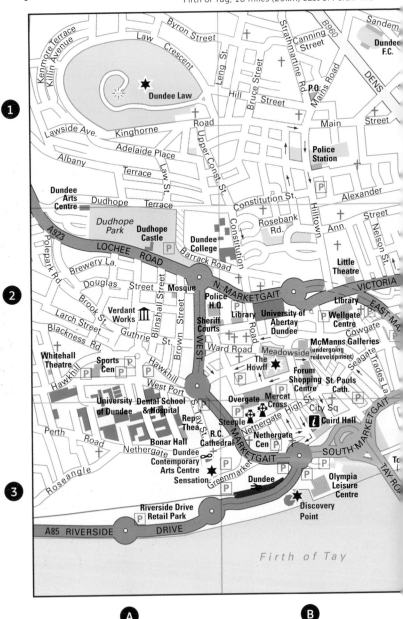

Index to street names

approach from the south via the Tay Road Bridge gives panoramic views of the city and the good road network north means there is also easy access to the surrounding countryside of the Grampian Highlands. Dundee is a city of considerable historical importance. Robert the Bruce was declared King of the Scots here in 1309, the city suffered severe damage in the civil war and again prior to the Jacobite uprising, before recovering in the 19th century to become one of Scotland's most important trade centres. The Overgate and Wellgate Centres at either end of the High Street provide a good range of shops. Dundee Contemporary Arts Centre which opened in 1997 has boosted the city's cultural standing and the Dundee Repertory Theatre shows contemporary plays. There are many museums and art galleries: three of the best are Discovery Point, Verdant Works and the McManus Galleries (undergoing redevelopment and due to reopen at the end of 2007).

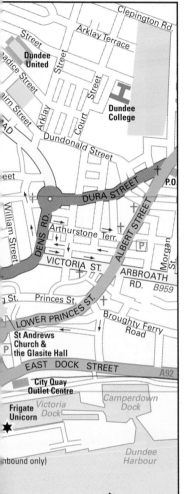

Useful information

Police
Tayside Police
4 West Bell Street
DD1 9JU
01382 223200

Hospital A & E
Ninewells Hospital
Ninewells Avenue
DD1 9SY
01382 660111

City centre Post Office
4 Meadowside,
DD1 4AA

Railway Station
South Union Street,
DD1 4BY

Bus Station
Seagate, DD1 2HR

Tourist Information Centre
21 Castle Street
Dundee
DD1 3AA
01382 527527

City website
www.dundeecity.gov.uk

Horse riding, Loch Tay

Tay Forest Park

10 mile (16km) long Loch Rannoch is dammed at its eastern end. Issuing from the loch is the River Tummel which runs on through Loch Tummel. Bordering both lochs is the Tay Forest Park which includes several forests. The Queen's View Visitor Centre on the northern shore of Loch Tummel is the main interpretive centre for the park and there is a fine view from there across the loch to the peak of Schiehallion.

Angus glens

The peaceful, heather-clad glens of Angus cut into the Grampian Highlands. Glen Shee and the steep sided glacial valley of Glen Clova are the most popular, but Glen Esk, Glen Prosen and Glen Isla are all also worth exploring.

Gleneagles golf course

Crieff

Population: 6023. This former spa town in the foothills of the Grampians above the River Earn became a popular resort in Victorian times with the arrival of the railway in 1856. It has retained much of its charm and character and is noted for its local crafts, many of which are available at the Crieff Visitors Centre. To the south east is the small town of Auchterader and the championship golf courses of Gleneagles.

Places to visit in Angus & Dundee

Angus and Dundee boast a variety of innovative and award-winning tourist attractions. See Verdant Works which illustrates Dundee's once thriving jute industry, Pictavia which explores the legacy of the Picts, Discovery Point, home to Captain Scott's polar exploration ship the R.R.S. Discovery, and the Sensation science centre.

R.R.S. Discovery, Dundee

The Pictish legacy

This area was part of the 8th century Pictish kingdom and many beautifully carved stones still stand as reminders of the past. See the sculptured stones at Aberlemno, St Vigeans, Meigle or the stones in Montrose Museum or Brechin Cathedral.

Sculptured Stone, Aberlemno

Aberdeenshire & Moray

This quiet corner of Scotland is rich in historic castles, royal connections and whisky distilleries.

There are miles of unspoilt coastline and the Grampian Mountains contain more peaks over 4000ft (1219m) than anywhere else in Scotland. As a gateway to Royal Deeside, the city of Aberdeen has much to offer the visitor. Follow the Castle Trail or the Royal Road along the beautiful Dee valley and visit Balmoral Castle.

Huntly Castle

Royal Deeside

Queen Victoria and Prince Albert began the Royal connection with Deeside when it became their favourite holiday retreat 150 years ago. The tradition continues today. The Victorian Heritage Trail links places of historical interest – including Balmoral, Ballater, Aboyne and Banchory – along a route through spectacular scenery.

Scotland's castle country

Grampian has more castles than any other area of the UK. There are fairy-tale castles with spires and towers, dramatic ruins and stately mansions. Follow the Castle Trail linking some of the region's finest examples - the castles of Huntly, Kildrummy, Corgarff, Craigievar, Fraser, Tolquhon, Fyvie, and Delgattie, and the mansions of Duff House, Haddo House and Leith Hall.

Ballater

Population: 1362. The former railway town of Ballater lies within magnificent scenery on the River Dee. It is only 8 miles (13km) east of Balmoral and there are many royal warrants displayed on the shop fronts in the town. It is a good touring centre and base for walking on Lochnagar, in Glen Muick to the south west and the woodlands of the Muir of Dinnet Nature Reserve to the east.

Deeside

Tourist board website for Aberdeen & Moray:
Aberdeen & Grampian Highlands
www.aberdeen-grampian.com

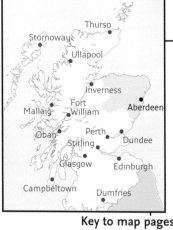

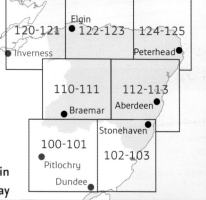

Key to map pages in
Aberdeenshire & Moray

Highland Games

Games are held throughout the region from June to early September. The events are a celebration of all things Scottish including massed pipe bands, highland dancing and international 'heavy' and 'track' events. The Braemar Gathering is held on the first Saturday in September and is always a highlight of the calendar.

Braemar Gathering

The Malt Whisky Trail

Over half of Scotland's distilleries are in Speyside. Scotland's Malt Whisky Trail follows a 70 mile (112km) signposted route linking seven of the world's most famous distilleries. - Glenfiddich, Glenlivet, Strathisla, Glen Grant, Dallas Dhu, Cardhu and Glenfarclas as well as the Speyside Cooperage where barrels are made. All distilleries on the trail have visitor centres and offer guided tours.

Lochnagar

The Lochnagar mountain ridge is popular with climbers. The steep north east facing cliffs comprise four distinct peaks, the highest of which is Cac Carn Beag at 3788 ft (1155m). Below the ridge is the small loch of Lochnagar.

Ben Macdui

Much of the Cairngorm area lies within the Highland region, but the summit of the range, Ben Macdui at 4296ft (1309m), is on the boundary of Moray and Aberdeenshire. It is the second highest mountain in Scotland.

Glenfiddich Distillery

Grampian gardens

The area's relatively mild climate has helped Aberdeen flourish as the 'Flower of Scotland'. It is renowned for its parks, gardens and floral displays. Away from the city are the gardens of Pitmedden, Crathes Castle and Leith Hall Rock Garden. To the north, Forres is also known as a 'floral town' because of its award winning parks and gardens.

Pitmedden Garden

The Speyside Way

The way-marked Speyside Way is an 84 mile (135km) long distance footpath linking the Moray coast at Buckie to the Grampian Mountains at Aviemore. It generally follows the valley of the River Spey using forest and riverside paths.

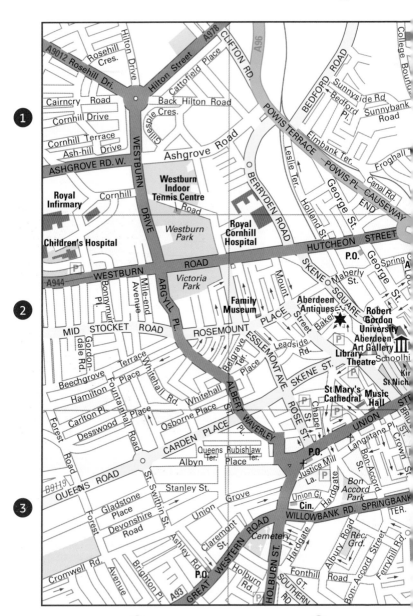

Index to street names

City of Aberdeen

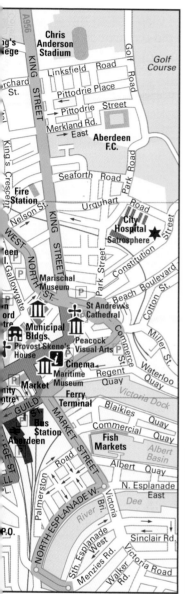

Aberdeen spires

Population: 189,707. Situated on the east coast 57 miles (92km) north east of Dundee, Aberdeen is the Capital of the Grampians. Since the 13th century the city has been an important centre for trade with the oil industry being the principal employer today. Widely known as 'The Granite City', as local stone was used in constructing many of the city's buildings, the sometimes austere look of the architecture is softened by the many flower gardens, of which the David Welch Winter Gardens is the most impressive.

Aberdeen has shopping for every taste, from busy shopping malls of designer boutiques and major chain-stores to speciality shops. The large transient population of students and oil workers means that Aberdeen has a bustling nightlife as well. A two mile (3km) long sweeping beach less than a mile (1.6km) from the centre is perfect for a bracing walk.

Useful information

Grampian Police
Headquarters
Queen Street, AB10 1ZA
0845 600 5700

Hospital A & E
Aberdeen Royal Infirmary,
Foresterhill, AB25 2ZN
0845 456 6000

City centre Post Office
St. Nicholas Shopping
Centre
St. Nicholas Street,
AB10 1HW

Railway Station
Guild Street, AB11 6LX

Bus Station
Guild Street AB11 6NA

Tourist Information Centre
23 Union Street
Aberdeen
AB11 5BP
01224 288828

City website
www.aberdeencity.gov.uk

Highlands & Skye

No single image can capture the scale and diversity of this region. From the soaring crags of Glen Coe to the wide rolling moors of Caithness, from the old pinewoods of upper Speyside to the spectacular Cuillin mountains of Skye, the north and west offer unmatched scenic splendour.

The Highlands of Scotland are rich in places to visit, with castles, battlefields and forts to remind you of a turbulent past, while distilleries, woollen mills and other crafts contribute to today's diverse Highland economy. Inverness, often called the capital of the Highlands, is a natural gateway to the north. At the other end of the Great Glen, Fort William stands in the shadow of Ben Nevis.

Skiing, Aonach Mor

Pony trekking

Outdoor activities

The Highlands provide year round opportunities for outdoor activities. Many hillwalkers return again and again to the region. Popular areas include the major peaks of Ben Nevis, Cairn Gorm, Glen Coe and Cuillin as well as the hills of Torridon, Wester Ross and Assynt. The three main centres for winter sports are the Nevis Range (Aonach Mor), Cairngorms and Glencoe. All three offer facilities for all grades of skiers and snowboarders. These are also the most important areas in the UK for ice climbing. The mountains around Torridon in the Northern Highlands are also worthwhile and even feature a gully route through a crashed World War II Lancaster bomber. In summer there are also facilities across the region for white water canoeing, paragliding, golf, birdwatching, pony trekking and water sports.

Fort William

Population: 10,391. Set at the foot of Ben Nevis, Fort William is the main tourist and mountaineering centre in the Highlands. The main attraction in winter is the Nevis Range ski centre on Aonach Mor. The attractions of the town itself include the Ben Nevis Distillery, the West Highland Museum and in the summer, a day trip on the Jacobite Steam Train across the 21 arch Glenfinnan Viaduct and on to Mallaig. The 84 mile round trip passes Loch Morar, the deepest loch in Britain at 1017ft (310m) and is part of the West Highland Line, one of the greatest railway journeys in the world.

Glen Coe

Steep sided Glen Coe is one of Scotland's most beautiful glens. It was the scene of a notorious massacre in 1692. The most well known peaks south of the glen road are the Three Sisters, whilst to the north the knife-edged ridge of Aonach Eagach is a challenge to mountaineers.

Glen Coe

Tourist board website for Highlands & Skye:
www.visithighlands.com

Key to map pages in Highlands & Skye

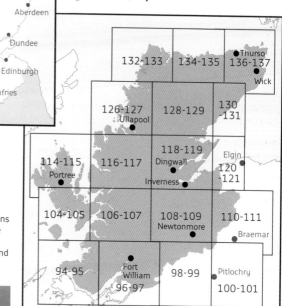

Ardnamurchan

A lighthouse on the Ardnamurchan peninsula marks the most westerly point on the British mainland. This peninsula and the neighbouring regions of Moidart and Morvern are excellent areas for walking, with coastal paths, woodland trails and mountain hikes.

Ardnamurchan Point

Mallaig

With a population of around 1000 Mallaig is a small yet busy fishing port at the western end of the Road to the Isles. The vehicle ferry to Skye leaves from here and there are ferries for foot passengers to Canna, Muck, Eigg and Rum.

Portree

Population: 2126. The port and chief town of Skye lies on Loch Portree on the east coast. It is the island's cultural centre, and has an attractive, colourful harbour. The Aros Experience

exhibition south of Portree gives a good introduction to the history of life on the island.

The Road to the Isles

The 46 mile (74km) route along the A830 between Fort William and Mallaig is a journey through dramatic loch and mountain scenery. It is also a journey steeped in history, with several places linked to the failed rebellion of Bonnie Prince Charlie. It was at Borrodale, near Arisaig that he first landed on the Scottish mainland in 1745 and a cairn less than a mile (1.5km) to the east marks the spot from which he escaped as a fugitive in 1746. The Glenfinnan Monument in its spectacular setting at the head of the Loch Shiel valley is a poignant memorial to the Highlanders who fought and died for his cause.

Glenfinnan Monument

Black Cuillins, Skye

Cuillin Hills

In the southern part of Skye the serrated peaks of the Cuillin Hills dominate the landscape. There are 11 Munros in the range, the highest being Sgurr Alasdair at 3258ft (993m). This is some of Britain's most spectacular walking and climbing country, although many of the routes are only for experienced climbers.

North East Skye

North from Portree the 20 mile (32 km) long Trotternish peninsula has some of the finest coastal scenery on Skye. Ancient landslides have created sheer cliffs and further inland the central spine of the peninsula is also studded with dramatic basalt outcrops. The most spectacular geological features are the Old Man of Storr, Kilt Rock and the pinnacles of the Quirang.

The Great Glen

The Great Glen or Glen Mor runs 60 miles (97 km) diagonally across the Highlands in a major geological fault running from Loch Linnhe at Fort William to the Moray Firth at Inverness. The lochs of the Glen are linked by the Caledonian Canal.

Trotternish Peninsula

Spean Bridge

The bridge was built by Thomas Telford in 1819 but nearby are the remains of an older bridge built by General Wade in 1736 to span the 100ft (30m) gorge. The area was used as a training ground by commandos during World War II and the Commando Memorial is set amongst stunning scenery to the north west of the village as a tribute to them.

Caledonian Canal, Fort Augustus

Ullapool

Population: 1231. An attractive fishing port and popular holiday resort on the eastern shore of Loch Broom. Although small it is the largest settlement in the north-western Highlands and is the ferry port for vehicles to Stornoway in the Western Isles. The town was founded in 1788 by the British Fisheries Society and laid out on a grid plan which is still visible today.

Commando Memorial

Ullapool

Thurso

Population: 8448. This small port at the mouth of the river Thurso is the most northerly town on the British mainland. In medieval times it was Scotland's main port for trade with Scandinavia. At the other side of Thurso Bay the port of Scrabster has a frequent ferry service to Orkney.

The East Coast

The small town of Dornoch is a peaceful holiday resort with good beaches, a golf course and a medieval cathedral. The coast route northwards winds through Golspie, Brora and Helmsdale. Highlights along the way include the baronial splendour of Dunrobin Castle, the Timespan Heritage Centre and the well-preserved broch of Carn Liath. North of Helmsdale is a fine viewpoint at the Ord of Caithness.

Dornoch

Dornoch Beach

Nairn

Population: 7892. The royal burgh and Victorian seaside resort of Nairn was once a busy fishing port. The harbour was built by Thomas Telford. It has since become known for its fine golf courses, beaches and impressive hotels along a seafront with many family leisure attractions.

The Pictish Trail

The Pictish trail is a signposted trail for motorists linking important sites of the 8th century Pictish period, including the collection of stones at Groam House Museum in Fortrose, the stone slab at Hilton of Cadboll and an exhibition of local finds at the Tarbat Discovery Centre.

Black Isle

The peninsula between Cromarty Firth and the Moray Firth is largely an area of farmland, crossed by many waymarked walks and cycle routes. There are several historic villages such as Avoch and Rosemarkie whilst the main centres are the small towns of Fortrose and Cromarty.

Black Isle

Cairngorms

This granite mountain mass of rounded summits includes some of Scotland's highest peaks. It is a popular area for hillwalkers, climbers and skiers. The Cairngorms are Britains only example of Arctic tundra vegetation and the area provides a habitat for populations of snow buntings and ptarmigans. Aviemore (population: 2214) is the commercial centre for the area. In winter the village is a mecca for skiers and in summer there are facilities for pony trekking, mountain biking, fishing, sailing, windsurfing and canoeing.

Cairngorms

City of Inverness

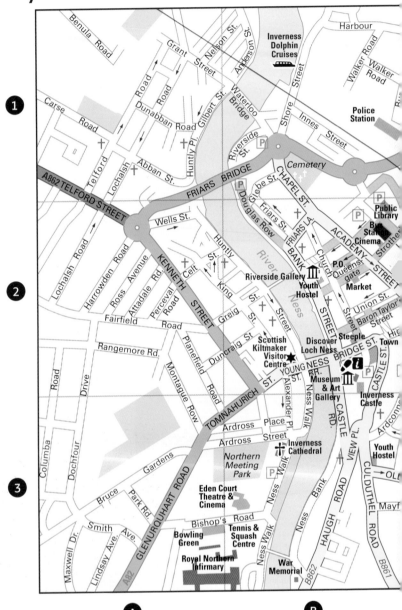

Index to street names

Population: 41,234. Sited at the mouth of the River Ness 113 miles (169km) north west of Edinburgh and surrounded by spectacular scenery, Inverness is the Capital of the Highlands and the Gateway to the North. Several major rail and road routes radiate from the city, making it an ideal base for exploring northern Scotland in all directions. It is an attractive cosmopolitan city with a compact centre. The imposing red sandstone Victorian castle is not open to the public but there are fine views over Inverness from the castle grounds. For evening entertainment the Eden Court Theatre is popular. For shopping try the modern Eastgate Centre, the Victorian style Market Arcade or the pedestrianised High Street. Beyond the city there is a diversity of attractions including dolphin watching in the Moray Firth, Cawdor Castle, Fort George and the battle site at Culloden.

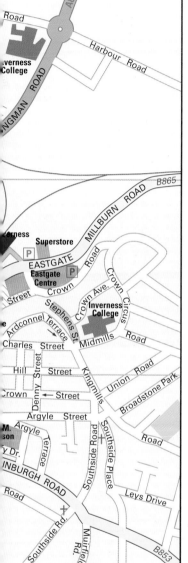

Useful information

Police
Burnett Road, IV1 1RL
01463 715555

Hospital A & E
Raigmore Hospital
Old Perth Road,
IV2 3UJ
01463 704000

City centre Post Office
14/16 Queensgate,
IV1 1AX

Railway Station
Station Square
Academy Street,
IV1 1LE

Bus Station
Margaret Street,
IV1 1LT

Tourist Information
Centre
Castle Wynd,
IV2 3BJ

City website
www.highland.gov.uk

Outer Islands

The Outer Islands are for those looking for a totally different holiday experience.

Although geographically separate, the Western Isles, Shetland and Orkney all share a remote scenic splendour. They also share a strong sense of history. Settlers arrived on the islands in Neolithic times and many of the archaeological remains from that era are renowned world-wide. For centuries Orkney and Shetland were also Viking strongholds and this heritage and ancestry is reflected in the people as well as their legends, myths and traditions. In the Western Isles the old Gaelic way of life lives on in crafts, language and music.

Tourist board regions for the Outer Islands:
Outer Hebrides www.visithebrides.com
Orkney www.visitorkney.com
Shetland www.visitshetland.com

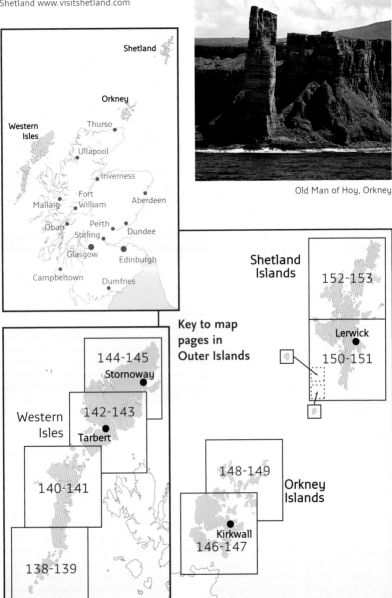

Old Man of Hoy, Orkney

Shetland

Orkney

Western Isles

Thurso

Ullapool

Inverness

Fort William

Mallaig

Aberdeen

Oban

Perth

Stirling

Dundee

Glasgow

Edinburgh

Campbeltown

Dumfries

Key to map pages in Outer Islands

Shetland Islands

152-153

Lerwick

150-151

Western Isles

144-145

Stornoway

142-143

Tarbert

140-141

138-139

Orkney Islands

148-149

Kirkwall

146-147

Western Isles

The Western Isles, a 130 mile (209km) long chain of islands lying to the north west of Scotland, offer a unique experience. The combination of land, sea and loch has produced landscapes which have been designated areas of outstanding scenic value.

Barra

A hilly island with silver sand beaches along a much indented coastline, Barra has often been called 'the Western Isles in miniature'. On the island's south coast is Castlebay, once a significant herring port and still the main settlement and ferry terminal. To the south the island of Vatersay is linked to Barra by a causeway.

Harris

South Harris

South Harris is joined to North Harris by a narrow neck of land to the south west of Tarbert, with West and East Loch Tarbert on either side. The landscape is dominated by craggy mountains, especially surrounding Beinn Dhubh, 1660ft (506m), in the north and the central An Coileach, 1266ft (386m). Harris is renowned for the woollen cloth Harris Tweed.

Harris from Taransay

North Harris

South of Loch Resort and west of Loch Seaforth lies the most mountainous part of the Outer Hebrides. The Forest of Harris is an area of mountains, streams and lochs which provide ample opportunity for walking and climbing.

St Kilda

Managed by the National Trust for Scotland, this most remote part of the British Isles lies 41 miles (66km) west of Benbecula and was Scotland's first World Heritage Site when it was designated in 1986. There are still remains of the village which was finally deserted in 1930. Getting there is not easy with charter boats available from Mallaig and Oban but can take 8 to 14 hours to reach the archipelago.

Isle of Lewis

The Isle of Lewis is the largest and most northerly island of the Outer Hebrides, measuring 61 miles (99km) north east to south west and a maximum of half that distance north west to south east. The name Lewis is generally given to the northern part of the island as distinct from North and South Harris. Much of Lewis consists of peat uplands containing many small lochs and streams in which salmon and trout abound. Stretches of rugged coastline are interspersed with uncrowded white sandy beaches. The most northerly point on the island is the windswept Butt of Lewis. Stornoway (population: 5975) is the main town on Lewis and is the commercial centre of the Outer Hebrides. The natural harbour was the scene of one of the worst disasters in UK maritime history when the Iolaire sank on New Years Eve 1918 with the loss of 200 lives.

Calanais Standing Stones, Isle of Lewis

Outer Islands

Rackwick, Hoy

Orkney Islands

Orkney is made up of 70 islands only 17 of which are currently inhabited. There is a population of 20,000 most of whom live in the towns of Kirkwall and Stromness. The islands are rich in historical and archaeological remains. Here you will find villages, burial chambers and standing stones built before the Great Pyramids of Egypt.

Kirkwall

Population: 6469. The capital and administrative centre of Orkney is a bustling market town and a ferry port for many of the northern isles. At its centre the sandstone cathedral of St Magnus is one of Scotland's finest medieval buildings. Learn about the history of island life at the Orkney Museum opposite the cathedral.

Southern Isles

Hoy is Orkney's most rugged isle with its steep western cliffs and the Old Man of Hoy rising to 449ft (137m). The 'flat isle' of Flotta lies to the east. Ferries link Hoy and Flotta to Mainland Orkney. Further east again South Ronaldsay, Burray and the small islets of Lamb Holm and Glimps Holm are connected to Mainland Orkney by the Churchill Barriers, a series of causeways built in World War II to block the eastern approaches to anchorage in Scapa Flow. Discover the history of Scapa Flow at the Lyness Interpretation Centre on Hoy.

Faraclett Head, Rousay

Northern Isles

Orkney's northern fringe of islands – Rousay, Egilsay, Wyre, Shapinsay, Stronsay, Eday, Sanday, Westray, Papa Westray and North Ronaldsay – each have their own character. Rousay is the most hilly and is known for its rich archaeological heritage. Sanday is the largest island and is renowned for its sweeping bays and white sandy beaches. Papa Westray, or Papay as it is known locally, can be reached by plane from Westray on the world's shortest scheduled flight at just two minutes long. North Ronaldsay is the most remote of the islands and this means many of the traditional ways of life still prevail.
All the islands are renowned for their tranquillity and as a haven for wildlife.

Stromness

Population: 1890. Although a port since Viking times, Stromness grew mainly in the 18th century and is now an important harbour town and ferry terminal. With its narrow, winding main street and houses facing gable-end to the sea, the town has a picturesque waterfront and is an attractive place to explore.

Wyre from Rousay

Shetland Islands

A cluster of over 100 islands set between Scotland and Scandinavia, Shetland shares something of the character of both countries, while guarding a rich local identity. Magnificent seascapes and fine seabird colonies are among the many features of these untamed islands.
Only 22,000 people live on the islands but the sheep population is over 300,000.

Shetland Race Week

South Mainland

24 miles (39km) south of Lerwick, Sumburgh Head is the southern extremity of Shetland. Rich in archaeology, the ancient settlements at Jarlshof and Old Scatness are both sites of international renown.

Lerwick

Population: 7336. The chief town of Shetland is a fishing port, service base for North Sea oilfields and a terminus for boat services to the Scottish mainland. It is also the focus of Shetland life. The annual festival of Up Helly Aa, held on the last Tuesday in January, is of pagan origin and pays homage to the traditional ceremonial burning of a Viking long ship. 5 miles (8km) west of Lerwick is Scalloway (population: 1056), the ancient capital of the isles and still an important fishing port.

North Shetland

Yell, Unst and Fetlar are all linked to each other and to Mainland Shetland by ferry. Green and fertile Fetlar is known as 'The Garden of Shetland', it is a sparsely inhabited island of pastoral farmland. Yell is an island of wild moor where coastal walks give the opportunity to spot whales, seals, otters and dolphins. Unst is the most northerly isle; its indented coastline offers both towering cliffs and beautiful beaches.

Sullom Voe

The long inlet of Sullom Voe almost separates the northern part of Shetland's Mainland from the rest of the island. It provides shelter and access to the Sullom Voe Oil Terminal, the largest facility of its kind in Europe.

Foula

26 miles (42km) west of Scalloway on Mainland Shetland lies Foula. Its high cliffs are home to thousands of seabirds, giving the isle its popular name of Bird Island.

Fair Isle

Sparsely populated Fair Isle is 24 miles (39km) south west of Sumburgh Head. Well known for its knitwear, it is also a place of great natural beauty.

Shetland Puffins

Unst

Battlefield sites are part of Scotland's national heritage. Some sites, such as Bannockburn and Culloden have visitor centres. Others may be marked by information panels or monuments which stand testament to thousands of lives lost several centuries ago.

Airds Moss 1680   67 D3
Site of skirmish between Royalists and Covenanters.

Alford 1645   112 A3
The site of the battle where the Royalist Marquis of Montrose defeated the Covenant army two months after his victory at Auldearn.

Ancrum Moor 1545   70 C3
The site of the battle in which the Scots repelled English raiders after a dispute following the death of James V over the betrothal of the infant Mary, Queen of Scots to Henry VIII's son, Edward. The decisive victory helped to unify Scotland.

Auldearn 1645   121 D4
The site of the Marquis of Montrose's tactical defeat of the Covenanters in the Civil War.

Bannockburn 1314   77 F1
Where the Scots under Robert the Bruce defeated the English under Edward II, gaining independence and national identity. The battle is commemorated at Bannockburn Heritage Centre.

Barra Hill 1308   112 C2
Battle where Robert the Bruce decisively defeated John Comyn on Christmas Eve.

Bothwell Bridge 1679   77 E5
The battle in which the Covenanters were heavily defeated by Scottish loyalists led by the Duke of Monmouth and Claverhouse.

Carbisdale 1650   128 C5
The scene of Montrose's defeat by the Earl of Sutherland. The main battle was fought on a craggy hill, Creag a' Choineachan.

Corrichie 1562   112 B4
The site where the Earl of Huntly was defeated by followers of Mary, Queen of Scots, led by Moray.

Culloden 1746   119 E5
Where the Jacobean cause led by Prince Charles Edward Stuart was finally defeated by the Duke of Cumberland on 16th April 1746. About 200 Jacobites were lost on the field, but around 2000 more were killed in the subsequent pursuit. Culloden was the last battle fought on British soil.

Dunbar 1296   80 B3
Site of the defeat of John Balliol by Edward I.

Dunbar 1650   80 B3
Battle where Cromwell defeated Charles, Prince of Wales, and his Scottish army under David Leslie, hampering the Royalists' campaign in the north.

Falkirk 1746   77 F3
The battle site where a Jacobite army of Highlanders defeated the Hanoverian army, led by Henry Hawley.

Glen Trool 1307   60 A2
Bruce's Stone marks the site of the rout of the English by Robert the Bruce's men in 1307.

Glencoe Massacre 1692   97 D4
The site where the MacDonald clan of Glencoe were killed on the orders of Sir James Dalrymple when they were six days late in signing their peace with William of Orange.

Glenshiel 1719   106 C3
Where the Jacobites, backed by Spain, were defeated by George I's army.

Harlaw 1411   112 C2
The site where Donald, Lord of the Isles, tried to claim the Earldom of Ross and was defeated by the Earl of Mar.

Haughs of Cromdale 1690   110 C2
The site where government forces defeated the Jacobites in 1690.

Inverlochy 1429, 1431 and 1645   97 D2
Inverlochy Castle was built in the 13th century and was the scene of battles in 1429, 1431 and 1645. In the last and most important battle the Covenanters, led by Argyll, were defeated by Montrose. This led to Charles I breaking off negotiations with Parliament and ultimately to his defeat.

Invernahavon 1370 or 1386   109 D5
A battle of uncertain date between Clan Cameron and the rival Clan Mackintosh, supported by Davidsons and Macphersons. The Mackintoshes and their followers suffered heavy losses, although the battle ended with the Camerons in flight.

Keppoch 1688   97 E2
The site of Scotland's last real clan battle, caused by a territorial dispute between the MacDonalds and the Mackintoshes.

Killiecrankie 1689   100 B3
The site of the battle where Government troops were defeated by the Jacobites in 1689.

Kilsyth 1645   77 E3
Battle site, now covered by Townhead Reservoir, where Montrose defeated the Covenanters, killing some 6000 of the enemy with the loss of only ten men.

Langside 1568   76 C4
The site where Mary, Queen of Scots' forces were defeated by Moray after her escape from Loch Leven.

Loudoun Hill 1307   67 E2
Battle site where Robert the Bruce defeated Earl of Pembroke.

Mauchline 1648   66 C3
On this battle site there was a skirmish between Covenanters and English troops, the outcome of which is uncertain.

Methven 1306   89 D3
Site where Robert the Bruce was defeated by the Earl of Pembroke.

THE BATTLE OF CULLODEN WAS FOUGHT ON THIS MOOR 16TH APRIL 1746. THE GRAVES OF THE GALLANT HIGHLANDERS WHO FOUGHT FOR SCOTLAND & PRINCE CHARLIE ARE MARKED BY THE NAMES OF THEIR CLANS.

Nechtanesmere 685   91 E1
Where Egfrith of Northumbria was killed by the Picts, ending Anglian incursions into this area.

Philiphaugh 1645   70 A3
On this site, after defeating the English, Scottish leader Sir David Leslie took prisoners to Newark Castle and murdered them in cold blood.

Pinkie 1547   79 E3
(Also known as the Battle of Inveresk or Musselburgh.) The Duke of Somerset, regent to Edward VI, sought to impose a betrothal treaty between English and Scottish monarchs, leading to battle in 1547. Although the English were victorious, they failed in their objective as Mary, Queen of Scots was sent to France to marry the Dauphin.

Prestonpans 1745   79 F3
The site of a battle where the English Government forces defeated the Jacobites as part of the 1745 Jacobite uprising.

Redeswire Fray 1575   71 D5
Site of the last significant Borders skirmish between the English and the Scots, marked by a stone.

Rullion Green 1666   79 D4
Battle site where 1000 Covenanters were defeated by superior Crown forces under General Dalziel.

Sherriffmuir 1715   88 B5
Where the Jacobite army under the Earl of Mar fought the army of George I, led by the Duke of Argyll.

Stirling Bridge 1297   77 F1
Where Scots under William Wallace routed the English under Warenne.

Strath Oykel 1369 or 1406   128 B4
A bloody battle of uncertain date between Clan Mackay and rival Clan Macleod, which ended with heavy losses for the Macleods. The conflict gave the name of Tuiteam Tarvach, meaning plentiful fall or great slaughter, to the vicinity.

Strathpeffer 1411   118 B5
Site of affray between Munros and Macdonalds and commemorated by the Eagle Stone.

Tibbermore 1644   89 D3
Site of first battle between the Royalist Marquis of Montrose and the Covenanters, in which Montrose was victorious, gaining control of Perth.

Turiff 1639   124 B4
Site of the first skirmish in the Civil War, known as 'Trot of Turiff', where Royalist Gordons defeated the Covenanters.

Munros

Sir Hugh T. Munro originally published *Tables of Heights over 3000 Feet* in the 1891 edition of the Scottish Mountaineering Club Journal. His name has given rise to these 284 Scottish mountain peaks higher than 914m.

Munro name	Height (m)	Map ref	Munro name	Height (m)	Map ref
Ben Nevis	1344	97 D2	Carn a' Coire Bhoidheach	1110	111 D6
Ben Macdui	1309	110 A5	Sgurr Mòr	1110	117 F2
Braeriach	1296	110 A4	Sgurr nan Conbhairean	1110	107 E3
Cairn Toul	1293	110 A5	Meall a' Bhùiridh	1108	97 E4
Sgor an Lochain Uaine	1258	110 A5	Stob a' Choire Mheadhoin	1106	97 F2
Cairn Gorm	1245	110 B4	Beinn Ghlas	1103	87 D1
Aonach Beag	1234	97 D2	Mullach Fraoch-choire	1102	107 D3
Carn Mòr Dearg	1223	97 D2	Beinn Eibhinn	1100	98 B2
Aonach Mòr	1221	97 D2	Creise	1100	97 E4
Ben Lawers	1214	87 D1	Sgurr a' Mhaim	1099	97 D3
North Top	1196	110 B4	Sgurr Chòinnich Mòr	1095	97 E2
Carn Eighe	1183	107 E2	Sgurr nan Clach Geala	1093	117 E2
Beinn Mheadhoin	1182	110 B4	Bynack More	1090	110 B4
Mam Sodhail	1180	107 E2	Beinn a' Chlachair	1088	98 B2
Stob Choire Claurigh	1177	97 E2	Stob Ghabhar	1087	85 F1
Ben More	1174	86 B3	Beinn Dearg	1084	117 F1
Leabaidh an Daimh Bhuidhe	1171	110 C4	Schiehallion	1083	99 E4
Stob Binnein	1165	86 B3	Sgurr a' Choire Ghlais	1083	117 F5
Beinn Bhrotain	1157	110 A5	Beinn a' Chaorainn	1082	110 B4
Cac Carn Beag	1155	111 D6	Beinn a' Chreachain	1081	86 A1
Derry Cairngorm	1155	110 B5	Ben Starav	1078	85 E1
Sgurr nan Ceathreamhnan	1151	107 D2	Beinn Dòrain	1076	86 A2
Bidean nam Bian	1150	97 D4	Beinn Heasgarnich	1076	86 B2
Sgurr na Lapaich	1150	117 E6	Stob Coire Sgreamhach	1072	97 D4
Ben Alder	1148	98 B2	Bràigh Coire Chruinn-bhalgain	1070	100 B2
Geal Charn	1132	98 B2	An Socach	1069	117 D6
Ben Lui	1130	85 F3	Meall Corranaich	1069	87 D1
Creag Meagaidh	1130	108 B6	Glas Maol	1068	101 D2
An Riabhachan	1129	117 E6	Sgurr Fhuaran	1068	106 C3
Binnein Mòr	1128	97 E3	Cairn of Claise	1064	101 D2
Ben Cruachan	1126	85 D2	Bidein a' Ghlas Thuill	1062	117 D1
Carn nan Gabhar	1121	100 B2	Sgurr Fiona	1059	117 D1
A' Chràlaig	1120	107 D3	Na Gruagaichean	1055	97 E3
An Stuc	1118	87 D1	Spidean a' Choire Leith	1054	116 C4
Meall Garbh	1118	87 D1	Toll Creagach	1054	107 E2
Sgor Gaoith	1118	110 A5	Sgurr a' Chaorachain	1053	117 D5
Stob Coire Easain	1116	97 F2	Stob Poite Coire Ardair	1053	108 B6
Stob Coire an Laoigh	1115	97 E2	Beinn a' Chaorainn	1052	108 A6
Aonach Beag	1114	98 B2	Glas Tulaichean	1051	100 C2
Monadh Mòr	1113	110 A5	Geal Charn	1049	108 C6
Tom a' Chòinich	1111	107 E2	Sgurr Fhuar-thuill	1049	117 F5

Munro name	Height (m)	Map ref	Munro name	Height (m)	Map ref
Carn an t-Sagairt Mòr	1047	111 D6	Conival	987	128 A2
Chno Dearg	1047	97 F2	Creag Leacach	987	101 D2
Creag Mhòr	1047	86 A2	Druim Shionnach	987	107 D4
Glas Leathad Mòr	1046	118 B3	Gulvain	987	107 D6
Beinn Iutharn Mhòr	1045	100 C2	Lurg Mhòr	986	117 D5
Cruach Ardrain	1045	86 B3	Inaccessible Pinnacle	986	105 D2
Stob Coir' an Albannaich	1044	85 E1	Ben Vorlich	985	87 D4
Meall nan Tarmachan	1043	86 C2	Sgurr Mhòr	985	116 B3
Càrn Mairg	1041	99 D4	An Gearanach	982	97 D3
Sgurr na Ciche	1040	106 C5	Ciste Dhubh	982	107 D3
Beinn Achaladair	1039	86 A1	Mullach na Dheiragain	982	107 D2
Meall Ghaordie	1039	86 C2	Creag Mhòr	981	87 D1
Sgurr a' Bhealaich Dheirg	1038	107 D3	Maol Chinn-dearg	981	107 D4
Carn a' Mhaim	1037	110 A5	Stob Coire a' Chairn	981	97 D3
Gleouraich	1035	107 D4	Beinn a' Chochuill	980	85 E2
Carn Dearg	1034	98 C2	Cona' Mheall	980	117 F1
Am Bodach	1032	97 D3	Slioch	980	117 D3
Beinn Fhada	1032	107 D3	Beinn Dubhchraig	977	86 A3
Carn an Righ	1029	100 C2	Meall nan Ceapraichean	977	117 F1
Ben Oss	1028	85 F3	Stob Bàn	977	97 E2
Càrn Gorm	1028	99 D4	Stob Coire Sgriodain	976	97 F2
Sgurr a' Mhaoraich	1027	106 C4	A' Mharconaich	975	99 D2
Sgurr na Ciste Duibhe	1027	106 C3	Carn a' Gheoidh	975	101 D2
Ben Challum	1025	86 A2	Carn Liath	975	100 B3
Sgorr Dhearg	1024	96 C4	Stuc a' Chroin	975	87 D4
Mullach an Rathain	1023	116 C4	Beinn Sgritheall	974	106 B3
Stob Dearg	1022	97 E4	Ben Lomond	974	86 A5
Aonach air Chrith	1021	107 D4	Sgurr a' Ghreadaidh	973	105 D2
Ladhar Bheinn	1020	106 B4	Meall Garbh	968	99 D4
Beinn Bheòil	1019	98 C2	A' Mhaighdean	967	117 D2
Carn an Tuirc	1019	110 C6	Sgorr nam Fiannaidh	967	97 D4
Mullach Clach a' Bhlàir	1019	109 F5	Ben More	966	83 D2
Mullach Coire Mhic Fhearchair	1019	117 D2	Sgurr na Banachdich	965	105 D2
Garbh Chioch Mhòr	1013	106 C5	Sgurr nan Gillean	965	105 D2
Cairn Bannoch	1012	111 D6	Carn a' Chlamain	963	100 B2
Beinn Ime	1011	85 F5	Sgurr Thuilm	963	106 C6
Beinn Udlamain	1010	98 C2	Meall nan Con	961	128 C1
Ruadh-stac Mòr	1010	116 C3	Beinn nan Aighenan	960	85 E1
Saddle, The	1010	106 C3	Meall Glas	960	86 B2
Sgurr an Doire Leathain	1010	107 D4	Sgorr Ruadh	960	116 C4
Beinn Dearg	1008	99 F2	Stuchd an Lochain	960	86 B1
Sgurr Eilde Mòr	1008	97 E3	Beinn Fhionnlaidh	959	85 D1
Maoile Lunndaidh	1007	117 E5	Saileag	959	107 D3
An Sgarsoch	1006	110 A6	Bruach na Frithe	958	105 D2
Carn Liath	1006	108 B5	Stob Dubh	958	97 D4
Beinn Fhionnlaidh	1005	107 E2	Tolmount	958	111 D6
Devil's Point, The	1004	110 A5	Carn Ghluasaid	957	107 E3
Sgurr an Lochain	1004	107 D3	Tom Buidhe	957	101 E2
Aonach Meadhoin	1003	107 D3	Sgurr nan Coireachan	956	106 C6
Sgurr Mòr	1003	106 C5	Stob na Broige	956	97 D4
Beinn an Dòthaidh	1002	86 A1	Sgòr Gaibhre	955	98 B3
Sàil Chaorainn	1002	107 E3	Am Faochagach	954	118 A2
Sgurr na Carnach	1002	106 C3	Beinn Liath Mhòr Fannaich	954	117 F2
Meall Greigh	1001	87 D1	Beinn Mhanach	954	86 A1
Sgorr Dhonuill	1001	96 C4	Meall Dearg	953	97 D4
Sgurr Breac	1000	117 E2	Sgurr nan Coireachan	953	106 C5
A' Chailleach	999	117 E2	Meall Chuaich	951	109 E6
Sgurr Choinnich	999	117 D5	Meall Gorm	949	117 F3
Stob Bàn	999	97 D3	Beinn Bhuidhe	948	85 F4
Ben More Assynt	998	128 A2	Sgurr Mhic Choinnich	948	105 D2
Broad Cairn	998	111 D6	Creag a' Mhaim	947	107 D4
Stob Diamh	998	85 D2	Driesh	947	101 E2
Glas Bheinn Mhòr	997	85 E1	Beinn Tulaichean	946	86 B4
Spidean Mialach	996	107 D4	Carn Bhac	946	110 B6
An Caisteal	995	86 A4	Meall Buidhe	946	106 B5
Carn an Fhidhleir	994	110 A6	Bidein a' Choire Sheasgaich	945	117 D5
Sgor na h-Ulaidh	994	97 D4	Carn Dearg	945	109 D4
Sgurr Alasdair	993	105 D2	Sgurr na Sgine	945	106 C3
Sgurr na Ruaidhe	993	117 F5	An Socach	944	110 B6
Spidean Coire nan Clach	993	116 C4	Sgurr Dubh Mòr	944	105 D2
Carn nan Gobhar (Lapaichs)	992	117 E6	Ben Vorlich	943	85 F4
Carn nan Gobhar (Strathfarrar)	992	117 F5	Stob a' Choire Odhair	943	85 F1
Sgairneach Mhòr	991	98 C2	Carn Dearg	941	98 B3
Beinn Eunaich	989	85 E2	Carn na Caim	941	109 D6
Sgurr Ban	989	117 D2	Beinn a' Chroin	940	86 A4

Munro name	Height (m)	Map ref
Mayar	928	101 E2
Meall nan Eun	928	85 E1
Moruisg	928	117 E4
Ben Hope	927	133 F4
Seana Bhraigh	927	117 F1
Beinn Narnain	926	85 F5
Geal Charn	926	108 C5
Meall a' Choire Leith	926	87 D1
Beinn Liath Mhòr	925	116 C4
Stob Coire Raineach	925	97 D4
Creag Pitridh	924	108 B6
Sgurr nan Eag	924	105 D3
An Coileachan	923	117 F3
Sgurr nan Each	923	117 E3
Tom na Gruagaich	922	116 B3
Sgaith Chuil	921	86 B2
An Socach	920	107 D2
Carn Sgulain	920	109 D4
Gairich	919	107 D5
A' Ghlas-bheinn	918	107 D2
Creag nan Damh	918	106 C3
Ruadh Stac Mòr	918	117 D2
Sgurr a' Mhadaidh	918	105 D2
Beinn a' Chleibh	917	85 F3
Carn Aosda	917	101 D2
Geal-chàrn	917	98 C2
Meall na Teanga	917	107 F5
Ben Vane	916	85 F5
Beinn Teallach	915	108 A6
Sgurr nan Ceannaichean	915	117 D5
Beinn a' Chlaidheimh	914	117 D2

Munro name	Height (m)	Map ref
Binnein Beag	940	97 E3
Luinne Bheinn	939	106 B4
Mount Keen	939	111 F6
Mullach nan Coirean	939	97 D3
Beinn na Lap	937	97 F3
Beinn Sgulaird	937	85 D1
A' Bhuidheanach Bheag	936	99 D2
Beinn Tarsuinn	936	117 D2
Am Basteir	935	105 D2
Sròn a' Choire Ghairbh	935	107 F5
Meall a' Chrasgaidh	934	117 E2
Beinn Chabhair	933	86 A4
Cairnwell, The	933	101 D2
Fionn Bheinn	933	117 E3
Maol Chean-dearg	933	116 C4
Meall Buidhe	932	98 B4
Beinn Bhreac	931	110 B5
Ben Chonzie	931	87 E2
A' Chailleach	930	109 D4
Bla Bheinn	928	105 E2
Eididh nan Clach Geala	928	117 F1

Golf courses

Golf is an extremely popular sport throughout Scotland. Below are contact details for the 18 hole courses.

Aberdour 01383 860080 — 78 C2
www.aberdourgolfclub.co.uk
Aboyne 01339 887078 — 112 A5
www.aboynegolfclub.co.uk
Airdrie 01236 762195 — 77 E4
www.airdriegolfclub.co.uk
Alford 01975 562178 — 112 A3
www.golf.alford.co.uk
Alloa 01259 722745 — 78 A1
www.alloagolfclub.co.uk
Alyth 01828 632268 — 90 B1
www.alythgolfclub.co.uk
Annanhill 01563 521644 — 66 C2
Arbroath Links 01241 875837 — 91 F2
Ardeer 01294 464542 — 75 F6
www.ardeergolfclub.co.uk
Auchmill 01224 714577 — 113 D4
Auchterarder 01764 662804 — 88 C4
www.auchterardergolf.co.uk
Baberton 0131 453 4911 — 78 C4
www.baberton.co.uk
Balbirnie Park 01592 752006 — 90 B5
www.balbirniegolf.com
Balfron 01360 550613 — 76 C2
www.balfrongolfsociety.org.uk
Ballater 013397 55567 — 111 E5
www.ballatergolfclub.co.uk
Ballochmyle 01290 550469 — 67 D3
Ballumbie Castle 01382 770028 — 91 D2
www.ballumbiecastlegolfclub.com
Balmore 01360 620284 — 76 C3
www.balmoregolfclub.co.uk
Balnagask 01224 876407 — 113 E4
Banchory 01330 822365 — 112 B5
www.banchorygolfclub.co.uk
Barshaw Park 0141 840 3106 — 76 C4
Bathgate 01506 630505 — 78 A4
www.bathgategolfclub.visps.com/

Beith 01505 503166 — 76 A5
www.beithgolfclub.co.uk
Belleisle 01292 616255 — 66 B4
www.golfsouthayrshire.com/belleisle.html
Bellshill 01698 745124 — 77 E5
www.bellshillgolfclub.com
Biggar Park 01899 220319 — 68 C2
Bishopbriggs, The 0141 772 8938 — 77 D3
www.thebishopbriggsgolfclub.com
Blairbeth 0141 634 3355 — 77 D5
www.blairbeth.co.uk
Blairgowrie 01250 872622 — 89 E1
www.theblairgowriegolfclub.co.uk
Boat of Garten 01479 831282 — 110 A3
www.boatgolf.com
Bonnyton 01355 302781 — 76 C5
www.bonnytongolfclub.com
Bothwell Castle 01698 801969 — 77 D5
www.bcgolf.co.uk
Braehead 01259 722078 — 77 F1
www.braehead.gc.btinternet.com
Braemar 013397 41618 — 110 C6
www.braemargolfclub.co.uk
Braid Hills 0131 447 6666 — 79 D4
www.edinburghleisure.co.uk/detail-74
Brechin 01356 625270 — 103 D3
www.brechingolfclub.co.uk
Brighouse Bay 01557 870509 — 60 C5
www.brighousebay-golfclub.com
Brodick 01770 302349 — 65 E2
Broomieknowe 0131 663 9317 — 79 E4
www.broomieknowe.com
Brora 01408 621417 — 130 C4
www.broragolf.co.uk
Brunston Castle 01465 811825 — 66 A5
www.brunstoncastle.co.uk
Bruntsfield Links 0131 336 1479 — 78 C3
www.sol.co.uk/b/bruntsfieldlinks

Buchanan Castle 01360 660330   76 B2
www.buchanancastlegolfclub.com
Buckpool 01542 832236   123 D3
www.buckpoolgolf.com
Burntisland 01596 872116   79 D2
www.burntislandhouseclub.co.uk
Caird Park 01382 438871   91 D2
Caldwell 01505 850329   76 B5
www.caldwellgolfclub.i8.com
Callander 01877 330975   87 D5
www.callandergolfclub.co.uk
Cally Palace Hotel 01557 814341   60 C4
www.callypalace.co.uk
Cameron House Hotel 01389 755565   76 A2
Camperdown 01382 431820   90 C2
Campsie 01360 310920   77 D3
www.campsiegolfclub.org.uk
Canmore 01383 728416   78 B2
www.canmoregolf.co.uk

Gleneagles Hotel Golf Course

Caprington 01563 521915   66 C2
Cardross 01389 841350   76 A3
www.cardross.com
Carluke 01555 770574   77 F5
Carnegie Club, The 01862 894600   119 E1
www.carnegieclub.co.uk
Carnoustie 01241 853789   91 E2
www.carnoustiegolflinks.co.uk
Carnwath 01555 840023   78 A6
www.carnwathgc.co.uk
Carrick Knowe 0131 337 1096   79 D3
www.edinburghleisure.co.uk/detail-75
Castle Park 01620 810733   80 A4
www.castleparkgolfclub.co.uk
Cathcart Castle 0141 638 3436   76 C5
Cathkin Braes 0141 634 0650   77 D5
www.cathkinbraesgolfclub.co.uk
Cawder 0141 761 1282   77 D3
www.cawder.co.uk
Charleton 01333 340505   91 D5
www.charleton.co.uk
Clober 0141 956 1685   76 C3
www.clober.co.uk
Clydebank & District 01389 383831   76 C3
www.clydebankanddistrictgolfclub.co.uk
Clydebank Municipal 0141 952 6372   76 B3
Coatbridge 01236 421492   77 E4
Cochrane Castle 01505 328465   76 B4
www.cochranecastle.com
Colonsay 01951 200290   72 C1
Colvend 01556 630398   61 E4
www.colvendgolfclub.co.uk
Colville Park 01698 262808   77 E5
www.colvillepark.co.uk
Cowal 01369 702395   75 E3
www.cowalgolfclub.com
Cowdenbeath 01383 511918   78 C1
www.fifegolf.org
Cowglen 0141 649 9401   76 C4
www.cowglengolfclub.co.uk
Craggan 01479 873283   110 B2
www.cragganforleisure.co.uk
Craibstone 01224 716777   113 D3
www.craibstone.com

Craigentinny 0131 554 7501   79 D3
www.edinburghleisure.co.uk/detail-77
Craigie Hill 01738 622644   89 E3
www.craigiehill.co.uk
Craigielaw 01875 870800   79 F3
www.craigielawgolfclub.com
Craigmillar Park 0131 667 2850   79 D3
www.craigmillarpark.co.uk
Crail 01333 450686   91 F5
www.crailgolfingsociety.co.uk
Crieff 01764 652909   88 B3
www.crieffgolf.co.uk
Crow Wood 0141 779 4954   77 D3
www.crowwood-golfclub.co.uk
Cruden Bay 01779 812285   125 E6
www.crudenbaygolfclub.co.uk
Culcrieff 01764 651622   88 B3
www.crieffhydro.com
Cullen 01542 840685   123 D3
www.cullengolfclub.co.uk
Dalmahoy Hotel 0131 333 1845   78 C4
Dalmilling 01292 263893   66 B3
www.golfsouthayrshire.com
Dalziel Park Hotel 01698 862862   77 E5
www.dalzielpark.co.uk
Deaconsbank 0141 638 7044   76 C5
Deer Park 01506 446699   78 B4
www.deer-park.co.uk
Deeside 01224 861041   113 D4
www.deesidegolfclub.com
Dollar 01259 742400   78 A1
www.dollargolfclub.com
Douglas Park 0141 942 0985   76 C3
www.douglasparkgolfclub.co.uk
Downfield 01382 825595   90 C2
www.downfieldgolf.co.uk
Drumoig Hotel 01382 541898   91 D3
www.drumoigleisure.com
Drumpellier 01236 424139   77 E4
Duddingston 0131 661 4301   79 D3
www.duddingstongolfclub.co.uk
Duff House Royal 01261 812062   123 F3
www.theduffhouseroyalgolfclub.co.uk
Dufftown 01340 820325   122 C6
www.dufftown.co.uk/dufftown_golf_club.htm
Duke's St. Andrews, The 01334 470214   91 D4
www.oldcoursehotel.co.uk/golf/dukes_landing.html
Dullatur 01236 723230   77 E3
www.dullaturgolf.com
Dumbarton 01389 732830   76 A3
www.dumbartongolfclub.co.uk
Dumfries & County 01387 268918   61 F2
www.thecounty.org.uk
Dumfries & Galloway 01387 263848   61 F2
www.dandggolfclub.co.uk
Dunaverty 01586 830677   64 A5
www.dunavertygolfclub.com
Dunbar 01368 862317   80 C3
www.dunbar-golfclub.com
Dunblane New 01786 821521   87 E5
www.dngc.co.uk
Dundonald 01294 314000   66 B2
www.lochlomond.com
Dunfermline 01383 729061   78 B2
www.dunfermlinegolfclub.com
Dunnikier Park 01592 205916   79 D1
www.dunnikierparkgolfclub.com
Duns 01361 882194   80 C5
www.dunsgolfclub.com
East Aberdeenshire 01358 742111   113 E3
www.eagolf.com
East Kilbride 01355 222192   77 D5
East Renfrewshire 01355 500206   76 C5
www.eastrengolfclub.co.uk
Easter Moffat 01236 843015   77 F4
Eastwood 01355 500280   76 C5
www.eastwoodgolfclub.co.uk
Edzell 01356 647283   102 C3
www.edzellgolfclub.net
Elderslie 01505 323956   76 B4
www.eldersliegolfclub.com

Elgin 01343 542884 122 B3
www.elgingolfclub.com
Elmwood 01334 658780 90 C4
www.elmwoodgc.co.uk
Erskine 01505 862108 76 B3
www.erskinegolfclublimited.co.uk
Esporta Dougalston 0141 955 2404 76 C3
Eyemouth 018907 50004 81 E4
www.eyegolfclub.co.uk
Fairmont St. Andrews 01334 837023 91 E4
www.standrewsbay.com
Falkirk 01324 611061 77 F2
www.falkirkcarmuirsgolfclub.co.uk
Falkirk Tryst 01324 562091 77 F2
www.falkirktrystgolfclub.com
Fereneze 0141 880 7058 76 B5
www.ferenezegolfclub.co.uk
Forfar 01307 463773 102 B4
www.forfargolfclub.com
Forres 01309 672250 121 E4
www.forresgolf.org.uk
Forrester Park 01383 880505 78 B2
www.forresterparkresort.com
Fort William 01397 704464 97 D2
www.fortwilliamgolf.com
Fortrose & Rosemarkie 01381 620529 119 E4
www.fortrosegolfclub.co.uk
Fraserburgh 01346 516616 125 E3
www.fraserburghgolf.org
Galashiels 01896 753724 70 B2
Garmouth & Kingston 01343 870388 122 C3
Girvan 01292 616255 65 F6
www.south-ayrshire.gov.uk
Glasgow Gailes 01294 311561 66 B2
www.glasgowgailes-golf.com
Glasgow Killermont 0141 942 2011 76 C3
www.glasgowgailes-golf.com
Gleddoch 01475 540704 76 A3
Glen 01620 892726 80 A2
www.glengolfclub.co.uk
Glenbervie 01324 562725 77 F2
www.glenberviegolfclub.com
Glencorse 01968 676481 79 D4
www.glencorsegolfclub.com
Glencruitten 01631 562868 84 B3
www.obangolf.com
Gleneagles Hotel, The 0800 3893737 88 C4
www.gleneagles.com
Glenrothes 01592 750063 79 D1
www.glenrothesgolf.org.uk
Golf House Club 01333 330301 79 F1
www.golfhouseclub.co.uk
Golspie 01408 633266 129 F5
www.golspie-golf-club.co.uk
Gourock 01475 636834 75 F3
www.gourockgolfclub.com
Grangemouth 01324 503840 78 A3
Grantown-on-Spey 01479 872079 110 B2
www.grantownonspeygolfclub.co.uk
Green Hotel, The 01577 863407 89 E5
www.green-hotel.com/leisure/golf.asp
Greenburn 01501 771187 78 A4
www.greenburngolfclub.co.uk
Greenock, The 01475 787236 75 F3
www.greenockgolfclub.co.uk
Greenock Whinhill 01475 724694 75 F3
www.greenockwhinhillgolfclub.com
Gullane 01620 842255 79 F2
www.gullanegolfclub.com
Haddington 01620 822727 80 A3
www.haddingtongolf.com
Haggs Castle 0141 427 3355 76 C4
www.haggscastlegolfclub.com
Hamilton 01698 282872 77 E5
www.hamiltongolfclub.com
Harburn 01506 871131 78 B4
www.harburngolfclub.co.uk
Hawick 01450 372293 70 B4
www.hawickgolfclub.com

Hayston 0141 775 0723 77 D3
www.haystongolf.com
Hazlehead 01224 321830 113 D4
Helensburgh 01436 675505 76 A2
www.helensburghgolfclub.co.uk
Hilton Park 0141 956 5125 76 C3
www.hiltonpark.co.uk
Hollandbush 01555 893646 68 A2
www.hollandbushgolfclub.co.uk
Hopeman 01343 830578 122 A3
www.hopemangc.co.uk
Huntly 01466 792643 123 E5
www.huntlygc.com
Inchmarlo 01330 826422 112 B5
www.inchmarlogolf.com
Insch 01464 820363 112 B2
www.inschgolfclub.co.uk
Inverallochy 01346 582000 125 E3
www.inverallochygolfclub.co.uk
Invergordon 01349 852715 119 E3
www.invergordongolf.co.uk
Inverness 01463 239882 119 D5
www.invernessgolfclub.co.uk
Inverurie 01467 672863 112 C2
www.inveruriegc.fsbusiness.co.uk
Irvine, The 01294 275979 76 A6
www.theirvinegolfclub.co.uk
Irvine Ravenspark 01294 276467 76 A6
www.irgc.co.uk
Jedburgh 01835 863587 70 C4
www.jedburghgolfclub.co.uk
Kames 01555 870015 78 A6
www.kames-golf-club.com
Keith 01542 886014 123 D4
www.keithgolfclub.org.uk
Kelso 01573 223009 71 D2
www.kelsogolfclub.co.uk
Kemnay 01467 642225 112 C3
www.kemnaygolfclub.co.uk
Kilbirnie Place 01505 684444 76 A5
www.kilbirnieplacegolfclub.co.uk
Kilmacolm 01505 872695 76 A4
www.kilmacolmgolfclub.com
Kilmarnock (Barassie) 01292 313920 66 B2
www.kbgc.co.uk
Kilspindie 01875 870358 79 F3
www.golfeastlothian.com
Kilsyth Lennox 01236 824115 77 E3
www.kilsythlennox.com

Glen Golf Club

King James VI 01738 632460 89 E3
www.kingjamesvi.co.uk
Kinghorn 01592 890978 79 D2
www.kinghorngolfclub.co.uk
Kings Acre 0131 663 3456 79 E4
www.kings-acregolf.com
King's Links 01224 632269 113 E4
Kingsbarns 01334 460860 91 F4
www.kingsbarns.com
Kingsknowe 0131 441 4030 79 D4
www.kingsknowe.com

54 Golf courses

Kingussie 01540 661600   109 E4
www.kingussie-golf.co.uk
Kintore 01467 632631   113 D3
www.kintoregolfclub.net
Kirkcaldy 01592 203258   79 D1
www.kirkcaldygolfclub.co.uk
Kirkcudbright 01557 330314   60 C4
www.kirkcudbrightgolf.co.uk
Kirkhill 0141 641 7972   77 D5
www.kirkhillgolfclub.co.uk
Kirkintilloch 0141 775 2387   77 D3
www.kirkintillochgolfclub.co.uk
Kirriemuir 01575 573317   101 F4
www.kirriemuirgolfclub.co.uk
Ladybank 01337 830814   90 C4
www.ladybankgolf.co.uk
Lagganmore Hotel 01776 810262   58 B4
www.lagganmoregolf.co.uk
Lamlash 01770 600296   65 E2
www.lamlashgolfclub.co.uk
Lanark 01555 662349   78 A6
www.lanarkgolfclub.co.uk
Langlands 01355 224685   77 D5
Largs 01475 673594   75 F5
www.largsgolfclub.co.uk
Lenzie 0141 777 7748   77 D3
www.lenziegolfclub.co.uk
Letham Grange Hotel 01241 890373   91 F1
Lethamhill 0141 770 6220   77 D4
Leven Links 01333 421390   90 C5
www.leven-links.com
Liberton 0131 664 1056   79 D3
www.libertongc.co.uk
Linn Park 0141 633 0377   76 C5
Littlehill 0141 772 1916   77 D4
Loch Lomond 01436 655555   76 A2
www.lochlomond.com
Loch Ness 01463 713334   119 D5
www.golflochness.com
Lochgelly 01592 782589   78 C1
Lochranza 01770 830273   74 C5
www.arran.uk.com/lochranza/golfcourse
Lochwinnoch 01505 843029   76 A5
www.lochwinnochgolf.co.uk
Longniddry 01875 852228   79 F3
www.longniddrygolfclub.co.uk
Longside 01779 821558   125 E5
Lothianburn 0131 445 2288   79 D4
www.lothianburngc.co.uk
Loudoun 01563 821993   67 D2
www.loudoungowfclub.co.uk
Luffness New 01620 843336   79 F2
www.luffnessgolf.com
Lundin 01333 320202   91 D5
www.lundingolfclub.co.uk
Macdonald Cardrona 01896 833701   69 E2
www.macdonaldhotels.co.uk/cardrona/index.htm
Machrie Hotel 01496 302310   72 C6
www.machrie.com
Machrihanish 01586 810277   64 A3
www.machgolf.com
McDonald 01358 722891   125 D6
www.ellongolfclub.co.uk
Meldrum House 01651 873553   113 D2
www.meldrumhousegolfclub.com
Melville 0131 663 8038   79 E4
www.melvillegolf.com
Merchants of Edinburgh 0131 447 1219   79 D3
www.merchantsgolf.com
Millport 01475 530 306   75 E5
www.millportgolfclub.co.uk
Milngavie 0141 956 1619   76 C3
www.milngaviegc.com
Minto 01450 870220   70 B3
www.mintogolf.co.uk
Moffat 01683 220020   68 C5
www.moffatgolfclub.co.uk

Monifieth 01382 532767   91 E2
www.monifiethgolf.co.uk
Montrose 01674 672932   103 E4
www.montroselinks.co.uk
Moray 01343 812018   122 B2
www.moraygolf.co.uk
Mortonhall 0131 447 6974   79 D4
www.mortonhallgc.co.uk
Mount Ellen 01236 872632   77 E4
Mouse Valley 01555 870015   78 A6
www.kames-golf-club.com
Muir of Ord 01463 870825   118 C5
Muirfield 01620 842123   79 F2
www.muirfield.org.uk
Murcar 01224 704354   113 E3
www.murcar.co.uk
Murrayfield 0131 337 3479   79 D3
www.murrayfieldgolfclub.com
Murrayshall 01738 552784   89 E3
www.murrayshall.com
Musselburgh 0131 665 7055   79 E3
www.themusselburghgolfclub.com
Nairn, The 01667 453208   119 F4
www.nairngolfclub.com
Nairn Dunbar 01667 452741   119 F4
www.nairndunbar.com
Newbattle 0131 660 1631   79 E4
www.newbattlegolfclub.com
Newburgh-on-Ythan 01358 789058   113 F2
www.newburgh-on-ythan.co.uk
Newmachar 01651 863002   113 D3
www.newmachargolfclub.com
Newton Stewart 01671 402172   60 A3
www.newtonstewartgolfclub.com
Newtonmore 01540 673878   109 E5
www.newtonmoregolf.com
Niddry Castle 01506 891097   78 B3
www.niddrycastlegc.co.uk
North Berwick 01620 895040   80 A2
www.northberwickgolfclub.com
North Inch 01738 636481   89 E3
Old Course Ranfurly 01505 613214   76 A4
www.oldranfurly.com
Oldmeldrum 01651 873555   113 D2
www.oldmeldrumgolf.co.uk
Orkney 01856 872457   147 D2
www.orkneygolfclub.co.uk
Paisley 0141 884 4114   76 B5
www.paisleygolfclub.co.uk
Palacerigg 01236 721461   77 E3
www.palacerigggolfclub.co.uk
Panmure 01241 852460   91 E2
www.panmuregolfclub.co.uk
Peebles 01721 720197   79 D6
www.peeblesgolfclub.co.uk
Peterculter 01224 735245   113 D4
www.petercultergolfclub.co.uk
Peterhead 01779 472149   125 F5
www.peterheadgolfclub.co.uk
Pines, The 01387 247444   61 F2
www.pinesgolf.com
Piperdam 01382 581374   90 C2
www.piperdam.com/golf-breaks.cfm
Pitlochry 01796 472792   100 B4
www.pitlochrygolf.co.uk
Pitreavie 01383 722591   78 C2
www.pitreaviegolfclub.co.uk
Pollok 0141 632 1080   76 C4
www.pollokgolf.com
Port Bannatyne 01700 504544   75 D4
www.portbannatynegolf.co.uk
Port Glasgow 01475 704181   76 A3
www.portglasgowgolfclub.com
Portlethen 01224 782571   113 E5
www.portlethengolfclub.com
Portpatrick 01776 810273   58 A4
www.portpatrickgolfclub.co.uk
Powfoot 01461 204100   62 B3
www.powfootgolfclub.com
Prestonfield 0131 667 9665   79 D3
www.prestonfieldgolf.com

St. Andrews Links

Road maps

M8	Motorway
full access / limited access	Motorway junction
Stirling / Harthill Bothwell	Motorway service area with off road / full / limited access
dual A71 single	Primary route
dual A93 single	'A' road
dual B778 single	'B' road
	Minor road
	Restricted access
	Road with passing places
	Road proposed or under construction
	Multi-level junction
	Roundabout
10	Road distance in miles
	Road tunnel
	Steep hill (arrows point downhill)
Toll	Level crossing / Toll
Lerwick 2½ hrs	Car ferry route & journey times
Speyside Way	Long Distance Footpath

	Railway line / station / tunnel
	National boundary
	National Park boundary
	Regional Park boundary
	Forest Park boundary
	Built up area
	Woodland
468 716	Spot / summit height in metres
Cairn Gorm 1245	Munro summit height in metres
	Beach
	Lake / Dam / River / Waterfall
	Canal / Dry canal / Canal tunnel
✈	Airport with scheduled services
Ⓗ	Heliport
Ⓟ	Park and Ride site (Operates at least 5 days a week)
□ □ ▫	Town / Village / Other settlement
Dunoon	Seaside destination

1 : 281,690
4.5 miles to 1 inch / 2.8 km to 1 cm

0		2		4			6 miles
0	2	4	6	8	10 km		

Height reference

	0	165	490	985	1640	2295	2950	ft
water	land 0 below sea level	50	150	300	500	700	900	m

City centre plans

M8	Motorway
dual A92	Primary route
dual A85	'A' road
dual B90	'B' road
dual	Other road
	Path / Footbridge
	Restricted access
	One way street
	Pedestrian street

Ⓟ	Car park
	Railway line / Station / Subway station
†	Ecclesiastical building
	Tourist building
	Important building
	Higher Education building
	Hospital
† †	Cemetery
	Recreational area / Open space

Places of interest & tourist features

★	Symbols highlighted in yellow are notable tourist attractions	⚓	Lighthouse
⚑	Ancient monument	🏆	Major sports venue
🐟	Aquarium	🏛	Museum / Art gallery
✕	Battlefield	🦜	Nature reserve
⛺	Campsite	🏃	Outdoor activity centre
🚐	Caravan site	£	Outlet / Shopping village
♖	Castle	🎋	Picnic site
🏞	Country park	🚢	Pleasure boat trip
🚲	Cycle trail	⋯⋯	Preserved railway
🍶	Distillery / Brewery	⛷	Skiing
✝	Ecclesiastical building	🎭	Theatre / Arts centre
❀	Garden	🎢	Theme park
⛳9ǀ18	Golf course 9 hole / 18 hole	𝒊 ⓘ	Tourist Information Centre (all year / seasonal)
●	Guided tour / Nature trail	☆☀	Viewpoint
⌂	Historic house (with or without garden)	Ⓨ	Wildlife park / Zoo
∪	Horse riding / Pony trekking centre	★	Other place of interest
		(NTS)	National Trust for Scotland

Key to pages

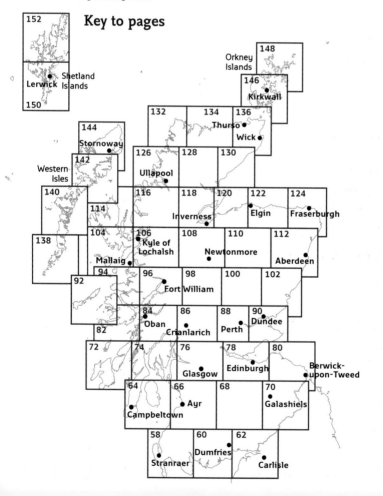

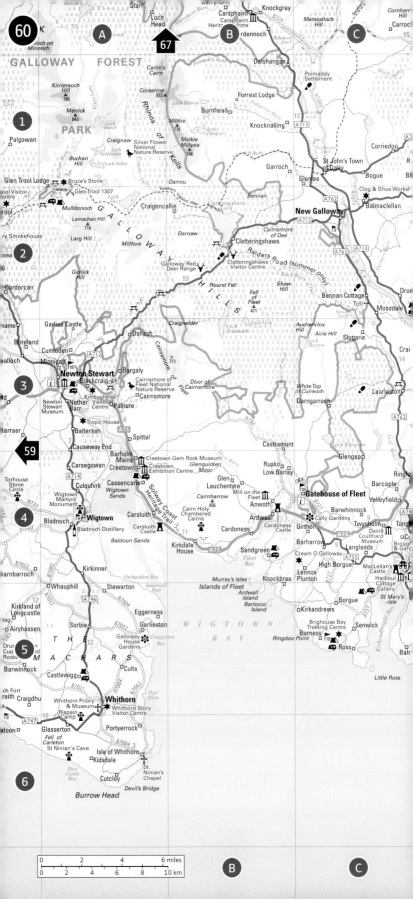

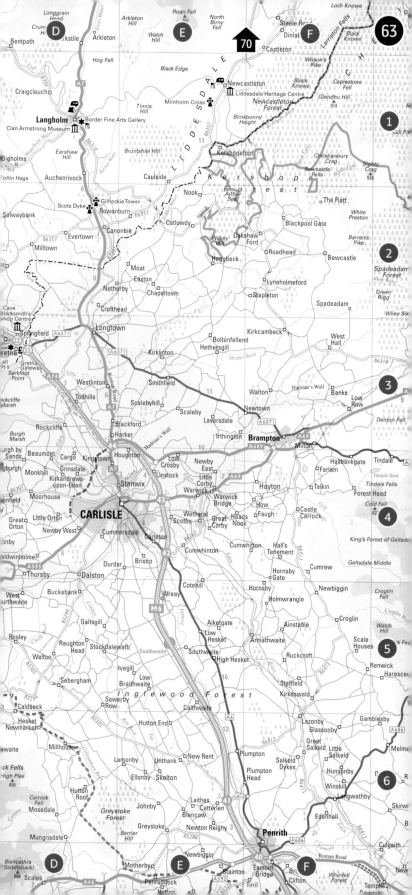

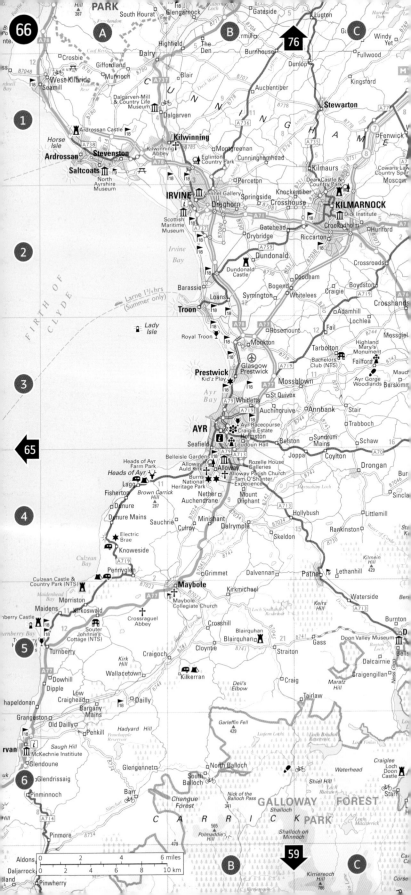

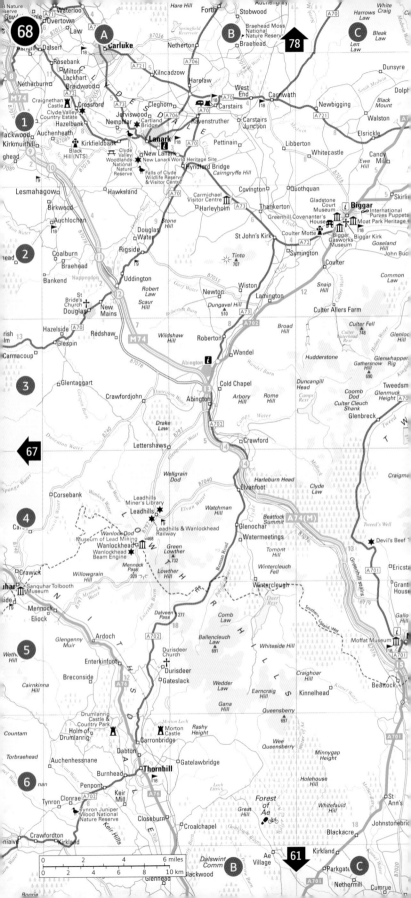

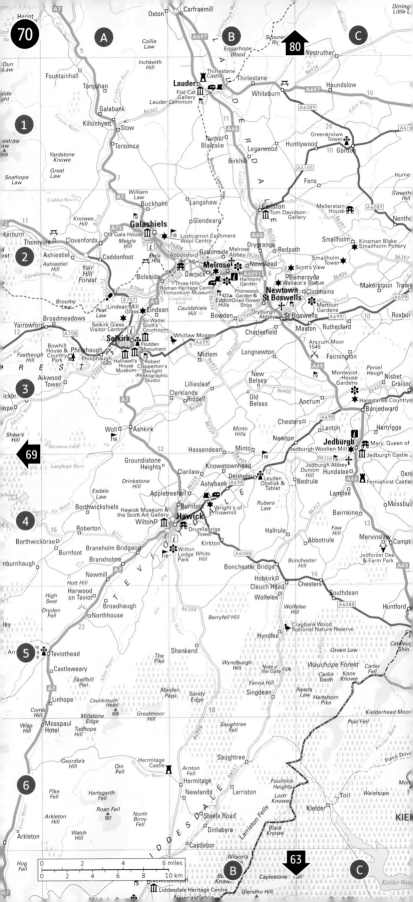

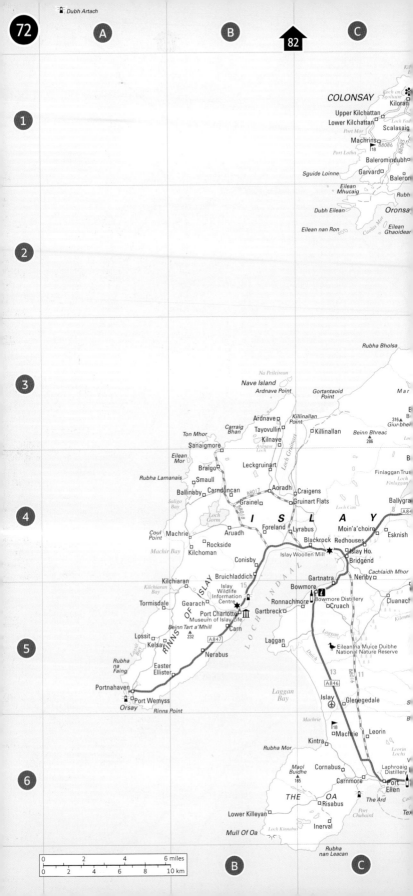

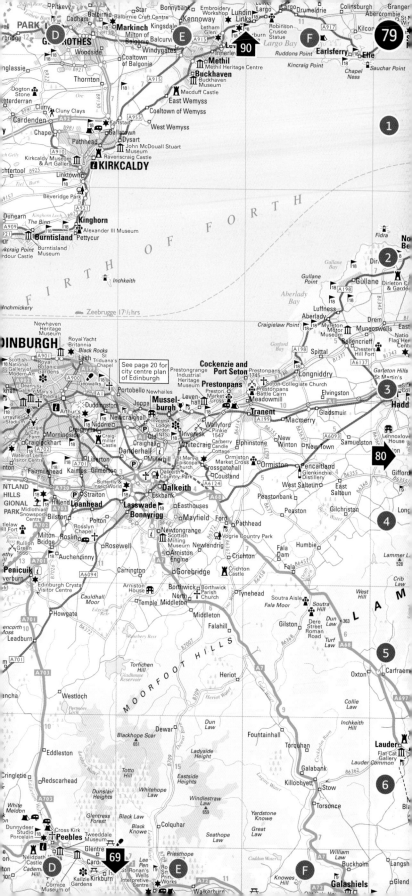

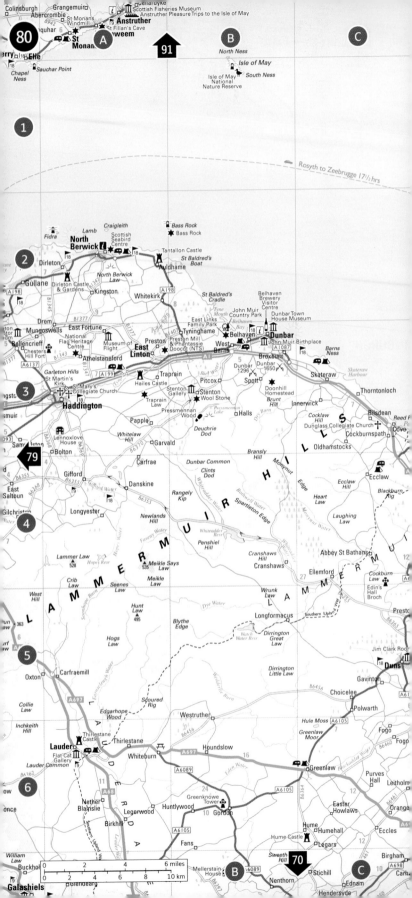

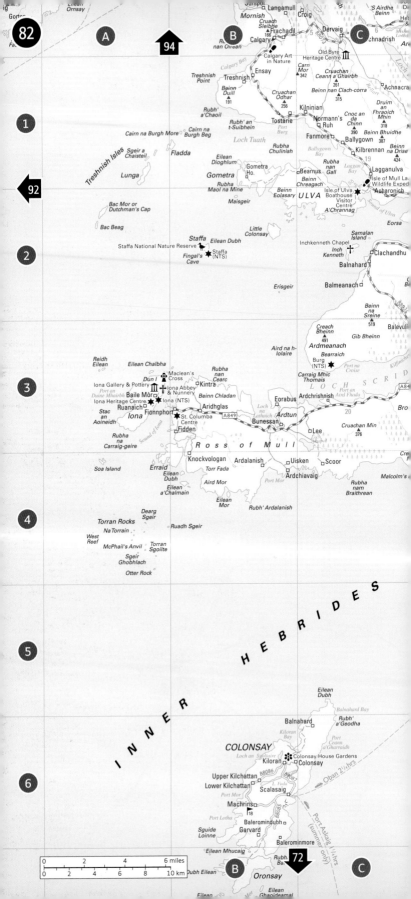

INNER HEBRIDES

Grishipoll Bay
Griship
Clabhach
Ballyhaugh
Ber Hog
104
Hogh Bay
Totam
Totronald
Arileod
Acha
Uig
C
Port Mine
Feall Bay
Gorton
Calgary Point
Crossapol
Friesk Bay
Crossupol Bay
Rubha Fasachd
Gunna
Soa
Loch Breachacha

Urvaig
Port a'Mhuirain
Miodar
Sgeir Bharrach
Salum Bay
Rubha Dubh
Vaul
Caolas
The Green
Balephetrish Bay
Balephetrish Hill
B8069
Ruaig
Port Ban
Coll - Tiree 1½ hrs
Brock
Hough Bay
5
Gott Bay
Rubha Liath
T I R E E
Scarinish
Soa
Kilkenneth
Tiree
B8068
Sandaig Island Life Museum
Moss
Crossapoll
B8065
Baugh
Heanish
Sandaig
Heylipoll
2
Hynish Bay
Barrapoll
3
B8067
Balemartine
Rinn Thorbhais
Balephuil
Mannal
Hynish
Story of Skerryvore

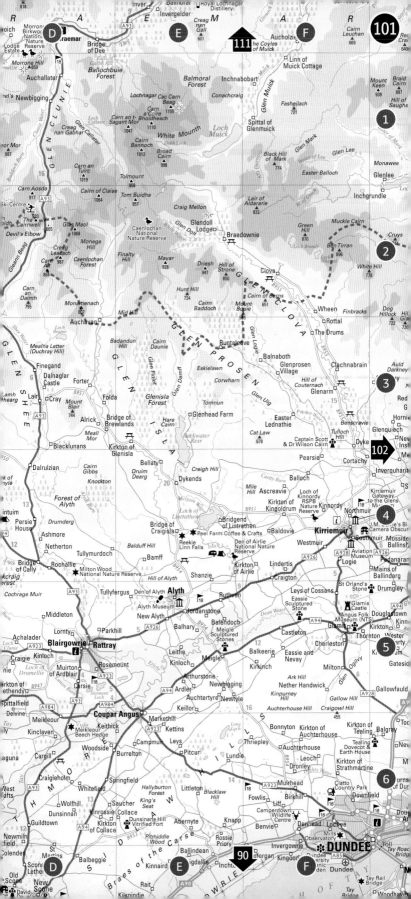

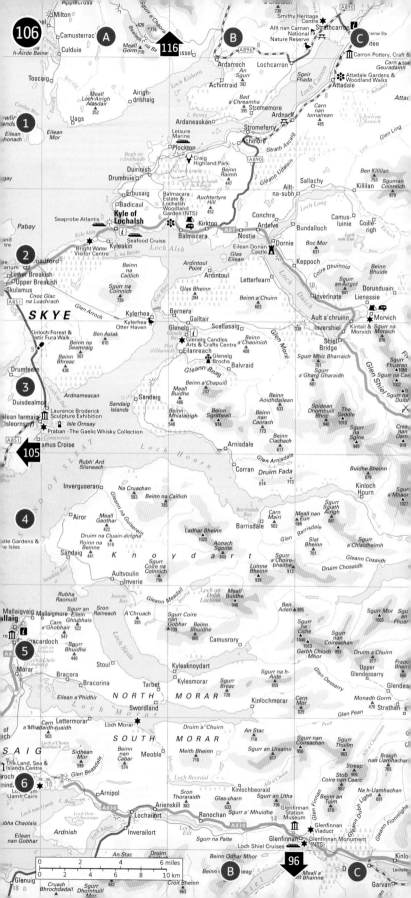

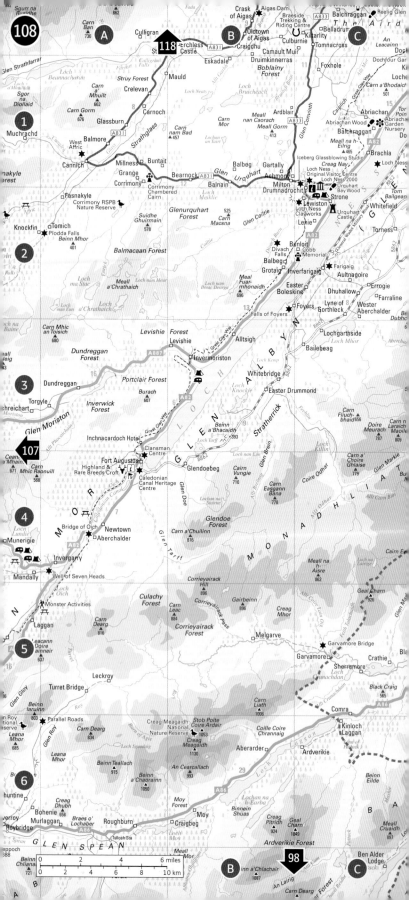

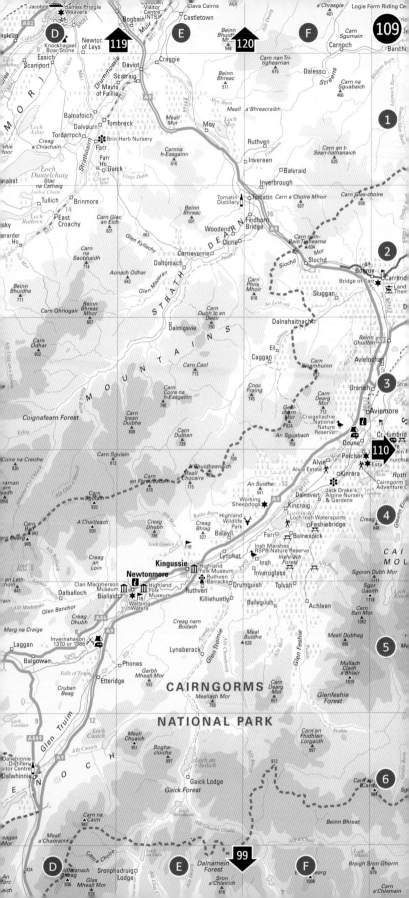

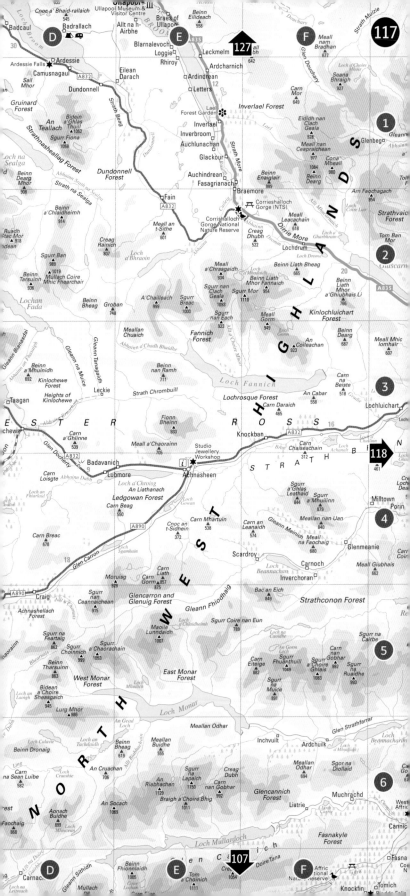

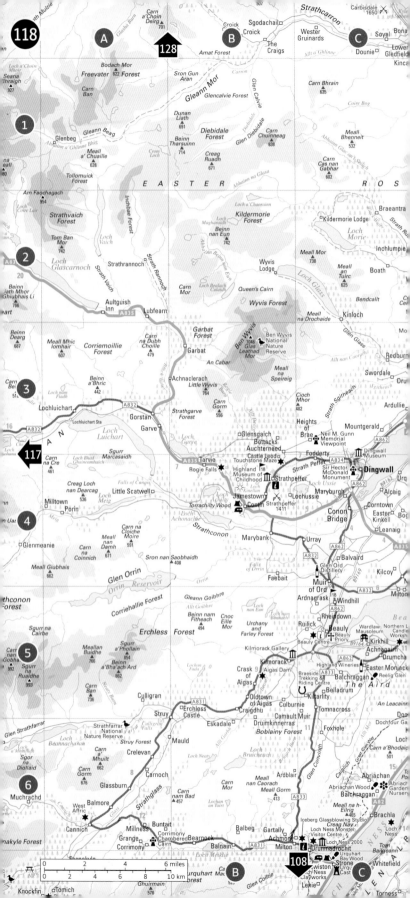

See page 42 for city centre plan of Inverness

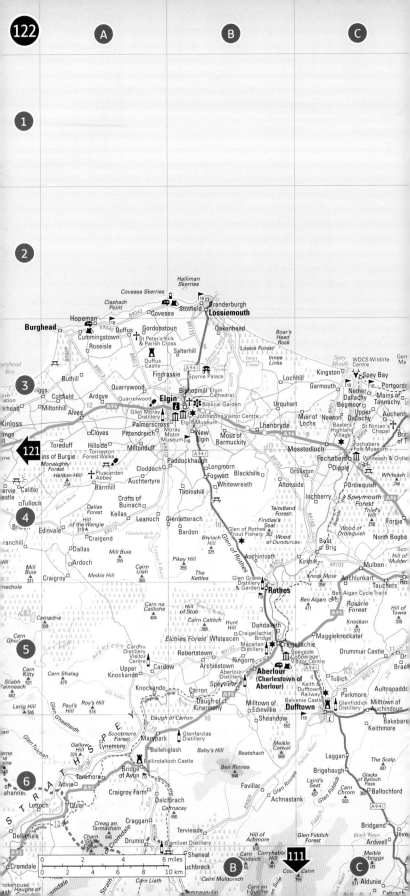

1

2

3

4

5

6

D

E

F

ehearty

Sandhaven
Fraserburgh
Heritage
Centre
Kinnaird
Head
Museum of Scottish Lighthouses
Broadsea
Fraserburgh
Sandhaven
Meal Mill
Peathill
Mid
Ardlaw
Pitblae
Cardno
Broomhead
Coburty
Maggie's
Hoosie
Fraserburgh
Bay
Cairnbulg Point
Cairnbulg
Inverallochy
Whitelinks Bay
Memsie
Charlestown
St Combs
Gowanhill
Inzie Head
Whitewell
Whitebog
Memsie
Cairn
Rathen
Cairness
Coralhill
South Inch
Craigellie
Loch of
Strathbeg
Strathbeg
Bay
Hillhead of
Auchentumb
Newburgh
Crimonmogate
Whitestripe
Waughton
Hill 234
Mormond Hill
230
Dartfield
Loch of
Strathbeg
RSPB
Nature
Reserve
Old
Rattray
Seatown
Rattray Head
Strichen
Crimond
Rattray Bay
Carnichal
New
Leeds
Upper
Ridinghill
Blackhill
North
Essie
Longhill
Backfolds
Leys
St Fergus
Moss
Kirktown
St Fergus
Gas Terminal
Scotstown Head
Denhead
Hythie
Rora Moss
Cuttyhill
Rora
Kirkton Head
Fetterangus
Forest
of Deer
Toux
Mains of
Pitfour
Aberdeenshire
Farming Museum
Millbank
Torterston
Inverugie
Lunderton
Craig Ewen
Ugie Salmon Fish House
Arbuthnot Museum
Peterhead
Maud
Waterhill of
Bruxie
Old Deer
Aden
Country
Park
Mintlaw
Longside
Inverquhomery
Flushing
Thunderton
Buchanhaven
Peterhead Maritime
Heritage Centre
Keith Inch
Bulwark
Stuartfield
Millbreck
Hillhead of
Cocklaw
Invernettie
Peterhead Bay
Nethermuir
Crichie
Clola
Nether
Kinmundy
Little
Dens
Blackhill
Stirling
Burnhaven
Sandford
Bay
Buchan Ness
Boddam
Kinnadie
Skelmuir
Knockie
Skelmuir Hill
Newton
Smallburn
Carse of
Balloch
Moss
of Cruden
Sandfordhill
Auchnagatt
Mill of
Elrick
Upper Hawkhillock
Ardallie
Greenheads
Aldie
Teuchan
Coldwells
Murdoch Head
Inkhorn
Milton of
Coldwells
Hill of
Dudwick
Muirtack
Auchiries
Erroliston
Gask
North Haven
Arthrath
Blindburn
Mains of
Dudwick
Waterloo
Hatton
Chapel Hill
Cruden Bay
Port Erroll
Bearnie
Hilton
Croft
Toll of Birness
Bogbrae
Bay of
Cruden
Invrebrie
Cookston
Broomfield
Leask
Kiplaw
Croft
The
Skares
Whinnyfold
Artrochie
Auchmacoy
Meikle
Loch
The
Veshels
Ellon
Kirkton of
Logie Buchan
Kirktown of
Slains
Clochtow
Cairnhill
Tipperty
Meikle
Tarty
Forvie
National
Nature
Reserve
St Catherine's Dub
Waterside
Forvie Ness
(Hackley Head)

113

A   B   C

1

2

3

Rubha
Coigeach

Feochag
Bay

Camas
Eilean
Ghlas

Reiff   Rubha N

Reiff

Eilean
Mullagrach   Loch an
Allltain Duibh   All
S

Isle
Ristol

Glas-leac Mor

Old

Cirean

Cluas

Stornoway 2¼hrs

THE MINCH

Tanera
Beg   Garadheanь

Summer Isles

4

Glas-
leac Beag

Priest
Island

Eilean
Dubh

Bottle Island

5

Greenstone
Point   Leac Mhor

Opinan   Rubha
Beag

Rubha Mor
Mellon Udrigle   Camus a Charraig

Cailleach
Head

Stattic
Point

Gruinard Island

Eilean
Furadh
Mor   Slaggan
Bay

Achgarve

Gruinard
Bay   Badluarach

Mungasdale

De

Rubha
Reidh   Camas
Mor

Cove

Loch a'
Draing

Chapel of Sand
Mellon
Charles
Ormiscaig   Laide

Coast   Second
Coast

A832

Little
Gruinard

An Cuaidh
296

Bualnaluib
Aultbea   Aultbea Woodcraft
& Hardwood Cafe
Drumchork

Isle
of
Ewe

Loch
Fada

Creag-
mheall
Beag
347

Melvaig

Aultgrishan

Loch
Sguod

Inverasdale

Midtown

Loch a'Bhaid-
luachrach

6

B8021

Cnoc Breac
293

Naast

Loch Ewe

Loch Thurnaig

Tuirnaig

Beinn
a'Chaisgein
Beag
680

Peterburn

Boor

Inverewe Garden
(NTS)

Meall
na
Meine
251

North Erradale

10

Londubh
Poolewe
Red Smiddy

Loch na
Moine

Beinn a'Cha
Mor

A832

Meall Aird
Mhic
Craidh
349

Loch na
Dubh
Loch

0   2   4   6 miles
0   2   4   6   8   10 km

Dearg

Auchtercairn

Strath
Bay

Gairloch

B

116

Beinn Airigh
Charr

Lochan
Beannach

C

Flowerdale

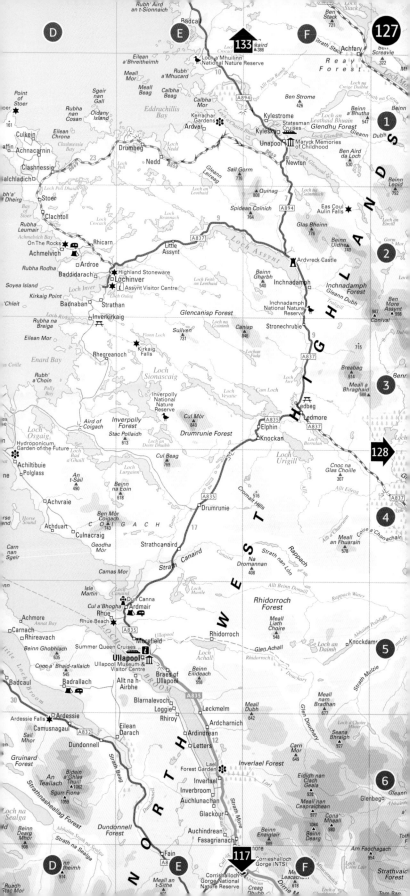

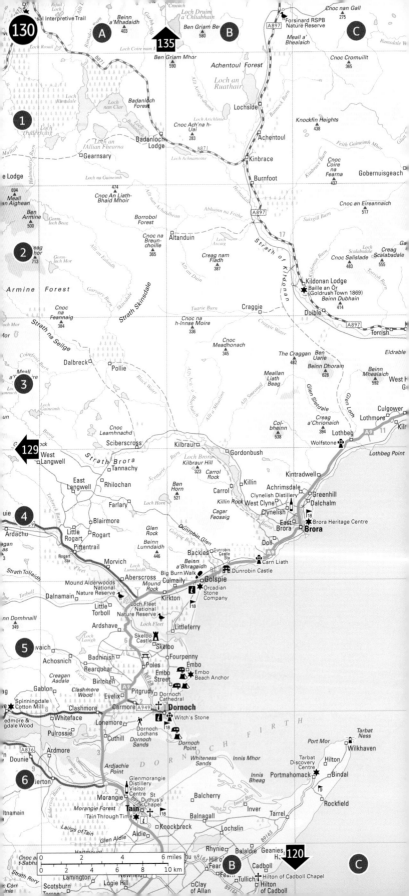

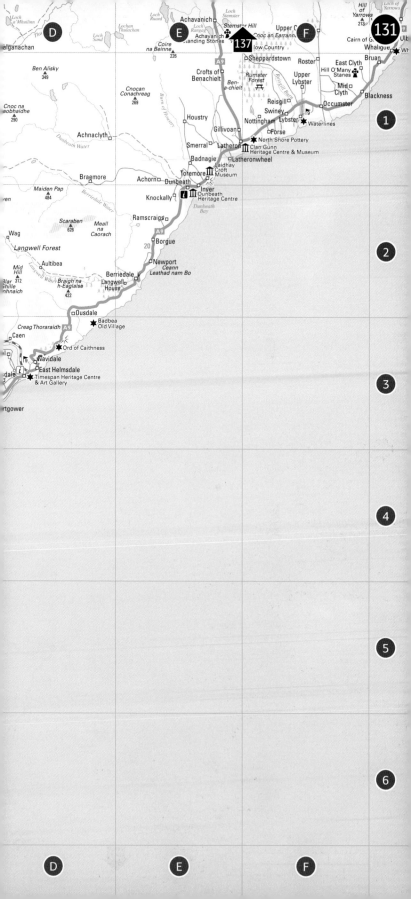

A B C

1

2

3

Am
Balg

Am Buach

Rubh' an Fhir Leithe

Sh
Balchrick

Eilean
an Roin Mor

Rubha na

Bagh Loch
an Roin

4

Loch Dr

Ardmore
Point

Rubha Ruadh

Fanagmore

Tarbet

Handa
Island   Handa
Island   Fo

Loch nam
Breac

Loch an
Laig Aird

A

Sound of Handa

Scourie Bay

5

Scourie More   Scourie   7
Rubh' Aird
an t-Sionnaich

Badca

Lo
Crocac

Loch a'Mh
National N

Eilean
a'Bhreitheimh   10

Meall   Rubh'
Mor   a'Mhucard

Meall   Calbha
Beag   Beag

Point
of Stoer   Sgeir
nan   Calbha
Old Man of Stoer   Rubha   Gall   Oldany   Mor
161   nan   Island
Cirean Geardail   Cosan   Eddrachillis
Bay   Kerrachar
6   Eilean   Gardens
Chrona   Ardvar
Culkein
Raffin   Clashnessie
Cluas Deas   Achnacarnin   Bay   Loch
Drumbeg   Nedd
Clashnessie   23   Nedd   Gleann
Loch   Leireag
Balchladich   Poll
Loch an
Leothaid

0   2   4   6 miles   h'a'
Dheirg   Loch   Lo
Clachtoll   Cnocach   Beannach
0 2 4 6 8 10 km   B   127   C   9
Rubha
Leumair

D   E   F

1

2

3

4

5

6

134

128

Duslic

Cape Wrath

Cape Wrath ★

Stack Clo Kearvaig ▲

An Garbh-eilean

Faraid Head

Kearvaig

Geodha Ruadh na Fola

Cnoc a'Ghiubhais 297

Sgribhis-bheinn 371

A'Ghoil

Faraid Head & Balnakeil Bay

Whiten Head

Bay of Keisgaig

Kearvaig

299

Inshore

Loch Inshore

Maovally

Balnakeil Bay

Sango Bay

Eilean Hoan

Cnoc Ard an t-Siuil

ore Beg

Sandwood Bay ★

Beinn Dearg 423

Fashven 457

Achiemore

Balnakeil

Durness ★

Balnakeil Craft Village

Keoldale

Pocan Smoo

Smoo Caves

Sangobeg

Leirinmore

Geodh a'Bhrideoin 183

Eilean Cluimhrig

Sandwood Bay

Sandwood Loch

Creag Riabhach 485

An Grianan 467

Meall na Moine 484

Beinn an Amair 278

Loch Airigh na Beinne

Sarsgrum

Loch Meadaidh

Beinn Ceannabeinne

Rispond

Strath Shinary

Beinn a'Chraisg 257

Ghlas-bheinn 332

Meall Meadhonach 422

ore Beg

Oldshore More

An Socach 358

Drochaid Mhor

Port-na-Con Souterrain

A838

Inverhope

Moine Ho.

Kinlochbervie ℹ

A838

Farrmheall 521

Meall a'Chraidh 490

Port-na-Con

Loch Eriboll

Hilam

A838 22

Lochside

265

Badcall

Achriesgill

19

Beinn Spionnaidh 772

Laid

Eilean Choraidh

Ben Arnaboll

230

Druim nan Cliar

Loch na Gainimh

Cranstackie 802

Polla

A838

Eriboll

Achlyness

Rhiconich

Gualin National Nature Reserve

Conamheall 482

An Lean-charn 521

Creag Riabhach Bheag 463

Ceathramh Garbh

Loch na h-Ula

Foinaven 915

Loch Udh am Tuim

Ben Hope 927

Cashel Dhu

Meallan Liath

Loch na Seilg

Loch a'Ghnbha Dhuibh

Strath Dionard

Creag Dionard 778

Loch Dionard

Ben Stack 721

Laxford Bridge

A838

Arkle 787

Meall a Chuirn

Allnacaillich

Strath More

Loch an Easain Uaine

Sabhal Mor 777

Dun Dornaigil Broch

Inabay

Loch a'Ghuirb Bhaid Mhor

Loch Stack

Sabhal Beag 729

Feinne-Bheinn Mhor 465

Glen Golly

Allnabad

Cnoc an Daimh Beag 295

Strath Stack

Achfary

Ben Screavie 322

Carn an Tionail 759

Cnoc a'Chraois 348

Loch Meadie

aird 388

Reay Forest

Loch More

Meallan Liath Coire Mhic Dhughaill 801

Carn Dearg

Druim nam Bad 346

Ben Strome 426

Loch an Leathaid Bhuain

Beinn a'Bhutha

Aultanrynie

Meall na Teanga 365

Kylestrome

Statesman Cruises

Glendhu Forest

Beinn Lice 470

Kinloch

Ben Hee 873

Meallan Liath Mor 683

Kylesku

Loch Glendhu

Dubh

A838

Loch a'Ghriomacho

Unapool

Maryck Memories of Childhood

Meall na Leitreach 566

Newton

Ben Aird da Loch 530

Meall a Fheur Loch 613

Loch Merkland

An Glas-loch

Meall an Fhuarain 473

Quinag

Eas Coul Aulin Falls ★

Beinn Leoid 792

750 ▲ Meallan a'Chuail

Loch Fiag

Glas Bheinn 776

A894 D

Corrykinloch

E

Cnoc a'Ghriama

F

Cnoc an Alaskie

NORTH WEST HIGHLANDS

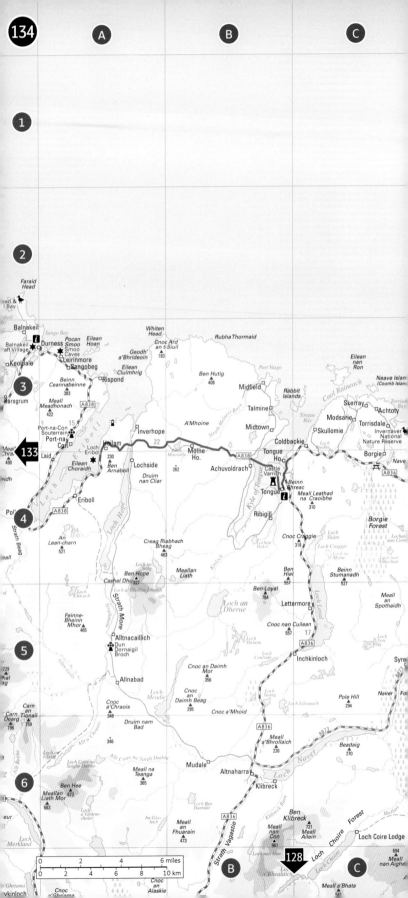

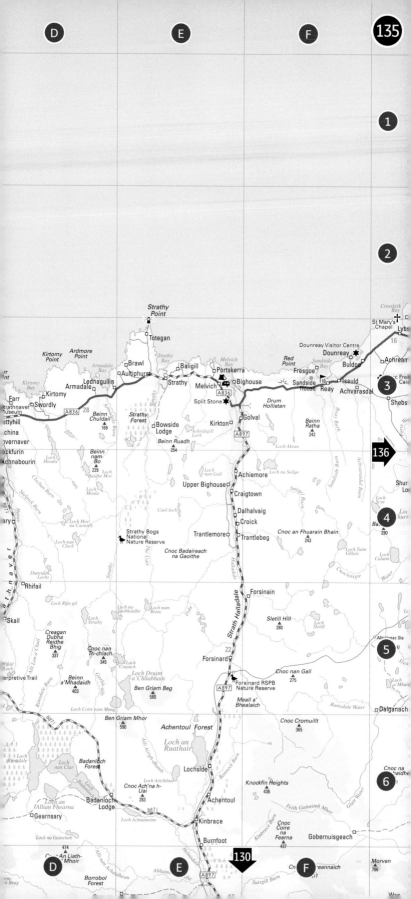

1

2

Crosskirk Bay

St Mary's Chapel

Lybs

16

Achrean

Dounreay Visitor Centre
Dounreay
Buldoo
Sandside Bay
Red Point
Fresgoe
Sandside House
Isauld
Reay
Achvarasdal
oc Fre Cai

3

Shebs

Strathy Point

Totegan

Kirtomy Point
Ardmore Point
Brawl
Aultiphurst
Armadale Bay
Lednagullin
Armadale
Kirtomy
Swordly
Kirtomy Bay

Strathy Bay
Baligill
Strathy
Melvich
Split Stone
Melvich Bay
Portskerra
Bighouse

Drum Hollistan

Farr
rath naver
useum
china
vernaver
ckfurin
chnabourin

ettyhill

A836
28
Beinn Chuldail
169
Strathy Forest
Bowside Lodge
Beinn Ruadh
254
Kirton
Golval
A897

Achridigill Loch
Beinn Ratha
242
Loch Akran

Roy Burn

136

Loch Meadie
Beinn nam Bo
229
Loch Baidhe Mor
Loch Meala

Loch nan Gall
Achiemore
Loch na Seilge

Smigel Burn

Achunabust Burn

Shur Lo

Upper Bighouse
Craigtown
Dalhalvaig
Croick
Trantlemore
Trantlebeg

Caol-loch

Cnoc an Fhuarain Bhain
243

Loch Cye
Loch Tuim Ghlais

Loch hurr

Ba
290

4

Loch Culuim Water

Strathy Bogs National Nature Reserve
Cnoc Badaireach na Gaoithe

Loch Mor na Caorach
Loch nam Clach

The Uair

Cnocloisgte

Rhifail

Skail

Loch na Saobhaidhe
Loch nam Breac

Loch Strathy

Dsic

Forsinain

Strath Halladale

Sletill Hill
280
Loch Sletill

Loch Rifa-gil

Clachan Burn

athnaver

Naver

ary

Creagan Dubha Reidhe Bhig
337
Cnoc nan Tri-chlach
345
Loch Crocach
Loch Druim a' Chliabhain

Forsinard
22
Cnoc nan Gall
275
Achnabreac Sta

u

5

Loch a' Mhoi

Rifail
Loch
erpretive Trail
Beinn a'Mhadaidh
403
Ben Griam Beg
580

Forsinard RSPB Nature Reserve
A897
Meall a' Bhealaich

Rumsdale Water

Dalganach

Ramsdale Burn

Loch Coire nam Mang

Ben Griam Mhor
590

Achentoul Forest
Loch an Ruathair

Cnoc Cromuillt
365

Cnoc na aidhe

6

B871
Loch Rumsdale
Badanloch Forest
Loch nan Clar

Cnoc Ach'na h-Uai
283
Loch Arichlinie

Lochside

Bannock Burn

Knockfin Heights
438

Badanloch Lodge
Gearnsary

B871
Loch Achnamoine
Achentoul
Kinbrace

Cnoc Coire na Fearna
437

Gobernuisgeach

Loch na Gaineimh
Feith Gaineimh Mhor

Gilan Water

An Liath-Mhoir
474

Burnfoot

Halladale
A897

130

Abhainn athe

Abhainn na Achaidhean

Cn eannaich
17

Morven
706

Borrobol Forest

Suisgill Burn

Wa

D E F

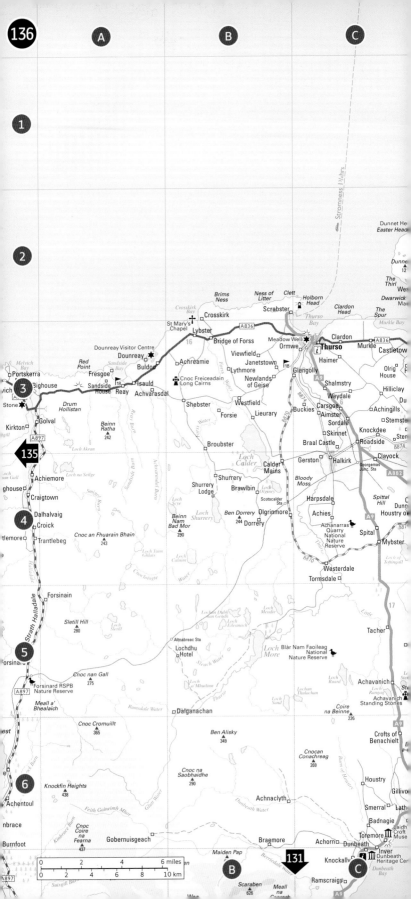

A   B   C

1

2

OUTER HEBRIDES

Rubh

Scurrival Pe

3

Greian
Head
Ben
Cliad
Cuidhir ▲207
Allathasdal
BARR
(BARRA)
B
Borve
Point
Rule
Borgh

Doirlinn Head
Ben
Tangaval
Heaval
▲383
Castlebay
(Bagh a'Chaisteil)
Barra H
Leidea
Aird a'Chaolais
▲333
Kisimul
Castle
Caolas
Heishival Mor
▲190
Castle
Bay

Vatersay
(Bhatarsaigh)
Vatersay Bay
Am
Meall
▲100

4

Vatersay
Sound of Sandray
Flodday
Cairn
Galtair
▲207
Sandray
(Sanndraigh)

Lingay
Sound of
Pabbay

Pabbay
(Pabaigh)
The Hoe
▲171

Sound of Mingulay

5

Guarsay
Mor
Macphee's Hill
▲224
Mingulay
(Miughalaigh)
Càrnan
▲273
Mingulay
Bay
Sron an
Duin
Sound of Berneray
Skate
Point
▲191
Nisam Point
Berneray
(Bearnaraigh)

6

0	2	4	6 miles
0	2 4	6 8	10 km

B   C

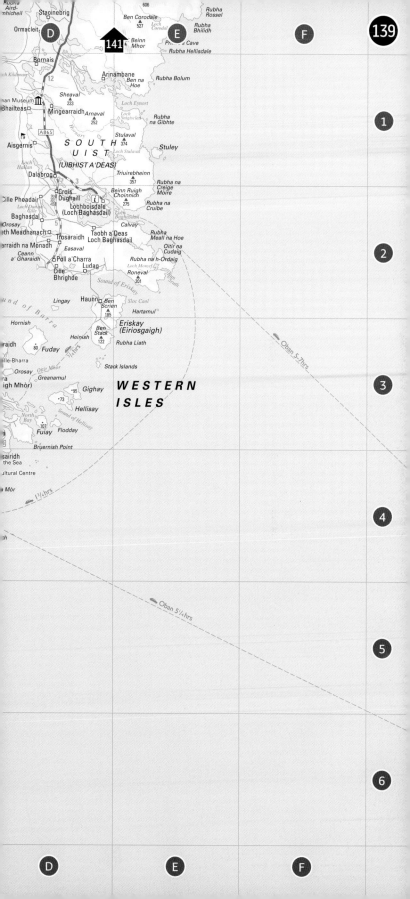

A **B** **C**

1

Haskeir Island

Haskeir Eagach

2

HEBRIDES

Griminis
Point

Valley

Scolpaig

A865

Valley
Strand

Balmartin
(Baile Mhartainn)
*Manish
Point*

Balelone

Loch
Hosta

Tigh a'Gearraidh

Hosta

Botarua

Hogha Gearraidh

Causamul

*Aird an
Runair*

Baile Raghaill

Ceann
a'Bhàigh

*Rubha
Port Scolpaig*

Paibeil

Baile
Mòr

Oitir
Mhòr

Clac
a'Ch

Deasker

*Rubha
Raouill*

Cladach Chircebost

3

Huskeiran

*Monach Islands
(Heisker Islands)*

Sound of Monach

Kirkibost Island

Ceann Iar

Hearnish

Stockay

Shillay

Monach Islands
National
Nature Reserve

Ceann Ear

Teanamachar

Sa

*Scrot
Mòr*

Baleshare

4

OUTER

Benbecula
(Baile a'Mhanaich)

Aird

Baln
(Baile

Baile nan Cailleach
Garry-a-siar

B E

Grimin

Torlum

Lionacl

Gualann

Hornish Point

Baile
Gharbhai

Gho

Ardivachar Point

Clachan

Io

Het
Jev

Aird
a'Mhachair

5

*Loch
Bee*

6

Geirninis

A865

Drimore

Groigearraidh

Stadhlaigearraidh

Tobha Mòr

Dr

S

Peighinn nan Aoireann

Snishival

*Rubha Aird-
mhicheil*

Staoinebrig

Ormacleit

6

0 ____ 2 ____ 4 ____ 6 miles
0 __ 2 __ 4 __ 6 __ 8 __ 10 km

B

Rubha

139

Bornais

C

Loch Kildonang

Kildonan Museum 🏛

Sheaval

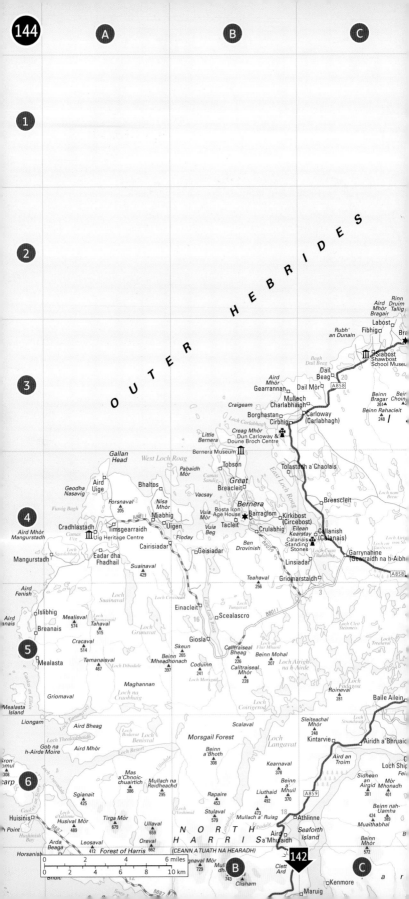

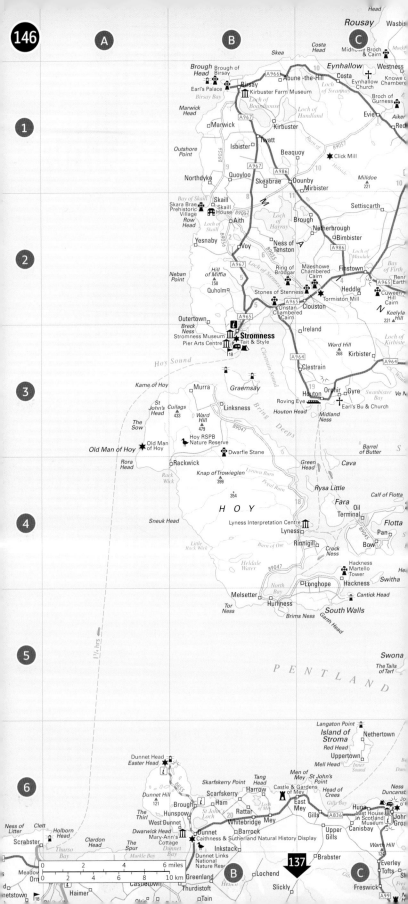

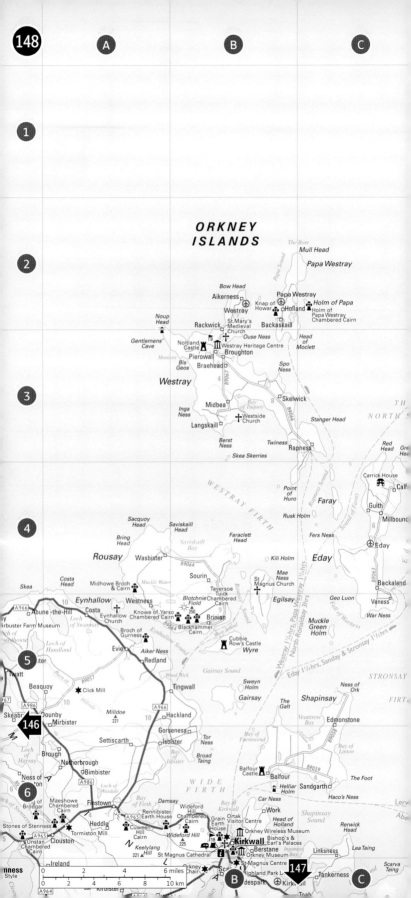

A   B   C

1

2

ORKNEY ISLANDS

The Bore

Mull Head

Papa Westray

Bow Head

Aikerness

Papa Westray

Knap of
Howar

Holm of Papa

Holland

Noup
Head

Westray

St Mary's
Medieval
Church

Backaskaill

Holm of
Papa Westray
Chambered Cairn

Rackwick

Ouse Ness

Head
of
Moclett

Gentlemens'
Cave

Noltland
Castle

Pierowall

Westray Heritage Centre

Broughton

Spo
Ness

Bis
Geos

Braehead

Monivey

Westray

3

Midbea

Bay of
Tuquoy

Skelwick

Inga
Ness

Westside
Church

Stanger Head

TH
NORTH

Langskaill

Red
Head

Gre
Hea

Berst
Ness

Twiness

Rapness

Skea Skerries

Carrick House

Calf

Point
of
Huro

Faray

Guith

WESTRAY FIRTH

Rusk Holm

Fers Ness

Millbown

Sacquoy
Head

Saviskaill
Head

Faraclett
Head

Eday

Bring
Head

Saviskaill
Bay

Kili Holm

Backaland

4

Rousay

Wasbister

B9064

Sourin

Mae
Ness

St
Magnus Church

Veness

Costa
Head

Midhowe Broch
& Cairn

Muckle Water

War Ness

Skea

Eynhallow

Westness

Taversoe
Tuick
Chambered
Cairn

Egilsay

Geo Luon

A966

Abune -the-Hill

Costa

Knowe of Yarso
Chambered Cairn

Blotchnie
Field

Brinian

Muckle
Green
Holm

Birbuster Farm Museum

Eynhallow
Church

250

Blackhammer
Cairn

andhouse

Loch of
Swannay

Broch of
Gurness

B9064

Cubbie
Row's Castle

Loch of
Handland

Evie

Aiker Ness

Wyre

5

Twatt

Redland

Wood Wick

Gairsay Sound

Sweyn
Holm

Ness of
Ork

STRONSAY

Beaquoy

B9057

Click Mill

Hillside

Tingwall

Gairsay

The
Galt

Shapinsay

FIRT

A986

Milldoe
221

A966

Hackland

Veantrow
Bay

Edmonstone

Skeabr

Dounby

Mirbister

Gorseness

Tor
Ness

Bay of
Linton

146

Settiscarth

Isbister

Broad
Taing

Brough

Netherbrough

Bay of
Isbister

Balfour
Castle

Balfour

Helliar
Holm

Sandgarth

The Foot

Haco's Ness

Lerv

Bimbister

A986

Loch of
Wasdale

WIDE
FIRTH

Bay of
Kirkwall

Car Ness

Work

Head of
Holland

Orkney Wireless Museum

Shapinsay
Sound

 Abe

Ness of
ton

Loch
of
Harray

Bay of
Firth

Damsay

Wideford
Hill
Chambered
Cairn

Grain
Earth
House

Ortak
Visitor
Centre

Rerwick
Head

6

Brodgar

Maeshowe
Chambered
Cairn

Finstown

A965

Rennibister
Earth House

Wideford Hill
225

Orkney Museum

Bishop's &
Earl's Palaces

Berstane

Linksness

Lea Taing

Stones of Stenness

A965

Tormiston Mill

Heddle

Cuween
Hill
Cairn

18

Kirkwall

Unstan
Chambered
Cairn

Clouston

Keelylang
Hill
221

St Magnus Cathedral

St-Magnus Centre

Scapa

Highland Park L

147

nness
Style

Ireland

Orkney
Chair

B

Tankerness

Scarva
Taing

A964

Kirbister

2   4   6 miles

Scarva

Toab

2   4   6   8   10 km

ndespark

Kirkwall

C

1

North Ronaldsay   Point of Sinsoss
Tor Ness
North
Ronaldsay   Linklet Bay
Hollandstoun
Bride's
Ness
South   Strom Ness
Bay

2

North Ronaldsay Firth

Tofts Ness
Whitemill
Point
Holms of Ire   Sandquoy   North Loch   Scuthvie
Bay
Scar
Burness   Start
Point
North Bay   Otters Wick   Bay of
Lopness
Broughtown   Sanday   Roadside   Newark
Cata   Sanday
Sand
Overbister

3

Kettletoft   Bay of
Newark
Backaskail   Quoy Ness   Sty Wick
Bay   Quoyness   Tres
Braeswick   Els   Chambered   Ness
Stove   Ness   Cairn

S A N D A Y
S O U N D

4

our Ness

Holm
of   Huip Ness
Huip   Papa
Stronsay   Stronsay
Odie   Whitehall
Stronsay
Mill Bay   Odness
St   Aith   Everbay
Catherine's   Odin
Bay   Grobister   Kirbister   Bay
olm   Bay of   Dishes   Burgh Head
Holland   Holland

5

Greenli   Bay
Ness   Tor Ness   of   Lamb Head
lm   Housebay
Ingale
Skerry

Auskerry Sound

Auskerry

6

hrs

hrs

Laxo
Marrister
Lisbister
Huxter
Whalsay
East Linga
Grif Skerry

D
E
F

Dury Voe
Go Water
970
Dury
Stava Ness
Clett Head

North Nesting
Laxfirth
Neap
East Kame
Bretabister
The Keen
South Nesting Bay
1

Catfirth
Skellister
Ling Ness
South Nesting
Freester
Moul of Eswick

Girlsta
Gletness
South Isle of Gletness

Skerries 2½ hrs

Hawks Ness

A970
iteness
ingwall
(Lerwick)
Laxfirth
Kebister Ness
Score Head
Gott
Aith Ness
2
Böd of Gremista
Gunnista
Bressay
Heogan
Loder Head
Holmsgarth
Up Helly Aa Exhibition
Maryfield
Setter
Clickimin Broch
Dim Riv Norse Longship Boat Trips
Lerwick
Brough
Noss National Nature Reserve
Shetland Museum
Fort Charlotte
Isle of Noss
Sound
Lerwick Town Hall
Grindiscol
Feadda Ness
alloway
Gulberwick
Ward of Bressay
Millburn Geo
astle
226
Uradale
Kirkabister
Brindister

Easter Quarff
Bard Head
3
Bergen 12½hrs (summer only)

Fladdabister
Okraquoy
A970
16

arkigarth
A970
Helli Ness
SHETLAND
Mail
Dedda Skerry
ISLANDS
rd of ester
Lamba Taing
257
Leebotten
Mousa
4
Hoswick
Sandwick
Hoswick Visitor Centre
Mousa Broch
orthpunds
Mousa Sound
Levenwick
No Ness

Blovid
Troswick Ness
am
and Crofthouse Museum
5
Lambhoga Head
oe
rgh
hof Prehistoric & e Settlement
utness

Sumburgh Head
6
disfjordur 31hrs (summer only)

D
E
F

1

2

3

SHETLAND ISLANDS

Ramna Stacks

Gruney

Garmus
Taing   Poin

Uyea   Hef

*South
Wick*   Isbister

A970

Hevdadale Head   North Roe

North   Burra Voe
Roe   Mu

The
Castle

River Water

4

The Faither
Muckle Ossa

Ronas
Hill
450

Housetter

Collafirth   Neap o
Skea

Ronas Voe   A970   Quey Firth

The
Clifts   Voe   Ollaberry

Hamnavoe   Scarff   Heylor

Head of Stanshi
Ure   *Eela Water*   Gluss
Esha Ness   Braehoulland   Isle

Tangwick Haa 10 Burnside   A970   Urafirth   B9079
Museum
B907B   Bardister

Stenness   Tangwick   Gluss

5   Hillswick   Burraland

Baa
Taing   A970

Isle of   Sullom
Nibon

Mangaster   Tronda

B9079
9

S T   Islesburgh   Bu
MAGNUS BAY   Mavis Grind   Brae   H

Erne Stack   Burravoe
Busta
Strom   Busta A970
Ness   Roesound   Voe

6   Ve   Wethersta
Skerries
Muckle   Olna Firth
Roe
Linga

Papa Stour
Gonfirth

Fogla Skerry   Papa
Biggings   Little

Papa Stour ⊕   Vementry
Swarbacks Minn   The

| 0 | | 2 | | 4 | | 6 miles |
| 0 | 2 | 4 | 6 | 8 | | 10 km |

Quilva
Taing   B   Burrafirth
Sandness   Burra   Brindister   Sca
Garth   Noonsbrough   Clousta   Fie
28
Sulma
B907

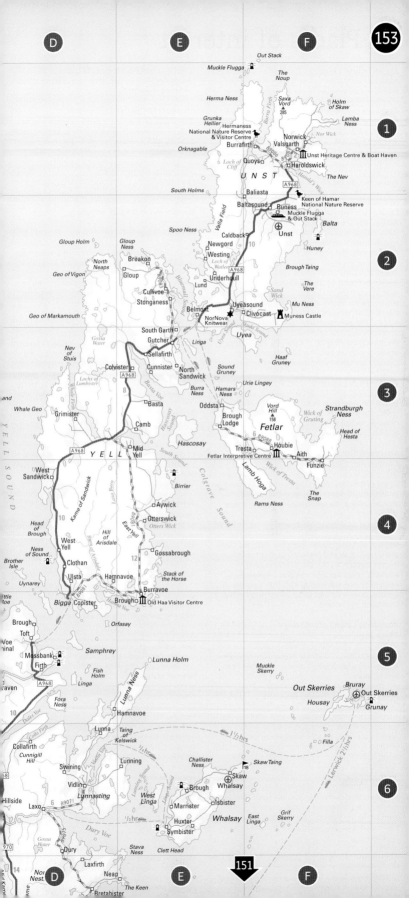

Abbot House Heritage Centre   78 B2
01383 733266 www.abbothouse.co.uk
Maygate, Dunfermline. In the restored 15th century
residence of the Abbot of Dunfermline. Learn
Scotland's story from Pictish to modern times and
find out about King Robert the Bruce, St Margaret
and other figures who played a role in the history of
Scotland's ancient capital.

Abbotsford   70 B2
01896 752043 www.scottsabbotsford.co.uk
Abbotsford, on the B6360 between Selkirk and
Melrose. The house which Sir Walter Scott, the 19th
century novelist, built in 1812 on the site of the
Cartley Hole farmhouse, and where he lived until he
died in 1832. Features Scott's collection of historical
relics, including armour and weapons, Rob Roy's gun
and Montrose's sword; his library with over 9000
rare volumes, and other rooms including the chapel.

Abercorn Church & Museum   78 B3
Hopetoun Estate, South Queensferry. 6 miles (10km)
west of South Queensferry off the A904. There has
been a church on this site for 1500 years. Abercorn
was the first bishopric in Scotland, dating from
AD681. The present church (dedicated to St Serf)
developed from the Reformation to the present day -
the present building, on the site of a 7th century
monastery, dates from the 12th century. The
museum contains Viking burial stones.

Aberdeen Art Gallery   36 B2
01224 523700 www.aagm.co.uk
School Hill, Aberdeen. Houses one of the finest art
collections in the UK dating from the 18th - 20th
centuries including British works by Spencer, Nash
and Bacon.

Aberdeen Exhibition & Conference Centre   113 E4
01224 824824 www.aecc.co.uk
Bridge of Don, Aberdeen. The foremost purpose-built
exhibition and events complex in the north of
Scotland. Venue for festivals, concerts and shows.

Aberdeen Maritime Museum   80 A3
01224 337700 www.aagm.co.uk
Shiprow, off Union Street, Aberdeen. Tells the story
of the city's long and fascinating relationship with
the sea through a collection of ship models,
artefacts, computer interaction and set-piece
exhibitions. A major display about the offshore oil
industry features a 28ft (8.5m) high model of the
Murchison oil platform.

Aberdeen University Zoology Museum   113 E4
01224 272850 www.abdn.ac.uk/zoologymuseum
Zoology Building, Tillydrone Avenue, Old Aberdeen.
A collection of zoological specimens ranging from
flies to whales.

Aberdeenshire Farming Museum   125 D5
01771 6229807 www.aberdeenshire.gov.uk
Aden Country Park, Mintlaw. Unique semi-circular
home farm steading where visitors can explore the
Aden Estate Story and the Weel Vrocht Grun
exhibitions, and visit Hareshowe, a working farm set
in the 1950s.

Aberdour Castle   78 C2
01383 860519 www.historic-scotland.gov.uk
Aberdour, 5 miles (8km) east of the Forth Bridges on
the A921. A 13th-century fortified residence
overlooking the harbour. Splendid residential
accommodation, terraced garden and fine circular
dovecot.

Aberlemno Sculptured Stones   102 C4
0131 668 8800 www.historic-scotland.gov.uk
At Aberlemno on the B9134, 6 miles (9.5km) north
east of Forfar. A magnificent upright cross-slab
sculptured with Pictish symbols stands in the
churchyard. As a conservation measure the stones
are boxed in winter.

Aberlour Distillery   122 B5
01340 881 249 www.aberlour.com
High Street, Aberlour. Book a place on a tour of this
distillery with a whisky tasting and an audio-visual
presentation.

Abernethy Round Tower   89 E4
0131 668 8800 www.historic-scotland.gov.uk
In Abernethy on the A913. One of two round towers
of the Irish style surviving in Scotland and dating
from the end of the 11th century.

Abriachan Garden Nursery   118 C6
01463 861232 www.lochnessgarden.com
North shore of Loch Ness, 9 miles (14.5 km) south
west of Inverness on the A82. Exciting garden on
Loch Ness side. A combination of native and exotic
plants in a beautiful woodland setting. Hardy
perennial plantings are a speciality. The adjacent
nursery sells many unusual plants.

Abriachan Wood   118 C6
www.wt-woods.org.uk/abriachanwood
On the shores of Loch Ness, 9 miles (15km) south of
Inverness. Abriachan means 'mouth of the steep
burn'. These are ancient woods, once coppiced for
hazel. The woods were used for commercial forestry
but are now under regeneration to return them to
native woodland. Waymarked trail and viewpoints.

Achamore Gardens   73 F6
01583 505328 www.gigha.org.uk
Isle of Gigha, Argyll. 1.5 miles (2.5km) from ferry.
Rhododendrons, camellias, azaleas and many semi-
tropical shrubs and plants may be seen at these
gardens which have been developed over the past 40
years. There is also a spring bank and a viewpoint
with fine views of Islay and Jura.

Achavanich Standing Stones   136 C5
Situated approximately 5 miles (8km) from Latheron
on the A9 to Thurso. The stones are set in an
unusual U shape and are thought to date from the
Bronze Age. Today 36 stones survive out of a
possible 54.

Achnabreck Cup & Ring Marks   74 B1
www.historic-scotland.gov.uk
Kilmartin Glen. 1.5 miles (2.5 km) north west of
Lochgilphead. The exposed crest of a rocky ridge
with well-preserved cup and ring marks. Bronze Age.

Adam's Grave   75 E3
Near Ardnadam Farm, 3 miles (3km) north of
Dunoon. Local name for a Neolithic cairn. Two
portals and one cap stone still remain and are
believed to date from 3500 BC.

Aden Country Park   125 D5
01771 622857 www.aberdeenshire.gov.uk
Mintlaw, 10 miles (16km) east of Peterhead on the
A92. A 215 acre (87ha) country park containing
woodland walks, nature trails, orienteering course,
sensory garden, adventure play area, lake and
caravan park.

Aigas Dam   118 B5
By the A831, between Beauly and Struy. This dam,
part of the River Beauly Hydro scheme, is by-passed
by a fish lift which allows the salmon to migrate
upstream to spawn.

Ailsa Craig   65 E6
Island in the Firth of Clyde, 10 miles (17km) west of
Girvan. A granite island rock, 1114ft (339.5m) high
with a circumference of 2 miles (3km). The rock itself
was used to make some of the finest curling stones
and the island has a gannetry and colonies of

guillemots and other sea birds.

Aiton Fine Arts   88 B3
01764 655423
63 King Street, Crieff. Family-run art gallery showing
contemporary Scottish artists' painting, prints and
sculpture.

Alexander III Monument   79 D2
By the A921, south of Kinghorn. On the King's Crag,
a monument marks the place where Alexander III
was killed in a fall from his horse in 1286.

Alford Heritage Centre   112 A3
019755 62906
Mart Road, Alford. Features the greatest collection of
rural bygones in north east Scotland. The exhibition
is designed to give the visitor an insight into the
rural life of the ordinary working people of Donside.

Alford Valley Railway   112 A3
07879 293934   www.alfordvalleyrailway.org.uk/
Alford Station, Alford. Narrow gauge railway running
a 30 minute trip from the restored Alford Station to
Haughton Caravan Park. Train collection includes a
former Aberdeen suburban tram, and two diesel
Simplex locomotives.

Allean Forest   99 F3
01350 727284   www.forestry.gov.uk
7 miles west of Pitlochry on the B8019. Magnificent
views of Loch Tummel and surrounding mountains
from waymarked walks through this working forest.

Alloa Tower   77 F1
01259 211701   www.nts.org.uk
Alloa Park on the A907 in Alloa. Formerly the
ancestral home of the Earls of Mar and Kellie for four
centuries. The present building dates from 1497 and
was built by the 3rd Lord Erskine. In the early 18th
century, the 6th Earl remodelled the tower to tie in
with the adjoining mansion house, which was
destroyed by fire in 1800. Impressive parapet walk
around the tower's battlements offering spectacular
views of the Forth. Fine family portraits, including
works by Jamesone and Raeburn.

Alloway Auld Kirk   66 B4
01292 443700   www.burnsheritagepark.com
Alloway, 2.5 miles (4km) south of Ayr on the B7024.
Ancient church, a ruin in Burns' day. William Burnes,
the poet's father, is buried in the churchyard. In the
poem, Tam o' Shanter, Burns described the 'warlocks
and witches in a dance, within Alloway's auld
haunted kirk'.

Alloway Parish Church   66 B4
www.allowaychurch.org
Alloway, 2.5 miles (4km) south of Ayr. Built between
1858 and 1890 by architect Campbell Douglas, this
church has a fine collection of stained glass

including works by Adam Small, W. and J. J. Kier,
Whall, Webster, Clayton, Bell and Susan Bradbury
(The Seasons and Robert Burns Memorial Window,
1996 and 2001).

Almond Valley   78 B3
01506 414957   www.almondvalley.co.uk
Millfield, Livingston Village. Off the A705, 2 miles
(3km) from junction 3 on the M8. The history and
environment of West Lothian brought to life in an
exciting and innovative museum combining a
working farm, restored watermill and a history
museum. Award-winning interactive displays for
children, indoor play areas, nature trail, trailer rides
and a narrow-gauge railway.

Almondell & Calderwood
Country Park   78 B3
01506 882254
On the B7015 at East Calder. Extensive riverside and
woodland walks in former estate, with large picnic
and grassy areas. The visitor centre, housed in an
old stable block, has a large freshwater aquarium,
displays on local and natural history, and a short
slide show. Ranger service, guided walks programme.

Aluminium Story Visitor Centre &
Library   97 D3
01855 831663
Linnhe Road, Kinlochleven. 7 miles (11km) from
Glencoe and 21 miles (34km) from Fort William at
the head of Loch Leven. The Aluminium Story uses
audio-visual displays and a video presentation
system to tell the story of the British Aluminium
Company which opened a smelter here in 1908.
Visitors can learn how the industry and the
company's hydro scheme altered the life of the area.

Alva Glen   77 F1
Situated above the village of Alva, at the foot of the
Ochil Hills. Formal gardens and a more rugged area,
offering views down into a steep gorge. Also the
remnants of an old dam that supplied the mills with
fast flowing water to drive their machines.

Alvie Estate   109 F4
01540 651255   www.alvie-estate.co.uk
Kincraig, Kingussie. On the B9152, 4 miles (6.5km)
south of Aviemore. A traditional Highland sporting
estate which has been in the same family since
1927. Now diversified into tourism - clay pigeon
shooting, fishing, horse riding, 4x4 off-road driving,
estate tours and corporate entertainment.
Spectacular views across the Spey Valley to the
Cairngorms.

Alyth Museum   90 B1
01738 632488
Commercial Street, Alyth. Displays of local history in
this interesting museum.

Sunset over Ailsa Craig

Amazonia Rainforest Experience 77 E5
0870 1123777
www.ama-zone-ia.com
Strathclyde Country Park. Indoor tropical rainforest with toucans, lizards, snakes and monkeys. Daily animal handling sessions.

An Cala Garden 83 F4
01852 300237
www.gardens-of-argyll.co.uk
Isle of Seil, Argyll. A garden laid out in the 1930s with many features redolent of that era, including streams, waterfall, ponds, herbaceous borders, rockeries and Japanese cherry trees.

Arduaine Garden

An Lanntair 145 E4
01851 703307
www.lanntair.com
Town Hall, South Beach, Stornoway, Isle of Lewis. On the seafront in Stornoway adjacent to ferry and bus station. The main public arts facility in the Western Isles since 1985. A forum for local, national and international arts, promoting a diverse year-round programme of exhibitions and events.

An Tairbeart Heritage Centre 74 B4
01880 820190
0.5 mile (0.8km) south of Tarbert. An Tairbeart explores the rich heritage of this unique coastline. Native woodland with hill and pasture and wonderful views, plus a wealth of wildlife. There is a varied programme of events, such as children's activities, local food tastings, rural skills demonstrations, storytelling, art exhibitions and ceilidhs.

An Tobar Arts Centre 94 C4
01688 302211
www.antobar.com
Argyll Terrace, Tobermory, Isle of Mull. Based in a renovated Victorian primary school, the building has retained its historic detail and atmosphere and commands breathtaking views over Tobermory Bay. Monthly touring local art and craft exhibitions. The best of traditional and contemporary music. Concerts and informal ceilidhs, usually on Tuesday and Friday evenings. Art, craft and music workshops with local and visiting artists. Shop and café.

An Tuireann Arts Centre 115 D5
01478 613306
www.antuireann.org.uk
On the B885, 0.5 mile (1km) from Portree centre. An exhibition gallery for the visual arts and crafts and related educational events.

Andrew Carnegie Birthplace Museum 78 B2
01383 724302
www.carnegiebirthplace.com
Moodie Street, Dunfermline. Weaver's cottage and the 1835 birthplace of Andrew Carnegie. Tells the rags to riches story of Andrew Carnegie, the weaver's son who emigrated to America and forged a fortune from the furnaces of the American steel industry.

Angus Folk Museum 90 C1
01307 840288
www.nts.org.uk
Kirkwynd, Glamis. The museum is within Kirkwynd Cottages, a row of six reconstructed early 18th century cottages with stone-slabbed roofs. The interiors display one of the finest folk collections of domestic relics in Scotland.

Annan Activities 62 C3
01461 800274
www.westlands-activities.co.uk
Westlands, on the B6357 between Annan and Kirkpatrick Fleming. The 70 acre (29ha) site has activities for all the family: quad bike tracks and safari, crazy golf, paintball, fishing pond, fly fishing lochans, clay pigeon shooting, go-karts for children and adults. Activities suitable for all ages. All equipment available for hire.

Annan Museum 62 B3
01461 201384
Historic Resources Centre, Bank Street, Annan. Local history museum with a regular programme of exhibitions.

Anstruther Pleasure Trips to the Isle of May 91 E5
01333 310103
www.isleofmayferry.com
The Harbour, Anstruther. Daily boat trips to the Isle of May nature reserve to view large numbers of sea birds, including puffins. Also colony of grey seals, remains of a 12th century monastery and lighthouses.

Antonine Wall 77 F3
www.historic-scotland.gov.uk
From Bo'ness to Old Kilpatrick, best seen off the A803 east of Bonnybridge, 12 miles (19km) south of Stirling. This Roman fortification stretched from Bo'ness on the Forth to Old Kilpatrick on the Clyde. Built circa AD142-143, it consisted of a turf rampart behind a ditch, with forts approximately every two miles. It was probably abandoned around AD163. Remains are best preserved in the Falkirk/Bonnybridge area.

Arbroath Abbey 91 F1
01241 878756
www.historic-scotland.gov.uk
Abbey Street, Arbroath. The substantial ruins of a Tironesian monastery founded by William the Lion in 1178. This was the scene of the signing of the Declaration of Arbroath in 1320, which asserted Scotland's independence from England.

Arbroath Art Gallery 91 F1
01241 872248
Arbroath. Two galleries feature changing displays from Angus Council's art collections. Also exhibitions from elsewhere and locally generated shows.

Arbroath Signal Tower Museum 91 F1
01241 875598
Signal Tower, Ladyloan, Arbroath. Housed in the shore station for the Bell Rock lighthouse, the museum features displays devoted to this renowned lighthouse as well as exhibits exploring the fishing community. Recreated 1950s schoolroom, Victorian parlour and wash house complete with noises and smells.

Arbuthnot Museum 125 F5
01771 477778
www.aberdeenshire.gov.uk
St Peter Street, Peterhead. One of Aberdeenshire's oldest museums. Features Peterhead's maritime history, Inuit art, Arctic whaling and animals, and one of the largest coin collections in northern Scotland.

Archaeolink Prehistory Park   112 B2
01464 851500   www.archaeolink.co.uk
Oyne, 1 mile from the A96. Discover Scotland's
prehistoric past - from Stone Age to Iron Age. Indoor
and outdoor displays make it a unique living history
experience.

Ardanaiseig Gardens   85 D3
01866 833333   www.ardanaiseig.com
Ardanaiseig Hotel, Kilchrenan, on the B845, 10 miles
(11.5km) east of Taynuilt. Ardanaiseig Gardens
comprises over 100 acres (40.5ha) of Victorian
woodlands on the shores of Loch Awe, under the
shadow of Ben Cruachan. Many exotic shrubs and
trees.

Ardbeg Distillery Visitor Centre   73 D6
01496 302244   www.ardbeg.com
3 miles (5km) east of Port Ellen on the southern tip
of Islay. Take a step back in time and experience the
history and mystique of the Ardbeg Distillery.
Visitors enjoy a personal guided tour and a dram of
Ardbeg's extraordinary malt whisky.

Ardchattan Priory   84 C2
www.historic-scotland.gov.uk
On the north side of Loch Etive, 6.5 miles (10.5km)
north east of Oban. The ruins of a Valliscaulian
priory founded in 1230 and later converted to
secular use. The meeting place in 1308 of one of
Robert the Bruce's parliaments. Burned by
Cromwell's soldiers in 1654. The remains include
some carved stones.

Ardchattan Priory Gardens   84 C2
01796 481355   www.gardens-of-argyll.co.uk
Ardchattan Priory, on the north shore of Loch Etive,
5 miles (8km) east of Connel. Four acres (1.6ha) of
garden surrounding Ardchattan Priory, a private
home, with a ruined chapel and interesting stones.
Herbaceous borders and extensive lawn facing the
loch. Rose, sorbus and many varieties of hebe.

Ardclach Bell Tower   121 D5
01667 460232   www.historic-scotland.gov.uk
Off the A939, 8.5 miles (13.5km) south east of
Nairn. A remarkable little two-storey fortified bell
tower built in 1655 on the hill above the parish
church of Ardclach. The ringing of the bell
summoned worshippers to the church and warned in
case of alarm.

Ardencraig Gardens   75 E4
01700 504644   www.gardens-of-argyll.co.uk
Ardencraig Lane, 2 miles (3km) from Rothesay, Isle
of Bute. A working greenhouse and garden which
produces plants for floral displays on Bute, built
between 1919 and 1923. Plus rare plants, an aviary
and fish ponds.

Ardessie Falls   117 D1
Beside the A832 at Dundonnel. A series of
spectacular waterfalls and impressive views of Little
Loch Broom.

Ardestie and Carlungie Earth Houses   91 D2
www.historic-scotland.gov.uk
Ardestie. Two examples of large Iron Age earth
houses attached to surface dwellings (both now
uncovered). At Ardestie the gallery is curved and
80ft (24m) in length. The Carlungie earth house is
150ft (45.5m) long and more complex.

Ardfearn Nursery   119 D5
01463 243250   www.ardfearn-nursery.co.uk
Bunchrew, 4 miles (6.5km) west of Inverness on the
A862. Horticultural adviser and broadcaster Jim
Sutherland and his son Alasdair have created a large
family nursery on the shores of the Beauly Firth.
Huge variety of plants of extreme hardiness,
attractive display beds containing over 1000 species

and cultivars, with easy access for all including
wheelchair users. Sales area with a wide selection of
plants. Panoramic views.

Ardgartan Visitor Centre   85 F5
01301 702432   www.forestry.gov.uk
Glen Croe, on the A83 west of Arrochar on the Cowal
Peninsula. Situated in Argyll Forest Park. Many
special events are held throughout the year
(nominal charge) and include Deer Watch, guided
walks on the hills to see local wildlife and
archaeology, and barbecues.

Ardkinglas Woodland Garden   85 E4
01499 600261   www.ardkinglas.com
Ardkinglas Estate in Cairndow, on the A83, 8 miles
(13km) north of Inveraray. One of the finest
collections of conifers in Britain, including Europe's
mightiest conifer and the tallest tree in Britain. Also
a spectacular display of rhododendrons and a
gazebo.

Ardnadam Heritage Trail   75 E3
Near the village of Sandbank, 3 miles (5km) north of
Dunoon. This is an excellent walk including a climb
to the Dunan viewpoint, approximately 2 miles
(3.2km) long.

Ardnamurchan Point Visitor Centre   94 C3
01972 510210   www.ardnamurchan.u-net.com
On the B8007, 6 miles (10km) west of Kilchoan.
Ardnamurchan lighthouse is set amongst
spectacular scenery on mainland Britain's most
westerly point, embracing world-class views of the
Hebrides and the Small Isles. Listen to the keepers'
radio conversations, learn how the light tower was
built, join in the centre's Whale Watch, visit the
beautifully restored original room and trace the
history of Ardnamurchan through anecdotes of
people past and present.

Ardrossan Castle   75 F6
Ardrossan, on a hill overlooking Ardrossan Bay. Mid
12th century castle with fine views of Arran and
Ailsa Craig. The castle was destroyed by Cromwell
and only part of the north tower and two arched
cellars remain.

Ardtornish Estate   83 F1
01967 421288   www.ardtornish.co.uk
Morvern, 40 miles (64km) south west of Fort William
via the Corran Ferry. Ardtornish estate is a 35,000
acre (14,164ha) Highland estate with 24 acres
(10ha) of established gardens around the Grade A
listed Ardtornish House. Fly-fishing for brown trout,
sea trout and salmon on three rivers and 16 hill
lochs. Free loch fishing to residents of estate's self
catering properties.

Arduaine Garden   83 F5
01852 200366   www.arduaine-garden.org.uk
Arduaine, on the A816, 20 miles (32km) south of
Oban. A 20 acre (8ha) garden on promontory with
fine views overlooking Loch Melfort. Noted for
rhododendrons, azaleas, magnolias and other
interesting trees and shrubs.

Ardunie Roman Signal Station   88 C4
www.historic-scotland.gov.uk
At Trinity Gask, 4 miles (6.5km) north of
Auchterarder. The site of a Roman watchtower, one
of a series running between Ardoch and the River
Tay.

Ardvreck Castle   127 F2
On the A837, 11 miles (18km) east of Lochinver, on
Loch Assynt. Built by the MacLeods, who in the mid-
13th century obtained Assynt through marriage, the
three-storeyed ruins stand on the shores of Loch
Assynt. After his defeat at Culrain, near Bonar
Bridge, in 1650, the Marquess of Montrose fled to
Assynt but was soon captured and confined here

before being sent to Edinburgh where he was then executed.

Ardwell Gardens   58 B5
01776 860227
On the A716, 10 miles (16km) south of Stranraer. Gardens surrounding an 18th century country house (not open to the public) with the formal layout around the house blending into the informality of woods and shrubberies. Daffodils, azaleas, camellias, rhododendrons. Walled garden and herbaceous borders. Walks and fine views over Luce Bay.

Argyll Adventure   85 D5
01499 302611   www.argylladventure.com
On the A83 2 miles (3km) south of Inveraray. An activity centre with clay pigeon shooting, a climbing wall and pony trekking for individuals and groups. Reservations are required for horse riding.

Argyll & Sutherland Highlanders
Regimental Museum   77 E1
01786 475165   www.argylls.co.uk
Stirling Castle, Stirling. A fine museum which brings alive the history of the Regiment from 1794 to the present day. Features weapons, silver, colours, uniforms, medals, pictures, music, World War I trench.

Argyll's Lodging   77 E1
01786 431319   www.historic-scotland.gov.uk
Castle Wynd, Stirling. A superb mansion built around an earlier core in about 1630 and further extended by the Earl of Argyll in the 1670s. It is the most impressive town house of its period in Scotland.

Ariundle Oakwood National
Nature Reserve   96 A3
                    www.snh.org.uk/nnr-scotland/
Follow signposts for Airigh Fhionndail car park, two miles north of Strontian. Ancient oakwoods where the trees are covered in mosses, ferns and lichens.

Armadale Castle Gardens &
Museum of the Isles   105 F4
Garden 01471 844305,   www.clandonald.com
Museum 01599 534454
Sleat, Isle of Skye. 0.5 mile (1km) north of Armadale. A 40 acre (16ha) garden set within the 20,000 acre (8094ha) Armadale Estate where some of the flora otherwise associated with warmer climes can be grown because of the gulf stream passing close to these shores. Woodland walks and meadows ablaze with wild flowers, seascapes around every corner. The Museum of the Isles has six interconnecting galleries which take you through 1500 years of the history and culture of the area with a seventh gallery hosting temporary special exhibitions.

Arniston House   79 E4
01875 830515   www.arniston-house.co.uk
Gorebridge, on the B6372, 1 mile (2km) from the A7

and 10 miles (16km) from Edinburgh. An outstanding example of the work of William Adam, built in the 1720s. Contains an important collection of furniture and Scottish portraiture.

Aros Experience   115 D5
01478 613649   www.aros.co.uk
On the A87 Viewfield Road south of Portree. The exhibition tells the story of Skye from 1700 to the present day. An audio-visual presentation introduces the scenery of Skye and a purpose-built auditorium is the location for regular shows on the Gaelic arts, including step dancing, singing and theatre. Walks through Portree Forest.

Arran Aromatics Visitor Centre   65 E2
01770 302595   www.arranaromatics.com
The Home Farm, 1 mile (1.5km) from Brodick on the road north to Lochranza. Visitors can watch the production of natural soaps and body care products. Set in a courtyard next to a cheese factory and seafood restaurant.

Arran Brewery   65 E2
01770 302353   www.arranbrewery.com
Cladach, 1 mile north of Brodick. Arran's first and only commercial craft brewery, producing three different real ales using traditional methods. Visitors may see the beer fermenting and watch the bottling and labelling. Displays explain the story of brewing and questions about the process are welcome.

Arthur's Seat   79 D3
Holyrood Park, Edinburgh. Rising to a height of 822ft (251metres), Arthur's Seat is the igneous core of an extinct volcano, now one of the most prominent landmarks of the city. A path leads from just outside Our Dynamic Earth along the base of the red cliffs and up to the summit. Panoramic views of Edinburgh, the Firth of Forth and the Pentland Hills.

Ascog Hall, Fernery & Gardens   75 E4
01700 504555   www.ascoghallfernery.co.uk
Ascog, 3 miles (5km) south of Rothesay on the A886. Built circa 1870, this magnificent Victorian fernery, with beautiful rock work and water pools, has been restored and restocked with an impressive collection of sub-tropical ferns. The only surviving fern from the original collection is said to be around 1000 years old.

Assynt Visitor Centre   127 D2
01571 844654
Lochinver. Interesting displays on the natural environment, history and culture of the area. Home of the local tourist information centre.

Atholl Country Life Museum   99 F3
01796 481232   www.blairatholl.org.uk
In Blair Atholl on the A924. Folk museum with lively displays showing past life in the village and glen,

Ardvreck Castle

including blacksmith's smiddy, crofter's stable, byre and living room.

Attadale Gardens & Woodland Walks 116 C6
01520 722603 www.attadale.com
On south shore of Loch Carron, 2 miles (3km) south of Strathcarron on the A890. Attadale House was built in 1755 by Donald Matheson. The gardens and woodlands were started in 1890 by Baron Schroder and planted with rhododendrons, azaleas and specimen trees. More recently old paths have been revealed, bridges have been built and water gardens have been planted with candelabra primulas, gunnera, iris and bamboo. Restored sunken garden, vegetable and herb gardens.

Auchagallon Stone Circle 65 D2
0131 668 8600 www.historic-scotland.gov.uk
4 miles (6.5km) north of Blackwaterfoot on the Isle of Arran. A Bronze Age burial cairn surrounded by a circle of 15 standing stones.

Auchentoshan Distillery 76 B3
www.auchentoshan.co.uk
On A82 west of Glasgow at Duntocher. One of only a few remaining lowland malt whisky distilleries it has been a landmark on the Glasgow horizon since 1823. Tours and tasting available.

Auchgourish Gardens & Arboretum 110 A3
01479 831464 www.auchgourishgardens.com
On the B970 between Boat of Garten and Aviemore. A botanic garden which began development in 2001 and is laid out in bio-geographic regions. It includes a large Japanese garden (the largest open to the public in the north of Scotland) and a winter garden with extensive rockeries. Other gardens include plants from Korea, the Himalayas, China, Asia and Europe.

Auchindrain Township Open Air Museum 85 D5
01499 500235
6 miles (10km) south west of Inveraray on the A83. Auchindrain is an original West Highland township of great antiquity and the only communal tenancy township in Scotland to have survived on its centuries-old site, much of it in its original form. The township buildings are as they would have done at the end of the 19th century and give visitors a fascinating glimpse of Highland life.

Auchingarrich Wildlife Centre 87 E4
01764 679469 www.auchingarrich.co.uk
2 miles (3km) south of Comrie on the B827. Wildlife centre set in 100 acres (40ha) of scenic Perthshire countryside. Abundance of animals and birds including foxes, otters, meerkats, deer, Highland cattle, birds of prey and wildcats.

Auchterarder Heritage Centre 88 C4
01764 663450
Auchterarder Tourist Office, 90 High Street, Auchterarder. History of the town and area told in descriptive panels using old photographs.

Auld Kirk Museum 77 D3
0141 5780144
The Cross, Kirkintilloch. The Auld Kirk Museum dates back to 1644 when it was the parish church of Kirkintilloch. Recently refurbished, it is now a museum describing the domestic and working life of people in the area. Temporary exhibition programme of crafts, photography and local history throughout the year.

Aultbea Woodcraft & Hard Wood Café 116 B1
01445 731394 www.eweview.com
Drumchork, off the A832, 6 miles (9.5km) north of Inverewe Garden. A wood-turning workshop, craft shop and tearoom with superb views over loch and mountains. Large display of wood-turning in native and exotic woods. Wood-turning tuition available.

Aurora Crafts 114 C5
01470 572208 www.craftsonskye.org.uk
In Ose, 0.25 mile (0.5km) off the A863, 6 miles (9.5km) south of Dunvegan. A craft shop where visitors can see demonstrations of lace-making on most days. Lace, embroidery, knitwear, spinning, wood-turned articles and other items made on the premises.

Aviation Museum 101 F4
01575 573233
Bellies Brae, Kirriemuir. The museum displays a large collection of ephemera associated with flight.

Ayr Gorge Woodlands 66 C3
At Failford, south of the A758 Ayr - Mauchline road. Gorge woodland, semi-natural, dominated by oak and some coniferous plantation. Situated by the River Ayr. Historic sandstone steps and extensive network of well-maintained footpaths.

Ayr Racecourse 66 B3
01292 264179 www.ayr-racecourse.co.uk
Ayr. Scotland's largest racecourse and venue for the Scottish National in April and the Ayr Gold Cup in September. The course was established on its current site in 1907. Corporate hospitality.

Ayton Castle 81 E5
01890 781212
Ayton, Eyemouth, 7 miles (11km) north of Berwick. Historic castle, built in 1846 and an important example of the Victorian architectural tradition. Ayton Castle has been restored in recent years and is lived in as a family home.

Bachelors' Club 66 C3
01292 541940 www.nts.org.uk
Sandgate Street, Tarbolton. Robert Burns and his friends founded a debating society here in 1780. Period furnishings.

Badbea Old Village 131 D3
North of Ousdale on the A9. Footpath leads from the lay-by to groups of ruined crofthouses perched above cliffs. Tenants evicted from inland straths during the infamous Clearances founded this lonely settlement. The site is very exposed - tradition has it that children and livestock had to be tethered to prevent them being blown over the cliffs. Many of the inhabitants emigrated to America or New Zealand, as the monument, erected in 1911, testifies.

Baille an Òr (Goldrush Town 1869) 130 C2
9 miles (14km) north west of Helmsdale, on the A897 Strath of Kildonan road. In 1868 permission was given to a prospector to pan for gold in the Helmsdale river - a large nugget of gold had been found 50 years earlier. Within a few months some 600 prospectors had arrived but by the start of 1870 none remained as the price of gold had fallen and the Duke of Sutherland wanted the men off his land. Gold panning still takes place and you can get all the necessary equipment from the craft shop in Helmsdale.

Balbirnie Craft Centre 90 B5
Balbirnie Park, Glenrothes. Independently owned craft workshops producing leather goods, wrought ironwork, paintings and prints, gold and silver jewellery and glass blowing.

Balfour Castle 147 D2
01856 711282 www.balfourcastle.co.uk
Shapinsay Island, Orkney. Guided tours by member of family around this Victorian castle with original furnishings and 3 acre (1.2ha) walled garden.

Ballindalloch Castle & Golf Course   122 A6
01807 500205   www.ballindallochcastle.co.uk
Near Aberlour, 13 miles (20km) north east of
Grantown-on-Spey. Exemplifies the transition from
the stark tower house of 16th century Scotland to
the elegant and comfortable country house so
beloved of Victorians in the Highlands.

Balloch Castle Country Park   76 A2
01389 722230   www.lochlomond-trossachs.org
Balloch, north of Dumbarton off the A811. Within
the boundaries of Loch Lomond and The Trossachs
National Park, the country park comprises 200 acres
(81ha) at the southern end of Loch Lomond. Mature
woodland, gardens, shore walks and wonderful
views. The castle, one of the first modern Gothic
style castles to be built in Scotland, houses a visitor
centre.

Ballygowan Cup & Ring Marks   74 B1
www.historic-scotland.gov.uk
Kilmartin Glen. 1 mile (2km) south west of Kilmartin,
near Poltalloch. Bronze Age cup and ring marks on
natural rock faces.

Balmacara Estate & Lochalsh
Woodland Garden   106 B2
01599 566325   www.nts.org.uk
Lochalsh House, Balmacara, on the A87, 3 miles
(4.8km) east of Kyle of Lochalsh. A beautiful
Highland estate where traditional crofting is still
carried out. Includes the village of Plockton, an
outstanding conservation area and location for the
television series Hamish Macbeth. The garden
provides sheltered lochside walks among pine, ferns,
fuchsias, hydrangeas and rhododendrons.

Balmichael Visitor Centre   65 D2
01770 860526   www.balmichael.com
Shiskine, Isle of Arran. 7 miles (11km) from Brodick
on the B880. Converted farm buildings and
courtyard including ice cream parlour and
jewellery/craft shop, working pottery, antique and
tapestry shops. Adventure playground and indoor
play barn. Quad biking for all abilities. Heritage area
with working mill wheel.

Balmoral Castle   111 D5
013397 42534   www.balmoralcastle.com
Balmoral, 8 miles (13km) west of Ballater. The
Highland holiday home of the Royal Family since
1852. Exhibition of paintings, works of art and royal
tartans in the Castle Ballroom. Wildlife, travel and
carriage exhibition in the carriage hall.

Balmoral Castle

Balnakeil Craft Village   133 E3
Balnakeil, 1 mile (1.5km) west of Durness, off the
single track road to Balnakeil Bay. Craft village
including print and painting galleries, pottery and
ceramic sculpture, weaving, spinning and feltwork,
clothes, enamelwork, basketry, woodwork and
bookshop.

Baluachraig Cup & Ring Marks   74 B1
www.historic-scotland.gov.uk
Kilmartin Glen. 1 mile (2km) south south-east of

Kilmartin, Argyll. Several groups of Bronze Age cup
and ring marks on natural rock faces.

Balvaird Castle   89 E4
01786 431324   www.historic-scotland.gov.uk
About 6 miles (9.5km) south east of Bridge of Earn.
A late 15th century tower on an L-plan, extended in
1581 by the addition of a walled courtyard and
gatehouse.

Balvenie Castle   122 C5
01340 820121   www.historic-scotland.gov.uk
Dufftown. Picturesque ruins of a 13th century
moated stronghold with 15th and 16th century
additions. Originally owned by the Comyns.

Banchory Museum   112 C5
01771 622906   www.aberdeenshire.gov.uk
Bridge Street, Banchory. Features the life of
Banchory-born musician and composer J. Scott
Skinner, the 'Strathspey King', commemorative
china, tartans.

Banff Museum   123 F3
01771 622807   www.aberdeenshire.gov.uk
High Street, Banff. One of Scotland's oldest
museums, founded in 1828. Features an electrotype
copy of the Deskford Carnyx, an Iron Age war
trumpet, natural history display, local geology,
important collections of Banff silver, arms and
armour.

Bannockburn Heritage Centre   77 E1
01786 812664   www.nts.org.uk
Glasgow Road, 2 miles (3.2km) south of Stirling on
the A872. Site of the famous battle in 1314 when
Robert the Bruce, King of Scots, defeated the English
army of Edward II. Colourful exhibition with life-size
figures of Bruce and William Wallace plus heraldic
flags. Equestrian statue of Bruce outside.

Bar Hill Fort   77 E3
www.historic-scotland.gov.uk
0.5 mile (1km) east of Twechar (signposted from the
village). The highest fort on the line of the Antonine
Wall, containing the foundations of the
headquarters building and bathhouse. A small Iron
Age fort lies to the east.

Barbara Davidson Pottery   77 F2
01324 554430   www.barbara-davidson.com
Muirhall Farm on the A88 on the north side of
Larbert. A working pottery in a picturesque
converted 17th century farm steading. Products are
hand-thrown stoneware, mostly functional.

Barcloy Barn   61 E4
01556 630341
Colvend, Dalbeattie. A Portuguese shop selling olive
oil produced in the Algarve, together with home-
made preserves, almonds, lavender and a large
range of Portuguese pottery.

Barn Gallery, The   145 F4
01851 870704
Eagleton, Lower Bayble (Pabail Iarach), Isle of Lewis.
6 miles (10km) from Stornoway on the Eye
Peninsula. A small gallery displaying the original
work of four artists, in watercolour, oil, pastel,
acrylic and liquid wax.

Barnaline Walks   84 C4
Dalavich, on an unclassified road along the west
shore of Loch Awe. Walks start from Barnaline car
park and picnic site, taking in Dalavich Oakwood
Forest Nature Reserve (an interpretive trail with
information point), Avich Falls and Loch Avich.

Barnluasgan Visitor Centre   74 A1
www.forestry.gov.uk
Near Lochgilphead. Follow the B8025 from
Bellanoch towards Tayvallich. This unstaffed centre
provides information on Knapdale Forest.

Balmacara Estate & Lochalsh Woodland Garden

Barochan Cross 68 A3
0131 668 8600   www.historic-scotland.gov.uk
In Paisley Abbey, in the centre of Paisley. A fine free-standing Celtic cross that formerly stood in Houston parish, west of Paisley.

Baron's Haugh RSPB
Nature Reserve 77 E5
01505 842663   www.rspb.org.uk
Motherwell. Baron's Haugh is an urban nature reserve with a variety of habitats: flooded meadow (or haugh), marshland, river, woodland and scrub.

Barra Heritage & Cultural Centre 138 C4
01871 810413
Dualchas, 0.3 mile (0.5km) west of Castlebay pier. Local history exhibition in Gaelic and English in a high tech environment. Art exhibitions. Local artefacts and old photographs. The centre also runs the Dubharaidlt Thatched Cottage Museum. This is a restored house in a magnificent secluded location 3 miles (5km) north west of Castlebay.

Barras, The 17 C3
0141 552 4601   www.glasgow-barrowland.com
Gallowgate, 0.25 miles (0.5km) east of Glasgow Cross. Glasgow's world-famous market, with an amazing variety of stalls and shops. Founded one hundred years ago, the Barras is now home to over 800 traders. Look out for the Barras archways, children's crèche and buskers. Numerous licensed premises and cafés.

Barry Water Mill 91 E2
01241 856761   www.nts.org.uk
North of Barry village between the A92 and A930, 2 miles (3km) west of Carnoustie. A working 19th century meal mill. Full demonstrations on weekend afternoons.

Barsalloch Fort 59 E5
0131 668 8600
    www.historic-scotland.gov.uk
Off the A747, 7.5 miles (12km) west north-west of Whithorn. Remains of an Iron Age hill fort on the edge of a raised beach bluff. Defended by a deep ditch in horseshoe form.

Barwinnock Herbs 59 D1
01465 821338
    www.barwinnock.com
Barhill, 12 miles (19km) north west of Newton Stewart, off the B7027 near Loch Maberry. A garden and nursery with a fascinating collection of culinary, medicinal and aromatic herbs. Also Rural Life exhibition describing herbs for healing and flavour, and the local countryside, its natural materials and wildlife.

Bass Rock 80 B2
Off North Berwick. A massive 350ft (106.5m) high rock whose many thousands of raucous sea birds include the third largest gannetry in the world.

Baxters Highland Village 122 C3
01343 820393   www.baxters.com
1 mile (1.5km) west of Fochabers. The story of the Baxter family began in 1868 when George Baxter opened a small grocery shop in Fochabers. See the Baxters Story and watch cookery demonstrations.

Bearsden Bathhouse 76 C3
    www.historic-scotland.gov.uk
On Roman Road, Bearsden, near Glasgow. The well-preserved remains of a bathhouse and latrine built in the 2nd century to serve a fort.

Beatrix Potter Exhibition 89 D1
01350 727674   www.birnaminstitute.com
Birnam Institute, Station Road, Birnam. A Victorian building erected in 1883. Visitors can enjoy the garden and woodlands where the famous author walked.

Beauly Centre 118 C5
01463 783444   www.beaulyandglens.com
Beauly. Local exhibition on Beauly Firth and the glens (Glen Affric, Glen Cannich, and Strathfarrer). There's also a recreation of an early 20th century Village Store and the Clan Fraser exhibition. Attractive gardens.

Beauly Priory 118 C5
01667 460232   www.historic-scotland.gov.uk
On the A9 in Beauly, 12 miles (19km) west of Inverness. Ruins of a Valliscaulian priory founded in about 1230, although much of the building was later reconstructed. Notable windows and window-arcading. Open by arrangement only.

Beecraigs Country Park 78 A3
01506 844516   www.beecraigs.com
The Park Centre, 2 miles (3km) south of Linlithgow. Nestled high in the Bathgate hills, Beecraigs offers a wide range of leisure and recreational pursuits within its 915 acres (370ha). Archery, orienteering, fly-fishing, walks and trails. Trim course, play area, all-terrain bicycle trail, picnic areas, barbecue sites, fish farm, horse route, deer farm, caravan and camping site. Ranger service.

Ben Nevis

Beinn Eighe National
Nature Reserve 117 D3
01445 760254   www.snh.org.uk/nnr-scotland
South of Loch Maree near Kinlochewe. The first National Nature Reserve in Britain, acquired primarily to protect an important remnant of Scotland's ancient pinewood. Red deer, roe deer, pine marten and wildcat all inhabit this area. Golden eagle, buzzard and other birds of prey may occasionally be seen. The mountain slopes of Beinn Eighe are also of great geological and botanical interest. Woodland and mountain trail.

Belhaven Brewery Visitor Centre 80 B3
01368 869200   www.belhaven.co.uk
Dunbar. Founded in 1719, Belhaven is the oldest surviving independent brewery in Scotland. Book guided tours in advance.

Bella Jane Boat Trips 105 E3
0800 731 3089   www.bellajane.co.uk
Elgol, Isle of Skye. 15 miles (24km) from Broadford on the B8083. Bella Jane run a three-hour trip from Elgol which sails to Loch Coruisk in the Cuillin Mountains, pausing to see a seal colony then landing ashore. Hot drinks and shortbread are

163

available on the return journey. Knowledgeable skipper and crew. Award-winning. Also day excursions aboard Celtic Explorer to the magical Isles of Rum and Canna.

Belleisle Estate   66 B4
01292 612000
Alloway, 1 mile south of Ayr on the A719. Country park and formal gardens with two spectacular golf courses open to the public. Pets' corner and deer park.

Bell's Cherrybank Gardens   89 D3
01738 472800   www.thecalyx.co.uk
Cherrybank on the western outskirts of Perth. The gardens contain the Bell's National Heather Collection. This is the largest collection in the UK and has over 900 varieties from all over the world, with plants flowering every month of the year.

Ben Aigan Cycle Trails   122 C5
01343 820223   www.forestry.gov.uk
Off the A95, 1.5 miles (2km) south of Mulben. Three forest mountain bike trails giving excellent views over the winding River Spey.

Ben Lawers National
Nature Reserve   87 D1
01567 820397   www.nts.org.uk
Off the A827, 6 miles (9.5km) north east of Killin. Perthshire's highest mountain (3984ft/1214m) noted for the rich variety of mountain plants and the bird population - birds include raven, ring-ouzel, red grouse, ptarmigan, dipper and curlew.

Ben Lomond   86 A5
01360 870224   www.nts.org.uk
Ardess Lodge, Rowardennan. Rising from the east shore of Loch Lomond to 3193ft (974m), the mountain offers exhilarating walking and spectacular views.

Ben Nevis   97 D2
2 miles (3km) from Fort William. Britain's highest (4406ft/1344m) and most popular mountain for both rock climber and hill walker. The Ben Nevis race every September sees runners tackling a course to the summit and back with a record time of 1 hour and 25 minutes. Ben Nevis is best seen from the north approach to Fort William, or from the Gairlochy Road, across the Caledonian Canal.

Ben Nevis Distillery Visitor Centre   97 D2
01397 700200   www.bennevisdistillery.com
Lochy Bridge, on the A82, 2 miles (3km) north of Fort William. Visitors can tour the distillery and taste the famous whisky, the Dew of Ben Nevis. Exhibition and video programme. Award-winning whiskies available.

Benmore Botanic Garden   75 E2
01369 706261   www.rbge.org.uk
Benmore, 7 miles (11km) north of Dunoon, on the A815. Some of Britain's tallest trees can be found here, as can over 250 species of rhododendrons and an extensive magnolia collection. Other features include an avenue of giant redwoods planted in 1863, a formal garden, and a variety of waymarked trails.

Bennachie Centre   112 C2
01467 681470   www.forestry.gov.uk
2 miles (3km) south of Chapel of Garioch. The centre describes the local social and natural history. Visitors can participate in guided walks, bat and bird box building, fungal forays and classes for beginners on countryside skills.

Bennie Museum   78 A3
01506 634944
9 - 11 Mansefield Street, Bathgate. Almost 5000 artefacts illustrating the social, industrial, religious

and military history of Bathgate, a former burgh town. Displays of postcards and photographs from the 1890s onwards. Fossils, Roman glass and coins, relics from Prince Charles Edward Stuart and the Napoleonic Wars.

Benromach Distillery   121 E3
01309 675968   www.benromach.com
Invererne Road, off the A96. Moray's smallest distillery. The attractive malt whisky centre describes 100 years of history and tradition in whisky making.

Bernera Museum   144 B4
01851 612331
Bernera, Isle of Lewis. On the B8059, 2 miles (3km) from Bernera Bridge. The museum displays information on genealogy, archaeology and historical sites. Also archives, old photographs and a lobster fishing exhibition in summer.

Beveridge Park   79 D1
01592 412945
Kirkcaldy, Fife. Public park with woodland, formal gardens and extensive leisure facilities.

Biblical Garden   122 B3
01343 557053   www.moray.gov.uk
King Street, Elgin. A 3 acre (1.2ha) garden created using the Bible as a reference. A desert area depicts Mount Sinai and the cave of resurrection. Planted with every species of plant mentioned in the Bible.

Big Burn Walk   129 F4
Start point of walk in Golspie. One of the finest woodland walks in Sutherland. The extensive and well-maintained paths cross the burn by a series of bridges and allow access up to a waterfall.

Biggar Gasworks Museum   68 C2
01899 221050   www.historic-scotland.gov.uk
On the A702 in Biggar. Typical of a small town coal-gas works, the only surviving example in Scotland (dates from 1839). Managed by the Biggar Museum Trust.

Biggar Kirk   68 C2
The Manse, High Street, Biggar. Cruciform 16th century church with fine examples of modern stained glass.

Birkhill Fireclay Mine   78 A3
01506 825855   www.srps.org.uk
3 miles (5km) west of Bo'ness. The caverns of Birkhill Fireclay Mine are set in the picturesque Avon Gorge. A mine guide takes visitors on a tour of the mine workings where you can discover how fireclay was mined. There are also fossils which are over 300 million years old. The mine can only be reached by descending 130 steps into the Avon Gorge so access for the disabled and elderly is difficult. Tour times are coordinated with the Bo'ness and Kinneil Railway timetable.

Birks of Aberfeldy   88 B1
Short walk from the centre of Aberfeldy. Robert Burns wrote The Birks of Aberfeldy here in 1878. A narrow path climbs to a bridge directly above the Falls of Moness, providing spectacular views.

Birnam Oak   89 D1
Birnam. An ancient tree believed to be the last surviving remnant of Birnam Wood, the great oak forest made famous in Shakespeare's Macbeth.

Bishop's & Earl's Palaces   147 D2
01856 875461   www.historic-scotland.gov.uk
Watergate, Kirkwall. The Bishop's Palace is a 12th century hall house, later much altered with a round tower built by Bishop Reid between 1541 and 1548. A later addition was made by the notorious Patrick Stewart, Earl of Orkney, who built the adjacent Earl's

Palace between 1600 and 1607 in a splendid Renaissance style.

Bishop's Glen 75 E3
Dunoon. Once the source of Dunoon's water supply, now a favoured beauty spot and delightful walk leading to the Bishop's Seat, 1655ft (504m).

Black Hill 77 F6
www.nts.org.uk
Off the B7018, 3 miles (5km) west of Lanark. This is the site of a Bronze Age burial cairn, Iron Age hill fort, and outlook point over the Clyde Valley.

Black Isle Wildlife & Country Park 119 D4
01463 731656 www.blackisle.org/wildlife_park.htm
The Croft, Drumsmittal. Feed the ducks, swans and geese on the ponds. There are also goats, sheep, pot-bellied pigs, rabbits and many more animals to see. Tearoom, gift shop and children's play area.

Black Spout Wood 100 B4
South of Pitlochry town centre off the A924. Attractive oak woodland deriving its name from the spectacular waterfall, the Black Spout.

Black Watch Monument 99 F4
Taybridge Drive in Aberfeldy. A cairn surmounted by a statue of Private Farquhar Shaw dressed in the uniform of the Black Watch Regiment. To commemorate the first muster of the regiment in May 1740.

Black Watch Regimental Museum 28 B1
0131 310 8530 www.theblackwatch.co.uk/museum
Balhousie Castle, Hay Street, Perth. The museum describes the regiments' history from 1740 to the present day.

Blackfriars Chapel 91 E4
www.historic-scotland.gov.uk
South Street, St Andrews. The vaulted side apse of a church of Dominican friars.

Blackhammer Cairn 147 D1
01856 751360 www.historic-scotland.gov.uk
North of the B9064 on the south coast of the island of Rousay, Orkney. A long Neolithic cairn bounded by a retaining wall with a megalithic burial chamber divided into seven compartments.

Blackhouse 145 D3
01851 710395 www.historic-scotland.gov.uk
At Arnol, on the A858. 15 miles (24km) north west of Stornoway. A traditional Hebridean thatched and chimneyless house dating from the 1870s with byre, attached barn and stackyard. Furnished with a peat fire in the hearth.

Blackness Castle 78 B3
01506 834807 www.historic-scotland.gov.uk
Blackness, on the B903, 4 miles (6.5km) north east of Linlithgow. A 15th century stronghold, once one of the most important fortresses in Scotland and one of the four castles which the Articles of Union left fortified. A state prison in Covenanting times; a powder magazine in the 1870s.

Blacksmith's Shop Centre, Gretna Green 63 D3
01461 338441 www.gretnagreen.com
On the Scottish/English border, 15 miles (24km) south of Lockerbie. The Blacksmith's Shop is famous around the world for runaway marriages. The unique Gretna Green Story involves the visitor in the legends of its romantic history and leads into the magnificent anvil and carriage museum. The Tartan Shop presents Scotland's finest independent collection of Scottish and UK merchandise - cashmere, tartans, crystal, luxury foods and gifts. Tartan information centre. Tax-free shopping and worldwide mailing services.

Bladnoch Distillery 60 A4
01988 402605 www.bladnoch.co.uk
Bladnoch, Wigtown. Scotland's most southerly distillery. Established in 1817 beside the River Bladnoch. Visitor centre, guided tours and gift shop.

Blair Atholl Distillery 100 B4
01796 482003
1 mile (1.5km) south of Pitlochry town centre on the A924. Established in 1798 in the popular Highland resort of Pitlochry, Blair Athol distillery makes the signature malt that is in Bell's, the biggest selling blended whisky in the UK.

Blair Atholl Water Mill & Tearoom 99 F3
01796 481321 www.blairathollwatermill.co.uk
Ford Road, Blair Atholl. Dating from 1613, this working museum produces oatmeal and flour which is on sale in the tearoom.

Blair Castle 99 F3
01796 481207 www.blair-castle.co.uk
Blair Atholl, 7 miles (11km) north of Pitlochry off the A9. A white turreted baronial castle, the traditional seat of the Dukes and Earls of Atholl. The oldest part, Cumming's Tower, dates back to 1269. Fine collections of furniture, portraits, lace, china, arms, armour, Jacobite relics and Masonic regalia. Deer park, woodland, riverside and mountain walks.

Blair Drummond Safari Park 77 E1
01786 841456 www.safari-park.co.uk
Blair Drummond, 4 miles (6.5km) towards Doune on the A84. Drive through wild animal reserves, boat safari around chimpanzee island, pets' farm, adventure playground. Giant astra-glide and flying-fox cable slide across lake. Five-seater pedal boats. Amusement arcade, bouncy castle, dodgem cars.

Blairquhan 66 B5
01655 770239 www.blairquhan.co.uk
Maybole, 14 miles (22.5km) south east of Ayr. Four families have lived at Blairquhan. The first tower-house was built in 1346. The new house was designed and built by the Scottish architect William Burn between 1821 and 1824. Walled garden with original glasshouse. Pinetum. Sir James Hunter Blair's Collection of Scottish Colourists.

Blairs Museum, The 113 E4
01224 863767 www.blairsmuseum.com
South Deeside Road, Blairs. Set in a former Catholic college, Scotland's Catholic Treasury houses a renowned collection of church metalwork, embroidered vestments and objects and paintings relating to the Stewarts and Mary, Queen of Scots.

Boath Doocot 121 D4
www.nts.org.uk
Auldearn, 2 miles (3km) east of Nairn, off the A96. A 17th century doocot on the site of an ancient motte. Montrose defeated the Covenanters nearby in 1645; battle-plan on display.

Böd of Gremista 151 D2
01595 695057 www.shetland-museum.org.uk/bod/
Gremista, 1.5 miles (2.5km) north of Lerwick town centre. A restored 18th century fishing booth, the birthplace of local shipowner and politician Arthur Anderson. Displays tell the story of Anderson's life and service to Shetland, and of the fisheries 200 years ago. Also recreated room interiors of the kitchen and bedroom.

Bolfracks Garden 88 B1
01887 820344 www.bolfracks.com
2 miles (3km) west of Aberfeldy on the A827. A garden overlooking the Tay Valley. Specialities are rhododendrons, mecanopsis, old and rambling roses, all contained within a walled garden and a less formal wooded garden with stream.

Bonawe Iron Furnace 85 D2

01866 822432   www.historic-scotland.gov.uk

At Bonawe, close to Taynuilt on the A85, 12 miles (19km) east of Oban. The restored remains of a charcoal furnace for iron smelting. Established in 1753, it functioned until 1876. The most complete example of its type.

Bo'ness & Kinneil Railway 78 A2

01506 822298   www.srps.org.uk

Bo'ness Station on the A904 and A706. Savour the nostalgia of the railway age and travel by steam train from Bo'ness to visit Birkhill Fireclay Mine. An exhibition tells the story of the movement of goods and people before motorway travel with a display of carriages, wagons and locomotives.

Bonhoga Gallery 150 C1

01595 830400

Weisdale, 12 miles (19km) west of Lerwick. Displays local, national and international art and craft exhibitions. Plus the Shetland Textile Working Museum.

Blair Drummond Safari Park

Border Fine Arts Gallery 63 D1

01387 383033   www.borderfinearts.com

Townfoot, Langholm, 20 miles (32km) north of Carlisle. Border Fine Arts have been producing high quality ceramic figurines for over twenty-five years and have many collectors throughout the world. Visitors can see an extensive display of sculptures which collectors find enthralling.

Borthwick Parish Church 79 E4

Borthwick, Gorebridge, 13 miles (21km) south east of Edinburgh. This church, which is largely Victorian, has an aisle and a vault dating from the 15th century, an apse originating in the 12th century, 18th and 19th century memorials (particularly the Dundas family), and two 15th century effigies thought to be the best preserved in Scotland. Associated also with the Borthwick family and clan. Commemorates the birthplace of the great 18th century Scottish Enlightenment figure, Principal William Robertson.

Bosta Iron Age House 144 B4

01851 612331

Great Bernera, at the end of the B8059, north west Lewis. The adjacent archaeological site was excavated in 1996 to reveal a complex of several Iron Age houses. A full-scale replica of one house has been built nearby, using authentic construction methods, and gives a fascinating insight into the way of life of the inhabitants 1500 years ago.

Bothwell Castle 77 D4

01698 816894   www.historic-scotland.gov.uk

At Uddingston off the B7071, 7 miles (11km) south east of Glasgow. In a picturesque setting above the Clyde valley, the largest and finest 13th century stone castle in Scotland. Much fought over during the Wars of Independence. Most of the castle dates from the 14th and 15th centuries.

Bowhill House & Country Park 70 A3

01750 22204

Bowhill, 3 miles (5km) west of Selkirk on the A708. For many generations Bowhill has been the Border home of the Scotts of Buccleuch. Inside the house, begun in 1812, there is an outstanding collection of pictures, including works by Van Dyck, Reynolds, Gainsborough, Canaletto, Guardi, Claude Lorraine, Raeburn. There is also a selection of the world-famous Buccleuch collection of portrait miniatures. Also porcelain and furniture, much of which was made in the famous workshop of Andrè Boulle in Paris. Restored Victorian kitchen. In the grounds are an adventure woodland play area, a riding centre, garden nature trails, bicycle hire.

Bowmore Distillery Visitor Centre 72 C5

01496 810671

     www.bowmore.co.uk

School Street, Bowmore, Isle of Islay. Malt whisky distillery, licensed since 1779. Guided tours. Across the entrance yard, a former warehouse, is now a swimming pool heated by waste energy from the distillery.

Bracklinn Falls 87 D5

1 mile east of Callander. A series of dramatic waterfalls on the Keltie Water. The falls are approached along a woodland walk from a car park by the Callander Crags at Callander.

Braehead 76 C4

0141 885 4600

     www.braehead.co.uk

Braehead, 5 miles (8km) from Glasgow city centre. Over 100 of the UK's top high street names in spacious shopping malls. Cafés, restaurants, a public ice skating rink, international arena, riverside boardwalk and Maritime Heritage Centre.

Brahan Seer Plaque 119 E4

On the shore near Chanonry Lighthouse, Fortrose, Black Isle. The Brahan Seer who lived in the first half of the 17th century made many prophecies about the Highlands including predicting the Battle of Culloden and the building of the Caledonian Canal. He was burned at the stake on the orders of the Countess of Seaforth who had been told by the Seer that her husband was a philanderer. This plaque was erected to commemorate the event.

Brander Museum 123 E6

01771 622906   www.aberdeenshire.gov.uk

The Square, Huntly. A display about author George Macdonald. Also extensive collection of communion tokens plus arms and armour from 19th century Sudan.

Brandsbutt Symbol Stone 112 C2

01667 460232   www.historic-scotland.gov.uk

Inverurie. An early Pictish symbol stone with an ogham inscription.

Branklyn Garden 89 E3

01738 625535   www.branklyngarden.org.uk

On the A85 Dundee Road near Perth city centre. Started in 1922 on the site of a former orchard, Branklyn is an outstanding 2 acre (0.8ha) garden with rhododendrons, alpines, herbaceous and peat garden plants.

Brass Rubbing Centre 20 D4
0131 556 4364 www.cac.org.uk
Chalmers Close, 81 High Street, Edinburgh. Just off
the Royal Mile opposite the Museum of Childhood.
Housed in the historic Trinity Apse, thought to have
been founded in 1460 by Queen Mary of Gueldres,
consort of King James II of Scotland. Offers a fine
collection of replicas moulded from ancient Pictish
stones, medieval church brasses and rare Scottish
brasses.

Breadalbane Folklore Centre 86 C2
01567 820254
www.breadalbanefolklorecentre.com
Falls of Dochart, Killin. Includes a Tourist
Information Centre, water wheel and healing stones.
History of local clans (MacLaren, MacNab, Campbell
and MacGregor). Artefacts on Killin heritage. Display
boards and visual display units tell the story of
Breadalbane. Visitors can also learn about St Fillan,
the local patron saint and healer, a 6th century
Celtic monk who preached from the original mill
building.

Brechin Bridge 103 D4
Known locally as the Auld Brig, this is one of the
oldest stone bridges in Scotland.

Brechin Castle Centre 102 C3
01356 626813 www.brechincastlecentre.co.uk
Haughmuir, at the southern Brechin junction off the
A90. Scottish breeds of domestic animals, pets'
corner and pheasantry, farm buildings and display
of traditional agricultural machinery and
implements.

Brechin Cathedral Round Tower 102 C4
www.historic-scotland.gov.uk
One of the two remaining round towers of the Irish
type in Scotland. Built in the late 11th century with
a remarkable carved doorway. Capped by a stone
roof added in the 15th century.

Brechin Town House Museum 103 D3
01356 625536
High Street, Brechin. Local collections tell the story
of the development of Brechin from the Celtic church
of the 10th century to the last days of the burgh in
1975.

Bridge of Allan Parish Church 77 E1
01786 834155
12 Keir Street, Bridge of Allan, 2 miles (3km) south
of exit 11 on the M9. An attractive 19th century
building with fine timbered roof and excellent
stained glass windows. The chancel furnishings,
consisting of pulpit, communion table, chair,
organ screen and choir rail, were designed in 1904
by Charles Rennie Mackintosh in light oak and
represent a unique aspect of Mackintosh's style.

Bridge of Carr 110 A2
Carrbridge. High and narrow single-arch bridge. Built
by John Niccelsone, mason, in the summer of 1717,
for Sir James Grant.

Bridge of Dee 113 E4
On the A90 south west of Aberdeen. Built in the
1520s. Seven arches span 400ft (122m). The
medieval solidity of the structure is enlivened by
heraldic carvings.

Bridge of Oich 108 A4
01667 460232 www.historic-scotland.gov.uk
On the A82, 4 miles (6.5km) south of Fort Augustus.
A splendid suspension bridge designed by James
Dredge in 1854. It employs a patented design of
double cantilevered chains with massive granite
pylon arches at each end.

Brig o' Balgownie 113 E4
Bridge of Don. Also known as the Auld Brig o'Don,

this massive arch, 62ft (19m) wide, spans the deep
pool of the river and is backed by fine woods.

Brighouse Bay Trekking Centre 60 C5
01557 870267
Borgue, 6 miles (10km) south west of Kirkcudbright.
Approved by the British Horse Society, the Trekking
Centre offers riding for all abilities. Hard hats are
provided. Riding is within the 1200 acre (486ha)
holiday/farm complex. Also holiday park.

Bright Water Visitor Centre 106 A2
01599 530040 www.eileanban.org
Kyleakin, approximately 1 mile (1.5km) west of
Skye Bridge on the Isle of Skye. Eilean Bàn is a 6
acre island nestling under the Skye bridge. It is a
haven for wildlife, especially otters and was home to
Gavin Maxwell, author of The Ring of Bright Water.
The island can be reached by boat from the Bright
Water Visitor centre which also has displays about
the cultural and natural heritage of the small
island.

Brin Herb Nursery 119 D6
0845 2265142 www.brinherbnursery.co.uk
Flichity, Farr, 7 miles (11km) from the A9 on Daviot
- Fort Augustus road. Over 300 varieties of herb and
wild flower plants are grown in the nursery at 700ft
(213m) above sea level. Display gardens give
planting ideas. Shop sells herb related products,
books, cards and gifts.

British Golf Museum 91 E5
01334 460046 www.britishgolfmuseum.co.uk
Bruce Embankment, St Andrews. Visitors encounter
many famous professionals and amateurs of status.
Touch screen videos allow visitors to look deeper into
the lives of champions and to test their skills and
knowledge of the game.

Broad Bay Ceramics 145 E3
01851 820219 www.broadbayceramics.co.uk
In township of Col on the B895, 6 miles (9.5km)
north east of Stornoway. A working pottery making
a wide range of items, from the unique marbled
ware of the Hebridean range and the traditional
figurines of the Highlands and Islands, to the
collectible range of MacKatts of Glen Kitloch.

Broch of Gurness 146 C1
01856 751414 www.historic-scotland.gov.uk
Evie, off the A966 at Aikerness, about 14 miles
(22.5km) north west of Kirkwall. An Iron Age broch
over 10ft (3m) high, surrounded by stone huts, deep
ditches and ramparts.

Brodick Castle 65 E2
01770 302202 www.nts.org.uk
2 miles (3km) north of Brodick on the Isle of Arran.
Mainly Victorian castle, built on the site of a Viking
fortress. Original parts date from the 13th century,
although much of it was destroyed in the 15th and
16th centuries. Fine collections of furniture,
paintings, porcelain and silver collected by the
Dukes of Hamilton. The castle contains collections of
artwork by Gainsborough and Turner. Beautiful
walled garden, and woodland garden with famous
rhododendron collection. The castle occupies a fine
site overlooking Brodick Bay, on the slopes of Goat
Fell (2866ft/873m). Nature trail and other walks in
country park.

Brodie Castle 121 D4
01309 641371 www.nts.org.uk
Brodie, Forres. The oldest parts of the castle are
16th century. Fine collections of furniture and
porcelain and a major art collection. Woodland walk,
4 acre (1.6ha) pond with wildlife observation hides.
Famous daffodil collection in spring.

Brora Heritage Centre 130 C4
01408 622024
Brora. Hands-on exhibition illustrating the history of

Brora with historical photographs and local artefacts. The story of the area is told from stone age times to the present day, including exhibits on the local whisky, coal and woollen industry, and genealogy. Dinosaur area. Fantastic views.

Brough of Birsay 146 B1
01856 841815 www.historic-scotland.gov.uk
On the island of Birsay, at the north end of mainland Orkney. 20 miles (32km) north west of Kirkwall. The remains of a Romanesque church and a Norse settlement.

Broughton Gallery 69 D2
01899 830234 www.broughtongallery.co.uk
On the A701 just north of Broughton village. Sells paintings and crafts by living British artists and makers in Tower House, designed in 1937 by Sir Basil Spence.

Broughton House & Garden 60 C4
01557 330437 www.nts.org.uk
12 High Street, Kirkcudbright. 18th century town house, home and studio (1901-33) of artist E. A. Hornel, one of the Glasgow Boys. Permanent exhibition of his work. Extensive collection of Scottish books including Burns' works. Attractive Japanese-style garden, added by Hornel, leading down to River Dee estuary.

Broughty Castle & Museum 91 D2
01382 436916
www.dundeecity.gov.uk/broughtycastle
Broughty Ferry. A 16th century tower adapted for changing defence needs during the 19th century. The castle houses a museum which has displays on the life & times of Broughty Ferry.

Brow Well 62 A3
On the B725, 1 mile (1.5km) west of Ruthwell. Ancient mineral well visited by Robert Burns in July 1796, when at Brow sea bathing under his doctor's orders.

Bruce's Stone 60 A1
North side of Loch Trool, unclassified road off the A714, 13 miles (21km) north of Newton Stewart. A massive granite memorial to Robert the Bruce's first victory over the English, which led to his subsequent success at Bannockburn. Fine views of Loch Trool and the hills of Galloway. Start of hill climb to the Merrick (2764ft/842.5m), the highest hill in southern Scotland.

Bucholie Castle 137 E3
South of Freswick on the A9 John o'Groats to Wick road. The 12th century stronghold of Sweyn Asliefson, the Norse pirate. Originally named Lambaborg, the Mowats brought the present name of Bucholie with them from their estates in Aberdeenshire. Only ruins remain standing on a promontory high above the sea.

Buckhaven Museum 79 E1
01592 412860
College Street, Buckhaven. Museum displays Buckhaven's history with a focus on the fishing industry. Stained glass windows made by local people.

Bunnahabhain Distillery 73 D3
01496 840646 www.bunnahabhain.com
Port Askaig, Isle of Islay. Visitors can see the malt whisky distillation process and sample the results. Individuals and groups welcome.

Burg 82 C3
www.nts.org.uk
Isle of Mull, 7 miles (11km) west of Tiroran off the B8035, then rough path. Car parking at Tiroran. Covering an area of 1405 acres (568.5ha), this is a spectacular and remote part of Mull. The high cliffs here are known as the Wilderness. MacCulloch's Fossil Tree is 50 million years old, and can be reached by a steep iron ladder down to the beach at low tide.

Burland Croft Trail 150 C3
01595 880430
Burland, Trondra, Shetland. 3 miles (5km) from Scalloway. Follow the waymarked route through this working croft. See the croft animals such as sheep, Shetland cattle, Tamworth pigs, and Shetland ducks and geese which have been re-introduced as a result of detailed research.

Burleigh Castle 89 E5
www.historic-scotland.gov.uk
Off the A911, 2 miles (3km) north east of Kinross. The roofless but otherwise complete ruin of a tower house of about 1500 with a section of defensive barmkin wall and a remarkable corner tower with a square cap-house corbelled out.

Burns House 61 F2
01387 255297
Burns Street, Dumfries. Five minute walk from Dumfries town centre. It was in this ordinary sandstone house that Robert Burns, Scotland's national poet, spent the last years of his brilliant life. Now a place of pilgrimage for Burns enthusiasts around the world. The house retains much of its 18th century character and contains many relics of the poet. Visitors can see the chair in which he wrote his last poems and many original letters and manuscripts. The famous Kilmarnock and Edinburgh editions of his work are also on display.

Burns House Museum 67 D3
01290 550045
Castle Street, Mauchline, 11 miles (18km) from Ayr and Kilmarnock. A museum with a gallery devoted to Burns memorabilia. On the upper floor is the room Burns took for Jean Armour in 1788. It has remained intact and is furnished in the style of the period. Models of Jean and Robert plus a full video presentation. Visitors can also see a large collection of Mauchline boxware and an exhibition devoted to curling and curling stones. Nearby is Mauchline churchyard in which are buried four of Burns' daughters and a number of his friends and contemporaries.

Burns National Heritage Park 66 B4
01292 443700 www.burnsheritagepark.com
Murdochs Lane, Alloway, 2 miles (3km) south of Ayr on the B7024. The Burns National Heritage Park was established in 1995. It embraces Burns' Cottage, Museum, Monument, Auld Brig o' Doon and Alloway Kirk together with the Tam o' Shanter Experience. The old and new are linked in time by a 5-minute walk which transports the visitor from 1759 (when Burns was born) to the exciting, humorous and action-filled Tam o' Shanter Experience.

Burnswark Hill 62 B2
By unclassified road, 1.5 miles (2.5km) north of the B725, Ecclefechan to Middlebie road. A native hill fort (circa 6th century BC) with extensive earthworks, flanked by a Roman artillery range. Thought to have been a series of Roman practice seige works, best seen from the hilltop. The excavated ditches and ramparts of Birrens Fort are nearby.

Burntisland Museum 79 D2
01592 412860
102 High Street, Burntisland. Permanent display about the Edwardian Fair that visited Burntisland every year, plus displays on the local history of Burntisland.

Burrell Collection, The 76 C4
0141 287 2550   www.glasgowmuseums.com
Pollok Country Park, 2060 Pollokshaws Road,
Glasgow. This award-winning building houses a
world-famous collection gifted to Glasgow by Sir
William Burrell. Visitors can see art objects from Iraq,
Egypt, Greece and Italy. Tapestries, furniture,
textiles, ceramics, stained glass and sculptures from
medieval Europe, and drawings from the 15th to
19th centuries. Regular temporary exhibitions.

Bute Museum 75 D4
01700 505067   www.butemuseum.org
Stuart Street, Rothesay, Isle of Bute. Custom-made
museum, gifted by the 4th Marquis of Bute in 1926.
A recognised source of information on the Island of
Bute.

Butterfly & Insect World 79 E4
0131 663 4932 www.edinburgh-butterfly-world.co.uk
Dobbies Garden World, Lasswade. Visitors can walk
through an indoor tropical rainforest inhabited by
thousands of the world's most beautiful butterflies.
Also Bugs and Beasties exhibition, featuring
hundreds of live creepy crawlies, snakes, lizards and
frogs. Daily 'meet the beasties' handling sessions.
Also garden centre, birds of prey centre and
children's play parks

Cadzow Castle 77 E5
0131 668 8600   www.historic-scotland.gov.uk
In the grounds of Chatelherault Country Park,
Hamilton. Constructed between 1500 and 1550, the
castle was known as 'the castle in the woods of
Hamilton'.

Caerlaverock Castle 62 A3
01387 770244   www.historic-scotland.gov.uk
Glencople, off the B725, 9 miles (14.5km) south of
Dumfries. One of the finest castles in Scotland - its
remarkable features are the twin-towered gatehouse
and the Nithsdale Lodging, a splendid Renaissance
range dating from 1638.

Caerlaverock Wildfowl & Wetlands Trust 62 A3
01387 770200   www.wwt.org.uk
East Park Farm, Caerlaverock, 9 miles (14.5km)
south east of Dumfries. A 1,350 acre (546ha) nature
reserve where many birds can be seen from hides
and observation towers. Trails in summer.

Cairn Holy Chambered Cairns 60 B4
0131 668 8600   www.historic-scotland.gov.uk
6.5 miles (10.5km) south east of Creetown. Two
remarkably complete Neolithic burial cairns situated
on a hill giving good views over Wigtown Bay.

Cairn o'Get 137 E5
01667 460232   www.historic-scotland.gov.uk
5 miles (8km) north east of Lybster. A horned and
chambered Neolithic burial cairn.

Cairn o'Mohr Fruit Winery 90 B3
01821 642781   www.cairnomohr.co.uk
East Inchmichael, Errol. Award winning fruit wines
are made from local berries, flowers and leaves.
Guided tours, wine tastings and a shop.

Cairnbaan Cup & Ring Marks 74 B1
www.historic-scotland.gov.uk
Kilmartin Glen. Near to the Cairnbaan Hotel on the
A841, 2.5 miles (4km) north west of Lochgilphead.
Cup and ring marks on a natural rock surface.

Cairngorm Mountain Railway 110 A4
01479 861261   www.cairngormmountain.com
Cairngorm Mountain, 9 miles (15km) east of
Aviemore. Scotland's only mountain railway, taking
visitors on a spectacular journey to Cairngorm
Mountain - the UK's fifth highest mountain. A safe
and comfortable adventure for all ages and abilities.
Exhibition on the natural history of the area.

Cairngorm Reindeer Centre 110 A3
01479 861228
www.reindeer-company.demon.co.uk
Reindeer House, Glenmore, 6 miles (10km) east of
Aviemore on the A951. Britain's only free-ranging
herd of reindeer. Visitors join the guide for a walk to
the reindeer's hillside grazing. For visitors unable to
make the walk, reindeer can also be seen at the
centre. Exhibition and gift shop. Opportunity to
adopt your own reindeer.

Cairngorm Ski Centre 110 A4
01479 861261   www.cairngormmountain.com
9 miles (15 km) south east of Aviemore. Scotland's
first commercial ski centre and host to Scottish
championships for snowboard and freestyle. Skiing
at 1800 - 3600ft (600 - 1267m) with one black,
nine red, six blue and ten green runs. Sheltered area
for beginners.

Cairngorm Sleddog Adventure Centre 109 F4
07767 270526   www.sled-dogs.co.uk
Moormore Cottage, Rothiemurchas, Aviemore. Enjoy
exciting sleddog rides, pulled by a team of 12
huskies and pointers. An exciting and unusual way
to see the scenery and wildlife of the Rothiemurchas

The Burrell Collection

Estate at the foot of the Cairngorm Mountains. Kennel tours, courses and a small museum.

Cairnpapple Hill   78 A3
01506 634622
www.historic-scotland.gov.uk
Near Torphichen, off the B792, 3 miles (5km) north of Bathgate. One of the most important prehistoric monuments in Scotland. It was used as a burial and ceremonial site from around 3000 to 1400 BC. Excellent views.

Caithness Glass Visitor Centre   137 E4
01738 492320
www.caithnessglass.co.uk
Inveralmond Industrial Estate, on the A9 Perth western bypass at the Inveralmond roundabout. See the fascinating process of glass-making. Also paperweight collectors gallery, audio-visual theatre and children's play area. Factory shop.

Calanais Standing Stones & Visitor Centre   144 C4
01851 621422   www.historic-scotland.gov.uk
At Calanais, off the A858, 12 miles (19km) west of Stornoway, Isle of Lewis. A unique cruciform setting of megaliths second in importance only to Stonehenge. Erected about 3000 BC. An avenue of 19 monoliths leads north from a circle of 13 stones, with rows of more stones fanning out to the south, east and west. Inside the circle is a small chambered tomb.

Calderglen Country Park   77 D4
01355 236644
Strathaven Road, 1 mile (1.5km) from East Kilbride. The park consists of over 440 acres (180ha) of attractive wooded gorge and parkland, including several fine waterfalls. Extensive network of paths and nature trails, visitor centre, conservatory, ornamental garden, children's zoo, toddler's play area and special needs play area centred around the historic Torrance House.

Caledonian Canal   119 D5
01463 233140
www.waterscape.com/caledonian_canal
Canal Office, Seaport Marina, Muirtown Wharf, Inverness. Designed by Thomas Telford and completed in 1822, the Caledonian Canal links the lochs of the Great Glen (Loch Lochy, Loch Oich and Loch Ness). It provides a coast to coast shortcut between Corpach near Fort William and Clachnaharry at Inverness and is the only Scottish canal capable of carrying ships up to 500 tons. The canal has been described as the most beautiful in Europe - the spectacular Highland scenery of lochs, mountains and glens is unusual for a canal. A wide variety of craft use the canal throughout the year and can usually be seen at close quarters as they pass through locks and bridges. There are a number of pleasure cruises available on the canal and small boats are available for hire.

Caledonian Canal Heritage Centre   108 A4
01320 366493
www.waterscape.com/caledonian_canal
Canalside, Fort Augustus. The centre describes the fascinating history of the Caledonian Canal, from its conception to its present day refurbishment. Visitors can see the dramatic lock flight in operation.

Caledonian Railway   103 D4
01356 622992   www.caledonianrailway.co.uk
The Station, 2 Park Road, Brechin. From the unique

Victorian terminus at Brechin, board a steam train and journey back in time as you travel the falling grade to the Bridge of Dun. Static display of model trains.

Calgary Art in Nature   94 B4
Calgary, Isle of Mull, 11 miles (18km) west of Tobermory. Twenty artworks by local artists are scattered throughout an intimate wood waiting to be discovered by the walker.

Callendar House   77 F3
01324 503770
Callendar Park, 1 mile (2km) east of Falkirk town centre. Encapsulates 600 years of Scotland's history from medieval times to the 20th century and was visited by great historical figures like Mary, Queen of Scots, Cromwell and Bonnie Prince Charlie. Permanent attractions include displays on the Story of Callendar House, and on the Falkirk area during the great social revolution of 1750 - 1850. The house's research centre contains an extensive archive.

Cally Gardens   60 C4
01557 815029   www.callygardens.co.uk
Gatehouse of Fleet, Castle Douglas. A specialist nursery in an 18th century walled garden. There is a unique collection of over 3500 varieties, mainly perennials, planted out in 32 large borders.

Cambo Gardens   91 F4
01333 450054   www.camboestate.com
Cambo Estate on the A917, 2.5 miles (4km) north of Crail. Walled garden full of romantic charm designed around the Cambo burn, which is spanned by ornamental bridges and a greenhouse.

Cambus o'May Forest   111 F5
01330 844537   www.forestry.gov.uk
2.5 miles (4km) east of Ballater on the A93. A wonderful forest with four waymarked walks and a permanent orienteering course.

Cambuskenneth Abbey   77 F1
www.historic-scotland.gov.uk
1 mile (2km) east of Stirling. Ruins of an abbey founded in 1147 as a house of Augustinian canons. Scene of Robert the Bruce's parliament in 1326 and the burial place of James III and his queen. The fine detached tower is the only substantial survivor, but extensive foundations of the rest remain.

Camera Obscura   20 D4
0131 226 3709   www.camera-obscura.co.uk
Adjacent to Edinburgh Castle at the top of the Royal Mile. Edinburgh's oldest attraction. An 1850s camera obscura captures a live panorama of the city below while guides tell Edinburgh's story. Visitors can spy on passers-by or pick vehicles up in the palm of their hand. Three-dimensional hologram

View from Camera Obscura looking north to the Firth of Forth

display (the largest in Europe) and photographs of old Edinburgh.

Camperdown Wildlife Centre 90 C2
01382 431806 www.camperdownpark.com/wildlife.htm
Camperdown Country Park, Coupar Angus Road, 3 miles (4km) north of Dundee on the A923. Over 80 species of native wildlife; brown bears, lynx, arctic foxes and other more unusual species, such as Britain's rarest mammal, the pine marten.

Camus a Charraig 126 B5
On the main road to Mellon Udrigle, north of Gairloch on the A832. A beautiful white sand beach which borders a broad sandy bay of sparkling blue-green waters surrounded by mountains.

Canna 104 B4
01687 462466 www.nts.org.uk
This beautiful Hebridean island offers spectacular views, interesting archaeological remains and fascinating birdlife. The small farming population still uses traditional crofting systems. There is a post office, but no shops, pubs or roads. For details of work camps and holiday accommodation, contact the NTS Head Office in Edinburgh on 0131 243 9300.

Canongate Kirk 20 D4
0131 556 3515 www.canongatekirk.com
The Kirk of Holyroodhouse, Canongate, Edinburgh. Opposite Huntly House Museum in the Royal Mile. Historic 300 year old Church of Scotland, recently renovated and restored. Parish church of the Palace of Holyroodhouse and Edinburgh Castle, with Frobenius organ and Normandy tapestry.

Caol Ila Distillery 73 D4
01496 302760
Port Askaig, on the A846, on the east side of the Islay. A distillery built in 1846 by Hector Henderson. It stands in a picturesque setting at the foot of a steep hill with its own small pier overlooking the Sound of Islay and Paps of Jura.

Cape Wrath 133 D2
www.capewrath.org.uk
12 miles (19.5km) north west of Durness. The most northerly point of Scotland's north west seaboard. A passenger ferry from Keoldale (summer only) connects with a minibus service to the cape. Also mainland Britain's highest sea cliffs at Clo Mor which stand 920ft (280.5m) high.

Captain Scott and Dr Wilson Cairn 101 F3
In Glen Prosen on unclassified road north west of Dykehead. The cairn replaces the original fountain which was erected in memory of the Antarctic explorers, Captain Scott and Dr Wilson.

Carberry Candle Cottage 79 E4
0131 665 5656
Carberry, Musselburgh. Visitors can see live and video demonstrations of candle manufacturing. There is also a factory shop.

Cardhu Distillery Visitor Centre 122 A5
01340 872555
Knockando, Aberlour. The origins of Cardhu go back to the heyday of illicit distilling, when farmers made use of their own barley and local water. Licensed since 1824, the Cumming family expanded and improved the distillery.

Cardoness Castle 60 B4
01557 814422 www.historic-scotland.gov.uk
On the A75, 1 mile (2km) south west of Gatehouse of Fleet. The well-preserved ruin of a 15th century tower house, the ancient home of the McCullochs of Galloway. Four storeys with a vaulted basement. Features include the original stairway, stone

Carfin Lourdes Grotto & Pilgrimage Centre 77 E5
01698 268941 www.carfin.org.uk
100 Newarthill Road, Carfin, Motherwell. 12 miles (19km) east of Glasgow. The Pilgrimage Centre is situated adjacent to Carfin Lourdes Grotto and offers a unique audio-visual and gallery exhibition tracing the history and tradition of pilgrimage worldwide.

Carleton Castle 58 C1
Off the A77, 6 miles (9.5km) south of Girvan. One in a link of Kennedy watchtowers along the coast. Now a ruin, it was famed in a ballad as the seat of a baron who got rid of seven wives by pushing them over the cliff, but who was himself disposed of by May Culean, his eighth wife.

Carmichael Visitor Centre 68 B2
01899 308336 www.carmichael.co.uk
Warrenhill Farm by Biggar, 4 miles (6.5km) south of Lanark on the A73. Scotland's only wax model collection tells Scotland's and Carmichael's story using Madame Tussaud quality models. The Clan Centre for southern Scotland concentrates on the Carmichaels but also includes information on many other southern Scottish families, as well as the history of the estate's agriculture and environment. Wind energy exhibit. Deer park. Adventure playground. Animal farm. Horse and pony trekking. Clydesdale horse and cart rides. Heritage walks. Orienteering and way-finding.

Carn Ban 65 D3
0131 668 8600 www.historic-scotland.gov.uk
3.5 miles (5.5km) north east of Lagg on the south coast of the Isle of Arran. One of the most famous Neolithic long cairns of south west Scotland.

Carn Liath, Skye 115 D4
Kensalayre. One of the best preserved Neolithic small chambered cairns on Skye.

Carn Liath, Sutherland 129 F4
01667 460232 www.historic-scotland.gov.uk
By the A9, 3 miles (5km) east north east of Golspie. A typical broch, surviving to first-floor level, with associated settlement.

Carnasserie Castle 84 B5
www.historic-scotland.gov.uk
Off the A816, 9 miles (14.5km) north of Lochgilphead, 2 miles (3km) north of Kilmartin, Argyll. A handsome combined tower house and hall, home of John Carswell, first Protestant Bishop of the Isles and translator of the first book printed in Gaelic. Fine architectural details of the late 16th century. The castle was captured and partly blown up during Argyll's rebellion in 1685.

Carnegie Museum 112 C2
01771 622807 www.aberdeenshire.gov.uk
Town Hall, The Square, Inverurie. Local archaeology including Beaker folk and Pictish carved stones and transportation.

Carrick House 148 C4
01857 622260
Eday, Orkney. Historic private house dating from the 17th century, built by John Stewart, Earl of Carrick. The house was the scene of the capture of Pirate Gow in 1725. It was renovated into a larger house in the mid 19th century. Built of local sandstone, harled and crow-stepped in the traditional Orkney style. The guided tours take in the house, garden and other parts of the island. Spectacular views.

Carron Pottery, Craft & Art Gallery 116 C4
01520 722321 www.carronpottery.co.uk
Cam-Allt, 1 mile (1.5km) south of Strathcarron railway station on the A890. Well-established craft

shop selling a wide range of Scottish and local crafts. Visitors can view the pottery attached to the shop. Art Gallery with work by local and professional artists. Occasional solo exhibitions. Sculptures and ceramics.

Carsaig Arches   83 D4
A 3 mile (5km) walk from Carsaig leads to these remarkable tunnels formed by the sea in the basaltic rock. Reached only at low tide. On the way is the Nun's Cave; it is said that nuns driven out of Iona at the time of the Reformation sheltered here. The west wall bears numerous incised carvings, including crosses of various shapes, some of which could be as old as the late 6th century.

Carsluith Castle   60 A4
On the A75, 7 miles (11km) west of Gatehouse of Fleet. The delightful and well-preserved ruin of a 16th century tower house with 18th century ranges of outhouses still in use by the farmer. One of its owners was the last abbot of Sweetheart Abbey.

Carsphairn Heritage Centre   66 C6
01644 460653   www.carsphairnheritage.co.uk
On the A713, 25 miles (40km) south of Ayr and 25 miles (40km) north of Castle Douglas. Carsphairn Heritage Centre houses a permanent display on the parish together with a temporary annual exhibition, featuring local history. There is also a reference section which pays particular attention to family history records relevant to the area and a small display of locally made articles for sale together with other relevant mementoes of the area.

Cartland Bridge   77 F6
On the A73 west of Lanark. An impressive bridge built by Telford in 1822 over a gorge, carrying the Mouse Water. It is one of the highest road bridges in Scotland.

Cassley Falls   128 B4
At Invercassley on the A837. An attractive series of cascading falls, particularly impressive after heavy rainfall, and walkway by Rosehall. Salmon can be seen leaping during the summer months.

Castle & Gardens of Mey   137 D2
01847 851473   www.castleofmey.org.uk
6 miles (10km) west of John o'Groats. 16th century Mey Castle was originally the seat of the earls of Caithness but between 1952 and 2002 became the Scottish summer holiday retreat of Her late Majesty Queen Elizabeth, The Queen Mother. It was built to a Z plan characteristic of its era, with towers and corbelled turrets. The walled garden is protected from wind and salt spray by the 12ft (3.7m) high Great Wall of Mey.

Castle Campbell & Garden   78 A1
01259 742408   www.historic-scotland.gov.uk
In Dollar Glen, 1 mile (2km) north of Dollar. Once known as Castle Gloom, the castle was built towards the end of the 15th century by the 1st Earl of Argyll. Burned by Cromwell in the 1650s. The original tower is well preserved. The 60 acres (24ha) of woodland in the glen make an attractive walk to the castle.

Castle Douglas Art Gallery   61 D3
01557 331643
Market Street, Castle Douglas. First opened in 1938, having been gifted to the town by Mrs Ethel Bristowe, a talented artist in her own right. The gallery now forms an excellent venue for an annual programme of temporary exhibitions, ranging from fine art and craft to photography.

Castle Fraser   112 C3
01330 833463   www.nts.org.uk
Sauchen, Inverurie. Magnificent castle completed in 1636 and one of the most sophisticated Scottish buildings of the period. Notable paintings and furnishings.

Castle House Museum   75 D3
01369 701422
                          www.castlehousemuseum.org.uk
Castle Gardens, Dunoon. The museum illustrates the history of Dunoon and district from pre-history to the recent past. Four rooms have been set aside to give the visitor a reflection of life in Victorian times. Set in pleasant gardens, opposite Dunoon's beautiful Victorian Pier with excellent views of the surrounding area.

Castle Keep   105 E3
01471 866376   www.castlekeep.co.uk
Strathaird Steading, Strathaird, Isle of Skye. Bladesmith making hand-forged swords, knives, dirks and traditional Scottish weaponry.

Castle Kennedy Gardens   58 C3
01776 702024   www.castlekennedygardens.co.uk
5 miles (8 km) east of Stranraer on the A75. Landscaped gardens famous for rhododendrons and azaleas, featuring terrraces and avenues set between two lakes.

Castle Menzies   99 F4
01887 820982   www.menzies.org/castle/
Weem, 1.5 miles (2.5km) west of Aberfeldy. Imposing 16th century castle, a fine example of the transition between a Z-plan clan stronghold and a later mansion house. Seat of the clan chiefs for over 400 years, Castle Menzies was involved in a number of historic occurrences.

Castle of Old Wick   137 E5
01667 460232   www.historic-scotland.gov.uk
1 mile (2km) south of Wick. Also known as the Old Man of Wick, this is one of the oldest surviving stone castles in Scotland. The castle is the ruin of an early Norse tower house on a spectacular site on a spine of rock, known as the Brig o' Trams, projecting into the sea between two deep narrow gulleys. Great care is required when visiting this site.

Castle of St John   58 B3
01776 705088
Charlotte Street, Stranraer. Medieval tower house built circa 1500. An exhibition tells the castle's story, highlighting its use by Government troops during the suppression of the Covenanters, and its Victorian use as a prison. Family activities.

Castle Semple Centre
(Clyde Muirshiel Regional Park)   76 B4
01505 614791   www.clydemuirshiel.co.uk
Castle Semple Outdoor Centre, Lochlip Road, just off the A760 in Lochwinoch. Located on the edge of Castle Semple Loch. Ranger service, woodland walks and nature trails in Parkhill Wood. Historical landmarks in the vicinity include Peel Castle, Collegiate Church, grotto, maze and fishponds. Outdoor activities available from the centre (for taught courses, taster sessions and equipment hire) include kayaking, sailing, rowing boats, mountain biking, hill walking, orienteering and archery. Fishing permits are also available.

Castle Semple Collegiate Church   76 A4
0131 668 8600   www.historic-scotland.gov.uk
At Castle Semple, 4 miles (6.5km) west of Howwood. A late gothic church with a three-sided east end with windows of an unusual style.

Castle Sween   74 A3
                          www.historic-scotland.gov.uk
On the east shore of Loch Sween, 15 miles (24km) south west of Lochgilphead. Probably the oldest stone castle on the Scottish mainland. Built in the mid 12th century with later towers in addition to now vanished wooden structures. Destroyed by Sir Alexander Macdonald in 1647.

Castle Varrich   134 B4
0.5 mile (1km) from the village of Tongue. Ruin located above Kyle of Tongue on a promontory. Steep path to castle accessible from the gate beside the Royal Bank of Scotland. A 14th century MacKay stronghold. Beautiful views along Kyle of Tongue.

Castlecary   77 E3
www.historic-scotland.gov.uk
On the B816, east of Castlecary village. The reduced earthworks of a fort on the Antonine Wall.

Castlelaw Hill Fort   79 D4
www.historic-scotland.gov.uk
1 mile (2km) north west of Glencorse, off the A702, 7 miles (11km) south of Edinburgh. A small Iron Age hill fort consisting of two concentric banks and ditches. An earth house is preserved in the older rock-cut ditch. Occupied in Roman times.

Caterthuns   102 C3
www.historic-scotland.gov.uk
Near the village of Menmuir about 5 miles (8km) north west of Brechin. Two spectacular large Iron Age hill forts. The Brown Caterthun has four concentric ramparts and ditches; the White Caterthun is a well-preserved fort with a massive stone rampart, defensive ditch and outer earthworks.

Cathedral Church of St Machar   113 E4
01224 485988   www.stmachar.com
The Chanonry, Aberdeen. A twin-towered granite building dating from 1350 - 1520 with stone pillars and impressive stained glass windows on three sides. Outside is the tomb of Bishop Gavin Dunbar.

Cawdor Castle   119 F5
01667 404401   www.cawdorcastle.com
5 miles (8km) south west of Nairn on the B9090 off the A96. Cawdor Castle is the name romantically associated by Shakespeare with Macbeth. The medieval tower and drawbridge are still intact and generations of art lovers and scholars are responsible for the eclectic collection of paintings, books and porcelain to be found in the castle. There are beautiful gardens, five nature trails and a nine-hole golf course and putting green.

Chapel Finian   59 D5
0131 668 8600   www.historic-scotland.gov.uk
5 miles (8km) north west of Port William. The foundation remains of a small chapel or oratory, probably dating from the 10th or 11th century, in an enclosure about 50ft (15m) wide.

Chapel of Sand   126 B5
In Laide, north of Gairloch. Said to have been constructed by St Columba in the 6th century. Parts of the intricately carved windows of the chapel are still intact and there is a large remnant of an arch.

Chatelherault Country Park   77 E5
01698 426213
Carlisle Road, Ferniegair, Hamilton. A magnificent hunting lodge and kennels built in 1732 by William Adam. Extensive country walks. Exhibition on the Clyde Valley, geology and natural history of the park, 18th century gardens and parterre.

Chesters Hill Fort   80 A3
www.historic-scotland.gov.uk
1 mile (2km) south of Drem on the unclassified road to Haddington, East Lothian. One of the best examples of an Iron Age hill fort with multiple ramparts. A souterrain is built into one of the ditches.

Church of the Holy Rude   77 E1
01786 475275   www.holyrude.org
St John Street, Stirling. Believed to be the only church in the United Kingdom apart from Westminster Abbey which has held a coronation,

that of James VI, son of Mary, Queen of Scots. John Knox preached the coronation sermon. Scottish monarchs of the 15th and 16th centuries worshipped here, and developed the church. Extensively renovated during the 1990s. Magnificent romantic organ.

Cille-Bharra   139 D3
01871 810336
At Eolaigearraidh (Eoligarry), at the north end of Isle of Barra. The ruined church of St Barr, who gave his name to the island, and the restored chapel of St Mary formed part of the medieval monastery. Among the preserved gravestones there was a unique stone carved with a Celtic cross on one side and Norse runes on the other. A replica of this stone now stands in Cille-Bharra.

City Art Centre   20 B2
0131 529 3993   www.cac.org.uk
2 Market Street, Edinburgh. Houses the City of Edinburgh's permanent fine art collection and stages a programme of temporary exhibitions from all over the world. Six floors of display galleries (with escalators and lifts). Education programme of workshops, lectures, events and educational publications.

City Chambers   16 B2
0141 287 4018
George Square, Glasgow. The City Chambers is the headquarters of Glasgow City Council and arguably Glasgow's finest example of Victorian architecture. The building was opened in 1888 by Queen Victoria and to this day has preserved all its original features.

Clachan Bridge   83 F4
B844 off the A816, 12 miles (19k) south west of Oban. This picturesque single-arched bridge, built in 1792 and linking the mainland with the island of Seil, is often claimed to be the only bridge to span the Atlantic (although there are others similar). The waters are actually those of the narrow Seil Sound, which joins the Firth of Lorne to Outer Loch Melfort, but they can, with some justification, claim to be an arm of the Atlantic.

Clan Armstrong Museum   63 D1
01387 381610   www.armstrongclan.org.uk
Lodge Walk, Castleholm. Off the A7 in Langholm, north of Carlisle. The world's largest Armstrong Museum, containing the most extensive Armstrong archives and displaying the history of this formidable Borders' family from the reiving days of the 15th and 16th centuries to the present.

Clan Cameron Museum   107 E6
01397 712090 / 712480   www.clan-cameron.org
Achnacarry, Spean Bridge.The history of the Cameron Clan, its involvement in the Jacobite Risings and the subsequent resurgence of the clan. Visitors can also learn about the story of Achnacarry and its wildlife. There are sections on the Queen's Own Cameron Highlanders and the Commandos who trained at Achnacarry during World War II. The building is on the site of a croft burned by Cumberland's soldiers in 1746.

Clan Gunn Heritage Centre & Museum   131 E1
01593 741700   www.clangunnsociety.org
Old Parish Church, Latheron. Information about one of the oldest clans in Scotland from its Norse origins to current times. Comprehensive records of clan genealogy are held and the centre is the base for the Clan Gunn Society which maintains the clan's traditions throughout the world.

Clan Macpherson Museum   109 E5
01540 673332   www.clan-macpherson.org
Clan House, Main Street, Newtonmore. 15 miles

(24km) south of Aviemore on the A86. Museum depicting the history of the Clan Macpherson with portraits, photographs and other Macpherson memorabilia.

Clansman Centre 108 A4
01320 366444   www.scottish-swords.com
Canalside, Fort Augustus. On the A82, 38 miles (61km) west of Inverness at the southern end of Loch Ness. See how the 17th century Highland clans lived, ate and survived inside a reconstructed turf house. Hear a live presentation by an authentically dressed clansman, including clothing and weapons demonstration. Craft shop and scottish armoury.

Clatteringshaws Visitor Centre 60 B2
01671 402420   www.forestry.gov.uk
New Galloway, Castle Douglas. Situated in Galloway Forest Park. Forest wildlife exhibition. Guided walks. Fishing (by permit). Waymarked walks and cycle trails.

Clatto Country Park 90 C2
01382 436505
3 miles (5km) north west of Dundee. Visitor centre, childrens' play areas, picnic sites, fishing, watersports and guided walks.

Clava Cairns 119 E5
01667 460232   www.historic-scotland.gov.uk
Near Culloden, off the B9006, 6 miles (10km) east of Inverness. Two chambered cairns and a ring cairn in a row, each surrounded by a circle of stones. Of late Neolithic or early Bronze Age date. An extensive and well-preserved site in a beautiful setting.

Claypotts Castle 91 D2
01786 431324   www.historic-scotland.gov.uk
South of the A92, near Broughty Ferry. An unusually complete 16th century tower house with circular towers at diagonally opposite corners corbelled out to form overhanging cap houses.

Click Mill 146 C1
01856 841815   www.historic-scotland.gov.uk
At Dounby, on mainland Orkney. The last surviving and working horizontal water mill in Orkney, a type well represented in Shetland and Lewis.

Clickimin Broch 151 D2
01856 841815   www.historic-scotland.gov.uk
About 1 mile (2km) south of Lerwick, Shetland. A good example of a broch tower with associated secondary buildings of Iron Age date.

Cloch Lighthouse 75 F3
A770, 3 miles (4.5km) south west of Gourock. This notable landmark stands at Cloch Point with fine views across the upper Firth of Clyde estuary. The white-painted lighthouse was constructed in 1797.

Clog & Shoe Workshop 60 C2
01644 420465   www.clogandshoe.co.uk
13 miles (21km) north of Castle Douglas in Balmaclellan. Rural workshop where visitors can watch ongoing work which includes the making of modern and traditional clogs, boots, sandals, baby footwear, bags and purses.

Clootie Well 119 D4
Munlochy, south of Fortrose, Black Isle. Wishing well dedicated to St Boniface (or Curidan). Although no trace of it can now be found there is said to have been a chapel on this site. The trees and fence around the well are draped with thousands of rags. To have your wish granted you must spill a small amount of water three times on the ground, tie a rag on a nearby tree, make the sign of the cross and then drink from the well. Tradition states that anyone removing a rag will succumb to the misfortunes of the original owner.

Cluny Clays 79 D1
01592 720374   www.clunyclays.co.uk
Cluny Mains, Cluny, 2 miles (3km) north of Kirkcaldy on the B922. Outdoor entertainment centre. Golf driving range and 9 hole golf course. Scotland's national clay pigeon shooting and archery centre. Children's playpark and electric trikes, off-road driving, falconry and highland games. Set in beautifully landscaped surroundings in open rolling countryside.

Cluny House Gardens 99 F4
01887 820795
3.5 miles (5.5km) north east of Aberfeldy on the minor road between Weem and Strathtay. Cluny is a Himalayan style woodland garden. Situated on a slope in the Strathtay valley where the climate and soil provide perfect conditions for growing a profusion of primulas, meconopsis, rhododendrons, lilies, trilliums and spring bulbs.

Clyde Marine Cruises 75 F3
01475 721281   www.clyde-marine.co.uk
Victoria Harbour, Greenock, 25 miles (40km) west of Glasgow. Cruises, with accommodation for up to 120 persons, to all the scenic lochs and resorts of the Upper Firth of Clyde. Pickups from Greenock, Helensburgh, Kilcreggan, Dunoon, Rothesay, Largs and Millport.

Clyde Muirshiel Regional Park (Barnbrock) 76 B4
01505 614791   www.clydemuirshiel.co.uk
Kilbarchan, 4 miles (6.5km) north of Lochwinnoch just off the B786. The site incorporates the headquarters of the Clyde Muirshiel Regional Park. Campsite, picnic area and easy access to nearby Locherwood Community Woodland.

Clyde Valley Country Estate 77 F6
01555 860691
Crossford, Carluke. Garden centre, narrow gauge railway, bird of prey centre, putting green, woodland walks.

Clydebank Museum 76 C3
0141 562 2400
          www.west-dunbarton.gov.uk/culture/
Town Hall, Dumbarton Road, Clydebank. 2 miles (3km) north west of Glasgow on the A814. Community museum describing local social and industrial history. Displays on ship building, engineering and sewing machines including the Singer Sewing Machine Collection. Technical archive on Singer machines. Display on the Clydebank blitz.

Clydebuilt 76 C4
0141 886 1013
          www.scottishmaritimemuseum.org
Scottish Maritime Museum. Clydebuilt tells the history of Glasgow's river, its ships and its people, over the last 300 years. Hands on and interactive computer activities. Also Kyles, the oldest Clyde built ship afloat in the UK.

Clynelish Distillery 129 F4
01408 623000
Brora, 58 miles (93km) north of Inverness on the A9. The original Clynelish Distillery was built in 1819 by the Marquis of Stafford, later to become Duke of Sutherland. The superb quality of Clynelish whisky was so much in demand that only private customers at home and abroad could be supplied. Trade orders were refused. The distillery was extended in 1896 by the Leith Whisky blenders, Ainslie and Co. In 1967 the new Clynelish Distillery was built alongside the original building with three times the production capacity. Clynelish is available as a 14-year old single malt and is the heart of Johnnie Walker's Gold Label blend.

Cnoc Freiceadain Long Cairns   136 B3
01667 460232   www.historic-scotland.gov.uk
6 miles (9.5km) west south-west of Thurso. There were originally several round cairns here which, at a later date, were combined to form these two unexcavated Neolithic long-horned burial cairns, set at right-angles to each other. Forecourt horns are still visible under the grass.

Coats Observatory   68 A3
0141 889 2013
49 Oakshaw Street West, Paisley. Designed by John Honeyman, Coats Observatory continues a tradition of astronomical, meteorological and seismic observing which started in 1883. Displays relate to the history and architecture of the building, astronomy and astronautics, meteorology and seismicity.

Cobb Memorial   108 C2
Between Invermoriston and Drumnadrochit by the A82. A cairn commemorates John Cobb, the racing driver, who lost his life near here in 1952 when attempting to beat the water speed record, with his jet speedboat, on Loch Ness.

Commando Memorial

Cobbler, The   85 F5
Part of the Arrochar Alps, overlooking Arrochar and Loch Long. So-called because of its curious rock formation summit, The Cobbler - or Ben Arthur - is one of Scotland's most distinctive peaks.

Coldstream Museum   81 D6
01890 882630
Coldstream. 15 miles (24km) west of Berwick-upon-Tweed. Local history displays and section on the Coldstream Guards. Temporary exhibition gallery.

Colfin Smokehouse   58 B4
01776 820622   www.colfinsmokehouse.co.uk
Colfin Creamery, 2 miles (3km) from Portpatrick on the A77 at Colfin. Visitors can observe the salmon smoking process in detail and purchase the product.

Collins Gallery   17 C2
0141 548 2558   www.collinsgallery.strath.ac.uk
University of Strathclyde, 22 Richmond Street, Glasgow. Temporary exhibition gallery showing annual programme including contemporary, fine and applied art, photography, technology and design, and multi-media installations.

Colonsay House Gardens   72 C1
01951 200211   www.gardens-of-argyll.co.uk
Kiloran, Isle of Colonsay. 2 miles (3km) from pier. Famous rhododendron garden of 30 acres (12ha), adjacent to Colonsay House, home of Lord Strathcona. In the woodland garden, native trees and rare rhododendrons, bluebells and mecanopsis

flourish together. Due to the mildness of the climate and the shelter of the woods, many tender and rare shrubs from all parts of the world grow happily including mimosa, eucalyptus and palm trees.

Columba's Footsteps   64 A5
West of Southend at Keil, Mull of Kintyre. Traditionally it is believed that St Columba first set foot on Scottish soil near Southend. The footsteps are imprinted in a flat topped rock near the ruin of an old chapel.

Colzium Estate   77 E3
01236 823281
Colzium Lennox Estate, Stirling Road, Kilsyth. Outstanding collection of conifers and rare trees in a beautifully designed small walled garden. All trees well labelled. Fabulous display of snowdrops and crocuses in spring. 17th century ice house, glen walk, 15th century tower house, arboretum, curling pond, clock theatre and pitch and putt course.

Commando Memorial   107 F6
Off the A82, 11 miles (17.5km) north east of Fort William. An impressive sculpture by Scott Sutherland, erected in 1952 to commemorate the commandos of World War II who trained in this area. The three gigantic bronze figures stand proud in battledress, woollen caps and climbing boots looking out across the Great Glen. Fine views of Ben Nevis and Lochaber.

Confectionery Factory Visitor Centre   96 C3
01855 821277
Old Ferry Road, North Ballachulish, on the A82, 13 miles (20km) south of Fort William. Displays of products and an explanation of the history of Islay tablet, its origins on Islay and reason for the use of goats' milk. Also speciality Scottish food shop. Scenic views of Ballachulish bridge.

Corgarff Castle   111 D4
01975 651460   www.historic-scotland.gov.uk
Corgarff, Strathdon. A 16th century tower house converted into a barracks for government troops in 1748 by being enclosed within a star-shaped loopholed wall.

Cornalees Centre (Clyde Muirshiel Regional Park)   75 F3
01475 521458   www.clydemuirshiel.co.uk
Loch Thom, Inverkip. Stepped boardwalk trails and woodland walks through Shellhill Glen, access to the Greenock Cut and Kelly Cut for scenic walks and views of the Clyde estuary. Natural and local history exhibitions. Indoor games with environmental themes. Navigation and orienteering courses. Children's activities in the summer, guided walks, ranger service.

Cornice Museum of Ornamental Plasterwork   69 E2
01721 720212
Innerleithen Road, Peebles. The museum is a plasterer's casting workshop virtually unchanged since the turn of the century and illustrates the main methods of creating ornamental plasterwork in Scotland at that time. It also displays probably the largest surviving collection of 'masters' in Scotland.

Corrieshalloch Gorge National Nature Reserve   117 F2
01445 781200   www.nts.org.uk
Braemore, 12 miles (19.5km) south east of Ullapool,

on the A835. Here is one of the finest examples of a box canyon in Britain, forming a spectacular 200ft (61m) deep, mile-long gorge. A viewing platform stretched across the gorge looks up towards the Falls of Measach.

Corrimony Chambered Cairn 118 A6
01667 460232 www.historic-scotland.gov.uk
In Glen Urquhart, 8.5 miles (13.5km) west of Drumnadrochit. A chambered burial cairn surrounded by a kerb of stone slabs, outside of which is a circle of standing stones.

Corrimony RSPB Nature Reserve 108 A2
01463 715000 www.rspb.org.uk
Off the A831 between Drumnadrochit and Cannich, with parking near Corrimony Cairn. A mixed woodland reserve designed to encourage black grouse. Access by foot only. There is a 5 mile (8km) round trip waymarked trail leading to Loch Comhnard which is a haven for a wide range of birdlife including sandpipers, lapwings and whooper swans.

Corryvreckan Whirlpool 83 E5
Between the islands of Jura and Scarba. This treacherous tide race, dangerous for small craft, covers an extensive area and may be seen from the north end of Jura or from Craignish Point. The noise can sometimes be heard from a considerable distance.

Coulter Motte 68 C2
0131 668 8600 www.historic-scotland.gov.uk
1.5 miles (2.5km) south west of Biggar. Early medieval castle mound, originally moated and probably surrounded by a palisade enclosing a timber tower.

Courthouse Museum 119 E3
01381 600418 www.cromarty-courthouse.org.uk
Church Street, Cromarty, 25 miles (40km) north of Inverness on the A832. The courthouse, which dates from 1773, has been converted into an award-winning museum interpreting the history of the well-preserved town of Cromarty. Displays include a reconstructed trial in the 18th century courtroom, prison cells, animated figures and costumes. A personal tape tour of the town is included in the admission price.

Cowane's Hospital 77 F1
01786 472247
Near Holyrood Church, Stirling. A former almshouse founded by John Cowane between 1637 and 1649, for the guildry members who fell on hard times.

Cowans Law Country Sports 76 B6
01560 700666 www.cowanslaw.com
Hemphill Road, Moscow, Galston. From the A77 take the A719 to Moscow. A4 acre (1.7ha) trout loch set in the heart of Ayrshire's farming country. Also clay shooting, archery and air rifle range. Families and beginners welcome.

Craig Highland Farm 116 B6
01599 544205
Situated between Plockton and Achmore on shore road. Rare breeds farm and animal sanctuary situated in bay on shore of Loch Carron. Visitors can feed the llamas, ponies, donkeys, goats and poultry and observe the owls, pigs and rabbits. Low tide gives access to Eilean na Creige Duibhe, a wooded craggy island which is home to a number of herons. The reserve is managed by the Scottish Wildlife Trust.

Craigellachie Bridge 122 B5
North of Craigellachie. One of Thomas Telford's most beautiful bridges. It has a 152ft (46m) main span of iron and two ornamental stone towers at each end.

Craigie Estate 66 B3
01292 612000
Craigie Estate, Ayr. Beside the River Ayr with pleasant woodland walks. The Horticultural Centre features tropical and temperate houses.

Craigievar Castle 112 A4
013398 83635 www.nts.org.uk
5 miles (8km) south of Alford. A 'fairytale' castle, which seems to grow out of the hillside. Fine collection of family portraits and 17th and 18th century furniture.

Craigluscar Activities 78 B1
01383 738429 www.craigluscar.co.uk
Craigluscar. 3 miles (5km) north of Dunfermline. All terrain quad biking on Craigluscar Hill, miniature hovercrafts and clay pigeon shooting. Outdoor activities for individuals, families and groups. Corporate bookings.

Craigmillar Castle 79 D3
0131 661 4445 www.historic-scotland.gov.uk
Craigmillar Castle Road, off the A68 (Dalkeith road), 2.5 miles (4km) south east of Edinburgh city centre. Imposing ruins of massive 14th century keep enclosed in the early 15th century by an embattled curtain wall. Within are the remains of the stately ranges of apartments dating from the 16th and 17th centuries. The castle was burned by Hertford in 1544.

Craignethan Castle 77 F6
01555 860364 www.historic-scotland.gov.uk
Blackwood, Lesmahagow. An extensive and well-preserved ruin of an unusual and ornate 16th century tower house. It is defended by an outer wall pierced by gun ports, also by a wide and deep ditch with a most unusual caponier (a stone vaulted chamber for artillery). Attacked and dismantled by the Protestant party in 1579. In a very picturesque setting overlooking the River Nethan.

Craigston Castle 124 B4
01888 551228
5 miles (8km) from Turriff. Completed in 1607 and still owned by the original family. The main exterior feature is a sculpted balcony unique in Scottish architecture. Interior decoration dates mainly from the early 19th century.

Craigtoun Country Park 91 D4
01334 473666
2.5 miles (4km) south west of St Andrews on the B939. Craigtoun Country Park was formerly the grounds of Mount Melville House. The park consists of 50 acres (20ha) including formal gardens, two ponds, landscaped areas, Dutch village and cypress walk.

Craigvinean 88 C1
01350 727284 www.forestry.gov.uk
1 mile west of Dunkeld, on the A9. Craigvinean (Gaelic for crag of the goats) is one of Scotland's oldest managed forests. A waymarked walk provides superb views over the Hermitage and Dunkeld to Craig a Barns.

Crail Guided Walks 91 F5
01333 450869
Crail Museum & Heritage Centre, Marketgate, Crail. Walking tours of the oldest parts of Crail, taking in buildings of architectural and historic interest.

Crail Museum & Heritage Centre 91 F4
01333 450869 www.crailmuseum.org.uk
62-64 Marketgate, Crail. The museum provides an insight into the past life of this ancient Royal Burgh. Visitors can learn about the seafaring tradition, 200-year-old golf club and HMS Jackdaw, a World War II Fleet Air Arm Station.

Crail Pottery   91 F5
01333 451212   www.crailpottery.com
75 Nethergate, Crail. Three generations of potters produce a huge variety of hand-thrown pottery from porcelain to gardenware, sculpture, teapots and jardinières.

Crail Tolbooth   91 F5
Marketgate, Crail. The Tolbooth dates from the early 16th century. In the striking Dutch Tower is a bell dated 1520, cast in Holland.

Crarae Gardens

Crarae Gardens   74 C1
01546 886614   www.nts.org.uk
Crarae, 10 miles (16km) south of Inveraray on the A83. A superb natural gorge with a series of waterfalls and extensive walks through a unique collection of rhododendrons, azaleas, conifers and eucalyptus.

Crathes Castle   112 C5
01330 844525   www.nts.org.uk
3 miles (5km) east of Banchory. 16th century castle with remarkable original painted ceilings and a collection of Scottish furniture. Famous walled garden contains eight separate gardens designed for colour combinations.

Cream o' Galloway   60 C4
01557 814040   www.creamogalloway.co.uk
Rainton, 4 miles (6.5km) south of Gatehouse of Fleet off the A75. Cream o' Galloway is a small farm-based ice cream manufacturer specialising in traditional quality ice cream and frozen yoghurt with unusual flavours. There is a farm shop and a viewing gallery where visitors can watch the manufacturing process. Also illustrated nature walks, extensive adventure playground, treasure hunt and nature quizzes.

Creetown Gem Rock Museum   60 A4
01671 820357   www.gemrock.net
Chain Road, Creetown, 7 miles (11km) east of Newton Stewart on the A75. The museum houses one of the finest collections of privately owned gemstones, crystals, minerals and fossils in Great Britain. Visitors can witness the spectacular volcanic eruption display, the Crystal Cave and a 15-minute audio-visual programme.

Creetown Heritage Museum   60 A4
01671 820471
     www.creetown-heritage-museum.com
Creetown, Newton Stewart. Creetown is portrayed from its origin as an 18th century fishing hamlet, through the growth and decline of its famous granite quarries, to the present day. Displays include a large collection of old photographs, wartime memorabilia, village shop, information on local nature reserve, work of local artists, woodcarver and sculptor.

Crichton Castle   79 E4
01875 320017   www.historic-scotland.gov.uk
Crichton, off the A68. A large castle built around a 14th-century keep. The most spectacular part is the arcaded range erected by the Earl of Bothwell between 1581 and 1591. This has a façade of faceted stonework in an Italian style.

Crichton Grounds   61 F2
South of Dumfries on the B725. Extensive public parkland covering 85 acres (34ha) with mature shrubs and trees and a large rock garden.

Crieff Visitor Centre   88 B3
01764 654014   www.crieff.co.uk
On the A85 Crieff to Comrie road. Traditional whisky flagons, tableware and glass paperweights. Visitors can view the production process and see craftsmen at work.

Crinan Canal   74 A1
01546 603210   www.waterscape.com/crinan_canal
Crinan to Ardrishaig, by Lochgilphead. Constructed between 1793 and 1801 to carry ships from Loch Fyne to the Atlantic without rounding Kintyre. The 9 mile (14.5km) stretch of water with 15 locks is now almost entirely used by pleasure craft. There are magnificent views to the Western Isles from Crinan. The Crinan basin, coffee shop, boatyard and hotel make a visit well worthwhile.

Crinan Wood   74 A1
     www.woodland-trust.org.uk
Crinan, 6 miles (9.5km) north west of Lochgilphead on the B841. Crinan Wood is categorised as a temperate rainforest, benefitting from sea mists and plentiful rain. Over 13 types of fern grow here, together with many varieties of mosses and lichens. Waymarked trails and good views of Jura and Corryvreckan to the west, Ben More to the north.

Croick Church   128 B5
     www.croickchurch.com
At Croick 9 miles (14.5km) west of Ardgay. Made famous in 1845, during the Highland clearances, when many of the tenants of nearby Glencalvie were evicted to make way for sheep. They took refuge in the churchyard and even now names scratched on the east window bear witness to their distress.

Crombie Country Park   91 E1
01241 860360
Monikie, Broughty Ferry. A Victorian reservoir with the appearance of a natural loch. Set in 250 acres (101ha). Wildlife hide, trails, displays and interpretation centre, ranger service, guided walks and child play park. Barbecue area.

Crookston Castle   76 C4
0141 883 9606   www.historic-scotland.gov.uk
Off Brockburn Road, Pollok. The altered ruin of an unusual 15th century castle. It consists of a central tower with four square corner towers, set within 12th century earthworks. Affords excellent views of south west Glasgow.

Cross Kirk   79 D6
0131 668 8800   www.historic-scotland.gov.uk
In Cross Road, Peebles. The remains of a Trinitarian friary founded in the late 13th century. Consists of nave, west tower and foundations of domestic buildings.

Cross of Lorraine   75 F3
Lyle Hill, Greenock (access via Newton Street). Monument to the contribution made by the Free French Navy during World War II. The Cross of Lorraine is situated at a popular viewpoint overlooking the Clyde.

Crossraguel Abbey   66 A5
01655 883113   www.historic-scotland.gov.uk
On the A77, 2 miles (3km) south west of Maybole. A Cluniac monastery built in 1244 by the Earl of Carrick. Inhabited by Benedictine monks until the end of the 16th century. Extensive and remarkably complete remains of high quality, including the church, cloister, chapter house and much of the domestic premises.

Croy Hill   77 E3
0131 668 8600   www.historic-scotland.gov.uk
Between Croy and Dullatur. The site of a Roman fort (not visible) on the Antonine Wall. Part of the wall ditch can be seen, beside two beacon platforms on the west side of the hill.

Cruachan Power Station   85 D3
01866 822618   www.visitcruachan.co.uk
Dalmally, 18 miles (29km) east of Oban on the A85. A guided tour takes visitors 0.5 mile (1km) inside Ben Cruachan to see a reversible pumped storage scheme. An exhibition houses touch screen and computer video technology.

Cruck Cottage   62 A2
Torthorwald, off the A709. An example of an early 19th century thatched cottage, restored using traditional skills and local materials.

Cruickshank Botanic Garden   113 E4
01224 272704
Aberdeen University, Aberdeen. Originally founded in 1898 as a teaching and research garden. The 11 acres (4.5ha) are laid out in an ornamental style. Rock garden and ponds, herbaceous border, rose garden, terrace and arboretum.

Cruise Loch Lomond   86 A5
01301 702356   www.cruiselochlomondltd.com
The Boatyard, Tarbet. Scheduled daily cruises around the fjord-like northern area of Loch Lomond. Private hire for corporate bookings and tailored itineraries available.

Cubbie Row's Castle   147 D1
01856 841815   www.historic-scotland.gov.uk
On the island of Wyre, Orkney. Probably the earliest stone castle authenticated in Scotland. Built circa 1145 by Norseman Kolbein Hruga, it consists of a small rectangular tower enclosed in a circular ditch. Nearby are the ruins of St Mary's Chapel, late 12th century in the Romanesque style.

Culbin Forest   121 D3
01343 820223
www.forestry.gov.uk
Signposted from the A96 between Nairn and Findhorn Bay. Planted from the 1920s to stabilise the drifting sands. Botanical trail. Five waymarked low level walks.

Culbin Sands RSPB Nature Reserve   121 D3
01463 715000   www.rspb.org.uk
Nine miles of coastline between Nairn and Findhorn Bay. The reserve has sandy beaches, saltmarsh, mudflats and shingle ridges. Thousands of ducks and waders winter here and in the summer you can see butterflies, dragonflies and wild flowers.

Culcreuch Castle & Country Park   77 D2
01360 860555   www.culcreuch.com
Fintry, Stirling. A 14th century castle, ancestral home of the Clan Galbraith, set in a 1600 acre estate. Woodland, river and moorland walks. Pinetum. Walled garden and children's play area.

Cullerlie Stone Circle   112 C4
01667 460232   www.historic-scotland.gov.uk
Near Echt, off the A944. A stone circle enclosing an area on which eight small cairns were later constructed. About 4000 years old.

Culloden Visitor Centre   119 E5
01463 790607   www.nts.org.uk
Culloden Moor on the B9006 5 miles (8km) east of Inverness. Site of the battle on 16 April 1746, when the forces of Bonnie Prince Charlie were defeated by the Hanoverian army, so ending the Forty-Five Jacobite uprising. Turf and stone dykes which played a crucial part in the battle have been reconstructed on their original site. Visitor centre with Jacobite exhibition, displays, audio-visual programme and bookshop.

Culross Abbey   78 A2
www.historic-scotland.gov.uk
Culross, off the A985, 12 miles (19km) west of Forth Road Bridge. The remains of a Cistercian monastery founded in 1217. The eastern parts of the Abbey Church form the present parish church.

Culross Palace   78 A2
01383 880359   www.nts.org.uk
Culross, off the A985, 12 miles (19km) west of Forth Road Bridge. Built 1597 - 1611 for local entrepreneur Sir George Bruce.

Culsh Earth House   112 A4
01667 460232   www.historic-scotland.gov.uk
On the B919 at Culsh. A well-preserved underground passage with roofing slabs intact over the large chamber and entrance. About 2000 years old.

Culzean Castle & Country Park   66 A5
0870 1181945   www.nts.org.uk
Maybole, on the A719, 12 miles (19km) south of Ayr. High on a cliff above the Firth of Clyde, Robert Adam's Culzean Castle is one of the most romantic in Scotland. Designed at the end of the 18th century, the elegant interior includes the spectacular Oval Staircase and the Circular Saloon. Fascinating associated buildings in the 563 acre (227ha) country park include the Fountain Court and the

Culzean Castle & Country Park

Camellia House. Swan pond, deer park, woodland and beach walks.

Cumbernauld Museum 77 E3
01236 725664
Cumbernauld Library. Tells the history of Cumbernauld from the setting of a Roman camp, to the parlour of a 1930s miner. Audio-visual techniques bring the past to life.

Cunninghame Graham Memorial 76 C1
www.nts.org.uk
Gartmore, 2 miles (3km) south west of Aberfoyle. A cairn commemorates the life of R. B. Cunninghame Graham (1852 - 1936). An interpretive panel shows he was a radical politician, writer, traveller and renowned horseman.

Cuween Hill Cairn 146 C2
01856 841815   www.historic-scotland.gov.uk
On the A965, 0.5 mile (1km) south of Finstown, Orkney. A low mound covering a Neolithic chambered tomb with four cells. When discovered, it contained the bones of men, dogs and oxen.

Dalbeattie Museum 61 E3
01556 610437
Southwick Road, Dalbeattie. Museum highlighting the history and heritage of the area with an emphasis on the planned village of Dalbeattie.

Daldon Border Collies 115 D4
01470 532331
Bernisdale on the A850 north of Portree. Sheepdog trial demonstrations and the opportunity to see traditional crofting skills.

Dalgarven Mill & Country Life Museum 75 F6
01294 552448   www.dalgarvenmill.org.uk
On the A737 between Dalry and Kilwinning. A 17th century restored water mill, set in a secluded hollow, housing an exhibition of traditional flour production. In the adjoining granary there is a museum of Ayrshire country life, with collections of farming and domestic memorabilia and local costume, including some good examples of Ayrshire whitework. Room reconstructions of 1880's lifestyle.

Dalkeith Country Park 79 E4
0131 654 1666   www.dalkeithcountrypark.com
In Dalkeith High Street. The 18th century planned landscape includes farm animals, working Clydesdale horses, adventure woodland play area, nature trails, woodland walks, orangery and ice house. Ranger service.

Dallas Dhu Historic Distillery 121 E4
01309 676548   www.historic-scotland.gov.uk
2 miles (3km) south of Forres. A picturesque small distillery built in 1898.

Dalmeny House 78 C3
0131 331 1888   www.dalmeny.co.uk
South Queensferry. The home of the Earls of Rosebery for over 300 years, but the present Tudor Gothic building, by William Wilkins, dates from 1815. Interior Gothic splendour of hammer-beamed hall, vaulted corridors and classical main rooms. Works of art include a magnificent collection of 18th century British portraits, 18th century furniture, tapestries, porcelain from the Rothschild Mentmore collection and the Napoleon collection. Lovely grounds and a 4.5 mile (7km) shore walk.

Dalmeny Parish Church 78 C3
0131 331 1479
Main Street, Dalmeny, 10 miles (16km) west of Edinburgh. The best preserved Romanesque (Norman) church in Scotland, dating from the 12th

century. Coach tours should book in advance.

Dalton Pottery Art Café 62 B2
01387 840236   www.daltonpottery.co.uk
Meikle Dyke, Dalton. Signposted on the B725, 1 mile (2km) towards Dalton from Carrutherstown (off the A75 between Dumfries and Annan). A working pottery where visitors can see a range of porcelain giftware being made and hand decorated. Choose from 40 styles of pot, pre-fired and glazed, and paint your own enamel design to take away. Showroom.

Dalwhinnie Distillery Visitor Centre 109 D6
01540 672219   www.newtonmore.com/dalwhinnie
Dalwhinnie, off the A9, 50 miles (80km) north of Perth. The highest distillery in Scotland at 1073ft (326m) above sea level, opened in 1898. Tour guides explain the secrets of distilling. The exhibition features the history and geography of the area, and the classic malts.

Dalzell Park 77 E5
01698 266155
Adele Street, Motherwell. Peaceful woodland with spectacular scenery and heritage monuments such as Dalzell House and Lord Gavin's Temple. Wildlife includes woodpeckers, roe deer and squirrels. Ranger service.

David Coulthard Museum 60 C4
01557 860050   www.davidcoulthardmuseum.co.uk
Twynholm, Kirkcudbright. The museum traces David Coulthard's motor racing career to date. Visitors can see six racing cars, David Coulthard's trophies, race suits and helmets. Also lots of photographs.

David Douglas Memorial 89 E3
Located in the grounds of the old church at Scone. David Douglas was one of the greatest plant hunters and explorers of America's north west. He introduced over 200 new plants to Britain.

David Livingstone Centre 77 D4
01698 823140   www.nts.org.uk
165 Station Road, Blantyre. In the tenement where Livingstone was born. Displays chart his life, from his childhood in the mills to his exploration of Africa.

David Welch Winter Gardens 113 E4
01224 585310   www.aberdeencity.gov.uk
Polmuir Road, Aberdeen. 2 acres (1ha) of covered gardens displaying plants from around the world. Features Bromeliad house, cacti and succulent hall, Victorian corridor and outside gardens, floral hall, corridor of perfumes and fern house.

Dawyck Botanic Garden 69 D2
01721 760254   www.rbge.org.uk
Stobo on the B712, 8 miles (13km) south west of Peebles. A specialist garden of the Royal Botanic Garden Edinburgh. A historic arboretum with landscaped walks. The mature trees include the unique Dawyck Beech. There are also many varieties of flowering trees, shrubs and herbaceous plants. Visitors can explore Heron Wood and the world's first Cryptogamic Sanctuary and Reserve to see non-flowering plants. Other notable features include the Swiss Bridge, stonework and terracing created by Italian craftsmen in the 1820s.

Dean Castle & Country Park 66 C2
01563 522702   www.deancastle.com
On the A77 Dean Road, Kilmarnock. A magnificent collection of buildings dating from the 1350s. For 400 years Dean Castle was the stronghold of the Boyds of Kilmarnock, and today important collections of arms and armour, musical instruments and tapestries are on display in public rooms. The country park comprises 200 acres (81ha) of mixed

woodland. Ranger service and programme of events.

Dean Gallery, The 79 D3
0131 624 6200 www.natgalscot.ac.uk
Belford Road, Edinburgh. Houses the Gallery of Modern Art's extensive collections of Dada and Surrealism. In 1994, Edinburgh-born sculptor Sir Eduardo Paolozzi offered a large body of his work to the National Galleries of Scotland. This collection of prints, drawings, plaster maquettes, moulds and the contents of his studio is now housed in the Dean Gallery. The gallery also accommodates a library and archive of artists' books, catalogues and manuscripts relating in particular to the Dada and Surrealist movement, but also to 20th century art as a whole.

Dee Valley Confectioners 111 E5
01339 755499 www.dee-valley.co.uk
Station Square, Ballater. Watch the process of colours and flavours being added to the candy, followed by the stretch and pull methods for stripes and lettering.

Deep Sea World

Deep Sea World 78 C2
01383 411880 www.deepseaworld.co.uk
North Queensferry. Visitors can enjoy a diver's eye view of our marine environment on an underwater safari; come face to face with sand tiger sharks and watch divers hand feed a spectacular array of sea life; touch the live exhibits in the large rockpools; and visit the stunning Amazonian Experience which features ferocious piranhas and electrifying eels.

Delgatie Castle 124 B4
01888 563479 www.delgatiecastle.com
3 miles (5km) north east of Turriff. An 11th century tower house. The castle contains late 16th century painted ceilings and has the widest turnpike stair in Scotland.

Den of Alyth 90 B1
Alyth. The Den of Alyth is a broadleaved woodland through which the Alyth Burn flows. Walks of varying length through shady woods in a steep sided valley.

Den Wood 113 D2
www.woodland-trust.org.uk
4 miles (6km) north of Inverurie. There are a range of woodland habitats and four circular trails offering panoramic views.

Denny Ship Model Experiment Tank 76 B3
01389 763444
www.scottishmaritimemuseum.org/dumbart.htm
Castle Street, Dumbarton. A ship model experiment tank constructed in 1882 and retaining many of its

original features. Fully restored to working order so that the original process can be demonstrated.

Dere Street Roman Road 79 F5
www.historic-scotland.gov.uk
On the B6438 (off the A68) beside Soutra Aisle. A good stretch of the Roman road which ran from Corbridge beside Hadrian's Wall to Cramond on the Firth of Forth. Beside the road are scoops, pits from which the gravel for building the road was taken.

Designs Gallery & Café 61 D3
01556 504552 www.designsgallery.co.uk
179 King Street, Castle Douglas, on the A75, 18 miles (29km) west of Dumfries. A focal point for arts and crafts in south west Scotland. Changing exhibitions of high quality crafts. Adjacent shop sells cards, prints, ceramics, knitwear, studio glass and jewellery.

Deskford Church 123 E3
01667 460232 www.historic-scotland.gov.uk
Off the B9018, 4 miles south of Cullen, Banffshire. Ruin of a small, late medieval church with a richly carved sacrament house characteristic of north east Scotland.

Devil's Beef Tub 68 C4
A701, 6 miles (9.5km) north of Moffat. A huge, spectacular hollow among the hills, at the head of Annandale. In the swirling mists of this out-of-the-way retreat, Borders reivers hid cattle lifted in their raids. Can be seen from the road.

Devil's Porridge 62 C3
01461 40460
www.devilsporridge.co.uk
St John's Church, Eastriggs, off the A75 between Gretna and Annan. An exhibition on the fascinating story of the 30,000 women and men who worked in HM Factory Gretna in World War I. Women munition workers mixed the Devil's Porridge, the name coined by Sir Arthur Conan Doyle for the highly explosive mixture of gun cotton and nitro-glycerine which was made into cordite for British shells and bullets. Photographs, video, murals, artefacts and supporting exhibitions including Children at War, the story of the World War II evacuation.

Dewars World of Whisky 88 B1
01887 822010 www.dewarswow.com
Aberfeldy Distillery, Aberfeldy. Celebrating the lives of the entrepreneurial Dewar family and the art of blending whisky, visitors will enjoy this interactive, contemporary attraction with a traditional working distillery tour.

Dick Institute 66 C2
01563 554343
Kilmarnock. Temporary and permanent exhibitions over two floors of this grand Victorian building. Fine art, social and natural history collections are upstairs, whilst galleries downstairs house the temporary exhibitions of visual art and craft.

Dim Riv Norse Longship Boat Trips 151 D2
01595 693097
Lerwick, Shetland. Harbour tours on a working replica of a Norse longship.

Dingwall Museum 118 C3
01349 865366
Town House, High Street, Dingwall. 11 miles (18km) north of Inverness via the A9 and A835. The award-

winning museum contains a reconstructed smiddy and kitchen; military room and artefacts relating to the history of the ancient burgh. Special attractions including giant jigsaws for children. Changing exhibitions and activities such as spinning and blanket stamping.

Dirleton Castle & Gardens 80 A2
01620 850330 www.historic-scotland.gov.uk
Off the A198 in Dirleton. A romantic castle dating from the 13th century with 15th to 17th century additions. First besieged in 1298 by Edward I. Destroyed in 1650. The adjoining gardens include an early 20th century Arts and Crafts garden and a restored Victorian garden. Also a 17th century bowling green.

Discover Loch Ness 42 B2
0800 7315564 www.discoverlochness.com
Departures from Inverness city centre. Innovative and informative guided tours by coach around Inverness, Loch Ness and into the Highlands. The tours integrate geology, wildlife, local heritage, history and culture. Full or half day excursions available, some including boat trips on Loch Ness.

Discovery Point 30 B3
01382 201245 www.rrsdiscovery.com
Discovery Quay, Dundee. Centred around Royal Research Ship Discovery, Captain Scott's famous polar exploration ship. Spectacular exhibits and special effects recreate her historic voyages. Visitors can step on board Discovery herself and experience life below decks.

Divach Falls 108 B2
A82 from Inverness through Drumnadrochit, turning right at Lewiston onto Balmacaan road (Falls signposted). Car park at top. A 100ft (30.5m) fall above the village of Drumnadrochit. The falls are overlooked by Divach Lodge where J. M. Barrie once stayed.

Dogton Stone 79 D1
www.historic-scotland.gov.uk
Off the B922, at Dogton farmhouse, near Cardenden. 5 miles (8km) north of Kirkcaldy. An ancient Celtic cross with traces of animal and figure
sculpture.

Dollar Glen 78 A1
www.nts.org.uk
Dollar. At the foot of the Ochil Hills, Dollar Glen is unmistakable with its imposing castle, Castle

Campbell, at its head. A path crosses Dollar Burn and follows the west side of the glen to emerge at the rear of the castle.

Dollar Museum 78 A1
01259 742895
Dollar. A small award-winning museum with frequently changing, temporary exhibitions. Also permanent exhibitions on the history of Dollar, Castle Campbell, Dollar Academy, the Devon Valley Railway and the prehistory of Dollar. Reading room with local history material, including many photographs.

Dolphin & Seal Centre 119 D5
01463 731866
Tourist Information Centre off the A9, just north of the Kessock Bridge. The Moray Firth contains a resident population of over 140 Bottlenose Dolphins and there are also large populations of Common and Grey Seals. This exhibition includes information about the dolphins, a video display, children's activities and a reference corner and interpretive staff. Visitors may watch the dolphins and hear them communicate and echo-locate their food through an underwater hydrophone system.

Doon Valley Museum 66 C5
01292 550633
Cathcartston, Dalmellington. Local history museum with a fine collection of photographs and maps illustrating the Doon Valley over the centuries. Also local history displays combined with changing art exhibitions and a weaving tableau.

Doonhill Homestead 80 B3
www.historic-scotland.gov.uk
Off the A1, 2 miles (3km) south of Dunbar. The site of a wooden hall of a 6th century British chief, and of an Anglian chief's hall which superseded it in the 7th century. A rare record of the Anglian occupation of south east Scotland.

Doonies Farm 113 E4
01224 875879 www.aberdeencity.gov.uk
Nigg, Aberdeen. A 182 acre (74ha) working farm populated with rare breeds.

Dornoch Cathedral 129 E5
01862 810357
Dornoch, on the A9, 40 miles (64km) north of Inverness. A small well-maintained cathedral founded in 1224 by Gilbert, Archdeacon of Moray and Bishop of Caithness. Partially destroyed by fire in 1570 and restored 1835-37, and again in 1924.

Drummond Castle Gardens

The fine 13th century stonework is still visible. There are 27 magnificent stained glass windows.

of Loch Tay.

Dornoch Lochans 119 E1
01862 810600 www.dornochlochans.co.uk
Davochfin Farm, 1 mile (2km) west of Dornoch on Cuthill Road. A trout fishery with four well-stocked ponds. Also pitch and putt, croquet and boule and golf driving range. All equipment can be provided.

Doune Castle 87 E5
01786 841742 www.historic-scotland.gov.uk
Off the A820 at Castle Road, Doune, 8 miles (13km) north west of Stirling. A magnificent late 14th century courtyard castle built for the Regent Albany. Its most striking feature is the combination of tower, gatehouse and hall with its kitchen in a massive frontal block. Later possessed by the Stuarts of Doune, Earls of Moray.

Dounreay Visitor Centre 135 F3
01847 802572
Dounreay, on the A836, 9 miles (14.5km) west of Thurso. The Dounreay Visitor Centre tells the story of the remarkable work carried out at this nuclear power station in the past, the present and looking into the future. Visitors can also hear how UKAEA Dounreay is developing world-class expertise in decommissioning, waste management and environmental reclamation of the site.

Druchtag Motte 59 E5
0131 668 8600 www.historic-scotland.gov.uk
At the north end of Mochrum village, 2 miles (3km) north of Port William. A well-preserved Norman motte castle.

Drum Castle & Gardens 112 C4
01330 811204 www.nts.org.uk
Drumoak, Banchory. The 13th century tower of Drum is one of the three oldest tower houses in Scotland. Jacobean and Victorian extensions make this a fine mansion house with notable portraits and furniture, much from the 18th century.

Drumcoltran Tower 61 E3
0131 668 8600 www.historic-scotland.gov.uk
Off the A711, 8 miles (13km) south west of Dumfries. The tower can be found among farm buildings. A well-preserved mid 16th century tower house. Simple and severe.

Drumlanrig Castle & Country Park 68 A6
01848 331555 www.buccleuch.com
3 miles (5km) north of Thornhill. A late 17th century castle built by William Douglas, 1st Duke of Queensbury. Contains fine French furniture, silver, porcelain, tapestries and a renowned art collection including works by Rembrandt and Holbein. The extensive grounds contain parkland, woodland walks, historical gardens and a cycle museum.

Drumlanrig's Tower 70 B4
01450 377615
1 Towerknowe, off the High Street in the centre of Hawick. This 15th century fortified tower house, stronghold of the Douglases, tells the story of Hawick and Scotland using period sets, costumed figures and audio-visuals. Themes include Border Reivers and Hawick's renowned knitwear industry.

Drummond Castle Gardens 88 B4
01764 681433 www.drummondcastlegardens.co.uk
Drummond Castle, Muthill, 2 miles (3km) south of Crieff. One of Scotland's largest formal gardens with magnificent early Victorian parterre, fountains, terracing and topiary.

Drummond Hill 87 E1
01350 727284 www.forestry.gov.uk
Kenmore, 4.5 miles west of Aberfeldy, off the A827. Drummond Hill has forest walks with stunning views

Drummond Trout Farm and Fishery 87 E3
01764 670500 www.drummondtroutfarm.co.uk
1 mile (2km) west of Comrie. Trout farm - feed the fish and see the salmon ladder. You can also fish for trout (two ponds for beginners, three for intermediate fishers and one for fly fishing).

Drumpellier Country Park 77 E4
01236 422257
Townhead Road, 2 miles (3km) from Coatbridge. Five hundred acres (202ha) of wood, heath and loch. There is a visitor centre, road train, angling, boating, nature trails, golf course and driving range, butterfly house, pets' corner and play areas.

Drumtochty Forest 103 E2
01330 844537 www.forestry.gov.uk
Between Auchenblae and the Cairn o'Mount on the B974. Two waymarked walks along an old mill lade leading through a beautiful small gorge.

Drumtroddan Cup & Ring Marked Rocks 59 E5
0131 668 8600 www.historic-scotland.gov.uk
Off the A714, 2 miles (3km) west of Port William. A group of Bronze Age cup and ring markings in bedrock. An alignment of three stones stands 400 yards (365m) south.

Dryburgh Abbey 70 B2
01835 822381 www.historic-scotland.gov.uk
Dryburgh, near Newtown St Boswells on the B6404, 5 miles (8km) south east of Melrose. The remarkably complete ruins of a Premonstratensian abbey. One of the four famous Border abbeys founded in the reign of David I by Hugh de Morville, Constable of Scotland. Mainly remains of transepts and cloisters. Sir Walter Scott and Field Marshall Earl Haig are buried here.

Dryhope Tower 69 E3
Off the A708 near St Mary's Loch, 15 miles (24km) west of Selkirk. A stout tower, now ruinous but originally four storeys high, rebuilt circa 1613. Birthplace of Mary Scott, the Flower of Yarrow, who married the freebooter Auld Wat of Harden in 1576 - ancestors Sir Walter Scott was proud to claim.

Duart Castle 83 F2
01680 812309 www.duartcastle.com
Off the A849 on the east of Mull. Built on a cliff overlooking the Sound of Mull this is one of the oldest inhabited castles in Scotland and the home of the 28th Chief of Clan Maclean. The keep was built in 1360 adjoining the original courtyard. After the 1745 Rising, it was used as a garrison for Government troops and then fell into ruin. It was restored by Sir Fitzroy Maclean in 1911. The keep contains dungeons with figures of prisoners from the Spanish Armada and exhibitions of clan history. Also an exhibition of The Swan, one of Cromwell's ships that sank directly below the castle in 1653.

Duff House 123 F3
01261 818181 www.duffhouse.org.uk
Between Banff and Macduff. One of the best examples of Georgian baroque architecture in Britain with a fine collection of paintings, furniture and artefacts.

Duffus Castle 122 A3
01667 460232 www.historic-scotland.gov.uk
5 miles (8km) north west of Elgin. Massive ruins of a fine motte and bailey castle with 14th century tower surrounded by a moat.

Dullatur 77 E3
www.historic-scotland.gov.uk
0.6 mile (1km) east of Dullatur. A well-preserved section of ditch. Part of the Antonine wall.

Dulsie Bridge 121 D5
Off the A939 from Ferness, take the B9007 south, turn right onto an unclassified road to Dulsie. An old stone bridge dating from 1764 spans the spectacular Findhorn Gorge at this well-known beauty spot.

Dumbarton Castle 76 B3
01389 732167 www.historic-scotland.gov.uk
Castle Road, off the A814 in Dumbarton on Dumbarton Rock. Spectacularly sited on a volcanic rock, the site of the ancient capital of Strathclyde. The most interesting features are the 18th century artillery fortifications, with the 19th century guns. Also mostly modern barrack, a dungeon, a 12th century gateway and a sundial gifted by Mary, Queen of Scots.

Dumfries & Galloway Aviation Museum 61 F2
01387 251623 www.dumfriesaviationmuseum.com
Heathhall, Dumfries. Opened in 1977 and regarded as one of the foremost volunteer run aviation museums in the UK. Various aircraft are on display and under restoration, including a Spitfire, Hawker Hunter and a Trident airliner. In the former control tower is a varied collection of memorabilia ranging from aero engines to uniforms and documentation.

Dumfries Museum & Camera Obscura 61 F2
01387 253374
The Observatory, 0.5 mile (1km) west of Dumfries centre. Situated in the 18th century windmill tower on top of Corbelly Hill with collections inaugurated over 150 years ago. Exhibitions trace the history of the people and landscape of Dumfries and Galloway. The camera obscura was installed in 1836 and gives a table-top panorama of Dumfries and the surrounding area. Note no wheelchair access to camera obscura.

Dun Beag Broch 114 C6
01667 460232 www.historic-scotland.gov.uk
1 mile (2km) west of Bracadale, Isle of Skye. A fine example of a Hebridean broch, apparently occupied until the 18th century. Visitors can see the remains of the stairway, a side cell and the gallery built into the 13ft (4m) thick walls.

Dun Canna 127 E5
Ardmair, north of Ullapool. The site of a Viking Fort. Also a flat pebble beach with good swimming.

Dun Carloway & Doune Broch Centre 144 B3
01851 643338 www.historic-scotland.gov.uk
On the A858, 1.5 miles (2.5km) south of Carloway and 16 miles (25.5km) west north-west of Stornoway, Isle of Lewis. This 2000 year old round defensive tower is one of the best preserved Iron Age brochs in Scotland. One wall rises over 70ft (21m). There is also an interpretation centre.

Dun Dornaigil Broch 133 F5
01667 460232 www.historic-scotland.gov.uk
10 miles (16km) south of Hope. A well-preserved broch standing to a height of 22ft (6.5m) above the entrance passage.

Dunadd Fort 74 B1
www.historic-scotland.gov.uk
Kilmartin Glen, 1 mile (2km) west of Kilmichael Glassary. A spectacular site occupied since the Iron Age. The well-preserved hill fort is part-Roman, when it was a stronghold of Dalraida, the kingdom of the Scots.

Dunagoil Vitrified Fort 75 D5
Isle of Bute. On a commanding site at the south of the island, this ancient fort is clear evidence of Iron Age habitation.

Dunaverty Rock 64 A5
At Southend, Mull of Kintyre, dominating beach and golf course. Formerly the site of Dunaverty Castle, a Macdonald stronghold. In 1647, about 300 people were put to death here by Covenanters under General Leslie. The rock is known locally as Blood Rock.

Dunbar Town House Museum 80 B3
01368 863734 www.dunbarmuseum.org
In Dunbar High Street, at the corner of Silver Street. A 16th century town house now containing a museum of local history and archaeology.

Dunbeath Heritage Centre 131 E2
01593 731233 www.dunbeath-heritage.org.uk
Old School, Dunbeath. Housed in the birthplace of author Neil M. Gunn. Historical detail has been extensively portrayed with a tableau of beautifully sculpted and dressed life size figures depicting Dunbeath inhabitants from the present back to its early settlers. The tableau is surrounded by displays, models and stained glass. Ancestral research, heritage trail, fishing and a bookshop.

Dunblane Museum 87 E5
01765 823440 www.dunblanemuseum.org.uk
The Cross, Dunblane, 6 miles (9.5km) north of Stirling. A museum located in barrel-vaulted rooms built in 1624. Contents include paintings, books, and artefacts which illustrate the life of the cathedral and its congregation from St Blane to the restoration in 1893. Large collection of communion tokens.

Duncansby Head 137 E2
The north east point of mainland Scotland, 18 miles (29km) north of Wick. The lighthouse on Duncansby Head commands a fine view of Orkney, the Pentland Skerries and the headlands of the east coast. A little to the south are the three Duncansby Stacks, huge stone needles in the sea. The sandstone cliffs are severed by great deep gashes (geos) running into the land. One of these is bridged by a natural arch.

Dunchraigaig Cairn 74 B1
www.historic-scotland.gov.uk
1.25 miles (2km) south of Kilmartin. A Bronze Age cairn excavated in the last century.

Duncryne Hill 76 B2
Between Balloch and Drymen, just off the A811 east of Gartocharn. Known locally as The Dumpling, due to its shape, this small hill can be climbed using a short steep path. The reward at the top is one of the best views of Loch Lomond.

Dundee Contemporary Arts 30 A3
01382 909252 www.dca.org.uk
152 Nethergate, Dundee. Centre for contemporary art and film with two galleries, cinema, print studio, craft shop, visual research centre and activity room.

Dundee Law 30 A1
The Law is the highest point in the city, and takes its name from the old Scots word for a hill. It is the remains of a volcanic plug and was later the site of an ancient hill fort. Atop the Law is a beacon which is lit four times a year.

Dundee University Botanic Garden 90 C3
01382 647190
www.dundeebotanicgarden.co.uk
Riverside Drive, Dundee. Botanic and teaching garden with a fine collection of trees and shrubs. Two large tropical and temperate plant houses.

Dundonald Castle 66 B2
01563 851489 www.dundonaldcastle.org.uk
Dundonald, on the A759, 5 miles (8km) west of Kilmarnock. A large prominent stone castle, built by

Robert Stewart in the 1370s, probably to mark his succession to the Scottish throne as Robert II in 1371. Two great feasting halls, one above the other, with great vaults beneath. The third medieval castle to be built on the site, preceded by a hill fort between 500 and 200 BC. Remains of an earlier, but equally grand 13th century castle of the Stewarts are visible.

Dundrennan Abbey   61 D5
01557 500262   www.historic-scotland.gov.uk
Dundrennan, on the A711, 6.5 miles (10.5km) south east of Kirkcudbright. The beautiful ruins, amid a peaceful setting, of a Cistercian abbey founded in 1142 by King David I. Includes much later Norman and transitional work. The east end of the church and the chapter house are of high quality. It is believed that Mary, Queen of Scots spent her last night in Scotland here in May 1568.

Dunfallandy Stone   100 B4
                      www.historic-scotland.gov.uk
1 mile (2km) south of Pitlochry. A fine Pictish sculptured stone with a cross on one face and figures on both faces.

Dunfermline Abbey & Palace   78 B2
01383 739026   www.historic-scotland.gov.uk
St Margaret Street, Dunfermline. The remains of the great Benedictine abbey founded by Queen Margaret in the 11th century. The foundations of her church are under the present nave, built in the 12th century in the Romanesque style. Robert the Bruce is buried in the choir, now the site of the present parish church. Of the monastic buildings, the ruins of the refectory, pend and guest house remain.

Dunfermline Museum   78 C1
01383 313838
Viewfield Terrace, Dunfermline. A museum of Dunfermline's social, natural and industrial history, particularly that of damask linen, the industry that made Dunfermline famous in the last century

Dunrobin Castle

Dunglass Castle & Henry
Bell Obelisk   76 B3
Ruined castle on the shore of the River Clyde near the village of Bowling. Former seat of the Colquoun family which dates back to the 14th century. Obelisk erected within the grounds to the memory of Henry Bell, first provost of Helensburgh and pioneer of the steam boat.

Dunglass Collegiate Church   80 C3
                      www.historic-scotland.gov.uk
Between Bilsdean and Cockburnspath. A handsome cross-shaped church with vaulted nave, choir and transepts, all with stone slab roofs. Founded in 1450 for a college of canons by Sir Alexander Hume.

Dunkeld   89 D1
01350 727460   www.nts.org.uk
The Ell Shop, Dunkeld. Attractive village with mostly ruined Gothic cathedral on banks of River Tay. The National Trust for Scotland owns many houses dating from the rebuilding of the town in 1689 after the Battle of Dunkeld.

Dunkeld Bridge   89 D1
Over the River Tay at Dunkeld. One of Thomas Telford's finest bridges, a seven-arched bridge and tollhouse built in 1809. An attractive riverside path leads from here downstream to the famous Birnam Oak, last relic of Macbeth's Birnam Wood.

Dunkeld Cathedral   89 D1
                      www.dunkeldcathedral.org.uk
High Street, Dunkeld. Beautifully situated on the banks of the River Tay. Originally 12th century, but nave and great north west tower from 15th century.

Dunnet Bay Natural
History Display   137 D2
01847 821531
          www.visitjohnogroats.com/ranger_services.htm
Dunnet Pavilion, Dunnet, Castletown. On the A836, 7 miles (11km) east of Thurso, next to caravan site. A display illustrating the natural history and wildlife of Caithness.

Dunnet Head   136 C2
B855, 12 miles (19km) north east of Thurso. This bold promontory of sandstone rising to 417ft (127m) is the northernmost point of the Scottish mainland. There are magnificent views across the Pentland Firth to Orkney and a great part of the north coast to Ben Loyal and Ben Hope. The windows of the lighthouse are sometimes broken by stones hurled up by the winter seas.

Dunninald House Gardens   103 E4
01674 674842   www.dunninald.com
2 miles south of Montrose. Set in a planned landscape dating from 1740, there is an attractive walled garden.

Dunnottar Castle   113 D6
01569 762173
On the A92, 2.5 miles (4km) south of Stonehaven. A spectacular ruin 160ft (48.5m) above the sea. The site for the successful protection of the Scottish crown jewels against the might of Oliver Cromwell's army.

Dunnydeer Studio Porcelain   79 D6
01721 722875
Peebles Craft Centre, Peebles. Part of a complex of workshops. Visitors can see a ceramic artist (Duncan Hood) at work and purchase finished products including sculptures and jewellery.

Dunrobin Castle   129 F4
01408 633177   www.highlandescape.com
Off the A9, 1 mile (2km) north of Golspie. Set in a great park with magnificent formal garden

overlooking the sea. Dunrobin Castle was originally a square keep, built circa 1275 by Robert, Earl of Sutherland, after whom it was named Dun Robin. For centuries this has been the seat of the Earls and Dukes of Sutherland. The present outward appearance results from extensive changes made 1845 - 50. Fine paintings, furniture and a steam-powered fire engine. Falconry displays and museum.

Dunsinane Hill Vitrified Fort   90 B2
South east of Collace, off the A94. Magnificent views from the summit, reached by a steep footpath beginning on the north side of the hill.

Dunskey Castle   58 B4
Located just to the south of Portpatrick. Impressive 16th century castle ruins in a dramatic cliff top setting overlooking the the Irish Sea. Reach the castle from the cliff top footpath which ascends from the old quarry at the south end of Portpatrick waterfront.

Dunskey Gardens & Woodland Walks   58 B4
01776 810905   www.dunskey.com
Dunskey House, 1 mile from Portpatrick. A charming, recently renovated 18th century walled garden with working greenhouses, interesting woodland walks, plant sales and tea room.

Dunskey Trout Lochs   58 B4
01776 810364   www.dunskey.com
Dunskey House, 1 mile from Portpatrick. Two exclusive trout lochs for fly-fishing only. Boat and bank fishing.

Dunstaffnage Castle & Chapel   84 B2
01631 562465   www.historic-scotland.gov.uk
Off the A85 by Loch Etive, 3.5 miles (5km) north of Oban. A fine, well-preserved 13th century castle built on rock. Nearby, ruins of what was an exceptionally beautiful chapel.

Dunvegan Castle   114 B5
01470 521206   www.dunvegancastle.com
On the A850, 1 mile (2km) north of Dunvegan village, Isle of Skye. Historic stronghold of the Clan Macleod, set on the sea loch of Dunvegan, the home of the chiefs of Macleod for 800 years. Possessions on view include books, pictures, arms and treasured relics. Trace the history of the family and clan from the days of their Norse ancestry through 30 generations to the present day. Boat trips from the castle jetty to the seal colony. Extensive gardens and grounds. Audio-visual room. Clan exhibition with items belonging to Bonnie Prince Charlie.

Durisdeer Church   68 A5
6 miles (9.5km) north east of Thornhill on the A702. Dating from 1699, the church houses the Queensberry Marbles, which represent the recumbent figures of the second Duke and Duchess of Queensberry. In the vault lie lead coffins, containing ancient remains of the Clan Douglas.

Dwarfie Stane   146 B3
01856 811397   www.historic-scotland.gov.uk
Towards the north end of the island of Hoy, Orkney. A huge block of sandstone in which a Neolithic burial chamber has been cut. No other known example in the British Isles.

Dyce Symbol Stones   113 D3
01667 460232   www.historic-scotland.gov.uk
Dyce Old Church, Dyce. Two fine examples of Pictish symbol stones in the ruined parish church, one with the older type of incised symbols, and the other with symbols accompanied by a Celtic cross.

Eagle Rock   78 C3
www.historic-scotland.gov.uk
On the shore of the River Forth about 2.5 miles

(0.5km) west of Cramond. A much-defaced carving on natural rock, said to represent an eagle.

Earl's Bu & Church   146 C3
01856 841815   www.historic-scotland.gov.uk
By the A964, 8 miles (13km) west south-west of Kirkwall, Orkney. Earl's Bu are the foundation remains of what may have been a Viking palace. Nearby are the remains of Scotland's only 12th century circular medieval church.

Earl's Palace   146 B1
01856 721205   www.historic-scotland.gov.uk
In Birsay at the north end of mainland Orkney, 11 miles (17.5km) north of Stromness. The gaunt remains of the courtyard palace built in the 16th century by Robert Stewart, Earl of Orkney.

Edinburgh Castle

Earthquake House   87 E3
01764 652578
The Ross, Comrie. Situated on the highland boundary fault line, Earthquake House contains replica and modern seismic measuring instruments. Explanatory boards are on the exterior of the building and there are large windows to view the seismometers.

Eas Coul Aulin Falls   127 F2
At the head of Loch Glencoul, 3 miles (4.5km) west of the A894 near Unapool. The tallest waterfall in Britain, dropping 658ft (200m). Seals and the occasional elusive otter may be seen on the loch.

Eassie Sculptured Stone   90 C1
www.historic-scotland.gov.uk
In Eassie churchyard, near Glamis. A fine elaborately carved monument with Celtic cross on one side and Pictish symbols and processional scenes on the reverse.

East Links Family Park   80 B3
01368 863607   www.eastlinks.co.uk
20 acre (8ha) park with narrow gauge train safari, woodland maze, farm animals and play areas.

Easter Aquhorthies Stone Circle   112 C2
01667 460232   www.historic-scotland.gov.uk
1 mile (2km) west of Inverurie. A recumbent stone circle about 4000 years old.

Eathie Burn   119 E4
Rosemarkie, north of Fortrose, Black Isle. Fossils may be found on this attractive foreshore.

Eden Estuary Centre   91 D4
01334 473047   www.snh.org.uk
Main Street, Guardbridge. By main entrance for paper mill. A small hide overlooking Eden Estuary local nature reserve.

Edinbane Pottery   114 C4
01470 582234   www.edinbane-pottery.co.uk
Edinbane, just off the A850. 14 miles (22.5km) from Portree, 8 miles (13km) from Dunvegan, 48 miles

(77km) from Skye bridge. Workshop and gallery, specialising in both wood-fired and saltglaze handmade functional pottery.

Edinburgh Canal Centre   78 C3
0131 333 1320   www.bridgeinn.com
The Bridge Inn, 27 Baird Road, Ratho. Built circa 1750, the inn became a canalside inn with the opening of the Union Canal in 1822. Canal boat restaurants cater for meals, dances, weddings, etc. Sightseeing cruises and Santa cruises in December.

Edinburgh Castle   20 A2
0131 225 9846   www.historic-scotland.gov.uk
In the centre of Edinburgh at the top of the Royal Mile. Battlements overlook the Esplanade where the floodlit Military Tattoo is staged each year. The oldest part, St Margaret's Chapel, dates from the Norman period. The Great Hall was built by James IV; the Half Moon Battery by the Regent Morton in the late 16th century. The Scottish National War Memorial was erected after World War I. The castle houses the Crown Jewels (Honours) of Scotland, the Stone of Destiny and the famous 15th century gun Mons Meg.

Edinburgh Crystal Visitor Centre   79 D4
01968 675128   www.edinburgh-crystal.co.uk
In Penicuik, south of Edinburgh. Visitors can watch and talk to the craftsmen, and discover the history of Edinburgh Crystal. Opportunity to try blowing and cutting crystal (must be booked in advance).

Edinburgh Dungeon   20 B2
0131 240 1000   www.thedungeons.com
Market Street, Edinburgh. The Edinburgh Dungeon transports visitors back to the darkest chapters of Scotland's history. Visitors come face to face with the notorious murderers, Burke and Hare, wander through the plague ravaged streets of old Edinburgh and join James VI on a one-way boat ride to confront the infamous cannibal Sawney Bean in Witchfynder.

Edinburgh Printmakers   20 B1
0131 557 2479
              www.edinburgh-printmakers.co.uk
23 Union Street. Edinburgh's main studio for practising artists who make limited edition prints. Visitors can watch artists at work. Courses in print-making.

Edinburgh University Collection of Historic Musical Instruments   20 B2
              www.music.ed.ac.uk/euchmi
Reid Concert Hall, Bristo Square & St. Celia's Hall, Niddry Street. Founded circa 1850 and opened to the public in 1982. The galleries, built in 1859 and still with their original showcases, are believed to be the earliest surviving purpose-built musical museum in the world. On display are 1000 items including string, woodwind, brass and percussion instruments from Britain, Europe and from distant lands. The history of the instruments of the orchestra, the wind band, theatre, dance, popular music, domestic music-making and brass bands is shown. Displays include many beautiful examples of the instrument-maker's art over the past 400 years. St. Celia's Hall houses the internationally important Russell Collection of Early Keyboard Instruments.

Edinburgh Zoo   79 D3
0131 334 9171
              www.edinburghzoo.org.uk
134 Corstorphine Road. Established in 1913 by the Royal Zoological Society of Scotland. Over 1000 animals, many threatened in the wild, all set in 80 acres (32ha) of beautiful hillside parkland. Animals range from tiny blue poison arrow frogs to massive white rhinos. The world's largest penguin pool and a magic forest, home to the tiniest primates. A Penguin Parade takes place April - September, daily at 1400.

Edin's Hall Broch   80 C5
0131 668 8600   www.historic-scotland.gov.uk
On the north eastern slope of Cockburn Law, off the A6112 about 4.5 miles (7km) from Grantshouse. One of the few Iron Age brochs in the Scottish Lowlands. Unusually large, sitting in a fort defended by ramparts and ditches, partially overlain with a later settlement. Occupied in Roman times.

Edradour Distillery   80 C5
01796 472095   www.edradour.co.uk
Edradour, on the A294, 2.5 miles (4km) east of Pitlochry. The smallest distillery in Scotland, established in 1825. Visitors can taste a hand-crafted single malt whisky.

Edrom Church   100 B4
0131 668 8600   www.historic-scotland.gov.uk
In Edrom churchyard, Berwickshire, off the A6015, 3.5 miles (5.5km) north east of Duns. A fine Norman chancel arch is carved in the church doorway built by Thor Longus circa 1105.

Edzell Castle & Garden   81 D5
01356 648631   www.historic-scotland.gov.uk
At Edzell, off the B966, 6 miles (9.5km) north of Brechin. Late medieval tower house incorporated into a 16th century courtyard mansion. Walled garden with a bathhouse and summerhouse laid out by Sir David Lindsay in 1604.

Eglinton Country Park   102 C3
01294 551776
Irvine. 990 acres (400ha) of countryside with a loch, woodland and gardens. Visitor centre.

Eileach An Naoimh   83 E5
              www.historic-scotland.gov.uk
On an island of that name in the Garvellach group, north of Jura. The ruins of beehive cells, a chapel and a graveyard. Associated by local tradition with St Columba.

Eilean Donan Castle   106 B2
01599 555202   www.eileandonancastle.com
Dornie, on the A87, 8 miles (13km) east of Kyle of Lochalsh. On an islet (now connected by a causeway) in Loch Duich, this picturesque and inhabited castle dates back to 1214. It passed into the hands of the Mackenzies of Kintail who became the Earls of Seaforth. In 1719 it was garrisoned by

Eilean Donan Castle

Spanish Jacobite troops and was blown up by an English man o' war. Now completely restored. Visitors can explore every part of the castle from the Banqueting Hall to the bedrooms. Includes a recreated kitchen with sights, sounds and smells.

Elcho Castle   89 E3
01738 639998   www.historic-scotland.gov.uk
Rhynd, 3 miles (5km) south east of Perth. A handsome and complete fortified 16th century mansion. Notable for its tower-like jambs or wings and for the wrought-iron grills protecting its windows.

Electric Brae   66 A4
On the A7, 20 miles (32km) south of Ayr (also known as Croy Brae). An optical illusion is created so that a car appears to be going up the hill when it is in fact going down.

Elgin Cathedral   122 B3
01343 547171   www.historic-scotland.gov.uk
In Elgin on the A96. The superb ruin of what was perhaps the most beautiful cathedral in Scotland. The octagonal chapter house is the finest in Scotland.

Elgin Museum   122 B3
01343 543675   www.elginmuseum.org.uk
High Street, Elgin. Museum interpreting the natural and human heritage of Moray. Internationally known for its fossils and Pictish stones.

Ellisland Farm   61 F1
01387 740426   www.ellislandfarm.co.uk
Holywood, off the A76, 6.5 miles (10.5km) north north-west of Dumfries. The farm which Robert Burns took over in 1788, building the farmhouse and trying to introduce new farming methods. Unsuccessful, he became an exciseman in 1789, and when the stock was auctioned in 1791 he moved to Dumfries. Burns wrote some of his most famous works at the farm, including Tam o' Shanter and Auld Lang Syne. The granary houses an audio-visual display and there are facilities for barbecues.

Embo Beach Anchor   129 F5
Embo, north of Dornoch. The anchor probably came from the Prussian barque Vesta which was wrecked in 1876. It came ashore 300 yards (275m) north of the village and Embo fishermen rescued all 11 crew.

Embroidery Workshop   90 C5
01333 423985   www.embroideredoriginals.co.uk
Blacketyside Farm, on the A915 coast road to St Andrews, 0.5 mile (1km) north of Leven. A tiny craft workshop and gift shop, housing an extensive range of original handmade designs. Visitors can watch craftspeople at work.

Eppie Callum's Tree   88 B3
Crieff. A 600 year old oak tree standing 70ft (21m) high. The tree is said to have once sheltered notorious outlaw Rob Roy Macgregor from his enemies.

Ettrick Bay   75 D4
West side of the Isle of Bute. This is a popular and safe beach.

Explorers, The Scottish Plant Hunters
Garden   100 B4
01796 484600   www.pitlochry.org.uk/garden.php
Pitlochry Festival Theatre, Port-na-Craig, Pitlochry. Scotland's newest garden celebrates 300 years of plant collecting by Scotsmen. Art and sculpture are combined with landscape features to provide a unique experience.

Eyemouth Museum   81 E5
01890 750678
Auld Kirk, Manse Road. The museum contains a

magnificent tapestry which was sewn by local ladies to commemorate the Great East Coast Fishing Disaster of 1881, when 189 local fishermen were drowned. Also exhibitions on farming, milling, blacksmith and wheelwright, in addition to local fishing heritage.

Eynhallow Church   146 C1
01856 841815   www.historic-scotland.gov.uk
On the island of Eynhallow, Orkney. The ruins of a 12th century church and a group of domestic buildings.

Fair Isle   150 A4
www.nts.org.uk
Between Orkney and Shetland. One of Britain's most isolated inhabited islands. Most famous for the intricately patterned knitwear which bears its name, a traditional craft which continues today. Fair Isle is important for birdlife, and offers many opportunities for ornithological study. The island also has much of archaeological interest, and traditional crofting is still in evidence.

Fairy Glen RSPB Nature Reserve   119 E4
01463 715000   www.rspb.org.uk
Rosemarkie, Black Isle, 16 miles (26km) from Inverness. One mile of attractive woodland glen with a stream and two waterfalls, on the edge of a coastal village. Lots of woodland plants to see, and breeding dippers and grey wagtails. The glen has many tales and legends connected with it and is reputed to be the home of a black witch.

Falconer Museum   121 E4
01309 673701   www.falconermuseum.co.uk
Tolbooth Street, Forres. Founded in 1871 and now containing a wealth of Moray heritage.

Falkirk Wheel   77 F2
01324 619888   www.thefalkirkwheel.co.uk
At the interchange between the Union and the Forth and Clyde canals, close to Tamfourhill, south Falkirk. A spectacular wheel reconnects the Union Canal up 82ft (25m) to the Forth and Clyde Canal. The wheel weighs 1300 tonnes and is equivalent in height to a nine-storey block of flats. Free visitor centre and park.

Falkland Palace, Garden & Old Burgh   90 B5
01337 857397   www.nts.org.uk
Falkland, Cupar. Country residence of the Stewart kings and queens. The gardens contain the original royal tennis court, built in 1539 and the oldest in Britain.

Falls of Acharn   87 E1
On the south east bank of Loch Tay, 4 miles (6km) from Kenmore. A 1 mile (1.5km) return walk starts from Acharn and leads to a man-made cavern from which the picturesque falls can be viewed.

Falls of Bruar   99 F3
At Bruar, 10 miles north of Pitlochry. Robert Burns visited the Bruar gorge in 1787 and wrote The Humble Petition of Bruar Water. When Burns died in 1796, the duke created a wild garden in his memory.

Falls of Clyde Wildlife Reserve &
Visitor Centre   77 F6
01555 665262   www.swt.org.uk
The Scottish Wildlife Trust Visitor Centre, New Lanark. One of Britain's most spectacular waterfalls set in a mosaic of ancient woodland, meadow and ancient monuments. Over 100 species of birds have been recorded on the reserve, with unsurpassed views of breeding peregrine falcons. The ranger service based at the visitor centre provides a comprehensive events programme, including badger watches, bat walks, insect expeditions and waterfall day walks.

Falls of Dochart   86 C2
Dramatic waterfalls rushing through the centre of the picturesque Highland village of Killin. On the island of Inchbuie in the river is the burial ground of Clan McNab.

Falls of Foyers   108 B2
Foyers, on the eastern shore of Loch Ness. Car park in village, then walk. These falls, which are particularly spectacular in spate, are surrounded by woodland trails. The falls were visited and written about by Robert Burns.

Falls of Glomach   107 D2
www.nts.org.uk
18 miles (28km) east of Kyle of Lochalsh, north east off the A87. At 370ft (112m), this is one of the highest waterfalls in Britain, set in a steep narrow cleft in remote countryside. The falls are well worth the 5 mile (8km) walk from the car park at Dorusduain.

Falls of Leny   86 C5
Falls on the River Leny west of Callander with surrounding woodland walks. The descent is popular with canoeists.

Falls of Shin   128 C5
01549 402231   www.fallsofshin.com
Lairg, off the A836, 5 miles (8km) north of Bonar Bridge. Waterfalls in a beautiful wooded section of the Achany Glen. Popular for watching salmon leaping as they migrate upstream on their annual journey to the spawning grounds in the headwaters of the River Shin. The salmon can be seen from April to November. The visitor centre is a popular stop.

Famous Grouse Experience   88 B3
01764 656565 www.famousgrouse.co.uk/experience/
The Hosh, on the A85 towards Comrie, 1.25 miles (2km) from Crieff. Glenturret is the oldest distillery in Scotland, established in 1775. Take a tour of the distillery to see how the single malt is made and view the interactive exhibit which explains how the Famous Grouse whisky is blended to make it one of Scotland's most popular.

Faraid Head & Balnakeil Bay   133 E2
North of Durness, the Balnakeil area is of outstanding nature conservation interest for its outcrops of Durness limestone and the associated plant communities. Faraid Head, behind the beautiful Balnakeil beach, is a narrow headland with dunes, coastal grasslands and steep cliffs. During the summer months a ranger service is operated from the Tourist Information Centre where advice on guided walks and local wildlife can be obtained.

Farigaig   108 C2
01320 366322   www.forestry.gov.uk
By Inverfarigaig on south side of Loch Ness, 18 miles (29km) south west of Inverness. Farigaig Forest offers excellent views over Loch Ness and across Inverfarigaig to Dum Dearduil, the site of a vitrified Iron Age fort dating from around 500 BC. The forest comprises large specimen conifers, introduced from America during the last century, and a mixture of native trees including birch, rowan, alder, ash, willow, hazel, elm and oak.

Faskally Forest   100 B4
01350 727284   www.forestry.gov.uk
1 mile north of Pitlochry on the B8019. Compact, wonderfully mixed woodland beside Loch Faskally.

Fast Castle   81 D3
Off the A1107, 4 miles (6.5km) north west of Coldingham. The scant and remote but impressive remains of a Home stronghold is perched on a cliff above the sea. The castle passed to the last Logan of Restalrig in 1580, who was outlawed for the Gowrie conspiracy (alleged plot to kill James VI).

Fergusson Gallery   28 C3
01738 441944
Marshall Place, Perth. An art gallery devoted to the work of the Scottish colourist painter, John Duncan Fergusson (1874 - 1961) and housing the largest collection of his work.

Ferniehirst Castle   70 C4
01835 862201
Lothian Estates Office, on the A86, 2 miles (3km) south of Jedburgh. A 16th century Border castle and Scotland's frontier fortress. The ancestral home of the Kerr family; restored by the clan chief, the Marquis of Lothian. Information centre, chapel, Kerr museum and private apartments.

Ferrycroft Countryside Centre   128 C4
01549 402160
A Tourist Information Centre in Lairg where visitors can learn about Sutherland. The audio-visual displays show the many changes to Sutherland's landscape from the Ice Age to the present day. Themes include forest cover, inhabitants, hydro-electric schemes, wildlife, conservation and archaeology. There are indoor puzzles and a play area for children. Visitors can also book accommodation, buy maps and books, exchange currency and obtain angling permits. Archaeological trail and forest walks.

Fetlar Interpretive Centre   153 F3
01957 733206   www.fetlar.com
Beach of Houbie, on the island of Fetlar, 4 miles (6.5km) from the car ferry. Museum and visitor information centre with interactive display on Fetlar's history, folklore, flora, fauna and geology. Extensive archive of photographs, audio recordings and historic local film. Award-winning exhibition on the history of antiseptic surgery.

Fettercairn Distillery Visitor Centre   103 D2
01561 340205
Distillery Road, 0.5 mile (1km) west of Fettercairn. Visitor centre with tours which describe the processes of whisky making. Includes a free dram of Old Fettercairn.

Fife Folk Museum   90 C4
01334 828180
The Weigh House, High Street, Ceres. A local museum housed in a 17th century tollbooth and 18th century cottages overlooking the Ceres Burn. The collection illustrates the social, economic and cultural history of rural Fife.

Finavon Doocot   102 C4
www.nts.org.uk
6 miles (10km) north of Forfar, off the A90. A 16th century dovecot, the largest in Scotland, Finavon Doocot had 2400 nesting boxes.

Findhorn Foundation   121 E3
01309 690311   www.findhorn.org
Findhorn, off the A96. The Findhorn Foundation Community was established in 1962. Visitors can see ecological barrel houses, turf roofs, innovative architecture, renewable energy sources such as a wind turbine and solar panels, and a Living Machine natural sewage treatment system.

Findhorn Heritage Centre & Ice House   121 E3
01309 690659
Northshore, Findhorn. Based in two salmon fishers' huts and an ice house. One hut is laid out as a salmon fishers' bothy of days gone by, the other is filled with exhibits which trace the development of Findhorn from pre-historic times.

Finlaggan Trust Centre   72 C4
01496 810629   www.finlaggan.com
The Cottage, Ballygrant, Isle of Islay. 2 miles (3km)

off the A846 from Port Askaig. Islay, known as the Cradle of Clan Donald and Finlaggan, is the main headquarters of the Lords of the Isles and a place of pilgrimmage for clan members today. The interpretive centre describes local history and details the archaeological finds.

Finlaystone Country Estate 76 A3
01475 540505 www.finlaystone.co.uk
A8 west of Langbank. A family run estate including 140 acres (57ha) of woodland with waterfalls, walking trails and adventure play areas. The extensive gardens overlook the Clyde and were originally laid out in 1900. The visitor centre has displays on the history of the clan MacMillan and Celtic art, natural history information and a doll museum.

Flat Cat Gallery 80 A6
01578 722808 www.flatcatgallery.co.uk
2 Market Place, Lauder. Changing exhibitions of paintings, sculpture, ceramics, jewellery and furniture by artists from the Borders and further afield. Also a resident restorer of middle-eastern rugs and textiles. A good stock of carpets on display.

Flodden Monument 70 A3
Located in Selkirk town centre, this monument was erected in 1913 on the 400th anniversary of the battle and is inscribed O Flodden Field. The memorial is the work of sculptor Thomas Clapperton, and commemorates the lone survivor of the 80 Selkirk men who marched to Flodden.

Floors Castle 71 D2
01573 223333 www.floorscastle.com
Located in Kelso, Floors Castle is the home of the Roxburghe family. It is the largest inhabited castle in Scotland. The apartments display an outstanding collection of French 17th and 18th century furniture, many fine works of art and tapestries, Chinese and Dresden porcelain and a Victorian collection of birds. The extensive parkland and gardens overlooking the River Tweed provide delightful walks and picnic areas. The walled garden contains splendid herbaceous borders and is best seen in July, August and September.

Floral Hall & Coffee Shop 119 D5
01463 713553 www.invernessfloralhall.com
Bught Lane, Inverness. In Bught Park, off the A82, 1.5 miles (2.5km) from city centre. The Floral Hall, Cacti House and gardens are part of a working horticultural nursery with professional staff. Visitors can stroll along winding paths through a sub-tropical landscape enhanced with a grotto, waterfall, fountain and tropical fish. Ferns and orchids flourish. Rare and fascinating tropical plants. Outside demonstration gardens consist of a number of landscaped areas.

Flow Country 137 D5
At Golticlay, just north of Rumster Forest on the Lybster to Achavanich road. A view of the open

peatlands of central Caithness. To the west, beyond Loch Rangag and Loch Ruard, these ancient peatlands have remained unchanged for thousands of years. Blàr nam Faoileag National Nature Reserve is visible and is part of the largest single expanse of actively growing blanket bog remaining in Britain. These peatlands, with their extraordinary surface patterns of pools and ridges, collectively form what is commonly known as the Flow Country.

Fochabers Folk Museum 122 C4
01343 821204
High Street, Fochabers. Shows the history of Fochabers over the past 200 years. Includes a large collection of horse-drawn carts and carriages.

Fordyce Joiner's Workshop & Visitor Centre 123 E3
01261 843322 www.aberdeenshire.gov.uk
Church Street, Fordyce. Learn about the importance of the rural carpenter to the local community over the last 150 years. Displays of early tools and machinery.

Forsinard RSPB Nature Reserve 135 E5
01641 571225 www.rspb.org.uk
RSPB Visitor Centre, Forsinard Station, Forsinard. On the A897, 26 miles (41.5km) inland from Helmsdale. A nature reserve forming 24,711 acres (10,000ha) of rolling peatland in the heart of the world-famous Flow Country. The unique blanket bogs contain thousands of bog pools, with insect-eating plants, dragonflies and many uncommon birds. Guided walks (May - Aug) and self-guided trail.

Fort Charlotte 151 D2
01856 841815 www.historic-scotland.gov.uk
In the centre of Lerwick in Shetland. A pentagonal artillery fort, with bastions projecting from each corner and towering walls. Built in 1665 to protect the Sound of Bressay from the Dutch, but taken by them and burned in 1673. Rebuilt in 1781.

Fort George 119 E4
01667 460232 www.historic-scotland.gov.uk
Visitor Centre, off the A96, by Ardersier, 11 miles (17.5km) east of Inverness. A vast site of one of the most outstanding artillery fortifications in Europe. It was planned in 1747 as a base for George II's army and was completed in 1769. Since then it has served as a barracks. It is virtually unaltered and presents a complete view of the defensive system. There is a reconstruction of barrack rooms in different periods and a display of muskets and pikes. Includes the Queen's Own Highlanders Regimental Museum.

Forth & Clyde Canal 76 C3
01324 671217 www.scottishcanals.co.uk
One of the biggest canal restoration projects in Europe, the Millennuim Link has brought the 69 miles (110km) of canal, from Glasgow to Edinburgh and the Forth to the Clyde, back to life. The towing path provides delightful walks through town and country with plenty of interest for both nature and history enthusiasts. Excursions by canal boat are available.

Forth Rail Bridge 78 C3
www.forthbridges.org.uk
South Queensferry. Opened on 4 March 1890 by the Prince of Wales. The bridge was designed on the cantilever principle with three towers 340ft (104m) high. The engineers were Sir John Fowler and Benjamin Baker.

Fortingall Yew 87 E1
Fortingall, 9 miles (14.5km) west of Aberfeldy. The surviving part of

Floors Castle

the great yew in an enclosure in the churchyard is reputedly over 3000 years old, perhaps the oldest tree in Europe. The attractive village is claimed to be the birthplace of Pontius Pilate and has been a religious centre since St Columban times.

Fortrose Cathedral 119 E4
01667 460232 www.historic-scotland.gov.uk
In Fortrose, 8 miles (13km) south south-west of Cromarty. The surviving fragments consist of the 13th century vaulted undercroft of the chapter house and the south aisle of the nave, a 14th century vaulted structure, both finely worked, with two canopied monuments and other memorials.

Fossil Grove 76 C4
0141 287 2000 www.glasgowmuseums.com
Victoria Park, Glasgow. Fossil stumps and roots of trees which grew here 350 million years ago. Discovered by accident and now designated a Site of Special Scientific Interest.

Foulden Tithe Barn 81 E5
0131 668 8600 www.historic-scotland.gov.uk
On the A6105, 4 miles (6.5km) south east of Chirnside. A two-storey tithe barn with outside stair and crow-stepped gables. View exterior only.

Fowlis Wester Sculptured Stone 88 C3
www.historic-scotland.gov.uk
In the church at Fowlis Wester, 6 miles (9.5km) north east of Crieff. A tall cross-slab carved with Pictish symbols, figure sculpture and Celtic enrichment. A replica stands in the village square.

Fraserburgh Heritage Centre 125 D3
01346 512888 www.fraserburghheritage.com
Quarry Road, Fraserburgh. The Centre describes the history of Fraserburgh from the bustling quayside to the haute couture of dress designer Bill Gibb.

Fruitmarket Gallery, The 20 B2
0131 225 2383 www.fruitmarket.co.uk
45 Market Street, in Edinburgh city centre adjacent to Waverley station. Originally built in 1938 as a fruit and vegetable market, the building now contains an acclaimed art gallery with a national and international reputation for diverse and challenging pro-active exhibitions. Art bookshop and restaurant.

Fyrish Monument 119 D3
Above village of Evanton on Fyrish Hill, off the A9. Curious monument erected in 1782 by Sir Hector Munro who rose from the ranks and distinguished himself at the relief of Seringapatam. The monument is a replica of the gates of the Indian city of Negapatam, the scene of one of Munro's military victories. It was built to provide work at a time of poverty and unemployment in the Evanton area. There are stunning views over the Cromarty Firth.

Fyvie Castle 124 B6
01651 891266 www.nts.org.uk
Fyvie. Probably the grandest example of Scottish baronial architecture. The five towers enshrine five centuries of history. The oldest part dates from the 13th century. Collection of portraits, arms and armour, and 17th century tapestries.

Gairloch Heritage Museum 116 B2
01445 712287 www.ghrm.freeserve.co.uk
Achtercairn, in Gairloch, on the A832 70 miles

(112km) north west of Inverness. A heritage centre displaying all aspects of life in a typical west Highland parish from the Stone Age to the present day, including archaeology, fishing, agriculture and domestic arts. Reconstructed crofthouse room, schoolroom, dairy and shop. The local lighthouse and preserved fishing boats are outside. Archive and library.

Gairloch Marine Life Centre & Cruises 116 B2
01445 712636 www.porpoise-gairloch.co.uk
At Gairloch harbour on the A832. Porpoise, dolphin and whale surveys have been conducted for the Sea Watch Foundation for over 15 years. At the centre, visitors can see photo displays, video and computer presentation, maps and charts along with survey records. The whole of marine life is covered, from jelly fish through to birds, seals and whales. Sail Gairloch Cruises take place daily subject to weather conditions and demand.

Gallery of Modern Art 16 B2
0141 229 1996 www.glasgowmuseums.com
Queen Street, Glasgow. The elegant Royal Exchange building displays works by living artists from around the world. A wide range of temporary exhibitions plus a programme of events including music, drama, dance and workshops.

Galloway House Gardens 60 A5
01988 600680 www.gallowayhousegardens.org.uk
On the A713, 10 miles north of Castle Douglas, on the shore of Loch Ken. Woodland garden with a number of walks through the grounds, leading down to the shore and sandy bay.

Galloway Hydro Visitor Centre 61 D4
01557 330114 www.scottishpower.plc.uk
Tongland, 2 miles (3km) north east of Kirkcudbright. Hydro-electric station, built in the 1930s, which provides a third of the power of south west Scotland. Visitor centre with exhibition room, 1930s style office and guided tours of the power station and dam.

Galloway Red Deer Range 60 B2
01671 402420
Laggan O'Dee, 10 miles (16km) from Newton Stewart and 9 miles (14.5km) from New Galloway on the A712. Created in 1977 to enable visitors to see red deer in a semi-natural habitat of 500 acres (200ha). Good photo opportunities.

Red Deer

Galloway Wildlife Conservation Park 61 D4
01557 331645 www.gallowaywildlife.co.uk
Lochfergus Plantation, 1 mile (2km) east of Kirkcudbright, on the B727. A varied collection of nearly 150 animals are found in the hillside woodland setting of this zoological park and wild

190

animal conservation centre: from pandas and monkeys to lynx and Scottish wildcats. On offer are guided tours of the zoo, pet-handling sessions, quizzes for children, animal sponsorship, and involvement in threatened species breeding and wildlife conservation both in the zoo and nature reserve. Also crazy golf.

Gartmorn Dam Country Park   78 A1
01259 452409
www.clacksweb.org.uk/visiting/gartmorndam
Sauchie, near Alloa. The country park is a peaceful retreat for visitors to walk, cycle or to enjoy horse riding or fishing, with an extensive network of paths. Gartmorn Dam itself is a 170 acre (69ha) reservoir engineered by Sir John Erskine to power pumps which drained mines.

Garvamore Bridge   108 C5
6 miles (9.5km) west of Laggan Bridge, 17 miles (27km) south west of Newtonmore. This two-arched bridge at the south side of the Corrieyairick Pass was built by General Wade in 1735.

Gateway Centre   76 A2
0845 345 4978   www.lochlomond-trossachs.org
Balloch. A visitor centre on the banks of Loch Lomond which provides the 'gateway' to the Loch Lomond and Trossachs National Park. There is a ranger service, woodland trails, information on local scenery and wildlife and interactive exhibitions.

Geilston Garden   76 A3
01389 849187   www.nts.org.uk
On the A814 at the west end of Cardross, 18 miles (29km) north of Glasgow. Small estate typical of those owned on the banks of the Clyde by tobacco barons and factory owners who made their money in 19th century Glasgow. Charming garden with walled area and wooded glen.

Glamis Castle

Gemini Explorer Marine Wildlife Tours   123 D3
07747 626280   www.geminiexplorer.co.uk
Boat departs from Buckie Harbour, Buckie. Take a 2.5 hour long boat trip along the Moray Firth Coast aboard the Gemini Explorer, an ex-lifeboat. Dolphins, porpoise and seals are regularly seen from the boat as well as occasional sightings of Minke whales and basking sharks.

Geoffrey (Tailor's) Tartan Weaving Mill   20 D4
0131 226 1555
www.geoffreykilts.co.uk/tartanweavingmill.htm
Beside Edinburgh Castle at the top of the Royal Mile. A working mill where visitors can see the production of tartan cloth and try weaving on a 60 year old pedal loom. Visitors can also have their photo taken

in ancient Scottish costume. Clans and tartans information bureau.

George Square   16 B2
Glasgow city centre. The heart of Glasgow with the City Chambers and statues of Sir Walter Scott, Queen Victoria, Prince Albert, Robert Burns, Sir John Moore, Lord Clyde, Thomas Campbell, Dr Thomas Graham, James Oswald, James Watt, William Gladstone and Sir Robert Peel.

George Waterston Memorial Centre & Museum   150 A4
01595 760244
Auld Schule, Fair Isle, Shetland. Maps the social history of the island with displays of agriculture, fishing, shipwrecks, textiles, natural history and archaeology.

Georgian House   20 A2
0131 226 3318   www.nts.org.uk
7 Charlotte Square, Edinburgh. A typical house in Edinburgh's New Town, designed by Robert Adam, furnished as it would have been by its first owners in 1796. Video programmes.

Geowalks   79 D3
0131 555 5488   www.geowalks.demon.co.uk
Discover extinct volcanoes, hidden views, stunning scenery, the secrets of the local landscape and over 400 million years of history. Explore the beautiful surroundings of Fife and the Lothians, and the dramatic cityscape of Edinburgh. Join Dr Angus Miller for a walk back in time. Walks vary from 2 - 5 hours.

Gilnockie Tower   63 D2
Hollows, on the A7, 2 miles (3km) north of Canonbie. A tower house built in 1525 by the Border freebooter Johnie Armstrong and originally called Holehouse (from the quarry beside which it stands). Managed by the Clan Armstrong Centre.

Gladstone Court Museum   68 C2
01899 221050
www.biggar-net.co.uk/museums
North Back Road, Biggar. On the A702, 26 miles (41.5km) south of Edinburgh. An indoor street museum of shops and windows. Grocer, photographer, dress maker, bank, school, library, ironmonger, chemist, china merchant, telephone exchange.

Gladstone's Land   20 D4
0131 226 5856   www.nts.org.uk
477b Lawnmarket, Royal Mile, Edinburgh. Typical example of the 17th century tenements of Edinburgh's Old Town, clustered along the ridge between the Castle and the Palace of Holyroodhouse - the Royal Mile. Completed in 1620 and originally home to a prosperous Edinburgh merchant, Thomas Gledstanes, the house contains original painted ceilings and some contemporary furniture.

Glamis Castle   90 C1
01307 840393   www.glamis-castle.co.uk
Glamis, on the A94, 6 miles (9.5km) west of Forfar. One of the oldest parts is Duncan's Hall, legendary setting for Shakespeare's Macbeth. The present castle was modified in the 17th century. Famous for being the childhood home of Queen Elizabeth, The Queen Mother, and birthplace of Princess Margaret. Fine collections of china, painting, tapestries and furniture. Two exhibitions, Coach House and Elizabeth of Glamis.

Glen Etive
97 E4

Off the A82 15 miles (24 km) north of Bridge of Orchy and
13 miles east of Glencoe. A single track road follows Glen
Etive for 14 miles through some of the most stunning
scenery in Scotland to the shores of Loch Etive.

Glasgow Botanic Garden   76 C4
0141 334 2422   www.glasgow.gov.uk
730 Great Western Road, Glasgow, 1.5 miles (2.5km)
west from the city centre. The gardens were formed
in 1817 to provide a source of plant material for use
in teaching medicine and botany. Today they are
valued by tourists and as a centre for education,
conservation and research. Specialist plant
collections include exotic Australian tree and filmy
ferns, orchids and tropical begonias.

Glasgow Cathedral   17 C2
0141 552 6891   www.historic-scotland.gov.uk
Cathedral Square, Cathedral Street. The only
Scottish mainland medieval cathedral to have
survived the Reformation complete (apart from its
western towers). Built during the 12th and 13th
centuries over the supposed tomb of St Kentigern.
Notable features are the elaborately vaulted crypt,
the stone screen and the unfinished Blackadder
Aisle. The parish church of Glasgow.

Glasgow School of Art   16 A1
0141 353 4500   www.gsa.ac.uk
167 Renfrew Street, Glasgow. Charles Rennie
Mackintosh's architectural masterpiece. The
Mackintosh Building has taken its place as one of
the most influential and significant structures of the
20th century. Regular guided tours let you
experience this famous and fascinating art school.

Glasgow Science Centre   76 C4
0141 420 5000   www.glasgowsciencecentre.org
On the south bank of the River Clyde. Three
attractions on one site. Scotland's first IMAX theatre,
a large screen format offering a 2D/3D sound and
visual experience. The Science Mall, four floors of
dynamic and engaging science exhibits. The
Glasgow Tower, which at 328ft (100m) high is the
highest free-standing structure in Scotland, and the
only 360 degree rotating structure in the world.

Glebe Cairn   74 B1
www.historic-scotland.gov.uk
In Kilmartin Glen. An early Bronze Age burial cairn
with two burial chambers (cists).

Glen Affric National Nature Reserve   107 E2
01320 366522   www.forestry.gov.uk
From the A831 at Cannich take the unclassified road
south to Loch Affric. Known as one of the most
beautiful glens in Scotland, Glen Affric is a mix of

high mountains, lochs, rivers and part of the ancient
Caledonian Pine forest. Main features include Dog
Falls in the lower Glen, Loch Affric and the wilder
West Affric owned by the National Trust for
Scotland. The glen is also an excellent place for all
types of walking.

Glen Esk Folk Museum   102 C2
01356 648070
The Retreat, Glenesk, Brechin. A museum housing
antiques, documents and artefacts reflecting the
history of Glen Esk and surrounding area. The
interpretive centre houses a large relief model of
Glen Esk, a stable in original form and displays on
past and present local life.

Glen Finglas   86 C5
01764 662554   www.woodland-trust.org.uk
Off the A821, 5 miles (8km) west of Callander. The
glen carries the Finglas water south east to the
Black Water between Loch Achray and Loch
Venacher. Acquired by the Woodland Trust in 1996,
there is an ongoing programme of restoration to
native woodland. Waymarked walking trails of
various grades.

Glen Garioch Distillery   113 D2
01651 873450   www.glengarioch.co.uk
Old Meldrum, 18 miles NW of Aberdeen. Tours of
Scotland's most easterly distillery which has been
producing whisky since 1797.

Glen Grant Distillery & Garden   122 B5
01542 783318
Rothes. Fine single malt whisky has been produced
here since 1840. Visitors can tour the distillery,
sample a dram in the study or pavillion and explore
the garden.

Glen Moray Distillery   122 A3
01343 500900   www.glenmoray.com
Bruceland Road, Elgin. Constructed in the classic
square layout of a Scottish farm, featuring a
courtyard surrounded by the buildings where the
whisky is produced.

Glen Nevis Visitor Centre
(Ionad Nibheis)   97 D2
01397 705922
1.25 miles (2km) up Glen Nevis, located 2 miles
(3km) east of Fort William. Information on the
history, geology, flora and fauna of Ben Nevis and

Glen Nevis

Glen Nevis. Ranger guided walks during June, July and August.

Glen of Rothes Trout Fishery   122 B4
01340 831888   www.glen-of-rothes.co.uk
8 miles (13km) south of Elgin on the A941. A fishery with 6 acres (2.4ha) of lochs. Visitors can fish for rainbow and brown trout from the banks.

Glen Ord Distillery Visitor Centre   118 C4
01463 872004
Just off the A832 on the outskirts of Muir of Ord, 15 miles (24km) west of Inverness. The sole survivor of nine distilleries which once operated around Glen Ord. Licensed in 1838. The tour and exhibition show the history of the Black Isle and the main processes of distilling. Complimentary tasting.

Glenarn Gardens   75 F2
01436 820493   www.gardens-of-argyll.co.uk
Rhu, by Helensburgh, Argyll and Bute. A west coast garden in a sheltered glen overlooking the Gareloch, famous for the collection of rare and tender rhododendrons. Also fine magnolias and many other interesting ericaceous plants. Colour all year round. A network of paths with small bridges connect the different parts of the garden - the pond, walled garden, woodland, greenhouse and the productive vegetable patch.

Glenbarr Abbey & the Clan MacAlister Visitor Centre   64 A2
01583 421247
Glenbarr, Tarbert, on the A83, 12 miles (19km) north of Campbeltown. A house in the 18th century Gothic Revival style, the seat of the lairds of Glenbarr since 1796, designed by James Gillespie Graham. Tours are conducted by the 5th laird, Angus Macalister, whose home this is. Among items displayed are 19th century fashions, Spode, Sèvres and Derby china, gloves worn by Mary, Queen of Scots, thimble collection.

Glenbuchat Castle   111 E3
01667 460232   www.historic-scotland.gov.uk
Bridge of Buchat. 14 miles (22.5km) west of Alford. A fine example of a Z-plan tower house, built in 1590.

Glencoe   97 D4
01855 811307   www.nts.org.uk
Visitor Centre, Glencoe, Ballachulish. On the A82, 17 miles (27km) south of Fort William. Dramatic and historic glen, scene of the 1692 massacre of part of the MacDonald clan by soldiers of King William. Its name translates as Valley of Weeping. Its steep sided mountains offer superb walking and climbing. Red deer, wildcat, golden eagle and rare arctic plants can be seen among the breathtaking peaks and spectacular waterfalls. Ranger service. Video programme on massacre. Display on history of mountaineering.

Glencoe & North Lorn Folk Museum   97 D4
01855 811664
Off the A82 in Glencoe village. A local museum in four heather-thatched buildings and two outbuildings. Many exhibits reflect Highland rural life, history, geology and wildlife.

Glencoe Mountain Resort   97 E4
01855 851226   www.glencoemountain.com
Kingshouse, Glencoe. On the A82, 30 miles (48km) south of Fort William, 12 miles (19km) from station at Bridge of Orchy. Scotland's original ski centre, Glencoe is renowned for its exhilarating skiing and friendly atmosphere. For skiers and boarders of all standards, Glencoe provides on-site facilities including ski and snowboard school and hire departments. A diversity of terrain for snowboarders includes jumps, drop-ins and wide open runs. The chairlift and restaurant are open in summer.

Glencripesdale National Nature Reserve   95 E4
www.snh.org.uk/nnr-scotland/
At the end of a 5 mile (8km) track off the A884 to Liddlesdale. Stunning views from this remote woodland across Loch Sunart with the possibility of seeing otters.

Glendale Toy Museum   114 B5
01470 511240   www.toy-museum.co.uk
Holmisdale House, Glendale, Isle of Skye. 7 miles (11km) west of Dunvegan. A unique display of toys, games and dolls from Bisque to Barbie, Victorian to Star Wars.

Glendronach Distillery   123 F5
01466 730202
Forgue, between Huntly and Inverurie. A traditional malt whisky distillery established in 1825 with its own floor maltings, peat fire and kiln.

Glenelg Brochs   106 B3
01667 460232   www.historic-scotland.gov.uk
About 8 miles (13km) south east of Kyle of Lochalsh. Two Iron Age broch towers, Dun Telve & Dunn Troddan standing over 33ft (10m) high, with well-preserved structural features.

Glenelg Candles Arts & Crafts Centre   106 B3
01599 522313   www.glenelgcandles.co.uk
In Glenelg, 2 miles (3km) from car ferry to Skye and 7 miles (11km) from Shiel Bridge on the A87. A candle workshop where visitors can see demonstrations of handmade Highland landscape candles, or browse among paintings by local artists, books and gifts.

Glenfarclas Distillery   122 B6
01807 500209   www.glenfarclas.co.uk
Glenfarclas, Ballindalloch, on the A95. Established in 1836. Glenfarclas means 'valley of green grass land'. Distillery tours and free tasting.

Glenfiddich Distillery   122 C5
01340 820373   www.glenfiddich.com
On the A941, 0.3 mile (0.5km) north of Dufftown. A distillery, opened in 1887, producing the only Highland single malt whisky that is distilled, matured and bottled at its own distillery. Visitors can tour the distillery. Free sample.

Glenfinnan Monument   106 C6
01397 722250   www.nts.org.uk
Information Centre, Glenfinnan, on the A830, 18.5 miles (30km) west of Fort William. Set amid superb Highland scenery at the head of Loch Shiel, the monument was erected in 1815 in tribute to the clansmen who died for the Jacobite cause. It is on the site where Bonnie Prince Charlie raised his standard in 1745. Displays and audio-visual programme in information centre.

Glenfinnan Station Museum   106 C6
01397 722295   www.road-to-the-isles.org.uk
Station Cottage at Glenfinnan station. Restored station containing a museum illustrating the history of the West Highland railway line through objects and photographs. Steam train runs from the station to Fort William and Mallaig during the summer. Woodland walk and viewpoint.

Glenfinnan Viaduct   106 C6
At Glenfinnan, near Loch Shiel. Spectacular 21 arched railway viaduct built in 1901 and one of the first large constructions made of concrete. The viaduct has featured in the Harry Potter films.

Glengoulandie Country Park 99 E4

01887 830495 www.glengoulandie.co.uk
Glengoulandie, Foss, on the B846, 8 miles (13km)
north west of Aberfeldy. Native animals housed in a
natural environment. Many endangered species are
kept, and there are fine herds of red deer and
Highland cattle.

Glengoyne Distillery 76 C2

01360 550254 www.glengoyne.com
Dumgoyne, Killearn, on the A81, 3 miles (5km)
north of Strathblane. First licensed in 1833, this is
Scotland's most southerly Highland distillery and
the closest to Glasgow. Nestling in the Campsie Hills,
it draws water from a waterfall. The distillery
produces Scotland's only unpeated whisky.
Conducted tours show the main process of distilling.
Heritage Room houses cooperage display, old
artefacts and shop. Visitors taste a dram in
reception room, overlooking dam, glen and
waterfall.

Glenkinchie Distillery 79 F4

01875 342004
2 miles (3km) from Pencaitland on the A6093.
Visitors can see all aspects of the traditional
distilling craft, with sample tasting. Exhibition
includes a scale model of a malt distillery made for
the British Empire Exhibition of 1924.

Glenlivet Distillery 122 A6

01340 821720 www.glenlivet.com
Ballindalloch, about 10 miles (16km) north of
Tomintoul. Situated in one of the most scenic and
romantic glens in the Scottish Highlands. The guided
tour also includes the chance to see inside a vast
bonded warehouse and to sample a dram.

Glenlivet Estate 110 C3

01807 580283 www.glenlivetestate.co.uk
Tomintoul, Ballindalloch. A large Highland estate
encompassing some of the finest landscapes of the
Grampian Highlands. A network of over 60 miles of
waymarked trails. Learn about the history,
countryside, wildlife and management of the area.

Glenluce Abbey 58 C4

01581 300541 www.historic-scotland.gov.uk
Off the A75, 2 miles (3km) north of Glenluce. The
remains of a Cistercian abbey founded circa 1192,
including a handsome early 16th century chapter
house. Includes an exhibition of objets trouvés.
Lovely tranquil setting.

Glenlyon Gallery 88 B1

01887 820202 www.glenlyongallery.com
Boltachan, Aberfeldy, 20 miles (32km) from
Aberfeldy. All works are by Alan B. Hayman who
specialises in wildlife art and sculpture.

Glenfinnan Viaduct

Glenmorangie Distillery Visitor Centre 119 E1

01862 892477 www.glenmorangie.com
On the A9, 0.5 mile (1km) north of Tain. Describes
150 years of the distillery's history. Personal and
informative tours, and free sample.

Glenmore Forest Park & Visitor Centre 110 A3

01479 861220 www.forestry.gov.uk
7 miles (11km) along Ski Road from Aviemore. The
Glenmore Forest Park is situated in the foothills of
the Cairngorm National Nature Reserve. Caravan
and camping site, visitor centre, car parks and picnic
areas. Waymarked walks, off-road cycle routes,
lochside activities, bird watching. Ranger services.
Guided walks and tours.

Glenshee Ski Centre 101 D2

013397 41320 www.ski-glenshee.co.uk
Cairnwell, Braemar. 2000-3504ft (610-1068m)
altitude ski area. 36 runs extending over three
valleys and four mountains with a diversity of
terrain for all standards of skiers and snowboarders.
Britain's largest ski lift system.

Glentrool Visitor Centre 59 E2

01671 840302 www.forestry.gov.uk
Glentrool, 8 miles north of Newton Stewart, 3 miles
west of Loch Trool and Stroan Bridge. The gateway
to Glen Trool, Scotland's largest forest park, covering
18,780 acres (7606ha) of forest, moorland and loch.
Exhibits on Loch Trool.

Glenwhan Gardens 58 C4

01581 400222 www.glenwhangardens.co.uk
Dunragit, off the A75, 6 miles (10km) east of
Stranraer. A beautiful 12 acre (5ha) garden
overlooking Luce Bay and the Mull of Galloway,
begun in 1979 and hewn from the hillside creating
two small lakes. A rich habitat for many tender
species, including alpines, scree plants and conifers.
Woodland with bluebells, snowdrops, specie
rhododendrons, azaleas and shrub roses. A
plantsman's garden. Also rare ducks, guinea fowl
and chickens, and a Primula Arena.

Glover House 113 E4

01224 709303 www.aberdeencity.gov.uk
79 Balgownie Road, Aberdeen. Home of Thomas
Blake Glover, the industrial pioneer who introduced
modern coal mining and shipbuilding methods to
19th century Japan. The house has been restored to
its original Victorian splendour.

Goat Fell 74 C6

01770 302462 www.nts.org.uk
Isle of Arran. Access from Cladach on the A841
Brodick to Lochranza road. At 2866ft (873m), Goat
Fell is the highest peak on Arran, dominating the

skyline of the island and affording impressive views from the top. The climb includes fine rock climbing and ridge walking.

Gordon Highlanders Museum 113 E4
01224 311200
www.gordonhighlanders.com
St Luke's, Viewfield Road, Aberdeen. Striking displays of the regiment's unique collection recalling 200 years of service and gallantry. Housed in the former home and studio of the famous Victorian artist Sir George Reid PRSA.

Gorgie City Farm 79 D3
0131 337 4202
www.gorgiecityfarm.org.uk
51 Gorgie Road, Edinburgh. A 2 acre (1ha) farm with various farm animals, commonly kept pets, herbs, vegetables and a wildlife garden. Special events throughout the year, craft classes, educational workshops and tours. Education centre.

Gracefield Arts Centre 61 F2
01387 262084
Edinburgh Road, Dumfries. Exhibitions of local, national and international contemporary art and craft.

Grain Earth House 147 D2
01856 841815
www.historic-scotland.gov.uk
At Hatston, about 1 mile (2km) north west of Kirkwall, Orkney. A well-built Iron Age earth house with an underground chamber supported on stone pillars.

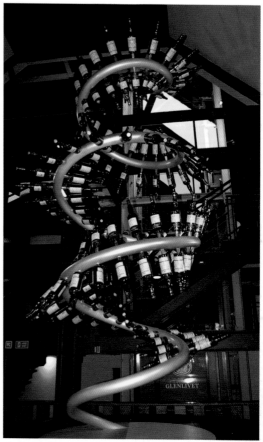
Glenlivet Distillery

Grampian Transport Museum 112 A3
019755 62292
www.gtm.org.uk
Alford, 25 miles (40km) west of Aberdeen. An extensive collection of historic road vehicles housed in a purpose-built hall. Climb-aboard exhibits for children. Driving simulator, video bus featuring motor sport and road transport history.

Grangemouth Museum 78 A2
01324 504699
Victoria Library, Bo'ness Road, Grangemouth. Display relating to the growth of Grangemouth. Exhibits on local industries, canals, shipping and ship building, and the world's first practical steamship, the Charlotte Dundas.

Grantown Museum 110 B2
01479 872478
www.grantownmuseum.co.uk
Burnfield House, Burnfield Avenue, Grantown-on-Spey. Located in a refurbished school originally built in 1865. The permanent exhibition tells the story of Sir James Grant's Town - a fine example of a planned town - bringing the history of Grantown-on-Spey to life through audio-visual and traditional displays.

Grassic Gibbon Centre 103 F2
01561 361668
www.grassicgibbon.com
Arbuthnott, Laurencekirk. Visitor centre dedicated to the life and times of the novelist Lewis Grassic Gibbon (James Leslie Mitchell).

Greenbank Garden 76 C5
0141 639 3281
www.nts.org.uk
Flenders Road, Clarkston, 6 miles (10km) south of Glasgow city centre. Attractive garden surrounding an elegant Georgian house. Wide range of ornamental plants - especially interesting for owners of small gardens.

Greenhill Covenanter's House 68 C2
01899 221050
Burnbraes in Biggar. Farmhouse, rescued in a ruinous condition and rebuilt, 10 miles (16km) from its original site. Exhibits include relics of local Covenanters, Donald Cargill's bed (1681), 17th century furnishings and costume dolls.

Greenknowe Tower 80 B6
0131 668 8600
www.historic-scotland.gov.uk
On the A6089, 0.5 mile (1km) west of Gordon on the Earlston road, Berwickshire. A handsome tower house on an L-plan, built in 1581 and still retaining its iron yett (gate).

Gretna Gateway Outlet Village 63 D3
01461 339100
www.gretnagateway.com
Gretna. Famous name brands in designer fashion at discounted prices. Over 20 outlets covering fashion, sports, gifts and home. Scotland's only outlet store for some brands.

Gretna Hall Blacksmith's Shop 63 D3
01461 337635
www.gretna-green-weddings.com
Gretna Green, 1 mile (1.5km) north of the border with England. Built in 1710, the Gretna Hall blacksmiths has an interesting history associated with weddings, which are still performed here.

Grey Cairns of Camster 137 D5
01667 460232
www.historic-scotland.gov.uk
Off the A9, on the Watten Road, 5 miles (8km) north of Lybster. Two Neolithic chambered burial cairns -

Off the A9, on the Watten Road, 5 miles (8km) north of Lybster. Two Neolithic chambered burial cairns - one long with two chambers and projecting 'horns'; one round with a single chamber.

Grey Mare's Tail Nature Reserve 69 D4
01683 222714   www.nts.org.uk
Adjacent to the A708, 10 miles (16km) north east of Moffat. Spectacular 200ft (61m) waterfall in landscape of geological interest and rich in wild flowers. Herd of wild goats.

Greyfriars Bobby 20 B2
www.greyfriarsbobby.co.uk
By Greyfriars churchyard on the corner of George IV Bridge and Candlemaker Row in Edinburgh. Statue of Greyfriars Bobby, the Skye terrier who, after his master's death in 1858, watched over his grave in the nearby Greyfriars Churchyard for 14 years.

Greyfriars Bobby

Greyfriars Kirk 20 B2
0131 226 5429   www.greyfriarskirk.com
2 Greyfriars Place, in Edinburgh Old Town. Edinburgh's first Reformed Church (1620). On display is the National Covenant (signed at the church in 1638), Scotland's finest collection of 17th and 18th century funeral monuments, fine 19th century windows by Ballantyne, Peter Collins' organ (1990) with carvings of Scottish flora and fauna, memorabilia about Greyfriars Bobby. Millennium window by Douglas Hogg and Millennium kneelers portraying kirk history.

Griselda Hill Pottery 90 C4
01334 828273   www.wemyss-ware.co.uk
Kirkbrae, Ceres, 3 miles (5km) south east of Cupar. Since 1985, the Griselda Hill pottery has revived the production of Wemyss Ware, beautifully hand-painted cats, pigs and other pottery in bright cheerful colours.

Groam House Museum 119 E4
01381 620961   www.groamhouse.org.uk
High Street in Rosemarkie on the A832, 15 miles (24km) north east of Inverness. Award-winning Pictish museum. The centre-piece in a stunning display of locally-found stones is the magnificent 8th century Rosemarkie cross-slab. Part of the nationally important collection of original work by George Bain, the artist responsible for the revival of Celtic art, is also exhibited. Temporary exhibitions of local history or Pictish interest.

HM Customs & Excise Museum & Exhibition 75 F3
01475 726331
Custom House, Custom House Quay, Greenock, 25 miles (40km) west of Glasgow. A magnificent building which has been used as a customs office since its completion in 1819. The museum shows the diverse and colourful history of the organisation and highlights the great variety of work undertaken by the department.

HM Frigate Unicorn 31 C3
01382 200900   www.frigateunicorn.org
Victoria Dock, Dundee. Launched at Chatham in 1824, the Unicorn is the oldest surviving British built warship still afloat. Never used in war she was never fitted out with masts and rigging and still today has the waterproof roof fitted soon after her launch. Visitors have access to four decks which give an idea of the cramped conditions the crew would have lived in.

Hackness Martello Tower 146 C4
01856 811397   www.historic-scotland.gov.uk
At Hackness, at the south east end of the island of Hoy, Orkney. An impressive tower (one of a pair) built between 1813 and 1815 to provide defence against the French and American privateers for the British convoys assembling in the sound of Longhope. Renovated in 1866 and used again in World War I.

Haddo House & Country Park 124 C6
01651 851440   www.nts.org.uk
Ellon, off the B999. Elegant house designed by William Adam in 1731. Much of the interior is Adam Revival, dating from the 1880s. Beautiful library. The adjacent country park features lakes, monuments, walks and wildlife.

Hailes Castle 80 A3
www.historic-scotland.gov.uk
Off the A1, 1.5 miles (2.5km) south west of East Linton. A beautifully-sited ruin incorporating a 13th century fortified manor which was extended in the 14th and 15th centuries. Includes a fine 16th century chapel and two vaulted pit-prisons.

Halistra Pottery 114 B4
01470 592347   www.halistra-pottery.co.uk
Halistra, Waternish, Isle of Skye. Situated on the Waternish peninsula, one of the craft centres of Skye, this is a purpose built gallery and open plan workshop allowing visitors to see the pottery being made. Wonderful views across Loch Dunvegan to the outer isles.

Halliwell's House Museum 70 A3
01750 20096
Market Place in Selkirk, 35 miles (56km) south of Edinburgh. A local museum in a row of 19th century

ironmongery in the country. Based on local history, the museum traces the growth of Selkirk, from the Stone Age to its role as an important textile-producing centre.

Hallmuir POW Chapel 62 B2
Hallmuir Camp, Dalton, Lockerbie. A simple army hut transformed into a chapel by Ukrainian prisoners of war between 1947 and 1950. The chapel is furnished with hand carved statues, crosses and furniture.

Hamilton Mausoleum 77 E5
01698 328232
In the centre of Hamilton, just off the M74. A grandiose family tomb commissioned by the 10th Duke of Hamilton in the 18th century. An enormous cupola, massive bronze doors, an octagonal chapel guarded by stone lions and an Egyptian sarcophagus crowning a marble pedestal. The chapel was never used for worship - it has a notorious resounding echo which lasts for 15 seconds.

Hamilton Park Racecourse 77 E5
01698 283806   www.hamilton-park.co.uk
Hamilton, 15 miles (24km) south east of Glasgow. Daytime, evening and weekend horse race meetings with annual themed events. Public enclosure with access to grandstand. Corporate hospitality.

Hamilton Toy Collection 87 D5
01877 330004
www.thehamiltontoycollection.co.uk
On the High Street in Callander. A family-run toy museum comprising five rooms of toys dating from between 1880 and 1980. Teddy bears, trains (running layout), dolls houses and accessories, cars, bygones, planes, ships, children's books, science fiction toys and associated memorabilia.

Hampden Park Stadium 76 C4
0141 620 4000   www.hampden.org.uk
Hampden Park, Glasgow. Scotland's national football stadium and home of Queen's Park FC. It has retained its oval shape since opening in 1903. Extensive redevelopment in the 1990s brought the capacity to 52,500.

Handa Island 132 C5
01971 502340   www.swt.org.uk
Handa Island, 6 miles (10km) north of Scourie, is internationally famous for its sea bird colonies including the largest breeding colony of guillemots in Britain. The island is also renowned for its magnificent Torridonian Sandstone cliffs, which rise to a height of 400ft (122m) along the dramatic northern edge of the island. The island is reached by ferry boat from Tarbet.

Harbour Cottage Gallery 60 C4
01557 330073
Castlebank, beside the harbour in Kirkcudbright. An 18th century cottage restored and opened in 1957 as a gallery exhibiting the work of artists in Galloway.

Harbour View Gallery 145 F1
01851 810735   www.abarber.co.uk
Near Butt of Lewis, 28 miles (45km) north of Stornoway on the A857. Artist's studio gallery in a scenic location at the northern tip of the Isle of Lewis. Contemporary, original watercolours by island based artist Anthony W. J. Barber. Also prints and cards.

Harestanes Countryside Visitor Centre 70 C3
01835 830306
Ancrum, off the A68, 3 miles (5km) north of Jedburgh. Housed in converted farm buildings and comprising both indoor and outdoor attractions. Changing exhibitions, walk routes and guided walks, activities and events. Wildlife garden and wooden games room. Waymarked walks include view of Waterloo Monument. This prominent landmark on the summit of Peniel Heugh (741 ft/226m high) was built after the battle of Waterloo by the Marquess of Lothian and his tenants. No access to interior.

Harmony Garden 70 B2
01721 722502   www.nts.org.uk
Opposite Melrose Abbey in Melrose. This attractive walled garden was built in the early 19th century, in a fine conservation area. The garden is lovely throughout the seasons, with a rich display of spring bulbs, colourful herbaceous and mixed borders, and fruiting apricots. The garden is set against the beautiful backdrop of Melrose Abbey ruins, with the Eildon Hills in the distance.

Harris Tweed & Knitwear 142 C4
01859 511217
www.harristweedandknitwear.co.uk
4 Plockropool, on Golden Road, 5 miles (8km) south of Tarbert. Visitors can see Harris tweed being woven. Also demonstrations of warping, bobbin winding and wool plying.

Hartmount Woodturning & Cabinet Making Studio 119 E3
01862 842511
Tigh an Fhraoich, Hartmount, off minor road to Scotsburn, 3 miles (5km) south of Tain. Family business (member of the Guild of Master Craftsman) with over 35 years experience. Custom-built woodworking shop and display area. Work produced to client's requirements. Courses throughout the year, one-to-one tuition.

Hawick Museum & the Scott Art Gallery 70 A4
01450 373457
Wilton Lodge Park, Hawick. This 200-year-old mansion house, set in over 100 acres (40ha) of award-winning parkland, houses Hawick's long-established museum and art gallery. A programme of museum and art exhibitions complements permanent displays on local industrial history, natural history, ethnography, domestic bygones and militaria.

Heads of Ayr Farm Park 66 A4
01292 441210   www.headsofayrpark.co.uk
Dunure Road, on the A719, 4 miles (6.5km) south of Ayr. Comprising 125 acres (50.5ha) with beautiful views over the Firth of Clyde. Animals include buffalo, wallabies, rhea and rabbits. Reptile house. Pony and buggy rides. Trampolines, toy tractors. Quad biking. Indoor and outdoor play areas.

Heatherbank Museum of Social Work 16 B1
0141 331 8637   www.lib.gcal.ac.uk/heatherbank
Glasgow Caledonian University, City Campus, Cowcaddens Road, Glasgow. Permanent and temporary exhibition to highlight public awareness of the social welfare needs of society through contemporary and historical issues. Book, picture resources and ephemera. Libraries and archives available for research.

Heathergems 100 B4
01294 313222
22 Atholl Road, Pitlochry. A Scottish jewellery factory and visitor centre. Visitors can see products being made. Seated video area and a large shop.

Hebridean Jewellery 140 C5
01870 610288   www.hebridean-jewellery.co.uk
Located at lochdar at the north end of South Uist near Benbecula. Celtic jewellery shop and workshop. Visitors can see five jewellers working with silver, gold and gemstones. Commissions undertaken.

Hebridean Whale & Dolphin Trust Visitor Centre
95 D4
01688 302620 www.hwdt.org
Tobermory, Isle of Mull. Visitor centre offering information on marine issues and local species. The trust carries out research projects such as eco-tourism and minke whale photo ID and educational activities.

Hermaness National Nature Reserve & Visitor Centre
153 F1
01595 693345 www.snh.gov.uk/nnr-scotland/
Shorestation, Burrafirth, Unst, Shetland. On the B9086, 3 miles (5km) north west of Haroldswick. Overlooking Muckle Flugga, the most northerly point in Britain, this reserve, with dramatic seacliffs and offshore stacks, is a haven for over 100,000 seabirds. The recommended walk takes between 3 and 4 hours. The neighbouring visitor centre is staffed during the summer and is useful for those unable to visit the reserve itself.

Hermitage, The
89 D1
01350 728641 www.nts.org.uk
Off the A9, 2 miles (3km) west of Dunkeld. Interesting walks in mixed woodland. The focus is a delightful folly, Ossian's Hall, in a gorge of the River Braan.

Hermitage Castle
70 A6
01387 376222 www.historic-scotland.gov.uk
In Liddesdale, 5.5 miles (9km) north east of Newcastleton. A vast eerie ruin of the 14th and 15th centuries, consisting of four towers and connecting walls, outwardly almost perfect. Much restored in the 19th century. Associated with the de Soulis family, but with the Douglases after 1341.

Hermitage Park
76 A2
Helensburgh. Formal gardens, play area, putting green, bowling green. Features a memorial bust to John Logie Baird, the inventor of the television, who was born in Helensburgh.

Highland Adventure Safaris
99 F4
01887 820071 www.highlandadventuresafans.co.uk
Drumduin, Aberfeldy. Explore the hills of Perthshire with a ranger led Land Rover safari. Wildlife watching trips and exciting off-road driving experiences available. Corporate bookings and special events can be arranged.

Highland & Rare Breeds Croft
108 A4
01320 366433 www.rarebreedcroft.freeserve.co.uk
Fort Augustus. Footpath walk around enclosed fields containing red deer, highland cattle, various breeds of sheep, goats, pigs, hens and pheasants, ducks and shetland ponies.

Highland Folk Museum, Kingussie
109 E4
01540 661307 www.highlandfolk.com
Duke Street, Kingussie, 12 miles (19km) south west of Aviemore off the A9. An open air museum, partly housed in an 18th century shooting lodge. Features a Black House from Lewis, a clack mill and exhibits of farming equipment. Indoors, a fine display of barn, dairy, stable and an exhibition on Highland tinkers. Special features on costume, musical instruments and Highland furniture. See also the other site of the museum at Newtonmore.

Highland Folk Museum, Newtonmore
109 E5
01540 661307 www.highlandfolk.com
Aultlarie, in Newtonmore off the A9, 15 miles (24km) south west of Aviemore; 65 miles (104km) north of Perth. A fascinating glimpse into 300 years of social history in the Highlands - an 18th century farming township with turf houses authentically furnished with box beds and cruisie lamps; an early 20th century school complete with many of its original fittings; a clockmakers workshop; curling hut and pond; and working croft. See also the other site of the museum at Kingussie.

Highland Mary's Monument
66 C3
At Failford, on the B743, 3 miles (4.5km) west of Mauchline. The monument commemorates the place where, it is said, Robert Burns parted from his Highland Mary, Mary Campbell. They exchanged vows, but she died the following autumn.

Highland Mary's Statue
75 E3
Castle gardens, near Dunoon pier. The statue of Burns' Highland Mary at the foot of the Castle Hill. Mary Campbell was born on a farm in Dunoon and exchanged vows with Burns. However, she died the following autumn and Burns went on to marry Jean Armour.

Highland Museum of Childhood
118 B4
01997 421031
www.highlandmuseumofchildhood.org.uk
The Old Station, Strathpeffer, on the A834, 5 miles (8km) west of Dingwall. Located in part of the old station, the museum tells the story of childhood in the Highlands over the last century. A fascinating collection of over 270 dolls from all over the world and an extensive display of toys and games including Victorian board games.

Highland Wildlife park

Highland Park Distillery
147 D3

01856 874619
www.highlandpark.co.uk
Holm Road, 1 mile (2km) outside Kirkwall, Orkney. A 200 year old distillery and the most northerly whisky distillery in the world. Visitors can tour the distillery and traditional floor maltings (still in use). Most days there is also a kiln burning.

Highland Stoneware
127 D2

01571 844376
www.highlandstoneware.com
Lochinver, Assynt, Sutherland. Highland Stoneware was formed in 1974, and has built an international reputation for quality and innovation. Visitors can watch the craftspeople at work to see the full range of making and decorating skills used in creating their unusual and distinctive pottery.

Hopetoun House

Highland Wildlife Park
109 F4
01540 651270
highlandwildlifepark.org
Kincraig, Kingussie, on the B9152, 7 miles (11km) south of Aviemore. Visitors can discover Scottish wildlife, from native species to those creatures long extinct, and explore themed habitats on foot. Cars can be driven around the main reserve (those without a car will be driven by staff). Brightwater Burn is an otter habitat with walkways and pools. Themed special events at weekends. Managed by the Royal Zoological Society of Scotland.

Highland Wineries
118 C5
01463 831283
www.moniackcastle.co.uk
Moniack Castle, off the A862, 7 miles (11km) west of Inverness. A family business in a 16th-century castle producing country wines, liqueurs, meat and game preserves, all made by hand. Tour, tastings, video and talk by tour guide.

Highlanders Regimental Museum
119 E4
01463 224380
At Fort George, 14 miles (22.5km) east of Inverness. A regimental museum with collections of medals, uniforms and other items showing the history of the Queen's Own Highlanders, Seaforth Highlanders, The Queen's Own Cameron Highlanders, and Lovat Scouts.

Hill House
75 F2
01436 673900
www.nts.org.uk
Upper Colquhoun Street, Helensburgh, off the B832, 23 miles (37km) north west of Glasgow. Charles Rennie Mackintosh designed this house for the publisher Walter Blackie in 1904. A masterpiece of domestic architecture synthesizing traditional Scottish style with avant-garde innovation, this extraordinary building still looks modern today. Mackintosh, with his wife Margaret, also designed the interiors and most of the furniture.

Hill o' Many Stanes
137 D6
01667 460232
www.historic-scotland.gov.uk
At Mid Clyth, 4 miles (6.5km) north east of Lybster. More than 22 rows of low slabs arranged in a slightly fan-shaped pattern, which may have formed a prehistoric astronomical observatory.

Hill Of Tarvit Mansion House & Garden
90 C4
01334 653127
www.nts.org.uk
Off the A916, 2.5 miles (4km) south of Cupar. Fine Edwardian house designed by Sir Robert Lorimer provides a setting for his important collection of French, Chippendale-style and vernacular furniture.

Superb paintings, including works by Raeburn and Ramsay. Formal gardens also designed by Lorimer.

Hilton of Cadboll Chapel
119 F2
01667 460232
www.historic-scotland.gov.uk
At Hilton of Cadboll, 12 miles (19km) north east of Invergordon. The foundation remains of a small rectangular chapel.

Hirsel Country Park
81 D6
01890 882834
www.hirselcountrypark.co.uk
North west Coldstream. Estate of the late Prime Minister Sir Alex Douglas Home. A museum in the grounds depicts the workings of the estate. Crafts centre, lake, picnic area and woodland walks.

Holm of Papa Westray Chambered Cairn
148 C2
01856 841815
www.historic-scotland.gov.uk
On the island of Holm of Papa, Papa Westray, Orkney. A massive tomb with a long narrow chamber divided into three, with 14 beehive cells opening into the walls.

Holmwood House
76 C5
0141 637 2129
www.nts.org.uk
61-63 Netherlee Road, off the B767 in Cathcart, Glasgow. Alexander Greek Thomson, Glasgow's greatest Victorian architect, designed this villa for a local mill owner in 1857. Many rooms are richly ornamented in wood, plaster and marble.

Holyrood Abbey
20 D4
www.historic-scotland.gov.uk
At the foot of Canongate (Royal Mile), Edinburgh, in the grounds of the Palace of Holyroodhouse. The ruined nave of the 12th and 13th century Abbey church, built for Augustinian canons. Administered by the Lord Chamberlain.

Holyrood Park
21 C2
0131 652 8150
www.historic-scotland.gov.uk
East of Holyroodhouse Palace, Edinburgh. There has probably been a royal park here since the Augustinian Abbey was founded in the early 12th century, but it was formally enclosed in 1541 during James V's reign. Within the park is a wealth of archaeology, including the remains of four hill forts, other settlements and round them a fascinating landscape of prehistoric and early-medieval farming activity.

Hopetoun House
78 B3
0131 331 2451
www.hopetounhouse.com
South Queensferry. The residence of the Marquis of Linlithgow. Set in 100 acres (40ha) of magnificent

parkland on the shore of the Firth of Forth with fine views of the famous bridges. Built 1699 - 1707 by William Bruce and extended by William Adam from 1721. Features original furniture, carriage collection, paintings by famous artists, 17th century tapestries, rococo ceilings and Meissen ceramics.

Hoswick Visitor Centre   151 D4
01950 431533
Hoswick, Sandwick, 14 miles (22.5km) south of Lerwick. Previously a weaving shed and now an exhibition of old weaving looms and radios. The history of the area is illustrated with photographs of mining, crofting, fishing and knitting.

House for an Art Lover   76 C4
0141 353 4770   www.houseforanartlover.co.uk
Bellahouston Park, 10 Dumbreck Road, 3 miles (5km) south of Glasgow city centre. A house designed in 1901 by Charles Rennie Mackintosh but not built until 1989-96. Exhibition and film showing the construction. Permanent exhibition of Mackintosh rooms. Sculpture park. Situated in parkland adjacent to magnificent Victorian walled gardens.

House of Dun   103 D4
01674 810264   www.nts.org.uk
On the A935, 3 miles (5km) west of Montrose. Beautiful Georgian house overlooking Montrose Basin, designed in 1730 by William Adam and with superb contemporary plasterwork. Home in 19th century to Lady Augusta Kennedy-Erskine. Many of her belongings remain, as well as her wool work and embroidery. Restored Victorian walled garden and attractive woodland walks.

House of Menzies   88 B1
01887 829666   www.houseofmenzies.com
Castle Menzies Farm, 2 miles out of Aberfeldy on the B846. Situated within an original doocot and cattle court, the House of Menzies features work by contemporary Scottish artists, potters and silversmiths.

House of the Binns   78 B3
01506 834255   www.nts.org.uk
Off the A904, 3 miles (5km) east of Linlithgow. Home of the Dalyell family since 1612. General Tam Dalyell raised the Royal Scots Greys here in 1681. The architecture reflects the early 17th century transition from fortified stronghold to spacious mansion. Elaborate plaster ceilings dating from 1630. Woodland walk to panoramic viewpoint over Firth of Forth. Famous for snowdrops and daffodils in spring.

Howff, The   30 B2
Meadowside, Dundee. An historic graveyard which was formerly the garden of Greyfriars Monastery, gifted to the people of Dundee by Mary, Queen of Scots.

Hoxa Tapestry Gallery   147 D4
01856 831395   www.hoxatapestrygallery.co.uk
Neviholm, Hoxa, Orkney. On Mainland 3 miles (5km) from St Margaret's Hope and 18 miles (29km) south of Kirkwall. The gallery shows the work of Leila Thomson who weaves in the High Gobelin technique. Her theme is the life and the landscape of Orkney. Visitors can watch her weaving, view her work and take tuition courses.

Hoy RSPB Nature Reserve   146 B3
01856 791298   www.rspb.org.uk
Ley House, Hoy, Orkney. RSPB site close to the Old Man of Hoy sea stack. Visitors will see and hear a wide range of birds, including skylarks, sea birds, peregrines and golden plovers. The site contains the highest hill in Orkney, natural field landscapes, lochans and a population of mountain hares. Also Racknier Crofting Museum, the remains of a Bronze

Age settlement and Berriedale, the remnants of Britain's most northerly woodlands.

Hub, The - Edinburgh Festival Centre   20 D4
0131 473 2015   www.thehub-edinburgh.com
348 Castlehill, on the Royal Mile, Edinburgh. The permanent home for the Edinburgh International Festival housed in the former Tolbooth Church. Many of the original, gothic interiors of the church have been maintained and are complemented by new, comtemporary interior design. The centre offers a booking office, exhibition area and café. Special culinary evenings and café concerts.

Hume Castle   80 C6
Hume, on the B6364, 6 miles (9.5km) north of Kelso. A ruined castle, destroyed by Cromwell and partially rebuilt by the Earl of Marchmont. Good views of the Tweed valley and beyond.

Hunter House   77 D4
01355 261261
Maxwelton Road, Calderwood, 3 miles (4.5km) east of East Kilbride town centre. An exhibition about the lives of John and William Hunter, pioneering 18th century medical surgeons. Audio-visual presentation on East Kilbride new town.

Hunterian Art Gallery   76 C4
0141 330 5431   www.hunterian.gla.ac.uk
82 Hillhead Street, in the west end of Glasgow. A prestigious art gallery housing many important works by old masters, impressionists and Scottish paintings from the 18th century to the present day. Includes works by Chardin, Rembrandt and Koninck and Whistler. The print gallery has a changing display from a collection of 15,000 prints. Also houses the Mackintosh House, a reconstructed interior of the architect's own house in Glasgow, using original furniture, prints and designs.

Hunterian Museum   76 C4
0141 330 4221   www.hunterian.gla.ac.uk
University of Glasgow in the west end of Glasgow. Scotland's first public museum was established in 1807 based on the vast collections of Dr William Hunter (1718-83). Many items from his valuable collections are on display.

Huntingtower Castle   89 D3
01738 627231   www.historic-scotland.gov.uk
Huntingtower, off the A85, 3 miles (5km) north west of Perth. A 15th century castellated mansion, known as Ruthven Castle until 1600. Two fine and complete towers, now linked by a 17th century range. There are fine painted ceilings.

Huntly Castle   123 E5
01466 793191   www.historic-scotland.gov.uk
Castle Street, Huntly. A magnificent ruin of a castle from the 12th century motte to the palace erected in the 16th and 17th centuries by the Gordon family. The architectural details and heraldic enrichments are particularly impressive.

Huntly Nordic & Outdoor Centre   123 E5
01466 794428   www.huntly.net/hnoc
Hill of Haugh, Huntly. Cross-country ski centre with year-round artificial ski track suitable for all the family. Fifteen miles (25km) of machine-prepared ski trails. Other activities include rollerskiing and mountain biking.

Huntly Peregrine Wild Watch Centre   123 E5
07880 780431   www.forestry.gov.uk
Bin Forest, 3 miles NW of Huntly on the A96. Visitor centre with wardens on duty, display boards and a television showing live pictures of the Peregrine falcons nesting in the quarry. There's also a hide overlooking the nesting point.

Hutchesons' Hall 16 B2
0141 552 8391 www.nts.org.uk
158 Ingram Street, in Glasgow city centre. Built
1802-5, this is one of the most elegant buildings in
Glasgow. Incorporates statues from an earlier
building (1641) of local philanthropists George and
Thomas Hutcheson. Enlarged in 1876.

Hydroponicum, Garden of the
Future 127 D4
01854 622202 www.thehydroponicum.com
Achiltibuie. A pioneering indoor garden created for
the 21st century, overlooking the beautiful Summer
Isles. Guided tours take visitors around modern
growing houses, each with different climatic zones.
Here lush, sub-tropical fruit trees, exotic flowers,
scented plants, vegetables and herbs all grow
without the use of soil or pesticides.

Iceberg Glassblowing Studio 118 C6
01456 450601
Victoria Buildings, in Drumnadrochit on the A82. A
glass-blowing studio manufacturing both solid and
hollow glassware, mostly small delicate pieces
including vases, Christmas decorations, animals, and
modern jewellery. Visitors can see the
manufacturing process.

Inchcailloch Nature Reserve 76 B1
01389 722100 www.snh.org.uk/nnr-scotland/
On Inchcailloch island, Loch Lomond, opposite
Balmaha. Protected oak woodland of European
importance. The island lies on the highland
boundary fault providing a great opportunity to see
the distinction between the lowland and highland
areas of Loch Lomond. Woodland birds, deer,
bluebell wood. Two miles of waymarked paths,
taking visitors to a beach with picnic and barbecue
facilities.

Inchcolm Abbey 78 C2
01383 823332 www.historic-scotland.gov.uk
On Inchcolm Island in the Firth of Forth. The ruins of
an Augustinian house founded circa 1123 and
including a 13th century octagonal chapter house.

Inchkenneth Chapel 82 C2
www.historic-scotland.gov.uk
On the island of Inch Kenneth off the west coast of
the Isle of Mull. A simple building of a distinctive

Inveraray Jail

west Highland type, with good medieval monuments
in the graveyard.

Inchmahome Priory 86 C5
01877 385294 www.historic-scotland.gov.uk
On an island in the Lake of Mentieth. The beautifully
situated ruins of an Augustinian monastery founded
in 1238, with much 13th century building surviving.
Briefly housed Mary, Queen of Scots as an infant in
1547.

Ingleby Gallery 21 C1
0131 556 4441 www.inglebygallery.com
Carlton Terrace, Edinburgh. Specialises in modern
British and contemporary art, with an emphasis on
painting, sculpture and photography. Artists include
Howard Hodgkin, Andy Goldsworthy, Ian Hamilton
Finlay, Sean Scully and Callum Innes.

Innerpeffray Chapel 88 C4
www.historic-scotland.gov.uk
Innerpeffray, 4 miles (6.5km) south east of Crieff. A
rectangular collegiate church founded in 1508. Still
retains its altar and evidence of its furnishings.

Innerpeffray Library 88 C4
01764 652819 www.innerpeffraylibrary.co.uk
Innerpeffray, on the B8062, 4 miles (6.5km) south
east of Crieff. The first lending library in Scotland,
founded in 1680. A collection of 3000 titles printed
between 1500 and 1800 now housed in a purpose-
built library completed in 1762. Many rare and
interesting volumes.

Insh Marshes RSPB Nature Reserve 109 F4
01540 661518 www.rspb.org.uk
Ivy Cottage, Insh, Kingussie. The most important
area of floodplain wetland in Britain with nearly
1000 pairs of wading birds breeding on the marshes.
This is an important wintering ground for wildfowl,
including whooper swans from Iceland. Varied
wetland plants. Otters. Flower rich meadows,
butterflies and other insects.

International Otter Survival Fund
Information Centre 105 F2
01471 822487 www.otter.org
On the A87 near Broadford on the Isle of Skye.
Guided walks by prior arrangement around the
island, with a description of the history, ecology and
conservation of the otter.

International Purves Puppets 68 C2
01899 220631 www.purvespuppets.com
Biggar Puppet Theatre, Broughton Road, Biggar. A
unique Victorian puppet theatre seating 100 and set
in beautiful grounds. Mysterious glowing scenery,
large-scale puppets, secret passages and magical
starry ceiling. Regular performances in many
languages for all ages. Backstage and museum
tours.

Inveraray Bell Tower 85 E5
01499 302259
The Avenue, Inveraray. This 126ft (38.5m) high
granite tower houses Scotland's finest ring of bells
and the world's second-heaviest ring of ten bells.
Excellent views, pleasant grounds. Opportunities to
see bells and ringers in action. Recordings always
available when tower open. Easy staircase to top
viewing gallery in bell chamber.

Inveraray Castle 85 D5
01499 302203 www.inveraray-castle.com
On the A83, 0.5 mile (1km) north of Inveraray. The
Duke of Argyll's family, the senior branch of the
Campbell Clan, moved from Loch Awe to Inveraray
in the first half of the 15th century. The present
building, in the style of a castle, was erected
between 1745 and 1790 to replace an earlier
traditional fortified keep, and marks the start of
more settled times. On display are the famous

more settled times. On display are the famous collections of armour, French tapestries, fine examples of Scottish and European furniture, and a wealth of other works of art together with a genealogical display in the Clan Room. The Formal Gardens open by appointment only.

Inveraray Jail   85 D5
01499 302381   www.inverarayjail.co.uk
Church Square, Inveraray. Award-winning attraction. Visitors can see a medieval punishment exhibition, listen to trials in the superb 1820 courtroom, visit the airing yards, talk with guides dressed as warders, prisoners and matron, experience life inside prison and try the crank machine, whipping table and hammocks, before comparing all this with a new exhibition In Prison Today.

Inveraray Maritime Museum   85 D5
01499 302213   www.inveraraypier.com
Arctic Penguin, The Pier, Inveraray. A fascinating collection of maritime displays, memorabilia, archive film and entertaining hands-on activities on board one of the last iron ships built (1911). Graphic tableaux in the hold depict the hardships suffered on emigrant ships during the Highland clearances. Scotland's last working Clyde Puffer (a small cargo vessel) takes visitors on a short cruise of Loch Fyne.

Inverbeg Galleries   76 B1
01436 860277   www.inverbeggalleries.co.uk
Inverbeg, Loch Lomond. On the A82, 3 miles (5km) north of Luss. An internationally renowned art gallery with one of the largest selections of oil and watercolour paintings and prints in the UK.

Inveresk Lodge Garden   79 E3
0131 665 1855   www.nts.org.uk
Inveresk. Attractive terraced garden in historic village of Inveresk. Excellent range of roses and shrubs and a beautiful display of colour in autumn.

Inverewe Garden   116 B1
01445 781200   www.nts.org.uk
Poolewe, on the A832, 6 miles (10km) north east of Gairloch. A world-famous garden created from a once-barren peninsula on the shore of Loch Ewe by Victorian gardener Osgood Mackenzie. Exotic plants from many countries flourish here in the mild climate created by the North Atlantic Drift. Spectacular lochside setting among pinewoods, with superb views.

Inverkeithing Museum   78 C2
01383 313838
The Friary, Queen Street, Inverkeithing. Local history of Inverkeithing and Rosyth. Small display on Admiral Greig, founder of the Russian navy.

Inverlochy Castle   97 D2
www.historic-scotland.gov.uk
2 miles (3km) north east of Fort William. A fine well-preserved 13th century castle of the Comyn family in the form of a square with round towers at the corners. The largest tower was the donjon or keep.

Inverness Cathedral   42 B3
Ardross Street, on the west bank of the River Ness, below Ness Bridge, ten minute walk from railway and bus stations. The cathedral church of the Diocese of Moray, Ross and Caithness, the first new cathedral to be completed in Britain since the Reformation. Built 1866 - 69 in the Gothic style to the design of Alexander Ross. Features twin towers with a ring of ten bells, octagonal chapter house, monolithic pillars of polished Peterhead granite, stained glass, sculpture, carved reredos, angel font after Thorvaldsen (Copenhagen), founder's memorial and icons presented by the Tsar of Russia. In beautiful riverside setting.

Inverness Dolphin Cruises   42 B1
01463 717900   www.inverness-dolphin-cruises.co.uk
Shore Street Quay, Shore Street, Inverness. The Moray Firth dolphins are the most northerly population in the world. Inverness Dolphin Cruises operate the M.V. Miss Serenity, which will carry 90 passengers in comfort. The company participates in the International Dolphin Watch programme. A good opportunity to see common and grey seals, porpoise, minke whales, terns, gannets, razor bills, kittiwakes and ospreys.

Inverness Museum & Art Gallery   42 B2
01463 237114
www.invernessmuseum.com
Castle Wynd, Inverness. Displays of natural and human history of Inverness and the Highlands. Features exhibition of Highland and Inverness silver, weapons and musical instruments. Temporary exhibitions and events.

Iona   82 A3
www.nts.org.uk
An island off the south west tip of the Isle of Mull. Car and coach parking at Fionnphort. The island where Columba began to spread the gospel in AD563. Superb long sandy beaches and turquoise seas. Unrivalled views.

Iona Abbey & Nunnery 82 A3
01681 700512
www.historic-scotland.gov.uk
On the Isle of Iona, off the south west tip of the Isle of Mull. Car and coach parking at Fionnphort. The site of St Columba's landing in AD563 and his original monastery. From here Christianity spread throughout Scotland and beyond. A Benedictine monastery was founded in 1203, but it fell into ruin at the Reformation in the 16th century. The cathedral was

Inveraray Maritime Museum

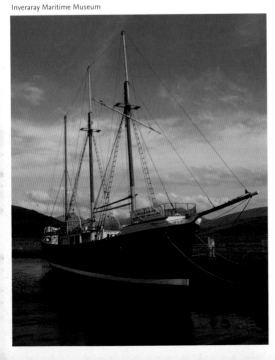

restored in 1910 and has a beautiful interior and carvings. The monastic buildings were later restored by the Iona Community who provide week-long programmes for guests. The abbey precincts contain the graves of many kings and chiefs, the restored St Oran's Chapel, and the 10th century St Martin's Cross.

Iona Gallery & Pottery 82 A3
01681 700439 www.ionagallery.com
Beside Iona Abbey. A working pottery where visitors can see work in progress. Displays both thrown and hand-built decorative stoneware. Late 19th century and early 20th century paintings and etchings, and contemporary landscapes. Also limited edition prints.

Iona Heritage Centre 82 A3
01681 700576
On the Isle of Iona, off the south west tip of the Isle of Mull, 0.3 mile (0.5km) from the ferry. Located in the old Telford Manse. Displays illustrate the lives of the islanders over the past 200 years.

Island Encounter, Wildlife/Birdwatch Safaris 83 D1
01680 300441 www.mullwildlife.co.uk
Located on the Isle of Mull, the Island Encounter wildlife/birdwatch safaris offer whole day trips for visitors wishing to see and experience wildlife and birds in areas of the island not usually visited. Binoculars, telescopes and lunch provided.

Islay Wildlife Information Centre 72 B5
01496 850288 www.islaywildlife.freeserve.co.uk
Port Charlotte, Isle of Islay. Displays on all aspects of Islay's wildlife and landscape, as well as an extensive reference library, a children's room and a laboratory where children and adults can try a number of hands-on activities such as dissecting owl pellets and making seaweed pictures. Family activity sessions during July and August.

Islay Woollen Mill 72 C4
01496 810563 www.islaywoollenmill.co.uk
On the Askaig Road, 1 mile (2km) from Bridgend. An early Victorian mill containing a tweed and woollen factory which produces tartan including all the tartans used in the films Braveheart and Rob Roy.

Isle of Arran Distillery Visitor Centre 74 C6
01770 830264 www.arranwhisky.com
Lochranza, Isle of Arran. 14 miles (22.5km) north of Brodick. This is the newest single malt whisky distillery in Scotland, and has been in production since August 1995. Tours explain how whisky is made. The visitor centre has interactive displays and a short film illustrating whisky production on Arran over the last 150 years. Audio-visual room set in mock 18th century crofter's inn.

Isle of Arran Heritage Museum 65 E2
01770 302636 www.arranmuseum.co.uk
Rosaburn, 1.5 miles (2.5km) north of Brodick Pier. An original 18th century croft farm with smiddy, cottage, coach house and stables. Extensive garden and special display area which is changed annually. Exhibits on shipping, geology, archaeology and local history.

Isle of Bute Discovery Centre 75 D4
01700 502151 www.visitbute.com
Esplanade Gardens, Rothesay. A visitor centre that highlights the cultural and historical heritage of Bute with a mix of multimedia, games and graphics. Genealogy Centre and Discovery Theatre.

Isle of Jura Distillery 73 E5
01496 820240 www.isleofjura.com
Craighouse, Isle of Jura. A distillery built in 1810 on a site where illegal distillation occurred for almost 300 years.

Isle of Mull Landrover Wildlife Expeditions 94 C4
01688 500121 www.torrbuan.com
Ulva Ferry, Tobermory. Explore Mull's wildlife and the island's immensly varied habitats, guided by a Hebridean wildlife expert. Visitors usually see otters, sea eagles, golden eagles, seals, deer, porpoises etc.

Isle of Mull Museum 95 D4
01688 302493
Main Street, Tobermory, Isle of Mull. An exhibition of items, facts and photos of Mull's history.

Isle of Mull Railway 83 F2
01680 812494 www.mullrail.co.uk
In Craignure, 0.25 mile (0.5km) south east of the ferry terminal. Scotland's only (narrow gauge) island passenger railway, running between Craignure and Torosay Castle. Scenic journey lasts 20 minutes. Steam and diesel locomotives.

Isle of Mull Weavers 83 F2
01680 812381 www.isleofmullweavers.com
The Steading, Torosay Castle, Craignure. Weaving demonstrations all day.

Inverewe Garden

Italian Chapel

Isle of Ulva Boathouse Visitor Centre   82 C2
01688 500241   www.ulva.mull.com
Ardalum House, Isle of Ulva. Off the west side of
Mull. Provides information on the history of Ulva
and also the local natural history. There is a restored
thatched croft house and five waymarked walking
trails.

Italian Chapel   147 D3
01856 781279
Lamb Holm, Orkney. On Mainland at St Mary's, 7
miles (11km) south of Kirkwall. Two Nissen huts
transformed into a chapel by Italian prisoners of war
during the construction of the Churchill Barriers in
World War II. A beautiful interior is the result of their
ingenuity and craftmanship. Painting of Madonna
and Child by Domenico Chioccetti.

J. M. Barrie's Birthplace &
Camera Obscura   101 F4
01575 572646   www.nts.org.uk
On A90/A926 in Kirriemuir. Birthplace of J. M.
Barrie, creator of Peter Pan. Exhibition about his
work, with his first theatre also on display. Camera
Obscura, within the cricket pavilion on Kirrie Hill,
presented to Kirriemuir by the author.

Jack Drake's Alpine Nursery
& Gardens   109 F4
01540 651287
                          www.drakesalpines.com
On the B970, 4 miles (6.5km)
south of Aviemore. Show garden
and alpine plant nursery growing
a wide range of alpines, heathers,
dwarf shrubs and dwarf
rhododendrons.

Jacobite   119 D5
01463 233999
              www.jacobite.co.uk
Tomnahurich Bridge,
Glenurquhart Road,1 mile
(1.5km) west of Inverness town

centre on the A82. Cruises and
coach tours in the Loch Ness area
including round trips, one-way
journeys to and from Urquhart
Castle, and combined coach and
cruise tours following the
Caledonian Canal. Enjoy dramatic
scenery along the way. See also
Caledonian Canal and Urquhart
Castle.

Jacobite Steam Train   97 D2
01524 737751 / 3
            www.steamtrain.info
Fort William railway station. This
round trip crosses the famous
Glenfinnan viaduct (stopping at
the village of Glenfinnan), passes
through the country's most
westerly mainland railway
station at Arisaig and the silver
beaches of Morar before reaching
Mallaig. Great views en route of
the Isles of Rum, Eigg, Muck and
Canna, and the southern tip of
Skye.

James Hogg
Monument   69 E4
By Ettrick, 1 mile (1.5km) west of
the B7009. A monument on the
site of the birthplace of James
Hogg (1770 - 1835), a friend of
Scott known as the Ettrick
Shepherd. His grave is in the
nearby church.

James Pringle Weavers   119 D5
01463 223311
Holm Mills, Dores Road. On the B862, 1.5 miles
(2.5km) south west of Inverness. Tartan is woven in
an original mill dating back to 1798. Weave your
own piece of tartan. Also cashmere, lambswool,
tweeds, whisky and golf equipment.

Jarlshof Prehistoric &
Norse Settlement   151 D6
01950 460112   www.historic-scotland.gov.uk
On the A970 at Sumburgh Head, 22 miles (35km)
south of Lerwick. An extraordinarily important site
with a complex of ancient settlements within 3 acres
(1.2ha). The oldest is a Bronze Age village of oval
stone huts. Above this there is an Iron Age broch and
wheelhouses, and even higher still an entire Viking
settlement. On the crest of the mount is a house
built around 1600. The displays explain Iron Age life
and the history of the site.

Jedburgh Abbey   70 C4
01835 863925   www.historic-scotland.gov.uk
Jedburgh. One of the Border abbeys founded by
David I circa 1138 for Augustinian canons. The
remarkable complete church is mostly Romanesque
and early Gothic. The west front has a fine rose

Jacobite Steam Train

window and there is a richly carved Norman doorway. The remains of the cloisters have recently been uncovered and finds from the excavations are displayed. An exhibition portrays life in the monastery.

Jedburgh Castle Jail & Museum   70 C4
01835 863254

Castle Gate, Jedburgh. A refurbished reform prison dating from 1824 standing on the site of Jedburgh Castle which was razed to the ground in the mid 1400s. Designed by Archibald Elliot to principles advocated by John Howard, the prison reformer. New displays in the Jailer's House provide an insight into the development of the Royal Burgh of Jedburgh, while the history of the jail itself is told in the two adjoining cell blocks.

Jedburgh Abbey

Jedburgh Woollen Mill   70 C3
01835 863585

In Jedburgh on the A68, 10 miles (16km) north of the English border. Visitors can trace their clan and tartan at the Clan Tartan Centre - fully authenticated by the Clan Chiefs of Scotland. A world of tartan from small mementoes to full Highland Dress, the choice is immense. Also golf equipment

Jedforest Deer & Farm Park   70 C4
01835 840364

Mervinslaw Estate, Camptown, on the A68, 5 miles (8km) south of Jedburgh. A Borders working farm with sheep, suckler cows, and red deer. Large display of rare breeds, including sheep, cattle, pigs, goats, poultry and waterfowl. Old and new breeds are compared. Emphasis on physical contact with animals and involvement with farm activities. Daily bulletin board, coded walks, adventure land, conservation and wet areas. Birds of prey with daily displays, hawk walks and tuition. Seasonal tractor rides and commentary. Educational resources material and guide book. Ranger-led walks and activities. Crazy golf.

Jim Clark Room   80 C5
01361 883960

44 Newtown Street, Duns, 15 miles (24km) west of Berwick-upon-Tweed. A museum devoted to the twice world motor racing champion, Jim Clark. A collection of trophies, photographs and memorabilia including a video presentation and souvenirs.

John Buchan Centre   69 D2
01899 880258   www.johnbuchansociety.co.uk

Broughton, on the A703, 6 miles (9.5km) east of Biggar and 28 miles (45km) from Edinburgh. The Centre tells the story of John Buchan, 1st Lord Tweedsmuir, author of The Thirty Nine Steps and also lawyer, politician, soldier, historian, and Governor-General of Canada. Broughton village was his mother's birthplace, and a much-loved holiday home.

John Hastie Museum   77 D6
01357 521257

8 Threstanes Road, 6 miles (10km) south of East Kilbride. A local history museum with displays on the town, weaving, commerce, Covenanters, ceramics.

John Knox House   20 D4
0131 556 9579 www.scottishstorytellingcentre.co.uk

43 - 45 High Street, Edinburgh. A picturesque 15th century house associated with John Knox, the

religious reformer, and James Mossman, keeper of the Royal Mint to Mary, Queen of Scots. The house contains many original features including the painted ceiling in the Oak Room, and an exhibition on the life and times of John Knox and James Mossman.

John McDouall Stuart Museum   79 D1
01592 412860

Rectory Lane, Dysart. An exhibition about the great 19th-century explorer of Australia, located in the house where he was born.

John Muir Birthplace   80 B3
01368 865899   www.jmbt.org.uk

126 High Street, Dunbar. The birthplace of John Muir, founding figure of the worldwide conservation movement. He was born in 1838. On the ground floor his father ran a business. His family emigrated in 1849. The flat has been furnished in period style to give an impression of the circumstances in which the family lived, without gas or running water. An audio-visual display tells the story of John Muir, both in Dunbar and the USA.

John Muir Country Park   80 B3

2 miles (3km) west of Dunbar. A coastal conservation area established in 1976 in honour of the conservationist John Muir. The park extends over 8 miles (12km) westward from the ruins of Dunbar Castle, where John Muir played as a boy and

John Knox House

includes rugged cliffs, saltmarshes and the sands of Belhaven Bay. Wildlife includes over 220 species of bird and 12 species of butterfly.

John o' Groats 137 E2
www.visitjohnogroats.com
Usually regarded as the most northerly place in Britain, it is in fact simply the one end of many end-to-end adventures (Land's End to John o' Groats). Dunnet Head a few miles to the west is in fact slightly further north. The settlement is named after Jan de Groot, a Dutch ferryman who settled here in the 16th century.

John Paul Jones Cottage Museum 61 F4
01387 880613 www.jpj.demon.co.uk
Arbigland, Kirkbean, off the A710, 14 miles (22.5km) south of Dumfries. Based around the cottage in which John Paul Jones, the Father of the American Navy, spent his first 13 years before becoming an apprentice in the merchant navy. The original building has been restored to the style of a gardener's cottage of the 1740s, with period furnishings, a replica of the cabin of the Bonhomme Richard, and a room containing a model of John Paul Jones and one of the cannons he is known to have used. The cottage gardens have been laid out in period style. Interpretive display and shop in former kennels.

Johnnie Armstrong's Grave 70 A5
Carlanrig, Teviothead. Take the A7 south from Hawick for 9 miles (14.5km) then turn right on to unclassified road. Memorial is 100 yards (91m) south on left next to churchyard. A stone marker marks the mass grave of the Laird of Gilnockie and his men, hanged without trial by King James V of Scotland in 1530.

Johnstons Cashmere Visitor Centre 122 B3
01343 554099 www.johnstonscashmere.com
Elgin. The only British mill to transform cashmere from fibre to garment. The story of luxury fine fibres interwoven with the 200-year history of the Johnstons is told through an audio-visual presentation, hands-on displays and information boards.

Jura House Walled Gardens 73 D4
01496 820315 www.jurahouseandgardens.co.uk
Ardfin, Craighouse, Isle of Jura. Interesting woodland and cliff walks with points of local historical interest and, for keen natural historians, abundant wildlife and flowers. The organic garden offers a wide variety of unusual plants and shrubs suited to the protected west coast climate, including a large Australasian collection.

Kailzie Gardens 69 E2
01721 720007 www.kailziegardens.com
2.5 miles (4km) east of Peebles on the B7062.

Kelvingrove Art Gallery & Museum

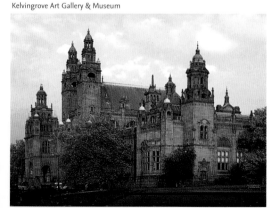

Seventeen acres (6.8ha) of gardens in the beautiful Tweed valley. The 1812 walled garden is semi-formal, with fine herbaceous borders and shrub roses. Formal rose garden and greenhouses. Woodland and burnside walks. Rhododendrons in season. Duck pond and stocked trout pond (rod hire available). Art gallery.

Keen of Hamar National Nature Reserve 153 F2
01595 693345 www.snh.gov.uk/nnr
Keen of Hamar, on the A968, 1 mile (1.5km) east of Baltasound. An important botanical site with unique habitat and landscape. A number of specialist plants grow on the serpentine soil.

Keills Chapel 73 F2
www.historic-scotland.gov.uk
6 miles (9.5km) south west of Tayvallich. A small west Highland chapel housing a collection of grave slabs and Keills Cross.

Keir Hardie Statue 67 D3
Cumnock town centre. Bust outside the Town Hall to commemorate James Keir Hardie (1856 - 1915), an early socialist leader, and founder of the Independent Labour Party in 1893.

Keith & Dufftown Railway 122 C5
01340 821181 www.keith-dufftown.org.uk
Dufftown Station, Dufftown. This picturesque 11mile (18km) branch line has been fully restored and trains can be boarded from either Keithtown Station or Dufftown.

Kelburn Castle & Country Centre 75 F5
01475 568685 www.kelburncountrycentre.com
On the A78, about 2 miles (3km) south of Largs. Historic home of the Earls of Glasgow, and still lived in today. The original Norman keep is now enclosed in a castle built in 1581. A new mansion (Kelburn House) was added to this in 1700, followed later by a Victorian wing. The buildings are surrounded by spectacular natural scenery including waterfalls. Breathtaking views over the Firth of Clyde. Activities include glen walks, riding, assault and adventure courses, and Scotland's most unusual attraction - the Secret Forest, with fantasy follies and hidden secrets. Exhibitions and ranger centre. Special events most weekends.

Kellie Castle & Garden 91 E5
01333 720271 www.nts.org.uk
On the B9171, 3 miles (5km) north of Pittenweem. The oldest part of Kellie Castle dates from 1360, and most of the present building was completed around 1606. It was sympathetically restored by the Lorimer family, who lived here in the 1870s.

Kelso Abbey 71 D2
0131 668 8600 www.historic-scotland.gov.uk
In Bridge Street, Kelso. The west end of the great abbey church of the Tironensians, who were brought to Kelso in 1128 by David I. One of the great Border abbeys - even in its fragmentary state, this is superb architecture.

Kelso Pottery 71 D2
01573 224027
In the centre of Kelso in the large car park behind the abbey. A workshop creating a range of simple, practical stoneware pottery, augmented by pit-fired ware.

Kelso Racecourse 71 D2
01668 280800
www.kelso-races.co.uk
North of Kelso off the A6089. The

first race was held at Kelso in 1822. The course now provides National Hunt racing in picturesque surroundings. Facilities include the original grandstand and two modern stands. Corporate hospitality.

Kelvingrove Art Gallery & Museum 76 C4
0141 276 9599
www.glasgowmuseums.com
Kelvingrove in the west end of Glasgow. This fine national art collection contains superb paintings and sculptures, silver and ceramics, European armour, weapons and firearms, clothing, and furniture. The natural history of Scotland is treated in depth and there are displays of relics from Scotland's history and prehistory. Activities for children and temporary exhibitions.

Kempock Stone 75 F3
Castle Mansions of Gourock. Granny Kempock's stone, of grey schist 6ft (2m) high, was probably significant in prehistoric times. In past centuries it was used by fishermen in rites to ensure fair weather. Couples intending to wed used to encircle the stone to get Granny's blessing.

Kerrachar Gardens 127 E1
01571 833288
www.kerrachar.co.uk
Kerrachar, Kylesku, Sutherland. On the south shore of Loch a' Chairn Bhain. Situated in an extremely remote and beautiful location, Kerrachar is only accessible by a 30 minute boat trip from Kylesku. The gardens contain a wide range of shrubs and perennials, including many unusual species, some of which are for sale. New areas are still under development.

Kerr's Miniature Railway 91 F1
01241 879249   www.geocities.com/kmr_scotland
West Links Park, Arbroath. The oldest miniature railway in Scotland complete with platforms, booking office, footbridge, signal box, turntable and locomotive shed. The 0.5 mile (1km) round trip includes a tunnel.

Kid'z Play 66 B3
01292 475215   www.kidz-play.co.uk
The Esplanade, Prestwick. An indoor adventure play area for children up to 12 years. Soft play adventure area for under 5s.

Kilberry Sculptured Stones 74 A4
www.historic-scotland.gov.uk
At Kilberry Castle off the B8024, 17 miles (27km) south south-west of Lochgilphead, on the west coast of Knapdale. A fine collection of late medieval sculptured stones gathered from the Kilberry estate.

Kilchurn Castle 85 E3
www.historic-scotland.gov.uk
At the north east end of Loch Awe, 2.5 miles (4km) west of Dalmally. A substantial ruin based on a square tower built by Colin Campbell of Glenorchy circa 1550, but much enlarged in 1693 by Ian, Earl of Breadalbane, whose arms are over the gateway with those of his wife. It incorporates the first purpose built barracks in Scotland. Spectacular views down Loch Awe. Access by boat only, phone 01866 833333.

Kildalton Cross 73 D6
www.historic-scotland.gov.uk
On the island of Islay, 2 miles (3km) east north-east of Port Ellen. The finest intact High Cross in Scotland, carved in the late 8th century.

Kilchurn Castle

Kildonan Museum 139 D1
01878 710343
8 miles (13km) north of Lochboisdale on the A865 to Lochmaddy, South Uist. Recently renovated, the museum displays information on local history. Craft shop. Occasional music performances in the evening, see local notices for details.

Kildrummy Castle 111 F3
01975 571331
www.historic-scotland.gov.uk
Kildrummy. Called the Queen of Highland castles, this was the headquarters for organising the 1715 Jacobite rising. Scotland's most complete 13th century castle.

Kildrummy Castle Gardens 111 F3
019755 71277
www.kildrummy-castle-gardens.co.uk
Off the A97, 10 miles (16km) west of Alford. The shrub and alpine garden in an ancient quarry are of interest to botanists for their great variety.

Kilmartin House Museum of Ancient Culture 74 B1
01546 510278   www.kilmartin.org
Kilmartin, on the A816, 9 miles (14.5km) north of Lochgilphead. Award-winning archaeological museum which examines the relationship between Scotland's richest prehistoric landscape and its people. Ancient monuments, local artefacts and bookshop.

Kilmartin Sculptured Stones 74 B1
www.historic-scotland.gov.uk
In Kilmartin Churchyard, Kilmartin, on the A816, 9 miles (14.5km) north of Lochgilphead. Carved west Highland grave slabs housed in a former mausoleum and in the church. One cross dates from the 16th century.

Kilmichael Glassary
Cup & Ring Marks 74 B1
www.historic-scotland.gov.uk
Kilmartin Glen. Near the schoolhouse in the village of Kilmichael Glassary, 5 miles (8km) north of Lochgilphead. Bronze Age cup and ring carvings on a natural rock outcrop.

Kilmorack Gallery 118 B5
01463 783230   www.kilmorackgallery.co.uk
Old Kilmorack Church, 2 miles (3km) west of Beauly along the Cannich road. Exhibition and sale of work by the Highland's leading artists. The gallery is housed in a spectacular 18th century church which remains largely unchanged since it was re-cast in 1835.

Kilmory Knap Chapel 74 B2
www.historic-scotland.gov.uk
On the shore between Loch Sween and Loch Caolisport in South Knapdale. A small medieval west Highland church with a collection of typical grave slabs. In the church is Macmillan's Cross, a splendid piece of medieval carving.

Kilmory Woodland Park 74 A3
01546 602127   www.gardens-of-argyll.co.uk
On the A83, 2 miles (3.2km) from the centre of Kilmory. The garden was started in the 1770s and included around 100 varieties of rhododendron - it supplied plants for Kew Gardens. Now attached to the local council buildings, the gardens have been restored, with woodland walks, nature trails, herbaceous borders and a sensory trail.

Kilmun (St Munn's) Church 75 E2
01369 703760   www.cowalshorechurches.org.uk
Kilmun, 6 miles (10km) from Dunoon on the A880. On the site of a 7th century Celtic monastery. The tower of a 15th century collegiate church still stands. The present building by Thomas Burns dates from 1841, with the interior re-modelled in 1899. Important stained glass. Water-powered organ. Ancient graveyard including fine 18th century carved stones. Mausoleum of Dukes of Argyll. Douglas vault. Grave of Elizabeth Blackwell, the first lady doctor.

Kilpatrick Dun 65 D2
0131 668 8600   www.historic-scotland.gov.uk
1 mile (2km) south of Blackwaterfoot, Isle of Arran. The ruins of a circular drystone homestead of unknown date, with a more recent enclosure wall.

Kilt Rock 115 E3
Off the A855, 17 miles (27km) north of Portree, Skye. 200ft (60m) high cliffs that look like the pleats of a kilt due to the way the rocks have been formed. A waterfall plunges down the cliffs into the sea.

Kilwinning Abbey 76 A6
0131 668 8600   www.historic-scotland.gov.uk
The ruins of a Tironensian-Benedictine abbey. Most of the surviving fragments, which consist of parts of the church and chapter house, appear to date from the 13th century.

King's Cave 64 C2
2 miles (3.2km) north of Blackwaterfoot, Arran. Reputedly the cave where Robert the Bruce was inspired by the determination of a spider in 1306.

King's Knot 77 E1
www.historic-scotland.gov.uk
Below the Castle Rock in Stirling. The earthworks of a splendid formal garden, probably made in 1628 for Charles I.

Kinkell Church 112 C3
01667 460232   www.historic-scotland.gov.uk
2 miles (3km) south of Inverurie. The ruins of a 16th century parish church with a fine sacrament house

dated 1524 and the grave slab of Gilbert of Greenlaw.

Kinloch Forest & Letir Fura Walk 105 F3
01320 366322   www.forestry.gov.uk
4 miles (6km) south of Skalamus at Sleat, Isle of Skye. Letir Fura is a ruined township located in Kinloch Forest, a fine example of native woodland. The 4 mile (6km) walk overlooks the Sound of Sleat providing excellent views and good opportunities to see local wildlife.

Kinlochlaich Gardens 84 C1
01631 730342   www.kinlochlaich-house.co.uk
Kinlochlaich House, on the A828, entrance beside the police station at Appin. A walled garden behind Kinlochlaich House surrounded by mature trees in outstanding Highland scenery. Built with the house at the end of the 18th century by John Campbell.

Kinneil House 78 A3
www.historic-scotland.gov.uk
On the western outskirts of Bo'ness. A 15th century tower set in a public park. Remodelled by the Earl of Arran between 1546 and 1550 and transformed into a stately home for the Dukes of Hamilton in the 1660s.

Kinneil Museum 78 A2
01506 778530
2 miles (3km) west of Bo'ness town centre. Displays on the history of Kinneil Estate and the social history of Bo'ness.

Kinnoull Hill Woodland Park 89 E3
01350 727284   www.forestry.gov.uk
1 mile (1.5km) east of Perth. Comprising five hills (Corsiehill, Deuchny Hill, Barnhill, Binn Hill and Kinnoull Hill). Kinnoull Hill, the highest and most impressive, offers spectacular views over the Ochil and Lomond hills.

Kinross House Gardens 89 E5
01577 862900   www.kinrosshouse.com
Kinross. Kinross House was built by the Surveyor General and Architect to Charles II, Sir William Bruce, as his own home and is one of the finest examples of late 17th century architecture in Scotland. It is set in formal walled gardens with rose gardens, yew hedges, topiary and herbaceous borders.

Kinsman Blake Smailholm Pottery 70 C2
01573 460666
Barn House, Smailholm. On the A68, 6 miles (9.5km) east of St Boswells. A small family pottery where visitors are welcome in the workshop to view demonstrations. Specialists in decorative techniques. Well-stocked showroom.

Kintail & Morvich 107 D3
01599 511231   www.nts.org.uk
16 miles (26km) east of Kyle of Lochalsh, north off the A87. A west Highland estate which includes the Falls of Glomach and the Five Sisters of Kintail, four of which are over 3000ft (914.5m). The site of the Battle of Glen Shiel, which took place in 1719, is within this area, 5 miles (8km) from Morvich. The best access to the mountains is from the Countryside Centre at Morvich.

Kippen Parish Church 77 D1
www.fkkt.org.uk
Fore Road, Kippen, off the A811, 9 miles (14.5km) west of Stirling. A church built in 1824, but modernised in 1924 under the guidance of Sir D. Y. Cameron RA. He and others donated works of art which, with distinguished Webster Windows, make it one of the most beautiful churches in Scotland.

Kirbuster Farm Museum 146 B1
01856 771268
Birsay, mainland Orkney. The farm museum is

based around a traditional rural dwelling with a central hearth and stone bed. Surrounding farm buildings and displays give an insight into Orkney farm life in days gone by. The museum includes a collection of farm implements and machinery and a cottage garden.

Kirk of Calder   78 B3
www.kirkofcalder.com
Mid Calder. This 16th century parish church won the West Lothian award for conservation in 1992. Famous visitors include John Knox, David Livingstone, Frederick Chopin and James 'Paraffin' Young. Fine stained glass windows. Visitors can learn about four centuries of Scottish history.

Kirk of St Nicholas   37 C2
01224 643494   www.kirk-of-st-nicholas.org.uk
Aberdeen. 15th century vaulted lower church, 18th century West Kirk, retaining its characteristic reformed layout, 19th century East Kirk, medieval effigies, medieval and 17th century carved woodwork, 17th century needlework, 48-bell carillon.

Kirkaig Falls   127 E3
Inverkirkaig, south of Lochinver. Popular beauty spot and walk, a 5 mile round trip from Inverkirkaig car park.

Kirkcaldy Museum & Art Gallery   79 D1
01592 412860
War Memorial Gardens, Kirkcaldy. A collection of fine and decorative arts of local and national importance. There is an outstanding collection of 18th-20th century Scottish paintings and probably the largest public collection of works (outside the National Galleries of Scotland) by William McTaggart and the Scottish colourist S. J. Peploe. There is also an award-winning museum display, Changing Places, which tells the story of the social, industrial and natural heritage of the area.

Kirkmadrine Early Christian Stones   58 B5
0131 668 8600   www.historic-scotland.gov.uk
In the Rhinns of Galloway, 2 miles (3km) south west of Sandhead. Three of the earliest Christian memorial stones in Britain, dating from the 5th or early 6th century, displayed in the porch of a former chapel.

Kirriemuir Gateway to the Glens Museum   101 F4
01575 575479
Kirriemuir. Housed in Kirriemuir's oldest building (1604). Exhibitions on Kirriemuir, with a stunning model of the town circa 1604. Also features on the western Angus Glens including a Highland wildlife display full of birds and animals.

Kirroughtree Visitor Centre   60 A3
01671 402165   www.forestry.gov.uk
Galloway Forest Park, Stronord, Newton Stewart. The visitor centre runs various activities during the year. Also waymarked cycle trails, walks and a forest drive.

Kisimul Castle   138 C4
01871 810313   www.historic-scotland.gov.uk
On a tiny island in the bay of Castlebay, Isle of Barra. For many generations, Kisimul was the stronghold of the Macneils of Barra, widely noted for their lawlessness and piracy. The castle is at least 550 years old. Restoration was commenced in 1938 by Robert Lister Macneil of Barra and completed in 1972.

Knap of Howar   148 B2
01856 872044   www.historic-scotland.gov.uk
On the west side of the island of Papa Westray, Orkney. Probably the oldest standing stone houses in north west Europe. Two Neolithic dwellings, approximately rectangular with stone cupboards and stalls.

Knapdale Forest   74 B1
www.forestry.gov.uk
Near Lochgilphead, Argyll. The name Knapdale is derived from Cnap (hill) and Dall (field). The forest is flanked to the north by the Crinan Canal and to the west by the Sound of Jura and Loch Sween. Historical and archaeological sites include ancient Castle Dounie. Waymarked walks and cycle rides, from where seals, otters and porpoises can be seen.

Knock of Crieff   88 B3
Within a short walk from the centre of Crieff. A mixed woodland site located in beautiful Strathearn.

Knocknagael Boar Stone   119 D5
01667 460232   www.historic-scotland.gov.uk
In Highland Council Offices, Glenurquhart Road, Inverness. On ground floor of council chambers. A rough slab incised with the Pictish symbols of a mirror-case and a wild boar.

Knowe of Yarso Chambered Cairn   147 D1
01856 841815   www.historic-scotland.gov.uk
On the island of Rousay, Orkney. A Neolithic oval cairn with concentric walls enclosing a chambered tomb divided into three compartments.

Kylerhea Otter Haven   106 A3
01320 366322   www.forestry.gov.uk
Kylerhea on the Isle of Skye is a superb place for otters - and from the hide you may be lucky enough to see them. Specially constructed paths are designed to protect the habitat and the wildlife, and visitors should keep to the designated paths and leave the shoreline undisturbed. Success in seeing an otter will be mostly down to your own skills in field craft, an element of luck, and patience. As well as otters, there are falcons, waders, sea birds and seals in the area.

Kyles of Bute   74 C3
Narrow arm of the Firth of Clyde, between Isle of Bute and Argyll. A 16 mile (25.5km) stretch of water which presents a constantly changing view of great beauty. It can perhaps be best appreciated from the A8003, Tighnabruaich to Glendaruel road, where there are two view indicators. The western indicator (Scottish Civic Trust) looks over the West Kyle and identifies many features. The east one (NTS) looks over Loch Ridden and the East Kyle.

Lady Gifford Statue   78 C5
Village clock, in West Linton, 17 miles (27km) south south-west of Edinburgh. A replica statue of Lady Gifford on the front of the village clock at West Linton. The original, now in the Graham Institute in West Linton, was carved in 1666 by the Laird Gifford, a Covenanter and skilled stonemason. The clock is on the site of a well, disused since Victorian times. Laird Gifford also executed panels (1660 and 1678) on a house opposite, depicting Lady Gifford and the entire family genealogy.

Lady Mary's Walk   88 B3
Walk from the centre of Crieff. A favourite walk of Lady Mary Murray, whose family owned the surrounding land in the early 19th century. It provides a peaceful stroll beside the picturesque River Earn, along an avenue of mature trees.

Ladykirk   81 D6
4 miles (6.5km) east of Swindon and 0.5 miles (0.5km) from Norham off the B6470. Ladykirk was built in 1500 by James IV, in memory of Our Lady who had saved him from drowning. As the border was only 300 yards away and in constant dispute, he ordered it built to withstand fire and flood - hence the all-stone construction of the kirk with no wooden

rafters and, until this century, stone pews. The Wardens of East March met regularly in the parish to resolve disputes between Scotland and England. In 1560, a copy of the last peace treaty between them was signed in Ladykirk, marking the end of sporadic warfare.

Lael Forest Garden   117 E1
01463 791575   www.forestry.gov.uk
6 miles (9.5km) south of Ullapool on the A835 to Inverness. Extending to 17 acres (7ha), the garden was set aside in 1933 for interesting and ornamental trees of native and foreign origin. The oldest specimen trees were planted around 1870 and there are now some 150 different trees and shrubs.

Lagavulin Distillery Visitor Centre   72 C6
01496 302730
Port Ellen on the Isle of Islay. 3 miles (5km) from the ferry on the A846. Home of the famous Lagavulin single malt, established in 1816. The distillery is set beside the ruins of Dun Naomhaig Castle, ancient stronghold of the Lords of the Isles. Tours and tastings.

Laggangairn Standing Stones   59 D2
0131 668 8600   www.historic-scotland.gov.uk
At Killgallioch, New Luce on the Southern Upland Way. Two stones carved with early Christian crosses.

Laidhay Croft Museum   131 E1
01593 731244
Laidhay, on the A9, 1 mile (2km) north of Dunbeath. An early 18th century croft complex with stable, dwelling house and byre under one rush thatched roof. Separate cruck barn with winnowing doors. Completely furnished in period style. Crofting hand tools, machinery and harness on view.

Laing Museum   90 B4
01337 883017
Newburgh, Fife. The museum was gifted to the town by Alexander Laing, and first opened in 1896. One gallery is devoted to Laing and his collections while the other holds temporary exhibitions with a local flavour.

Lamont Memorial   75 E3
Dunoon. Stone Celtic Cross erected in 1906 to mark the massacre of the Lamonts by the Campbells in 1646.

Land, Sea & Islands Centre   105 F6
01687 450263   www.arisaigcentre.co.uk
Arisaig. An exhibition celebrating the social and natural history of the area. Photographic displays and artefacts relating to the community, crofting, fishing, marine life and the special operations forces who trained here during World War 2. The centre is located on the site of a derelict smithy and the display includes a renovated forge.

Landmark Forest Theme Park   110 A2
0800 731 3446   www.landmark-centre.co.uk
Carrbridge, on the B9153 (old A9), 7 miles (11km) north of Aviemore. Scotland's most exciting heritage park with wild watercoaster ride, nature trail, treetop trail, Clydesdale horse, steam-powered sawmill demonstrations, forestry skill area, viewing tower, maze, adventure play area and microworld exhibition.

Laphroaig Distillery   72 C6
01496 302418   www.laphroaig.com
Port Ellen on the Isle of Islay. A working distillery illustrating the whisky making process in depth.

Largs Museum   75 F5
01475 687081
Kirkgate House, Manse Court, Largs. The museum

holds a small collection of local bygones and a library of local history books and photographs, put together by the local history society. Holds the key to Largs Old Kirk, adjacent, which belongs to Historic Scotland.

Largs Old Kirk   75 F5
01475 672450   www.historic-scotland.gov.uk
In Bellman's Close, off High Street in Largs. A splendid mausoleum with a painted ceiling illustrating the seasons. Added to the parish church in 1636 by Sir Robert Montgomerie of Skelmorlie. Contains an elaborate carved stone tomb in Renaissance style.

Last House in Scotland Museum   137 E2
01955 611250
John o' Groats, Caithness. A local history museum featuring photographs and a collection of artefacts. Also photographs of shipwrecks in the Pentland Firth, Scapa Flow and views of Stroma. All postcards purchased are stamped with the Last House in Scotland and John o' Groats' postmarks.

Laurence Broderick Sculpture Exhibition   106 A3
01767 650444   www.laurencebroderick.co.uk
Gallery An Talla Dearg, Eilean Iarmain, Isle Ornsay, Isle of Skye. On the A851 between Broadford and Armadale, 8 miles (13km) from Broadford. A gallery displaying the work of the sculptor, especially carvings of otters. Work in various stones, including Skye marble, and in bronze. Sculptor usually available to discuss his work and to do demonstrations.

Lauriston Castle   79 D3
0131 336 2060   www.cac.org.uk
Cramond Road South, Edinburgh. Set in 30 acres (12ha) this 16th century tower house with extensive 19th-century additions was built about 1590 by Archibald Napier whose son John invented logarithms. In the early 18th century Lauriston was owned by financier John Law who held high office in the court of pre-revolution France. The last private owners were the Reid family, and the castle contains William Reid's extensive collections of furniture and antiques - a snapshot of the interior of a Scottish country house in the Edwardian era.

Leadhills & Wanlockhead Railway   68 A4
01573 223691   www.leadhillsrailway.co.uk
Leadhills, 6 miles (9.5km) from the M74. Britain's highest adhesion railway, reaching 1498ft (456.5m) above sea level. Originally built in 1900 for the transport of refined lead to central Scotland. The diesel hauled journey takes approximately 25 minutes through picturesque countryside.

Leadhills Miners' Library   68 A4
01659 74456   www.lowtherhills.fsnet.co.uk
15 Main Street, Leadhills. The lead miners' subscription library established in 1741 with rare books, detailed 18th century mining documents and local records.

Lecht, The   111 D3
01975 651440   www.lecht.co.uk
Lecht 2090, Strathdon. 2090-2500ft (640-823m) altitude ski area. 20 runs. Snowboarding funpark. Dedicated snowtubing area. Summer activities include dry ski/snowboard slope, Deval karting track, quad bike circuit and chairlift ride.

Ledmore & Migdale Wood   119 D1
                          www.wt-woods.org.uk
Spinningdale, between Dornoch and Bonar Bridge on the A949. One of the largest oakwoods and colony of juniper bushes in the north of Scotland. Also Scots pine, birch, hazel, willow, and ash trees. An area of great archaeological interest - to date 28 different

features have been recorded, including several chambered cairns dating from over four thousand years ago. There are also waymarked trails.

Leighton Library   87 E5
01786 822296

In the centre of Dunblane, 0.25 mile (0.5km) from the station. One of the oldest libraries in Scotland, dating from 1684. Robert Leighton (1611 - 1684) Bishop of Dunblane and later Archbishop of Glasgow left his collection of 1400 books with instructions that they were to be available for the use of the clergy and provided money for a chamber to be built to house the collection. The library later became a subscription lending library from 1734 to circa 1840, with the collection increasing to 4500 books, mainly first editions.

Leisure Marine   116 B6
01599 544306
www.lehnanet.com/leisuremarine/

32 Harbour Street, Plockton, 6 miles (9.5km) north of Kyle of Lochalsh. Calum's Seal Trips at Plockton, made famous by the television programme Hamish Macbeth. Views of seals guaranteed, or money back. Spectacular scenery. Boat hire and private charter.

Leith Hall, Garden & Estate   112 A2
01464 831216   www.nts.org.uk

Huntly, on the B9002. Mansion house in a 286 acre (116ha) estate which was home to the Leith family for 300 years. Exhibition on family's military history.

Lennoxlove House   80 A3
01620 823720   www.lennoxlove.org

Lennoxlove Estate, on the B6369, 1 mile (2km) from Haddington. The home of the Duke of Hamilton. It features a 14th century keep originally built for Maitland of Lethington, Secretary of State to Mary, Queen of Scots, and houses mementos belonging to Mary, together with furniture, paintings and porcelain once part of the Hamilton Palace collection.

Lerwick Town Hall   151 D2
01595 744505   www.shetland.gov.uk

In Lerwick town centre on a commanding site on the ridge in the older part of the town known as Hillhead. The chief attraction is the series of stained glass windows representing leading personalities in the early history of the islands, from Norwegian inhabitation in the 9th century to the pledging of the islands to Scotland in 1469.

Letham Glen   90 C5

On the A915, Sillerhole Road on the outskirts of Leven. The nature centre displays information and pictures about wildlife. Nature trail through the glen.

Levegrove Park   76 A3

Dumbarton. Beautiful open park stretching to the shores of the River Clyde. Formal flower gardens and magnificent trees. Contains the ruins of an old parish church and the burial place of the Dixon family. Putting green, crazy golf.

Lewis Loom Centre   145 E4
01851 704500

3 Bayhead, Stornoway, Isle of Lewis. An enjoyable introduction to the history of Harris tweed. Information on sheep breeds, plant dyes, hand spinning, looms and all aspects of producing finished cloth. Craft shop selling mostly local produce, tweeds and knitwear.

Leyden Obelisk & Tablet   70 B4

Denholm, on the A698 north east of Hawick. The village was the birthplace of John Leyden (1776-1811), poet, orientalist and friend of Sir Walter Scott. An obelisk was set up in 1861 and a tablet on a thatched cottage records his birth there. Another famous son of Denholm was Sir James Murray, editor of the Oxford English Dictionary, whose birth is commemorated on a tablet on a house in Main Street, Denholm.

Liddesdale Heritage Centre   63 E1
01387 375259
www.liddesdaleheritagecentre.scotshome.com

Townfoot Kirk, South Hermitage Street, Newcastleton. Liddesdale Heritage Association is a voluntary community group who run Liddesdale Heritage Centre and Museum in the former Congregational Church (built in 1804) within the planned village of Newcastleton (built 1793). Displays on the history of Liddesdale and its people, and a unique commemorative bicentenery tapestry. Many books and articles on the Borders region. Facilities available for genealogical research. Waverley Line railway memorabilia.

Lighthouse, The   16 B2
0141 221 6362
www.thelighthouse.co.uk

11 Mitchell Lane, in Glasgow city centre. The Lightouse is Scotland's Centre for Architecture, Design and the City and is the long term legacy of Glasgow 1999 UK City of Architecture and Design. It is the imaginative conversion of Charles Rennie Mackintosh's first public commission. Mackintosh Interpretation Centre, interactive play environment for young children, IT hotspot and the Young Designers Gallery.

Lime Tree Studio Gallery   97 D2
01397 701806   www.limetreefortwilliam.co.uk

The Old Manse, Achintore Road, Fort William. Houses a continually changing exhibition of landscape paintings, mainly of north west Scotland. Extensive workshop programme and stained glass exhibition. Accommodation also available.

Lincluden Collegiate Church   61 F2
0131 668 8600   www.historic-scotland.gov.uk

In Abbey Lane, on western outskirts of Dumfries, 1 mile (2km) from the A76. The rich remains of a collegiate church founded in 1389 by Archibald the Grim, 3rd Earl of Douglas. The splendid chancel was probably added by his son, Archibald, the 4th Earl, and houses the exquisite monumental tomb of his wife, Princess Margaret, daughter of King Robert III.

Lindean Mill Glass   70 A2
01750 20173   www.lindeanmillglass.co.uk

Lindean Mill, Galashiels, 1 mile (2km) north of Selkirk. Scotland's premier glass studio where visitors can watch glassware being made by hand. Shop.

Linlithgow Canal Centre   78 A3
01506 671215   www.lucs.org.uk

Canal Basin, Manse Road, Linlithgow. On the Edinburgh and Glasgow Union Canal with small museum in former stable. Boat trips on the Victoria (1/2 hour town trip) and St Magdalene (2 1/2 hour trip to Avon Aqueduct).

Linlithgow Palace   78 B3
01506 842896   www.historic-scotland.gov.uk

Kirkgate, Linlithgow. The ruin of a great royal palace beside Linlithgow Loch. The Great Hall and Chapel (late 15th century) are particularly fine. The quadrangle has a richly-carved 16th century fountain. A favoured residence of the Stewart monarchs from James I. Works commissioned by James I, III, IV, V and VI can be seen. Both King James V and Mary, Queen of Scots were born here.

Linlithgow Story, The   78 A3
01506 670677   www.linlithgowstory.org.uk

Annet House, 143 High Street, Linlithgow. A small museum of local history which tells the story, not only of the Stewart kings of Scotland who built and

Loch Eriboll

lived in Linlithgow Palace, but also of the ordinary people who lived and worked in the burgh. Housed in a late 18th century merchant house.

Linn Botanic Gardens & Nursery 75 F2
01436 842242

Cove, Helensburgh, on the B833, 10 miles (16km) from Garelochhead. A garden developed since 1971 around a listed Clyde coast villa in the style of Greek Thompson. Thousands of unusual, exotic and rare plants, extensive water garden, formal ponds and fountains, herbaceous borders, glen with waterfall, cliff garden and rockery.

Linn of Tummel 100 B3
01796 473233 www.nts.org.uk

Walk from Garry Bridge, 2.5 miles (4km) north of Pitlochry on the B8019. Follow a riverside nature trail through mixed woodland to the meeting place of the Rivers Garry and Tummel. The Linn of Tummel (pool of the tumbling stream) comprises a series of rocky rapids in a beautiful setting.

Literary Pub Tour 20 B2
0131 226 6665 www.edinburghliterarypubtour.co.uk

The Beehive Inn, Grassmarket, Edinburgh. This two hour promenade performance, led by professional actors, begins at the Inn and follows a route through the streets and old taverns. Scotland's great poets, writers and colourful characters from the past 300 years are described, from Robert Burns and Walter Scott to Muriel Spark and Trainspotting.

Little Gallery 114 C6
01478 640254 www.the-little-gallery.co.uk

7 Portnalong, Isle of Skye, 3 miles (5km) west of Talisker distillery on the B8009. Overlooking Loch Harport, the gallery displays etchings, prints and watercolours depicting the Cuillin, Skye landscapes and the native flora and fauna.

Loanhead Stone Circle 112 C2
01667 460232 www.historic-scotland.gov.uk

Near Daviot, 5 miles (8km) north west of Inverurie. The best known of a group of recumbent stone circles about 4000 to 4500 year old. Encloses a ring cairn.

Loch-an-Eilein Pottery 109 F4
01479 810837 www.penspots.co.uk

Rothiemurchas, 3 miles (5km) south west of

Aviemore on the Loch-an-Eilein road. Small rural craft pottery making terracotta domestic wares, glazed in blues and greens. The pottery is situated on the Rothiemurchus estate near Aviemore. Hands-on make your own pot activity on Tuesdays and Thursdays.

Loch Awe Steam Packet 85 E3
01866 833333

25 miles (40km) east of Oban and 2 miles (3km) west of Dalmally on the A85. Steamboat rides to Kilchurn Castle and cruises around Loch Awe on the steamers Lady Rowena and the Flower of Scotland.

Loch Doon Castle 66 C6
0131 668 8600 www.historic-scotland.gov.uk

Off the A713, 10 miles (16km) south of Dalmellington. An early 14th century castle with an eleven-sided curtain wall of fine masonry. Once known as Castle Balliol. Originally it stood on an island in Loch Doon but it was moved to its present site in the 1930s before its original site was flooded during the construction of a hydro-electric scheme.

Loch Eriboll 133 F4

Situated between Tongue and Durness in the north of Sutherland. Reputedly the deepest sea loch or inlet in Britain. Both the loch itself and its shores are steeped in history. Despite the inhospitable landscape of today, archaeological remains indicate that people have lived here for at least the last 4000 years.

Loch Garten Osprey Centre 110 A3
01479 831476 www.rspb.org.uk

Off the B970, 8 miles (13km) north east of Aviemore. A public viewing facility overlooking the tree-top nest of ospreys. Direct viewing with telescopes or binoculars; CCTV transmits pictures of the nest to the centre.

Loch Insh Watersports 109 F4
01540 651272 www.lochinsh.com

Kincraig, 7 miles (11km) south of Aviemore. Watersports include sailing, windsurfing, canoeing, salmon/trout fishing and rowing. Dry ski slope skiing, mountain biking, archery. Hire and instruction. The 2 mile (3km) interpretation/fun trail and stocked fishing lochan were especially designed with wheelchair users in mind. Children's adventure area.

Loch Lomond   76 A2
Loch Lomond, the largest stretch of inland water in Britain, and framed by lovely mountain scenery, is a popular centre for all watersports. Cruises are available around the banks and attractive small islands.

Loch Lomond & the Trossachs National Park   76 A2
0845 345 4978   www.lochlomond-trossachs.org
Balloch. Loch Lomond and the Trossachs National Park was inaugurated in 2002 as Scotland's first National Park. It includes a landscape of farmland, wooded hills, lochs, mountains and glens. The Gateway Centre on the banks of Loch Lomond provides a 'gateway' for visitors to the Park.

Loch Lomond Aquarium   76 A2
01389 721500   www.sealifeeurope.com
Loch Lomond Shores, Balloch. A collection of marine creatures from around the world as well as features on local marine life including otters.

Loch Lomond Shores   76 A2
0845 580 885   www.lochlomondshores.com
Balloch. A purpose built attraction with shops, restaurants and features including Drumkinnon Tower, designed to look like the modern equivalent of a medieval castle, and the National Park Gateway centre..

Loch Morar   106 A6
South east of Mallaig. Said to be the deepest freshwater loch in Britain and the home of Morag, a monster with a strong resemblance to the Loch Ness Monster.

Loch Nam Uamh Cairn (The Prince's Cairn)   105 F6
Off the A830, south of Arisaig. The loch is famous for its association with Bonnie Prince Charlie. The memorial cairn on the shore marks the spot from

Loch Ness

where Prince Charles Edward Stuart sailed for France on 20 September 1746, after having wandered round the Highlands as a fugitive with a price of £30,000 on his head.

Loch Ness   118 C6
This striking 24 mile (38.5km) long loch in the Great Glen forms part of the Caledonian Canal which links Inverness with Fort William. Up to 700ft (213m) deep, the loch contains the largest volume of freshwater of any lake in the British Isles. Famous worldwide for its mysterious inhabitant, the Loch Ness Monster, it is also ideal for cruising and sailing.

Loch Ness 2000   118 C6
01456 450573   www.loch-ness-scotland.com
In Drumnadrochit on the A82, 15 miles (24km) south of Inverness. A fully automated multi-room presentation takes visitors through themed areas describing Loch Ness from the pre-history of Scotland, exploring the cultural roots of the story in Highland folklore; and into the present controversy and all the phases of investigation and exploration. Also Loch Ness boat trips aboard Deepscan, a research vessel, and themed shops.

Loch Ness Clayworks   108 C2
01456 450402
Bunloit, Drumnadrochit. Situated in a beautiful area with stunning views, this is a small and prolific pottery producing a wide range of colourful artistic and domestic pieces including mugs, bowls, plates, jugs, vases, oil lamps, night lights and more. Items can be purchased.

Loch Ness Monster Visitor Centre   108 C2
01456 450342   www.lochness-centre.com
Drumnadrochit. The story of Loch Ness, the monster, and other mysteries of the area is presented in a wide-screen cinema. Various gift shops.

Loch of Kinnordy RSPB Nature Reserve   101 F4
01738 630783   www.rspb.org.uk
Loch of Kinnordy, 0.5 miles (0.8km) west of Kirriemuir. Visitors can view wildlife at close quarters from three comfortable hides. There are short trails between the hides and interpretation materials within the hides and at the car park.

Loch of Strathbeg RSPB Nature Reserve   125 E4
01346 532017   www.rspb.org.uk
1 mile (1.5km) from Crimond. The 544 acre (220ha) loch is the largest dune loch in Britain, surrounded by marshes, reedbeds, grassland and dunes.

Loch of the Lowes Visitor Centre   89 D1
01350 727337   www.swt.org.uk
2 miles (3km) north east of Dunkeld. A visitor centre with wildlife displays and small aquaria. Observation hide at lakeside with fitted binoculars and telescopes. Birds include breeding ospreys, great crested grebe, tufted duck, coot, mallard, and occasionally cormorants, heron and goldeneye duck.

Loch Shiel Cruises   106 B6
01687 470322
      www.highlandcruises.co.uk
On the A830, 15 miles (24km) north west of Fort William. Pleasure cruises from Glenfinnan

214 Loch a'Chairn Bhain   132 C6
Tranquil sea loch near the A894 between Kylesku and Scourie.

and Acharacle on Loch Shiel, one of Scotland's most beautiful and historic lochs. A wide variety of rare wildlife, best seen from the water.

Loch Sloy Hydro-Electric Station   86 A5
0845 755 2233
By Inveruglas on the A82, Loch Lomondside. Opened in 1950, Loch Sloy was the first of the Hydro-Electric Board's major generating plants to come into service. The station is open to organised parties on application (there is a charge). Interesting walk to Loch Sloy dam across the road.

Loch Tay Pottery   88 B1
01887 830251
Fearnan, Aberfeldy. A showroom and workshop in a former croft. Andrew Burt produces a wide variety of stoneware pots.

Lochcarron Cashmere Wool Centre   70 B2
01896 751100   www.lochcarron.com
Waverley Mill, Huddersfield Street, Galashiels. A woollen mill manufacturing cashmere from spun yarn to finished garment. Produces a huge range of pure wool tartans. Tour of mill and museum illustrating the history of Galashiels and its trade.

Lochindorb   121 D6
Unclassified road off A939, 10 miles (16km) north west of Grantown-on-Spey. On an island in this lonely loch stand the ruins of a 13th century castle, once a seat of the Comyns. It was occupied in person by Edward I in 1303 and greatly strengthened. In 1336 Edward III raised the siege in which the Countess of Atholl was beleaguered by the Regent Moray's troops. In 1371 the castle became the stronghold of the Wolf of Badenoch, the vicious Earl of Buchan who terrorised the area. The castle was dismantled in 1456.

Lochleven Castle   89 E5
07778 040483   www.historic-scotland.gov.uk
On an island in Loch Leven, by Kinross. A late 14th or early 15th century tower on one side of an irregular courtyard. The prison of Mary, Queen of Scots in 1567. The castle is reached by boat.

Lochmaben Castle   62 A1
0131 668 8600   www.historic-scotland.gov.uk
On the south shore of Castle Loch, by Lochmaben. Off the B7020, 9 miles (14.5km) east north-east of Dumfries. The ruins of a royal castle, originally built by the English in the 14th century but extensively rebuilt during the reign of King James VI. Surrounded by extensive remains of earthworks, including a rectangular peel (timber pallisaded enclosure).

Lochore Meadows Country Park   78 C1
01592 414300   www.lochore-meadows.co.uk
Crosshill, Lochgelly. Green and pleasant countryside around a large lake reclaimed from coal mining waste in the 1960s. A slide show, displays and ranger-guided walks tell the story of the reclamation. Ancient historical remains.

Lochranza Castle   74 C5
0131 668 8600   www.historic-scotland.gov.uk
At Lochranza on the north coast of the Isle of Arran. A fine tower house, probably a 16th century reconstruction of an earlier building. Reputed to be where King Robert the Bruce landed on his return in 1307.

Lochwinnoch RSPB Nature Reserve   76 A4
01505 842663   www.rspb.org.uk
Lochwinnoch, south west of Glasgow. A varied nature reserve encompassing marshland, open water and woodland. A range of wildlife can be seen all year round, including great-crested grebes and the elusive otter. Visitor centre.

Logan Botanic Garden   58 B5
01776 860231   www.rbge.org.uk
Port Logan, 14 miles (22.5km) south of Stranraer, off the B7065. Experience the southern hemisphere in Scotland's most exotic garden. Logan's exceptionally mild climate allows a colourful array of tender plants to thrive. Tree ferns, cabbage palms, unusual shrubs, climbers and tender perennials are found within the Walled, Water, Terrace and Woodland Gardens. The Discovery Centre provides activities and information for all ages and the Soundalive self-guided tours enable visitors to make the most of the garden. Logan Botanic Garden is one of the National Botanic Gardens of Scotland.

Logan Fish Pond & Marine Life Centre   58 B5
01776 860300   www.loganfishpond.co.uk
Port Logan, off the B7056, 14 miles (22.5km) south of Stranraer. A fully restored Victorian fish larder in a unique setting - a tidal pool created by a blowhole which formed during the last Ice Age. The rock fissure through which the tide flows is now the setting for the unusual cave marine aquarium, containing a large variety of species from the Irish Sea.

Logie Farm Riding Centre   121 D5
01309 651226
Logie Farm, Glenferness, on the A939, 10 miles (16km) from Nairn. A riding centre with quality horses and ponies. Traffic-free riding, stunning scenery, an extensive cross-country course, show jumping and dressage areas, outdoor arena and first class instruction. Riding holidays for adults or unaccompanied children.

Logie Steading   121 E4
01309 611278   www.logie.co.uk
6 miles (10km) south of Forres. Originally built as a model farm in the 1920s, now converted to house an unusual visitor centre. Potter, textiles and glass engraving.

Loudoun Castle Theme Park   67 D2
01563 822296   www.loudouncastle.co.uk
Galston, on the A719 between the A77 and the A71. Set in over 500 acres (202ha) of parkland and woods, in the grounds of the imposing ruins of Loudoun Castle. Thrilling rides, including Galaxy Rollercoaster, road trains, woodland walks, games, stalls, go-carts and pony rides.

Loudoun Hall   66 B3
01292 612948
Ayr town centre. Loudoun Hall is one of Ayr's oldest and finest buildings, dating back to the late 15th century. Once the site of a brew house and bake house, the hall has been redeveloped. The forecourt is a public space with integrated art works.

Low Parks Museum   77 E5
01698 328232
129 Muir Street, Motehill, Hamilton. Combines the former Hamilton District Museum with the Cameronians (Scottish Rifles) Regimental Museum. Displays on the Hamilton Estate, coal mining, textiles, agriculture and Covenantors.

Luib Croft Museum   105 E2
01471 822427
Luib on the Isle of Skye. On the Broadford to Sligachan road, 36 miles (57.5km) from Dunvegan in the heart of the Cuillins. Depicts living conditions in the early 20th century. Exhibition of maps from 1750 - 2000 and information about a recently discovered Viking Farm.

Lunderston Bay (Clyde Muirshiel Regional Park)   75 F3
01475 521129   www.clydemuirshiel.co.uk
Lunderston Bay on the Clyde Coast. Panoramic

views to the Cowal peninsula, ranger service, coastal walks, rock pools, children's play area, beach and picnic spots.

Lyness Interpretation Centre 146 C4
01856 791300   www.scapaflow.co.uk
Lyness, Hoy, Orkney. Exhibition of photographs and artefacts cover the period when Scapa Flow was a key anchorage for the British Royal Navy in both World Wars. Housed in a converted pump house at the former Lyness naval base. There is a Naval Cemetery nearby.

Lyth Arts Centre 137 D3
01955 641270   www.lytharts.org.uk
Lyth, 4 miles (6.5km) off the A99 between Wick and John o' Groats. Regular performances by touring drama, music and dance companies, presenting the work of professional British and international artists. Up to ten new exhibitions of contemporary fine art shown simultaneously each season, ranging from local landscapes to the work of established British and foreign artists.

Mabie Farm Park 61 F2
01387 259666   www.mabiefarm.co.uk
Burnside Farm, Mabie. Lots of animals including donkeys, horses and ponies, chicks and guinea pigs. Also adventure playground, giant flume slide, zip-wire, go-carts, quad bikes and bouncy castles.

Macallan Distillery 122 B5
01340 872280   www.macallan.com
Craigellachie. Single malt distillery with 21 small stills. Visitor centre, guided tours and shop.

McCaig's Tower 84 B2
On a hill overlooking Oban. McCaig was a local banker who tried to curb unemployment by using local craftsmen to build this tower (1897 - 1900) as a memorial to his family. Its walls are 2ft (0.5m) thick and from 30 - 47ft (9 - 14m) high. The courtyard within is landscaped and the tower is floodlit at night in summer. An observation platform on the seaward side was added in 1983.

MacDuff Castle 79 E1
East Wemyss, beside the cemetery overlooking the sea. Reputed to be home of MacDuff of Shakespeare's Macbeth, now in ruins.

Macduff Marine Aquarium 124 B3
01261 833369   www.marine-aquarium.com
High Shore, Macduff. A series of displays covering the marine habitats of the Moray Firth, including rock pools, touch pools and splash tank. Featuring a wave machine and living kelp reef, the main display is the deepest open-topped tank in Scotland.

Machrie Moor Stone Circles 65 D2
0131 668 8600   www.historic-scotland.gov.uk
3 miles (5km) north of Blackwaterfoot on the west coast of the Isle of Arran. The remains of five Bronze Age stone circles. One of the most important sites of its kind in Britain.

McKechnie Institute 65 F6
01465 713643
Girvan. The red standstone building with its octagonal tower has been a local landmark since 1888 - reopening as a local museum in 1982, with changing exhibitions on local history and fine art.

Mackinnon Mills 77 E4
01236 440702   www.mackinnonmills.co.uk
Kirkshaws Road, Coatbridge, 10 miles (16km) east of Glasgow. Factory shopping with knitwear, designer label garments and everything for the golfer.

McLean Museum & Art Gallery 75 F3
01475 715624
15 Kelly Street, Greenock. A museum showing local history, maritime exhibits, ethnography, Egyptology, big game mounts and fine art. Also items relating to James Watt. Programme of temporary exhibitions in the art galleries.

Maclean's Cross 82 A3
www.historic-scotland.gov.uk
On the island of Iona, off the west coast of Mull. A fine 15th century free-standing cross.

MacLellan's Castle 60 C4
01557 331856   www.historic-scotland.gov.uk
Off the A711 High Street in Kirkcudbright. A handsome castellated mansion overlooking the harbour, dating from 1577, complete except for the roof. Elaborately planned with fine detail. A ruin since 1752.

Maeshowe Chambered Cairn 146 C2
01856 761606   www.historic-scotland.gov.uk
Stenness, off the A965, 9 miles (14.5km) west of Kirkwall, Orkney. The finest megalithic (Neolithic) tomb in the British Isles, consisting of a large mound covering a stone-built passage and a large burial chamber with cells in the walls. Runic inscriptions were carved in the walls by Vikings and Norse crusaders. Admission, shop and tearoom are at the nearby 19th century Tormiston Mill.

Magdalen Chapel
(Scottish Reformation Society) 20 B2
41 Cowgate, Edinburgh. Built in 1541, the chapel was used by various denominations and also as a guildhall by the Incorporation of Hammermen until 1862, when it was sold to the Protestant Institute of Scotland. Since 1965, it has been in the possession of the Scottish Reformation Society and used as their headquarters with regular services. Features stained glass (the only medieval examples still in the original setting and situation), bell and clock dating from early 17th century.

Maggie Walls Monument 89 D4
1 mile (1.5km) west of Dunning, on the B8062. The monument marks the spot where Maggie Wall was allegedly burned as a witch in 1657. It is constructed from rough field boulders and a plinth stone topped with a cross.

Maggie's Hoosie 125 E3
01346 514761
26 Shore Street, Inverallochy, Fraserburgh. A preserved but and ben fisher cottage with earth floor, box beds and original furnishings.

Maid of the Loch 76 A2
01389 711865   www.maidoftheloch.co.uk
Balloch Pier. Maid of the Loch is the largest UK inland waterways vessel ever built, a paddle steamer originally launched in 1953 and laid up in 1981. Now under restoration, visitors can see an exhibition and watch the restoration underway.

Maiden Stone 112 C2
01667 460232   www.historic-scotland.gov.uk
Near Chapel of Garioch, north west of Inverurie. A 9th century Pictish cross-slab bearing a Celtic cross on one side and a variety of Pictish symbols on the other.

Maison Dieu Chapel 103 D3
0131 668 8800   www.historic-scotland.gov.uk
Maison Dieu Lane, Brechin. Part of the south wall of a chapel belonging to a medieval hospital founded in the 1260s, with finely-detailed doors and windows.

Mallaig Heritage Centre 105 F5
01687 462085   www.mallaigheritage.org.uk
Station Road in Mallaig centre between railway station and Marine Hotel, off the A830. Exhibits and displays all aspects of the history of Mallaig and West Lochaber - social history, crofting, fishing,

Mellerstain House

railway archaeology, maritime history, and the Knoydart clearances. Children's quizzes.

Malleny Garden   78 C4
0131 449 2283   www.nts.org.uk
Balerno. Dominated by four 400 year old clipped yew trees, this peaceful garden features fine herbaceous borders and a large collection of old-fashioned roses. The National Bonsai Collection for Scotland is also housed here.

Manderston   81 D5
01361 883450   www.manderston.co.uk
Off the A6105, 2 miles (3km) east of Duns. An Edwardian stately home set in 56 acres (22.6ha) and surrounded by formal gardens, stables, dairy, lake and woodland garden. Features include the sumptuous staterooms, the only silver staircase in the world, a racing room and the first privately-owned biscuit tin museum. Domestic quarters in period style.

Mar Lodge Estate   110 C5
013397 41433   www.nts.org.uk
5 miles (8km) west of Braemar. Part of the core area of the Cairngorms, internationally recognised as the most important nature conservation landscape in Britain. The estate contains four of the five highest mountains in the UK.

Marischal Museum   37 C2
01224 274301   www.abdn.ac.uk/diss/historic
Marischal College, Broad Street, Aberdeen. Displays the collections of graduates and friends of Aberdeen University over 500 years. Exhibitions include Collecting the World and the Encyclopedia of the North-East.

Marrbury Smokehouse   77 E1
01671 840241   www.visitmarrbury.co.uk
On the A714, 9 miles north west of Newton Stewart, near Glentrool. Traditional Scottish smokehouse run by the Marr family, net and cobble salmon fishermen on the local River Cree since 1920. Visitors can enjoy a guided tour of the smoking process. A visitor centre sells smoked food and offers recipes and tips.

Mar's Wark   37 C2
                www.historic-scotland.gov.uk
At the top of Castle Wynd, Stirling. A remarkable Renaissance mansion built by the Regent Mar in 1570, of which the façade is the main surviving part.

Mary-Ann's Cottage   137 D2
01847 851765
At Dunnet, 10 miles (16km) east of Thurso. A

cottage built in 1850 by John Young. The croft was successively worked by three generations of the family, ending with Mary-Ann and James Calder. All the furniture, fittings and artefacts are original, the way of life and working practices changing little over the generations.

Mary, Queen of Scots Visitor Centre   70 C3
01835 863331
Queen Street, Jedburgh. A 16th century castle which is now a visitor centre devoted to the memory of Mary, Queen of Scots, who stayed here in 1566 while she was ill.

Maryck Memories of Childhood   127 F1
01971 502341
Unapool, on the A874, 0.5 mile south of Kylesku bridge, midway between Ullapool and Durness. The exhibition includes dolls, doll's houses, teddy bears and toys from 1880 to the present day. The craft shop has a range of items for sale, most made in Scotland and some handmade locally. Toys and dressing up opportunities for the under 8s (parental supervision required).

Maybole Collegiate Church   66 B5
0131 668 8600   www.historic-scotland.gov.uk
South of the A77 in Maybole. The roofless ruin of a 15th century church built for a small college established in 1373 by John Kennedy of Dunure.

Meadow Well   136 C3
Located in Thurso this was once a major source of the local water supply and where the local fishwives gathered to sell fresh fish.

Meffan, The   102 B4
01307 464123
20 West High Street, Forfar. Two art galleries featuring art from contemporary Scottish artists and the Angus collections. The Forfar Story features original Pictish stones from Angus, an interactive guide to the stones, a walk through an old Forfar vennel with its shops and a witch burning scene.

Meigle Sculptured Stones   90 B1
01828 640612   www.historic-scotland.gov.uk
On the A94 in Meigle, 12 miles (19km) west south-west of Forfar. One of the most notable collections of Dark Age sculpture in Western Europe.

Meikleour Beech Hedge   89 E2
10 miles (16km) east of Dunkeld on the A93. An incredible living wall of beech trees, 100ft (30m) high and one third of a mile (530m) long. Now officially recognised in the Guinness Book of Records as the highest hedge in the world.

Mellerstain House   70 C2
01573 410225   www.mellerstain.com
Gordon, off the A6089, 7 miles (11km) north west of Kelso. A superb Georgian mansion designed by William and Robert Adam. Features exquisite plaster ceilings, beautiful interior decoration, fine period furniture, marvellous art collection. Award-winning terraced garden and grounds.

Melrose Abbey   70 B2
01896 822562   www.historic-scotland.gov.uk
Main Square, Melrose, off the A7 or A68. The ruins of

the Cistercian abbey founded by King David I circa 1136. It was largely destroyed by an English army in 1385 but rebuilt in the early 15th century. It is now probably the most famous ruin in Scotland because of the elegant and elaborate stonework which remains. The Commendator's House contains a large collection of objets trouvés.

Melville Monument   87 E3
6 miles (9.5km) west of Crieff. The obelisk in memory of Lord Melville stands on Dunmore, a hill of 840ft (256m), with delightful views of the surrounding countryside.

Memsie Cairn   125 D3
01667 460232   www.historic-scotland.gov.uk
Near Rathen, 3.5 miles (5.5km) south of Fraserburgh. A large stone-built cairn, possibly Bronze Age, but enlarged during field clearance in the last two centuries.

Mercat Cross   30 B3
Nethergate, Dundee. Standing on the south side of St Mary's Tower, this is a replica of Dundee's old mercat cross which formerly stood in the Seagate. On top of the shaft is a unicorn sculpted by Scott Sutherland, RSA.

Mercat Walking Tours   20 B2
0131 225 5445   www.mercattours.com
These dramatised history and ghost tours of Edinburgh leave from the Mercat Cross beside St Giles Cathedral on the Royal Mile. Visit the wynds and closes of Old Edinburgh, the vaults beneath the South Bridge and the world-famous Mary King's Close.

Merkland Cross   62 B2
0131 668 8600   www.historic-scotland.gov.uk
At Merkland Smithy, near Ecclefechan. A fine carved wayside cross, dating from the 15th century.

Mertoun Gardens   70 B2
01835 823236
On the B6404, 2 miles (3km) east of Newtown St Boswells. Twenty-six acres (10.5ha) of beautiful grounds with delightful walks and river views. Fine trees, herbaceous borders and flowering shrubs. Walled garden and well-preserved circular dovecot. Dogs not permitted.

Methil Heritage Centre   79 E1
01333 422100
272 High Street, Methill, 8 miles (13km) east of Kirkcaldy. A lively community museum, interpreting the social and individual history of the area.

Michael Bruce's Cottage   89 E5
01592 840255
The Cobbles, Kinnesswood, Kinross. An 18th century pantiled weaver's cottage and a museum since 1906. Houses collection relating to the life of the poet, and local history including the manufacture of vellum and parchment.

Midhowe Broch & Cairn   148 A4
01856 841815   www.historic-scotland.gov.uk
On the west coast of the island of Rousay, Orkney. An Iron Age broch and walled enclosure situated on a promontory cut off by a deep rock ditch. Adjacent is Midhowe Stalled Cairn, a huge and impressive Neolithic chambered tomb in an oval mound with 25 stalls. Now protected by a modern building.

Midlothian Snowsports Centre   79 D4
0131 445 4433   www.ski.midlothian.gov.uk
Hillend, just south of Edinburgh. Europe's longest and most challenging artificial ski slope. Two main slopes, a fun slope and two nursery slopes. Equipment hire, skiing/snowboarding, coaching and instruction for all levels, chair lift and two ski tows. Chairlift open to all visitors, with terrific views.

Mill on the Fleet   60 B4
01557 814099   www.millonthefleet.co.uk
High Street, Gatehouse of Fleet, Castle Douglas. An exhibition housed in a restored 18th century cotton mill, telling the history of the town. Temporary and permanent exhibits.

Mill Trail Visitor Centre   77 F1
01259 769696
West Stirling Street, Alva, on the A91, 8 miles (13km) east of Stirling. An exhibition telling the story of spinning and weaving in Clackmannan (the Wee County). Features the experience of a 12-year-old working in the mills. Original weaving and knitting looms. Shop sells wide variety of local craft goods, books and knitwear.

Miller House & Hugh Miller's Cottage   119 E3
01381 600245   www.nts.org.uk
Off the A832 in Church Street, Cromarty, 22 miles (35km) north east of Inverness. Birthplace of Hugh Miller (1802 - 56), famous stonemason, geologist, writer and church reformer. Furnished thatched cottage, built circa 1698, with restored cottage garden. Miller House, a Georgian villa built by Miller's father, now houses a museum dedicated to his life.

Mills Observatory   90 C2
01382 435967   www.dundeecity.gov.uk/mills
Balgay Park, Dundee. Constructed in 1935 for the people of Dundee, the Mills Observatory is today Britain's only full-time public observatory. Located in picturesque wooded surroundings, it houses a 10 inch (25cm) refracting telescope.

Milnholm Cross   63 E1
One mile (1.5km) south of Newcastleton. Erected circa 1320, and owned by the Clan Armstrong Trust, Milnholm Cross is a memorial to Alexander Armstrong who was murdered in Hermitage Castle some 4 miles (6.5km) away. It faces the ruin of Mangerton Castle, seat of the Armstrong chiefs for 300 years.

Mine Howe   147 E3
01856 861234   www.orkneydigs.org.uk
Veltitigar Farmhouse, Tankerness, Orkney. Unique to Europe, this mysterious Iron Age archaeological site was re-discovered in 1999 and further excavated in 2000 by television's Time Team. 26ft (8m) underground, down deep steps, there is a small chamber with two side chambers. Related to the site there is a broch, round howe and long howe.

Moat Park Heritage Centre   68 C2
01899 221050
Kirkstyle, Biggar. A former church adapted to display the geology and history of the Upper Clyde and Tweed Valleys, from the days of the volcano and the glacier to the present. A fine collection of embroidery, including the largest known patchwork cover containing over 80 figures from the 1850s. Archaeology collection.

Moffat Museum   68 C5
01683 220868
The Old Bakehouse, The Neuk, Church Gate, Moffat. Located in an old bakehouse with a Scotch oven. Tells the story of Moffat and its people, border raids, Covenanters, education, sports and pastimes, famous people. Includes a short video presentation.

Moffat Woollen Mill   68 C5
01683 220134
Ladyknowe, Moffat. Visit the working weaving exhibition. The mill offers a good selection of cashmere, Aran, lambswool and traditional tartans and tweeds. Trace Scottish clan history and heraldry at the Clan History Centre and receive a certificate illustrating your clan ancestry.

Moirlanich Longhouse 86 C2
01567 820988 www.nts.org.uk
Off the A827, 1 mile (1.5km) north west of Killin. An outstanding example of a traditional cruck-frame cottage and byre dating from the mid 19th century. Inhabited until 1968, the house retains many original features and is furnished according to archaeological evidence.

Moncreiffe Hill Wood 89 E3
www.woodland-trust.org.uk
South of Perth, off the M90 at junction 9, take the minor road to Rhynd following tourist signposting. A visit to this spectacular 333 acre (134ha) wood will allow visitors to enjoy outstanding views along the River Tay and Strathearn and you may also catch a glimpse of the wildlife which inhabits the wood.

Monikie Country Park 89 E2
01382 370202
www.monikie.org.uk/cntryprk.htm
Main Lodge, Monikie, off the B962 between Dundee and Arbroath. The country park comprises 185 acres (75ha), with reservoirs, woodland and grassland. Instruction and hire for windsurfing, sailing, canoeing.

Monreith Animal World 59 E5
01988 700217
www.monreithanimalworld.zoomshare.com
Low Knowck Farm, on the A747, 0.5 mile (1km) from Monreith. Collection of animals and birds, including otters, pigmy goats, owls, waterfowl and small mammals, in natural spacious surroundings. Reptile collection.

Snowy Owl

Monster Activities 108 A5
01809 501340 www.monsteractivities.com
Great Glen Water Park, South Laggan on the A82 between Spean Bridge and Fort Augustus. Whitewater rafting all year round for individuals and groups. Also Canadian canoeing, kayaking, windsurfing and sailing on Loch Oich. Land based activities include archery, abseiling, mountain biking and guided treks.

Monteviot House Gardens 70 C3
01835 830704
Monteviot, off the B6400, 4 miles (6.5km) north of Jedburgh (off the A68). Gardens on the bank of the River Teviot with several feature areas - river garden, rose terraces and a water garden.

Montrose Air Station Heritage Centre 103 E4
01674 678222
Waldron Road, Montrose. RFC/RAF and wartime artefacts and memorabilia housed in the wartime

RAF Montrose HQ. Various aircraft on display outside, also pillbox and Anderson shelter.

Montrose Basin Wildlife Centre 103 D4
01674 676336 www.montrosebasin.org.uk
Rossie Braes, 1 mile (1.5km) south of Montrose on the A92. Unique displays show how a tidal basin works and the routes of migrating birds. Magnificent views of wildlife on the basin through telescopes and binoculars. Interactive displays.

Montrose Museum 103 E4
01674 673232
Panmure Place, Montrose. Tells the story of Montrose from prehistoric times, including local geology and wildlife. On show are various Pictish stones, pottery, whaling and Napoleonic artefacts.

Monument Hill 85 E3
Off the old road to Inveraray, 2 miles (3km) south west of Dalmally. Monument to Duncan Ban Macintyre (1724 - 1812), the Burns of the Highlands, who was born near Inveroran.

Moonstone Miniatures 61 D2
01556 650313
4 Victoria Street, Kirkpatrick Durham. 14 miles (22.5km) west of Dumfries, 4 miles (6.5km) east of Castle Douglas off the A75 at Springholm. Cabinets of miniature marvels at one-twelfth scale, including stately homes, shops and humble cottages.

Morag's Fairy Glen 75 E3
Dunoon. This delightful glen was gifted to the town by Bailie George Jones.

Moray Motor Museum 122 B3
01343 544933
Bridge Street, Elgin, 30 miles (48km) west of Inverness. Unique collection of high quality cars and motorbikes housed in an old mill building.

Morton Castle 91 D3
0131 668 8600
www.historic-scotland.gov.uk
On the A702, 17 miles (27km) north north-west of Dumfries. Beside Morton Loch. The well-preserved ruin of a fine late 13th century hall house, a stronghold of the Douglases.

Morven Gallery 145 D2
01851 840216
www.morvengallery.com
Upper Barvas, 12 miles (19km) west of Stornoway, Isle of Lewis. Fine art by local painters and sculptors. Ceramics, tapestry, carvings and designer knitwear. Talks, slide shows and conference facility. Workshops and children's activities.

Moss Farm Road Stone Circle 65 D2
0131 668 8600 www.historic-scotland.gov.uk
3 miles (5km) north of Blackwaterfoot, Isle of Arran. The remains of a Bronze Age cairn surrounded by a stone circle.

Mossburn Animal Centre 62 A2
01387 811288 www.mossburn.org
Hightae, Lockerbie. Off the B7020 from Lochmaben. Mossburn is an animal welfare centre where you can see and handle rescued animals, from pigs and horses to Thai water dragons, who now live in a healthy, happy and secure environment.

Motherwell Concert Hall & Theatre 77 E5
01698 302999
Civic Centre, Motherwell. Venue for performances by

some of the foremost stars of theatre, television and stage. Doubles as Motherwell Moviehouse showing a programme of popular films.

Motherwell Heritage Centre   77 E5
01698 251000
www.motherwellheritage.freeservers.com
1 High Road, Motherwell. A superb attraction, telling the story of the Motherwell area from Roman times to the present day. Visit the Technopolis interactive media display and walk through time to see the industrial heyday of the area, social and political upheavals and the development of the modern town.

Motoring Heritage Centre   76 A2
01389 607862   www.motoringheritage.co.uk
Main Street, Alexandria. A motor heritage centre situated in what was once the world's largest motor car works, now Loch Lomond Factory Outlets. Display traces the history of the once-famous Argyll marque and the story of Scottish motoring. Visitors can sit in a Model T Ford, see unique archive film and fascinating carts.

Motte of Urr   61 E3
Off the B794, 5 miles (7.5km) north east of Castle Douglas. The most extensive motte and bailey castle in Scotland, dating from the 12th century AD, although the bailey may have been an earlier earthwork of hillfort type.

Mount Stuart   75 E5
01700 503877   www.mountstuart.com
Mount Stuart, Isle of Bute. 5 miles (8km) south of Rothesay. Spectacular Victorian Gothic house, the ancestral home of the Marquess of Bute. Splendid interiors, art collection and architectural detail. Mature Victorian pinetum, arboretum and exotic gardens, waymarked walks. Three hundred acres (121ha) of ground and gardens. Audio-visual presentation.

Mousa Broch   151 D4
01856 841815   www.historic-scotland.gov.uk
On the island of Mousa, Shetland. The finest surviving Iron Age broch tower, standing over 40ft (12m) high. The stairs can be climbed to the parapet.

Muckle Flugga & Out Stack   153 E3
01806 522447   www.muckleflugga.co.uk
Depart from the harbour in Baltasound, Unst. All-day guided tour by motor boat to the seal islands of Yell Sound, the sensational cliffs of the west coast of Unst, around Muckle Flugga lighthouse and Out Stack at the northern tip of Shetland and on to the Scottish Natural Heritage Centre at Hermaness National Nature Reserve at Burrafirth.

Mugdock Country Park   76 C3
0141 956 6100
www.mugdock-country-park.org.uk
Craigallian Road, Milngavie, 10 miles (16km) north of Glasgow. Eight hundred acres (323ha) of beautiful countryside - lakes, woodland and moorland. Mugdock and Craigend Castles. Countryside events - orienteering, archery. Craigend stables and bridle routes. Also garden centre, craft shops, play areas, walks and Victorian walled garden

Muir O' Fauld Signal Station   88 C4
www.historic-scotland.gov.uk
East of Ardunie. The site of a Roman watch tower.

Muiravonside Country Park   78 A3
01506 845311
The Loan, Whitecross, Linlithgow. On the B825. 170 acres (68ha) of woodlands, parkland and gardens of the Muiravonside Estate, home of the Stirling family for 150 years. Exhibition in visitor centre. Auditorium and ranger office. Relics of industrial

past. Dovecot, burial ground and summer house. Children's farm.

Muirshiel Centre
(Clyde Muirshiel Regional Park)   76 A4
01505 842803   www.clydemuirshiel.co.uk
4 miles (6.5km) north west of Lochwinnoch, off the B786. In Calder Glen, originally a Victorian sporting estate. Woodland, riverside and waterfall walks and coded trails, picnic and barbecue sites and boardwalk access to scenic viewpoint, Windyhill. The area is rich in archaeological sites including a barytes mine.

Mull of Galloway RSPB
Nature Reserve   58 C6
www.mull-of-galloway.co.uk
Mull of Galloway. The RSPB reserve surrounds the Mull of Galloway lighthouse. A visitor centre to the east of the lighthouse has audio and visual displays of local wildlife and provides information on local history and geology.

Mull of Galloway Visitor Centre &
Lighthouse   58 C6
www.mull-of-galloway.co.uk
Mull of Galloway. Scotland's most southerly lighthouse, built in 1828. Guided tours are available on summer weekends. The Visitor Centre building originally housed the workmen who built the lighthouse.

Muness Castle   153 F2
01856 841815   www.historic-scotland.gov.uk
At the south east corner of the island of Unst, Shetland. A late 16th century tower house with fine detail and circular towers at diagonally opposite corners. The most northerly castle in the British Isles.

Murrayfield Stadium   79 D3
0131 346 5044   www.scottishrugby.org
Murrayfield, Edinburgh. The 67,000 capacity stadium for Scotland's international rugby union team and the venue for home matches during the Six Nations Championship. Built in 1925 by the Scottish Rugby Union and extended and modernised in 1936, 1983 and 1994. Stadium tours available, must be booked in advance

Museum of Abernethy   89 E4
01738 850889
www.abernethymuseum.free-online.co.uk
Abernethy. An independent museum housed in a restored 18th century cattle byre and stable in the centre of the historic village of Abernethy. The museum depicts life in the parish of Abernethy from Pictish times to the present day.

Museum of Childhood   20 D4
0131 529 4142   www.cac.org.uk
42 High Street, Edinburgh. This unique museum has a fine collection of childhood-related items including toys, dolls, dolls' houses, costumes and nursery equipment.

Museum of Edinburgh   20 D4
0131 529 4143   www.cac.org.uk
142 Canongate. A restored 16th century mansion with period rooms and reconstructions relating to the city's traditional industries. There are also collections of Edinburgh silver and glass, Scottish pottery, shop signs and relics relating to Field Marshall Earl Haig, the World War I general.

Museum of Fire   20 B2
0131 228 2401
Lothian and Borders Fire Brigade Headquarters, Lauriston Place, Edinburgh. The history of the oldest municipal fire brigade in the United Kingdom and the development of fire fighting is shown in an

exciting and educational way. Displays a range of fire engines from 1806. Phone for an appointment before visiting.

Museum of Flight 80 A3
01620 897240   www.nms.ac.uk/flight
East Fortune Airfield, North Berwick. Scotland's national museum of aviation with a large collection of over 40 aircraft (including Britain's oldest aeroplane, a Spitfire and a Vulcan bomber) in the hangars of a wartime airfield. Special exhibitions on space flight, concorde, early aviation, air traffic control and the R34 airship.

Museum of Islay Life 72 B5
01496 850358   www.islaymuseum.freeserve.co.uk
Off the A847 in Port Charlotte. The museum illustrates life on Islay from prehistoric times to the early 20th century. Also the Gordon Booth Library, where archives, photographs and books relating to island life may be consulted. In the Wee Museum of Childhood there are hands-on activities and quizzes for all ages.

Museum of Lead Mining 68 A4
01659 74387   www.leadminingmuseum.co.uk
Wanlockhead, Biggar, on the B797 between Abington (A74) and Mennock (A76). A museum tracing 300 years of lead mining in Scotland's highest village set in the dramatic Lowther Hills. Features heritage trail, beam engine, tours of a lead mine, period cottages, miners' library, displays of minerals. Gold panning centre (you can take some gold home).

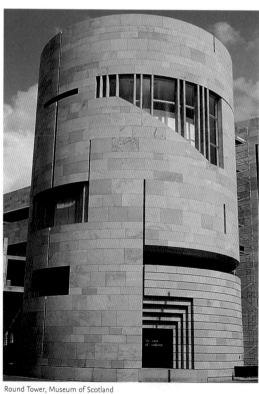
Round Tower, Museum of Scotland

Museum of Scotland 20 B2
0131 247 4422   www.nms.ac.uk/scotland
Chambers Street, Edinburgh. The Museum of Scotland tells the history of Scotland from its geological beginnings to the present day.

Spectacular views of the city from the rooftop. Opened in 1998 as an extension to the Royal Museum of Scotland. A striking piece of architecture to hold the treasured objects of Scotland's past and present.

Museum of Scottish Country Life 77 D4
0131 247 4377   www.nms.ac.uk/countrylife
East Kilbride. This unique museum offers visitors an insight into the working lives of people in rural Scotland and shows how the countryside was once worked by generations of farmers. The museum houses the national collection of country life exhibits, an events area and the original Georgian farmhouse and steading. The farm follows a pattern of seasonal work to show ploughing, seed time, haymaking and harvest. Special events are held throughout the year.

Museum of Scottish Lighthouses 125 D3
01346 511022   www.lighthousemuseum.org.uk
Kinnaird Head, Fraserburgh. A museum housed in a former castle which became the first lighthouse built by the Northern Lighthouse Board in 1787, now a monument to Scotland's lighthouse service. Tour to the top of the lighthouse.

Museum of the Cumbraes 75 E5
01475 531191
Garrison, Millport, Isle of Cumbrae. The museum tells the story of the islands Great and Wee Cumbrae. Displays show how the town of Millport developed and celebrate Millport's heyday as a holiday resort.

Museum of Transport 76 C4
0141 287 2720   www.glasgowmuseums.com
Kelvin Hall, 1 Bunhouse Road, Glasgow. The history of transport on land and sea with vehicles from horse-drawn carriages to motorcycles, fire engines, railway engines, steam and motor cars. The Clyde Room contains ship models. Also a recreated Glasgow street circa 1938, and a reconstructed underground station.

Museum on the Mound 20 B2
0131 529 1372   www.museumonthemound.com
Bank of Scotland Head Office, The Mound, Edinburgh. Between the Old and New Towns, just off the Royal Mile. A small but unusual museum telling the 300 year story of Scotland's first bank set against the economic development of the country. Features early adding machines, banknotes and forgeries, bullion chests and gold coins, maps, plans and photographs. Free postcards.

Muthill Old Church & Tower 88 B4
www.historic-scotland.gov.uk
On the A822 in Muthill. 5 miles (8km) south of Crieff on the A822. The ruins of a 15th century parish church with a tall Romanesque tower at its west end.

Muthill Village Museum 88 B4
01764 652578
Station Road, Muthill, 5 miles (8km) south of Crieff on the A822. Collection of local objects from yesteryear. Model castle and steam railway display.

Myreton Motor Museum   79 F3
01875 870288
Myreton, off the A198 just east of Aberlady. A varied
collection of road transport from 1897, including
motor cars, cycles, motorcycles, commercials, World
War II military vehicles and automobilia. Catalogue
and children's quiz book.

Nairn Museum   119 F4
01667 456791   www.nairnmuseum.co.uk
On the A96, 15 miles (24km) from east of Inverness.
A local history museum with five rooms of displays
and a changing exhibition each month. Local and
family history research room and children's area.

National Flag Heritage Centre   80 A3
01620 880306
Behind Athelstaneford Church. A 16th century
dovecot restored to house an audio-visual
dramatisation of the battle in AD832 at which an
army of Picts/Scots encountered a larger force of
Saxons under Athelstan. The appearance of a cloud
formation of a white saltire (the diagonal cross on
which St Andrew had been martyred) against a blue
sky inspired the Scots to victory. Since that time, the
St Andrew's Cross has been the national flag of
Scotland. There is a viewpoint overlooking the battle
site, and visitors can also inspect the Saltire
Memorial, the Book of the Saltire, and walk through
the historic churchyard.

National Gallery of Scotland   20 B2
0131 624 6200   www.natgalscot.ac.uk
The Mound, Edinburgh. It was designed by William
Henry Playfair and the foundation stone laid by
Prince Albert in 1850. The gallery opened to the
public in 1859. Contains outstanding paintings,
drawings and prints by the greatest artists from the
Renaissance to Post-Impressionism, including
Velásquez, El Greco, Titian, Vermeer, Constable,
Monet and Van Gogh. It also houses the national
collection of Scottish art featuring works by Taggart,
Wilkie, Ramsay and Raeburn.

National Library of Scotland   20 B2
0131 226 4531   www.nls.uk
George IV Bridge, Edinburgh. Founded in 1682, the
library is a treasure house of books and manuscripts,
with reading rooms open for research to scholars.
For the general public and visitors, it has a
programme of exhibitions on Scottish themes.

National Monument   21 C1
Calton Hill, Edinburgh. Unfinished memorial to Scots
lost in the Napoleonic Wars.

National Park Centre Balmaha   76 B1
01389 722100   www.lochlomond-trossachs.org
Balmaha, on the A811 north west of Drymen. Visitor
centre offering information on Loch Lomond and

Trossachs National Park. Audio-visual show and
exhibition.

National Park Centre
Luss   76 A1
01389 722120   www.lochlomond-trossachs.org
Luss, off the A82, 8 miles from Balloch. Visitor
centre offering information on Loch Lomond and the
Trossachs National Park. Audio-visual show and
exhibition. There is also an information point at
Inveruglas.

National Piping
Centre   16 B1
0141 3530220   www.thepipingcentre.co.uk
30-34 McPhater Street, Cowcaddens. In Glasgow
city centre. A national and international centre of
excellence for the bagpipes and their music,
incorporating a school with rehearsal rooms and a
performance hall, a museum and interpretation
centre, a reference library and conference facilities.
Housed in a fine listed building.

National Wallace Monument   77 F1
01786 472140
www.nationalwallacemonument.com
Abbey Craig, Hillfoot Road, Stirling. The National
Wallace Monument takes visitors back 700 years in
time to the days of Scotland's first struggle for
independence. The story of William Wallace,
freedom fighter and national hero, is told along with
background and events that shaped this period of
history. Climb the 246 steps of the 220ft (67m) high
tower for superb views.

National War Museum of Scotland   20 D4
0131 225 7534   www.nms.ac.uk/war
Within Edinburgh Castle. Explores the Scottish
experience of war and military service over the last
400 years, housed in mid 18th century buildings.

Necropolis   17 C2
0141 287 3961
Castle Street, behind Glasgow Cathedral.
Remarkable and extensive burial ground laid out in
1833, with numerous elaborate tombs of 19th
century illustrious Glaswegians and others; of
particular interest is the Menteith Mausoleum of
1842.

Neidpath Castle   69 E2
01721 720333
One mile (2km) west of Peebles on the A72. A rare
example of a 14th century castle converted into a
tower house in the 17th century. Displayed in the
great hall is an exhibit of beautiful batiks depicting
the life of Mary, Queen of Scots. The Laigh Hall
contains informative displays. Good views from the
parapet walks. Neidpath Castle is often used as a
film location. Resident ghost, the
Maid of Neidpath.

Neil M. Gunn Memorial
Viewpoint   118 C3
Heights of Brae, Strathpeffer.
Memorial viewpoint for the
author Neil M. Gunn, who lived
nearby.

Nelson Monument   21 C1
www.cac.org.uk
On Calton Hill in Edinburgh,
above Waterloo Place. One of the
first monuments to Admiral
Nelson, built between 1807 and
1815. A telescope-shaped tower
with a time-ball on the top that is
wound up every day (except
Sunday) and dropped at 1300.
The timeball, like the 1 o'clock

Neptune's Staircase

gun at Edinburgh Castle, acted as a signal to ships in Leith docks to set their chronometers, enabling them to calculate longitude. Nelson's Trafalgar signal is flown on 21 October. Good views from the top.

Nevis Range

Nelson Tower 121 E4
01309 673701
www.moray.gov.uk
Grant Park, Forres, 11 miles (17.5km) west of Elgin. Nelson Tower was built to commemorate Nelson's victory at Trafalgar. Displays on Lord Nelson and views of old Forres. There are also spectacular views of the Moray Firth from the tower.

Neptune's Staircase 97 D2
www.waterscape.com/caledonian_canal
Off the A830 at Banavie, 3 miles (4.5km) north west of Fort William. A picturesque series of eight locks, built between 1805 and 1822, which raises Telford's Caledonian Canal 64ft (19.5 m) in less than 0.5 mile (1km). There are stunning views of Ben Nevis.

Ness Heritage Centre 145 F1
01851 810377
www.c-e-n.org
Towards the Butt of Lewis, 28 miles (45km) from Stornoway on the A857. A unique insight into the social and cultural heritage of the Western Isles. Over 500 artefacts and 7000 photographs illustrate the lifestyle of a people carving out an existence on the very edge of Europe. Genealogical information spanning 250 years is an invaluable resource to visitors tracing their family histories.

Ness of Burgi 151 F4
www.historic-scotland.gov.uk
At the south eastern point of Scatness, Shetland, about 1 mile (2km) south west of Jarlshof. A defensive stone blockhouse, probably from the Iron Age, with some features resembling a broch.

Nether Largie Cairns 74 B1
www.historic-scotland.gov.uk
Kilmartin Glen, between Kilmartin and Nether Largie. One Neolithic and two Bronze Age cairns. There is access to the chamber in the north cairn.

Neverland Adventure Play Centre 61 F2
01387 249100
Park Lane, Dumfries. Adventure play centre for children aged up to ten. Themed on J.M. Barrie's story of Peter Pan, the boy who would never grow up. There are rope bridges, slides, a ball pool, Indian encampment and Captain Hook's pirate ship. Special area for under fours. Located beside the River Nith, with a pleasant seating area for adults overlooking the river. Parent/guardian supervision is required.

Nevis Range 97 D2
01397 705825
www.nevis-range.co.uk
Torlundy, on the A82, 7 miles (11km) north of Fort William. Britain's only mountain gondolas take passengers to 2150ft (655m) on Aonach Mor beside Ben Nevis. Spectacular views of the Highlands and islands. Mountain restaurant, bar and shop at 2150ft (655m). Walks. Britain's largest downhill mountain bike track with gondola access. Scotland's highest winter ski and snowboard area, ski school and ski hire (Dec - May).

New Abbey Corn Mill 61 F3
01387 850260
www.historic-scotland.gov.uk
On the A710, in New Abbey, 8 miles (13km) south of Dumfries. A carefully renovated water-driven oatmeal mill in working order and demonstrated regularly to visitors in the summer months.

New Lanark World Heritage Site 77 F6
01555 661345
www.newlanark.org
1 mile (2km) south of Lanark. New Lanark is the best example in Scotland of an industrial heritage village. Founded in 1785 by Scottish industrialist David Dale, it was the scene of early social experiments by Dale's son-in-law Robert Owen (1771-1858), whose far-reaching ideas on the care of his workers and the formation of man's character made New Lanark famous. The award-winning visitor centre gives visitors a glimpse of life under Owen's paternalistic management, especially through the New Millennium Experience, an innovative dark ride. Passport ticket also includes the Millworkers' House, Village Store, Robert Owen's House and Robert Owen's School.

Newark Castle 76 A3
01475 741858
www.historic-scotland.gov.uk
On the A8 in Port Glasgow. A large turreted mansion house in a remarkably good state of preservation, with a 15th century tower, a courtyard and hall.

Newbarns Project 61 E4
www.sat.archaeologyit.co.uk
Newbarns, Colvend, south of Dalbeattie on the A170. Site of a Neolithic cairn later used as a crannog. The excavation is organised by the Stewartry Archaeological Trust.

Newhailes 79 E3
0131 653 5599
www.nts.org.uk
Newhailes Road, Musselburgh. A dignified 17th century house, with 18th century additions, Newhailes has survived with much of its original interior decoration intact. The library, once the largest private collection in Scotland, was built in 1718 by Sir David Dalrymple who was a prominent figure in Scottish Enlightenment. The grounds surrounding the house are also worth a look.

Newhaven Heritage Museum 79 D3
0131 551 4165
www.cac.org.uk
24 Pier Place, Edinburgh. This museum is situated in the historic fishmarket overlooking the harbour. Find out about fishing and other sea trades, customs and superstitions. Displays tell the stories of the Society of Free Fishermen and the development of this tightly-knit community. Reconstructed sets of fishwives and fishermen, displays of objects and photographs, and first-hand written and spoken accounts of people's lives. Hands-on exhibits, music and video.

Newton Hill Country Sports 90 C3
01382 330519
www.newtonhilltv.co.uk
Newton Farm, Wormit, on the B946. Clay shooting, quad bikes, off-road driving and fly fishing.

Newton Stewart Museum — 60 A3
01671 402472
York Road, Newton Stewart. Contains a wealth of historical treasures and exciting and interesting displays of the natural and social history of Galloway.

Niel Gow's Oak — 89 D1
Walk from the Hermitage, near Dunkeld. Famous fiddle player Niel Gow (1727-1807) lived nearby and, according to local folklore, liked to sit here and play.

Nigg Bay Bird Reserve — 119 E2
01463 715000 — www.rspb.org.uk
Cromarty Firth, north of Invergordon. Bird reserve. The best access is along the shore from Barbaraville.

Noltland Castle — 148 B3
01856 841815 — www.historic-scotland.gov.uk
On the island of Westray, Orkney. A fine ruined Z-plan tower built between 1560 and 1573, but never completed. Remarkable for the large number of gun loops and the impressive winding staircase.

NorNova Knitwear — 153 E2
01957 755373 — www.nornova.co.uk
Muness, Uyeasound, Unst, Shetland. Hand spinning, knitting and all things to do with wool. Lace knitting for shawls and stoles. Shetland sheep.

North Ayrshire Museum — 75 F6
01294 464174
Manse Street, Saltcoats. Local history museum housed in a mid 18th century parish church. Displays feature cottage life, Ayrshire whitework, fine art, maritime history, archaeology and natural history. Good reference and photographic collection. Children's activity and discovery area.

North East Falconry Centre — 123 D5
01466 760328 — www.huntly-falconry.co.uk
3 miles (5km) north west of Huntly. The centre has almost 65 birds of prey ranging from owls to eagles. None of the birds are caged and they are all clearly visible. Regular flying displays.

North Glen Gallery & Workshop — 61 E4
01556 600200
North Glen, Palnackie, off the A711 between Dalbeattie and Auchencairn. Gallery, workshop and home base of international artist Ed Iglehart who works with many collaborators to produce individual works of glass. Glass-blowing demonstrations. Chandeliers, experimental structures, wine goblets and many other objects. Starting point for many walks.

North Shore Pottery — 137 D6
01593 741777
Mill of Forse, Latheron, south east Caithness. Studio and showroom located in a restored oatmeal mill. Visitors can see the potter at work, creating hand thrown pots, salt-glazed and reflecting the local landscape.

North Third Trout Fisheries — 77 E2
01786 471967 www.north-third-trout-fishery.co.uk
Greathill, 5 miles (8km) south west of Stirling. A rainbow trout fly-only fishery with over 120 acres (48ha) of water set in magnificent surroundings and offering both boat and bank angling. Famed for producing large numbers of fish weighing over 10lb (4.5kg) each. Expert advice is available.

Northern Lights Candles Workshop — 118 C5
01463 831132
Lentran, 5 miles (8km) west of Inverness on the A862 towards Beauly. Located in a converted crofters cowshed made from railway sleepers. Family business where a large variety of candles are handmade using simple tools, moulds and methods.

Visitors can watch candles being made.

Noss National Nature Reserve — 151 E2
01595 693345 — www.snh.org.uk/nnr
Noss Island, Shetland. On an island off the east coast of Bressay by Lerwick. A unique three-hour tour of some of Europe's finest scenery and wildlife habitats. Visitors can see up to 100,000 sea birds and dozens of seals at close range. Spectacular caves, sea statues and rock arches. Entertaining commentary on geology, local history and folklore of Bressay and Noss islands. Puffins visible before second week in August.

Puffins on Shetland

No. 28 Charlotte Square — 20 A2
0131 243 9300 — www.nts.org.uk
In Edinburgh city centre. An attractive gallery overlooking Charlotte Square and displaying a collection of 20th century Scottish paintings.

Oban Distillery Visitor Centre — 84 B3
01631 572004
Stafford Street, Oban. Take a guided tour and learn about the ancient craft of distilling. Visitor centre with exhibition tells the history of Oban.

Oban Rare Breeds Farm Park — 84 B3
01631 770608 — www.obanrarebreeds.com
2 miles (3km) from Oban along the Glencruitten Road. Displays rare breeds of farm animals - cattle, sheep, pigs, poultry, goats. Pets' corner. Woodland walk and beautiful views.

Ochil Hills Woodland Park — 78 A1
0.5 miles north of the A91 between Alva and Tillicoultry. The remains of the grounds of Alva House (now demolished). Woodland walks and children's play area.

Oiseval Gallery — 145 D2
01851 840240 — www.oiseval.co.uk
James Smith Photography, Brue, Isle of Lewis. An exclusive collection of photographic landscapes and seascapes of the Outer Hebrides, including images of St Kilda.

Old Bridge House Museum — 61 F2
01387 256904
In Dumfries town centre on the west bank of the River Nith at Devorgilla's Bridge. Built in 1660, the house is furnished in period style to illustrate life in Dumfries over the centuries. Rooms include kitchens of 1850 and 1900, a Victorian nursery and a dental surgery dating from 1900. Devorgilla's Bridge was originally built circa 1280 by Lady Devorgilla Balliol, who endowed Balliol College, Oxford.

Old Byre Heritage Centre — 82 C1
01688 400229
1.5 miles (2.5km) south west of Dervaig on the Isle of Mull. A genuine stone byre which has been converted into a museum, tearoom and gift shop. The social history of Mull has been created in miniature.

Oldshoremore Beach

133 D4

Steps down to this scenic beach a few miles north west of Kinlochbervie.

Old Gala House 70 A2
01750 20096
Scott Crescent, 0.25 mile (0.5km) from Galashiels town centre. Dating from 1583 and set in its own grounds, the former home of the Lairds of Gala is now an interpretive centre. Displays tell the story of the house, its inhabitants and the early growth of Galashiels. Features painted ceilings (1635), a painted wall (1988) and the Thomas Clapperton Room. The Christopher Boyd Gallery hosts an exciting programme of visual art exhibitions.

Old Haa Visitor Centre 153 E5
01957 722339
Burravoe, Yell, Shetland. The oldest building on Yell, with exhibitions on local flora and fauna, arts and crafts, and local themes of historic interest. Photographs, video and sound recordings of local musicians plus story telling. Genealogical information by arrangement. Craft shop and art gallery.

Old Man of Hoy 146 A3
North west coast of Isle of Hoy, Orkney. A 450ft (137m) high isolated stack (pillar) standing off the magnificent cliffs of north west Hoy. The Old Man of Hoy can also be seen from the Scrabster to Stromness ferry. A challenge to experienced climbers.

Old Man of Stoer 127 D1
2 mile (3km) walk from Stoer Lighthouse, north of Lochinver. A 200ft (60m) high sea stack of Torridonian stone. This is the most westerly point of Sutherland and on a clear day it is possible to see the Hebridean Island of Lewis.

Old Parish Church, Hamilton 77 E5
01698 281905   www.hopc.fsnet.co.uk
Strathmore Road, Hamilton. The oldest building in Hamilton, a Georgian masterpiece designed by William Adam 1732-34, and the only church designed by him. Embroidery work and exceptionally detailed glass windows depicting the history of the church. Well-preserved 11th century Netherton Cross.

Old Place of Mochrum 59 E4
Off the B7005, 11 miles (17.5km) west of Wigtown. Known also as Drumwalt Castle, this is a mainly 15th and 16th century construction with two picturesque towers.

Old Royal Station 111 E5
013397 55306
Ballater. Restored Victorian railway station containing displays on the 100 year history of royal

use. Unique royal waiting room built for Queen Victoria.

Old Scatness Iron Age Village 151 F4
01595 694688
             www.shetland-heritage.co.uk/amenitytrust
A970 Virkie, Sumburgh, Shetland. Iron Age Broch and village with excavations in progress. Some of the buildings stand over one storey high. Replicas of some buildings. During excavations (July - August) living history and displays.

Old Steeple 30 B3
Nethergate, Dundee. Scotland's highest surviving medieval tower (154ft/47m), originally part of the great medieval church, is Dundee's oldest building dating from 1485. The tower consists of the ground floor with a vaulted ceiling 50ft (15m) high, four internal levels, bell ringing chamber, belfry and clock room.

On the Rocks 127 D2
01571 844312
Achmelvich, 3 miles (5km) north west of Lochinver. Paintings and crafts by local artists. Courses in water colour painting and gemstone cutting.

Orbost Gallery 114 B5
01470 521207   www.orbostgallery.co.uk
4 miles (6.5km) south of Dunvegan off the A863. Paintings and prints of the landscape of Skye and adjacent highlands. Also caligraphy, wood engravings and a selection of antique prints. Picture framing service available and artist's materials on sale.

Orcadian Stone Company 129 F5
01408 633483   www.orcadianstone.co.uk
Main Street, Golspie. The ground floor includes highland rocks, minerals and fossils, a geological model of Assynt, a diorama of Glencoul and interpretive panels. The upper floor contains worldwide minerals, chosen for beauty and scientific interest. Gift shop specialises in mineral specimens, stone giftware, semi-precious stone jewellery, geological books and maps.

Orchardton Tower 61 E4
0131 668 8600   www.historic-scotland.gov.uk
Off the A711, 6 miles (9.5km) south east of Castle Douglas. A charming and unique circular 15th century tower house. Built by John Cairns.

Ord of Caithness 131 D3
At the hairpin bends on the A9, north of Helmsdale. From here there are spectacular views of the Caithness coastline. In the early morning or late

Our Dynamic Earth

evening, herds of red deer can often be seen.

Ord Summit 128 C4

West of Lairg village, Sutherland. Dotted with burial mounds, hut circles, a burnt mound (a type of ancient barbecue) and topped by two chambered cairns dating back 5000 years. The view from the summit of the Ord is stunning.

Orkney Chair 147 D3

01856 873521   www.orkney-chairs.co.uk

St Ola, Kirkwall, Orkney. In Orphir Road (A964), 1.5 miles (2.5km) from town centre. See craftspeople at work making traditional Orkney chairs.

Orkney Museum 147 D2

01856 873191   www.orkney.gov.uk

Tankerness House, Broad Street, Kirkwall. Opposite St Magnus Cathedral. The museum describes island life through 6000 years, with additional special exhibitions. It is housed in a merchant-laird's mansion, with courtyard and gardens, dating from 1574.

Orkney Wireless Museum 147 D2

01856 874000   www.owm.org.uk

Kiln Corner, Junction Road, Kirkwall, Orkney. A museum explaining Orkney's wartime history which involved an intense communications network of radio and telephones to protect the home fleet in Scapa Flow. Details of a secret radar station. Also displays of domestic receivers, valves, rare equipment, gramophones, transistors. Special display of Italian POW crafts.

Ormiston Market Cross 79 F4

www.historic-scotland.gov.uk

On the B6371 in Ormiston. A 15th century cross on a modern base in the main street. A symbol of the right of the inhabitants to hold a market.

Ortak Visitor Centre 147 D2

01856 872224   www.ortak.co.uk

Hatston Industrial Estate, Kirkwall, Orkney. A permanent exhibition with a video presentation describing how modern jewellery is made and telling the story of Ortak. In July and August visitors can watch a silversmith at work.

Our Dynamic Earth 21 C2

0131 550 7800   www.dynamicearth.co.uk

107 Holyrood Road, Edinburgh. Through dramatic special effects, stunning wrap-around images and state-of-the-art interactives, visitors discover the story of the planet, from the start of time to an unknown future. See the Restless Earth volcano erupt, walk through the tropical rainforest thunderstorm and meet an ever-changing menagerie of animals. Take a dramatic helicopter flight over the magnificent Scottish mountains and feel the chill of ice in the polar region.

Our Lady of the Isles 141 D4

North of South Uist, Western Isles. On Reuval Hill - the Hill of Miracles - is the statue of the Madonna and Child, erected in 1957 by the Catholic community with contributions from all over the world. The work of Hew Lorimer, it is 30ft (9m) high.

Our Lady of the Sea 138 C4

Heaval, on the Isle of Barra, Western Isles. Heaval is the highest point in Barra at 1257ft (383m), and on the slopes of the hill is erected an attractive statue of the Madonna and Child, symbol of the islanders' faith.

Overtoun Estate 76 B3

www.overtounhouse.com

Dumbarton. Historic gardens, picnic areas, spectacular views, Victorian architecture, wildlife. Guided walks through the summer.

Paisley Abbey 76 B4

0141 889 7654   www.paisleyabbey.org.uk

Abbey Close, Paisley. A fine Cluniac abbey church founded in 1163. Some 12th century walls remain, but most of the nave dates from the 14th and 15th centuries. Restored transept and choir. Fine medieval carvings in St Mirin Chapel, stained glass and Cavaille-Coll Organ. The Abbey contains the Barochan Cross, a weathered Celtic cross attributed to the 10th century.

Paisley Museum & Art Galleries 76 B4

0141 889 3151   www.renfrewshire.gov.uk

High Street, Paisley. Displays a world-famous collection of Paisley shawls. Also the local, industrial and natural history of Paisley and Renfrewshire. Important ceramic collection and many 19th century Scottish paintings.

Palace of Holyroodhouse 21 C2

0131 556 5100   www.royalcollection.org.uk

Canongate in Edinburgh. The official residence of The Queen in Scotland. The oldest part is built against the monastic nave of Holyrood Abbey, little of which remains. The rest of the palace was reconstructed by the architect Sir William Bruce for Charles II. Home of Mary, Queen of Scots for six years and where she met John Knox. Prince Charles Edward Stuart held court here in 1745. The State Apartments house tapestries and paintings. The Picture Gallery has portraits of over 80 Scottish kings painted by De Wet 1684 - 6.

Palacerigg Country Park 77 E3

01236 720047   www.northlan.gov.uk

Palacerigg Road, 3 miles (5km) east of Cumbernauld. A 700 acre (283ha) country park with a Scottish and north European animal collection. Home to populations of roe deer, owls, bison, wildcat, lynx and moufflon. Nature trails, bridle paths and golf course.

Panbride Church 91 E2

Panbride, Carnoustie. The first mention of Panbride was in 1178 when William I gave the church and parish to Arbroath Abbey. At the church gates is a loupin stane used to assist church-goers mounting horses. By the loupin stane there is a footpath which heads north to Muirdrum. Follow this footpath for a few hundred yards and you are at the top of the fairy steps. You are supposed to make a wish on the third step.

Parallel Roads 108 A6

Glen Roy, unclassified road off the A86, 18 miles (29km) north east of Fort William. Stretching for miles in a horseshoe curve around Glen Roy these parallel roads are gravel terraces about 30ft (9m) wide. They mark the three progressively lower levels of an ice age loch which slowly drained as the glacier damming it melted.

Parent Larch 89 D1

Close to Dunkeld Cathedral. The sole survivor from a group of larches planted here as seedlings over 250 years ago. The young trees had been collected from the Tyrol mountains in central Europe in 1738.

Parish Church of St Cuthbert 20 A2

0131 229 1142   www.st-cuthberts.net

Below Edinburgh Castle. This is the seventh church on this site. Tradition has it that St Cuthbert had a small cell church here at the head of the Nor'Loch. Recorded history tells that King David I, gifted lands to 'the Church of St Cuthbert, hard by the Castle of Edinburgh'. The present building was built in 1894 to a design by Hippolyte Blanc, but retained the 1790 tower. Interior was reorganised in 1990 by Stewart Tod. Features Renaissance style stalls, marble communion table, alabaster mural, stained glass by Tiffany. Famous names in graveyard.

People's Story, Canongate Tolbooth, Edinburgh

Parliament House & Law Courts 20 B2
0131 225 2595
11 Parliament Square, Edinburgh. Behind the High Kirk of St Giles, Royal Mile. Built 1632 - 9, this was the seat of Scottish government until 1707, when the governments of Scotland and England were united. Now the Supreme Law Courts of Scotland, Parliament Hall has a fine hammer beam roof and portraits by Raeburn and other major Scottish artists. Access to the splendid Signet Library on an upper floor is by prior written request only, to: The Librarian, Signet Library, Parliament House, Edinburgh. Outside is the medieval Mercat Cross, which was restored in 1885 by W. E. Gladstone. Royal proclamations are still read from its platform.

Pass of Killiecrankie
Visitor Centre (NTS) 100 B3
01796 473233 www.nts.org.uk
On the B8079, 3 miles (5km) north of Pitlochry. Site of the 1689 battle of Killiecrankie, won by the Highland Jacobites under Bonnie Dundee. Visitors can see Soldiers Leap, where a fleeing government soldier made a spectacular jump over the River Garry during the battle.

Paxton House & County Park 81 E5
01289 386291 www.paxtonhouse.co.uk
Paxton, on the B6461, 5 miles (8km) west of Berwick-upon-Tweed. Winner of several tourism awards and one of the finest 18th century Palladian houses in Britain. Designed by John and James Adam and built in 1758 by Patrick Home for his intended bride, Sophie de Brandt, an aristocrat from the court of King Frederick the Great of Prussia. Interiors by Robert Adam. The largest collection of Chippendale furniture in Scotland, and fine Regency furniture by Trotter of Edinburgh. The largest art gallery in any Scottish house or castle, an outstation of the National Galleries of Scotland. Over 80 acres (32ha) of grounds and gardens, including a mile of the River Tweed.

Peacock Visual Arts 37 C2
01224 639539 www.peacockvisualarts.com
Castle Street, Aberdeen. A gallery hosting an annual programme of national and international art exhibitions.

Peel Farm Coffee & Crafts 101 E4
01575 560718 www.peelfarm.com
Off the B954, 20 miles (32km) north of Dundee. A working farm in an unspoilt area of rural Angus close to the majestic Reekie Linn waterfall. Craft demonstrations.

Peel Ring of Lumphanan 112 A4
01667 460232 www.historic-scotland.gov.uk
0.5 mile (1km) south west of Lumphanan. A major early medieval earthwork 120ft (36.5m) in diameter and 18ft (5.5m) high. The site of a fortified residence.

People's Palace 17 C3
0141 271 2968 www.glasgow.gov.uk
Glasgow Green, Glasgow. Opened in 1898, this collection displays the story of Glasgow and its people, and its impact on the world from 1175 to the present day. Important collections relating to the tobacco and other industries, stained glass, ceramics, political and social movements including temperance, co-operation, woman's suffrage and socialism. Photographs, film sequences and reminiscences bring to life the city's past.

People's Story 20 D4
0131 529 4057 www.cac.org.uk
In the picturesque Canongate Tolbooth, built in 1591. A lively museum which tells the story of the life, work and pastimes of the ordinary working people of Edinburgh from the late 18th century. Sights, sounds and smells. Room reconstructions, rare artefacts and everyday objects.

Perth Museum & Art Gallery 28 C2
01738 632488
George Street, Perth. Collections of local history, fine and applied art, natural history and archaeology. Changing programme of temporary exhibitions.

Perth Sculpture Trail 28 C2
Perth. Perth Sculpture Trail extends through 1 mile (1.5km) of riverside parkland. Permanent public artworks have been specially created by national and international artists.

Perth Theatre & Perth Concert Hall 28 B2
0845 612 6324 www.horsecross.co.uk
Perth. Perth Theatre has been in existence for over a hundred years and offers a wide variety of events by the Perth Theatre Company and visiting companies. Perth Concert Hall, opened in 2005, is a much larger modern venue which hosts concerts, shows and Threshold, which is a digital art space with continuously running exhibitions.

Peterhead Maritime Heritage 125 D5
01771 622807 www.aberdeenshire.gov.uk
The Lido, South Road, Peterhead. Tells the story of Peterhead maritime life in sound and vision. Observation box with telescope views across Peterhead Bay.

Phoenix Boat Trips 119 F4
01667 456078 www.phoenix-boat-trips.co.uk
Departures from Nairn Harbour to view the beauty and the wildlife of the Moray Firth.

Picardy Symbol Stone 123 F5
01667 460232 www.historic-scotland.gov.uk
Near Mireton, Insch. One of the oldest Pictish symbol stones, possibly 7th century.

Pictavia 102 C3
01356 626241 www.pictavia.org.uk
By Brechin Castle Centre, Haughmuir. Discover Scotland's ancient past through the legacy of the ancient Picts. Pictavia offers an insight into the

culture and heritage of these enigmatic people who were central to the foundation of what is now known as Scotland. Interactive exhibits, replicas and artefacts.

Pier Arts Centre 146 B3
01856 850209 www.pierartscentre.com
Victoria Street, Stromness, Orkney. Former merchant's house (circa 1800), coal store and fishermen's sheds which have been converted into a gallery. Permanent collection of 20th century paintings and sculpture as well as changing exhibitions.

Pitlochry Festival Theatre 100 B4
01796 484626 www.pitlochry.org.uk
Port-na-Craig, Pitlochry. One of Scotland's most admired repertory theatres with a resident company. Beautifully situated overlooking the river. Art gallery.

Pitmedden Garden 113 D2
01651 842352 www.nts.org.uk
Pitmedden, 14 miles (22km) north of Aberdeen near Ellon. Pitmedden's centrepiece is the Great Garden, originally laid out in 1675 by Sir Alexander Seton.

Pitmuies Gardens 91 E1
01241 828245 www.pitmuies.com
House of Pitmuies, Guthrie, 7 miles (11km) east of Forfar. Two walled gardens lead down to a small river with an informal riverside walk with fine trees and two unusual buildings - a turreted dovecote and a Gothic washhouse.

Pittencrieff House Museum 78 B2
01383 722935
Pittencrieff Park, Dunfermline. A 17th century mansion, converted by Sir Robert Lorimer into three galleries. Displays on the history of the house and park.

Pittencrieff Park 78 B2
01383 313700
Dunfermline High Street. Beautifully landscaped and maintained park. The glasshouses are planted with a mixture of perennial and seasonal plants.

Plodda Falls 108 A2
From Drumnadrochit take the A831, turning left before Cannich onto the unclassified road to Tomich. Waterfalls 100ft (30.5m) high in the spectacular surroundings of well-established broadleaf and pine forest., south of the village of Tomich. They are particularly impressive when in spate. There are viewing platforms above and below the falls.

Pluscarden Abbey 122 A4
www.pluscardenabbey.org
By the B9010, 6 miles (9.5km) south west of Elgin. Originally a Valliscaulian house, the monastery was founded in 1230. Monastic church services open to the public.

Polkemmet Country Park 78 A3
01501 743905
On the B7066 west of Whitburn. A public park with mature woodland, a 9-hole golf course, golf driving range and bowling green. Also barbecue site (bookable) and large children's play area (the Fantasy Forest). Rhododendrons in summer. Reception and restaurant/bar at the Park Centre.

Pollok House 76 C4
0141 616 6410 www.nts.org.uk
Pollok Country Park, 2060 Pollokshaws Road, 3 miles (5km) south of Glasgow city centre. Built in 1740 and extended in 1890 by Sir John Stirling Maxwell. Set within Pollok Country Park (not NTS), the house contains a renowned collection of paintings and furnishings appropriate to an Edwardian country house.

Polmaddy Settlement 60 C1
01671 402420
6 miles north of New Galloway on the A713. The last settlement in this area before the clearances of the 19th century. A short waymarked trail has interpretation boards explaining the layout of the settlement. There are some remaining features such as foundations.

Port-na-Con Souterrain 133 F3
0.5 miles (1km) north of Port na Con pier, near Durness. Marked by two cairns at the east side of the road, this is a well preserved souterrain (Iron Age store room). Take extreme care and enter at your own risk.

Portmoak Moss 89 E5
www.woodland-trust.org.uk
Between Kinnesswood and Scotlandwell, off the A911. Once a peat bog, today it is under restoration to encourage regeneration of native trees such as birch, rowan, willow and Scots pine. Circular walk within the wood.

Pràban - The Gaelic Whisky Collection 106 A3
01471 833496 www.gaelicwhisky.com
An Oifig, Eilean Iarmain, Sleat, Isle of Skye. On the A851, 8 miles (13km) south of Broadford. Pràban na Linne (meaning 'the little whisky centre by the Sound of Sleat') is the only whisky company with its headquarters in the Hebrides. An exhibition about whisky is located in historic buildings, once the Isle Ornsay harbour shop.

Pressmennan Wood 80 B3
www.wt-woods.org.uk
1 mile (2km) south of Stenton. Purchased by the Woodland Trust in 1988, the wood comprises 210 acres (85ha), formerly part of the Biel and Dirleton Estate. Pressmennan Lake was formed artificially in 1819 by constructing a dam at the eastern end of a narrow, marsh glen. Waymarked walks and forest tracks.

Preston Market Cross 79 E3
www.historic-scotland.gov.uk
0.5 mile (1km) south of Prestonpans. The only surviving example of a market cross of its type on its original site. A fine early 17th century design with a cylindrical base surmounted by a cross-shaft headed by a unicorn.

Preston Mill & Phantassie Doocot 80 A3
01620 860426 www.nts.org.uk
East Linton. Picturesque mill with stone buildings dating from the 18th century. The water wheel and grain milling machinery are still intact and visitors can see them in operation. Attractive surroundings with millponds and a short walk through fields to a 16th century Phantassie Doocot, once home to 500 pigeons.

Prestongrange Industrial Heritage Museum 79 E3
0131 653 2904 www.prestongrange.org
Morison's Haven, Prestonpans. A museum telling the story of many local industries. Displays include a historic Cornish beam engine. Steam days.

Prestonpans Battle Cairn 79 F3
East of Prestonpans on the A198. The cairn commemorates the victory of Prince Charles Edward Stuart over General Cope at the Battle of Prestonpans in 1745.

Priorwood Garden & Dried Flower Shop 70 B2
01896 822493 www.nts.org.uk
Off the A6091 in Melrose. A unique garden overlooked by the ruins of Melrose Abbey,

specialising in plants suitable for drying. Visitors can watch and learn about the drying process and buy or order dried flower arrangements in the shop. The adjacent orchard includes many varieties of historic apple trees.

Provand's Lordship   17 C2
0141 552 8819   www.glasgowmuseums.com
3 Castle Street, Glasgow. The oldest dwelling in Glasgow, built in 1471 as a manse for the St Nicholas Hospital. Period displays and furniture. Tranquil recreated medieval/renaissance herb garden.

Provost Skene's House   37 C2
01224 641086   www.aagm.co.uk
Guestrow, off Broad Street. Splendid room settings including a suite of Georgian rooms, an Edwardian nursery, 17th century ceilings and wood panelling. The painted gallery houses the most important cycle of religious painting in north east Scotland.

Puck's Glen   75 E2
6 miles north of Dunoon on the A815, near Benmore Botanic Gardens. A delightful natural walk with a viewpoint and picnic area.

Pulteney Distillery   137 E4
01955 602371   www.oldpulteney.com
Huddart Street, Wick. Distillers of the single malt Old Pulteney at the most northerly distillery on the Scottish mainland. The visitor centre describes the historical process of whisky making and gives an insight into the seafaring history of Wick.

Quarrelwood   122 A3
01343 820223   www.forestry.gov.uk
0.5 mile (1km) from the A96, west of Elgin. Oakwood and pine forest. Two waymarked trails lead to monuments and to Cutties Hillock, the site of dinosaur finds.

Quarrymill Woodland Park   89 E3
On the outskirts of Perth along the A93 Blairgowrie road. Twenty seven acres of woodland around the Annety Burn. Paths specially designed for disabled visitors.

Queen Elizabeth Forest Park
Visitor Centre   86 C5
01877 382383   www.forestry.gov.uk
Located in Aberfoyle, the Queen Elizabeth Forest Park was first designated a Forest Park by the Forestry Commission in 1953, to mark the coronation of Queen Elizabeth II. It encompasses mountain and moorland, forest and woodland, rivers and lochs, and is home to a rich variety of animal and plant life. The visitor centre is situated on a hillside above Aberfoyle, with spectacular views in all directions, and provides information on all aspects of the forest and activities throughout the year. Resident woodcarver. Orienteering routes.

Queen's Cross Church   76 C4
0141 946 6600   www.crmsociety.com
870 Garscube Road, Glasgow. The only church designed by Charles Rennie Mackintosh and now the headquarters of the Charles Rennie Mackintosh Society. Built 1898-9 in a perpendicular Gothic style.

Queen's Gallery   21 C2
0131 556 5100   www.royalcollection.org.uk
Palace of Holyrood House, Edinburgh. Built in the shell of the former Holyrood Free Church and Duchess of Gordon's School, this state-of-the-art gallery enables exhibitions of the most delicate works of art from the Royal Collection to be shown. There is a programme of changing exhibitions, focusing primarily on works from the Royal Library at Windsor Castle.

Queen's View, Loch Lomond   76 C2
Off the A809, 12 miles (19km) north north-west of Glasgow. From the west side of the road a path leads to a viewpoint where, in 1879, Queen Victoria had her first view of Loch Lomond.

Queen's View Visitor Centre   99 F3
                                 www.forestry.gov.uk
Strathtummel, 7 miles (11km) west of Pitlochry on the B8019. The centre, close to the viewpoint, is the focal point of the Tay Forest Park and provides an ideal introduction, describing the history of the people and forests in Perthshire. The view across Loch Tummel to the mountain of Schiehallion and beyond is stunning.

Queensferry Museum   78 C3
0131 331 5545   www.cac.org.uk
53 High Street, South Queensferry. The town is named in honour of the saintly Queen Margaret (died 1093), who encouraged pilgrims to use the ferry crossing to travel to the shrine of St Andrew in Fife. Describes the development of this Passage, the growth of the former Royal Burgh and the building of the Forth Bridges. Displays on life, work and pastimes, including the annual Ferry Fair and a life-size model of the Burry Man.

Quendale Water Mill   151 F3
01950 460969   www.quendalemill.shetland.co.uk
Quendale, Dunrossness, Shetland. 4 miles (6.5km) from Sumburgh Airport. A restored 19th century over-shot water mill with displays of old croft

Loch Tummel from Queen's View Visitor Centre

implements, photographs and family history.
Souvenirs and local crafts in reception area.

Quirang 115 D3
Off unclassified Staffin to Uig road, 19 miles
(30.5km) north of Portree, Isle of Skye. An
extraordinary mass of towers and pinnacles into
which cattle were driven in times of trouble. A rough
track zigzags up to the Needle, an imposing obelisk
120ft (36.5m) high. Beyond the Needle, in a large
amphitheatre, stands the Table, a huge grass-
covered rock mass where it is said that Shinty used
to be played. Impressive views.

Quoyness Chambered Cairn 149 D4
01856 872044 www.historic-scotland.gov.uk
On the east side of Els Ness on the south coast of
the island of Sanday, Orkney. A megalithic tomb
with triple retaining walls containing a passage with
a main chamber and six secondary cells. Neolithic.

Raasay Outdoor Centre 115 E6
01478 660266 www.raasayoutdoorcentre.co.uk
Raasay House, on Raasay, an island off Skye. A
variety of activities are on offer at the centre,
complemented by the island's abundance of wildlife,
forestry, scenic mountains and landscapes. Qualified
instruction in windsurfing, sailing, kayaking, rock
climbing, abseiling, mountain biking, expeditions,
forest trails, archery and orienteering. The centre, set
in a Georgian Mansion is surrounded by four acres
(1.6ha) of woodland and lawns.

Rabbie's Trail Burners 20 D4
0131 226 3133 www.rabbies.com
207 High Street, Edinburgh. Scottish Highland
minicoach tours depart all year to all areas of the
Highlands.

Rammerscales House 62 A2
01387 810229
Hightae, on the B7020, 2.5 miles (4km) from
Lochmaben. An 18th century Georgian manor house
with magnificent views over Annandale. In Adam
style and mostly unaltered. Contains rare
contemporary art and a library with 600 volumes.
Extensive and attractive grounds with walled garden.

Randolph's Leap 121 E5
7 miles (11km) south west of Forres. Impressive
views of the River Findhorn winding through a deep
sandstone gorge.

Ravens Rock Forest Walk 128 C5
www.forestry.gov.uk
At Linsidemore on the A837. A delightful and under-
frequented walk alongside the deep gorge of the Allt
Mor Burn, through old mixed woods of mature
conifers and beech trees. The paths are easy and
there is plenty to keep children interested. The
partially suspended path leads you upward to
magnificent views over the burn towards
Strathoykel.

Ravenscraig Castle 79 D1
www.historic-scotland.gov.uk
Kirkcaldy, Fife. Extensive ruins of a 15th century
castle built by James II(of Scotland) consisting of
two towers linked by a cross range. The castle sits
inside Ravenscraig Park which has pleasant
woodland and coastal footpaths.

Real Mary King's Close 20 D4
08702 430160 www.realmarykingsclose.co.uk
Warriston's Close, The Royal Mile. Step back in time
to walk through a warren of narrow streets and
closes which once lay concealed beneath the Royal
Exchange. Guided tours present an interpretation of
life in Edinburgh from the 16th to the 19th century
and recount dramatic episodes from the past.

Red Castle 103 D4
Off the A92, 7 miles (11km) south of Montrose. This
red stone tower on a steep mound beside the
sandhills of Lunan Bay probably dates from the
15th century.

Red Kite Viewing 119 D5
01463 731505
On the Black Isle at the north end of Kessock Bridge,
Inverness, off the A9 northbound. The red kite is one
of the most beautiful birds of prey in Europe. Using a
closed-circuit television camera system, live pictures
are beamed back to a monitor in the North Kessock
Tourist Information Centre where RSPB staff are on
hand to assist. From the comfort of the Tourist
Information Centre, and safe in the knowledge that
these rare birds are not being disturbed, you may
have the chance to see close-up pictures of wild red
kites nesting in the Highlands.

Red Smiddy 116 B1
Poolewe, north east of Gairloch on the A832.
Poolewe was an important centre for early
ironworking and the remains of Scotland's earliest
blast furnace - the red Smiddy - lies close to the
village on the banks of the River Ewe.

Reekie Linn Falls 101 E4
South west of Kirriemuir on the B954. Spectacular
waterfall in the natural gorged woodland, its spume
effect accounts for its smoky description.

Reelig Glen 118 C5
01463 791575 www.forestry.gov.uk
At Moniack, 8 miles from Inverness. 1 mile (0.5km)
south of the A862 Inverness to Beauly road.
Woodland walk with viewpoint and picnic place. A
feature is the number of specimen trees on the walk,
with some of the tallest trees in Britain.

Renfrew Museum 76 C4
0141 886 3149 www.renfrewshire.gov.uk
41 Canal Street, Renfrew. Located in the former
Brown Institute building, the museum illustrates
local history.

Rennibister Earth House 146 C2
01856 841815 www.historic-scotland.gov.uk
On the A965 about 4.5 miles (7km) west north-west
of Kirkwall, Orkney. A good example of an Orkney
earth house, consisting of a passage and
underground chamber with supporting roof pillars.

Rennie's Bridge 71 D2
Situated in Kelso, this is a fine five-arched bridge
built over the River Tweed in 1803 by Rennie to
replace one destroyed by the floods of 1797. On the
bridge are two lamp posts from the demolished Old
Waterloo Bridge in London, which Rennie built in
1811. There is also a fine view to Floors Castle.

Rest & Be Thankful 85 F5
At the head of Glen Croe, 4 miles (6km) north west
of Ardgartan. Aptly named steep road pass, linking
Glen Kinglas and Glen Croe. The original General
Wade road, completed in 1750, can still be seen.
This was where cattle drovers enjoyed a well
deserved break after a tough climb. Also a viewpoint.

Restenneth Priory 102 B4
www.historic-scotland.gov.uk
Off the B9113, 1.5 miles (2.5km) east north-east of
Forfar. The ruins of an Augustinian priory church.
The lower part of the tower is early Romanesque.

Revack Estate 110 B2
01479 872234
Revack Lodge, on the B970, 1 mile (2km) south of
Grantown-on-Spey. Ten miles of woodland walks
and trails, adventure playground, walled garden,

ornamental lakes, exotic orchid houses, stocked fishing and a garden centre in a 350 acre (141ha) sporting and farming estate.

Rhue Beach 127 D5
West of Ullapool. A good family beach, with safe swimming and also the possibility of catching a glimpse of seals and various sea birds.

Ri Cruin Cairn 74 B1
www.historic-scotland.gov.uk
Kilmartin Glen, 1 mile (2km) south west of Kilmartin. A Bronze Age burial cairn with the covering removed to reveal three massive cists. Axe heads are carved on one of the cist slabs.

Ring of Brogar 146 B2
01856 841815   www.historic-scotland.gov.uk
Between Loch of Harray and Loch of Stenness, 5 miles (8km) north east of Stromness, Orkney. A magnificent circle of upright stones with an enclosing ditch spanned by causeways. Neolithic.

Rispain Camp 60 A6
0131 668 8600   www.historic-scotland.gov.uk
Behind Rispain Farm, 1 mile (2km) west of Whithorn on the A746. A rectangular settlement defended by a bank and ditch. 1st or 2nd century AD.

Riverside Gallery 42 B2
01463 224781   www.riverside-gallery.co.uk
11 Bank Street, in Inverness town centre by the River Ness. Original paintings and prints by local artists. Scottish landscapes, sporting, natural history and still life are all featured.

Rob Roy & Trossachs Visitor Centre 87 D5
01877 330342   www.robroyvisitorcentre.com
Ancaster Square in Callander, 16 miles (25.5km) north west of Stirling on the A84. Discover the truth behind the remarkable life of notorious outlaw Rob Roy MacGregor in an exciting exhibition, which includes a replica black house and the opportunity to dress as a highlander. Audio-visual presentation.

Rob Roy's Grave 86 C3
West end of Balquhidder Churchyard, off the A84, 14 miles (22.5km) north-west of Callander. Three flat gravestones enclosed by railings are the graves of Rob Roy, his wife and two of his sons. The church itself contains St Angus' Stone (8th century), a 17th century bell from the old church.

Rob Roy's Statue 113 D4
Peterculter by the A93. Statue of Rob Roy standing above the Leuchar Burn.

Robert Burns Centre 61 F2
01387 264808
Mill Road, Dumfries. Situated on the west bank of the River Nith. Award-winning centre illustrates the connection between Robert Burns, Scotland's national poet, and the town of Dumfries. Situated in the town's 18th century watermill, the centre tells of Burns' last years spent in the busy streets and lively atmosphere of Dumfries in the 1790s. Film theatre shows feature films in the evening.

Robert Clapperton's Daylight Photographic Studio 70 A3
01750 20523
The Studio, 28 Scotts Place. One of the oldest surviving daylight photographic studios in the UK. The studio is set up as a working museum and photographic archive, in the building originally used by Robert Clapperton in 1867. Photographic equipment, cameras and prints. Demonstrations of black and white print processing in the original dark room can be arranged. Archive photographs and postcards for sale.

Robert Smail's Printing Works 69 F2
01896 830206   www.nts.org.uk
7-9 High Street, Innerleithen, 30 miles (48km) south of Edinburgh. Restored printing works using machinery and methods of the early 20th century. Visitors can watch the printer at work and try setting type by hand. Victorian office with many historic items. Reconstructed waterwheel.

Robert the Bruce's Cave 62 C2
01461 800285
Kirkpatrick Fleming, 3 miles (5km) north of Gretna Green. Situated in an 80 acre (33ha) estate high above the River Kirtle, the cave is reputed to be where Robert the Bruce hid for three months in 1313.

Robinson Crusoe Statue 91 D5
Lower Largo. Bronze statue of Alexander Selkirk, the real life mariner on whom Daniel Defoe based his famous character.

Rockcliffe 61 E4
01556 5023702   www.nts.org.uk
7 miles (11km) south of Dalbeattie, off the A710. The NTS owns several sites in and around the picturesque village of Rockcliffe on the Solway Firth. These include the Mote of Mark which is an ancient

Royal Botanic Garden

hill fort, Rough Island which is a bird sanctuary with access on foot at low tide, and Muckle Lands and Jubilee Path which is a beautiful stretch of coastline between Rockcliffe and Kippford.

Rogie Falls 118 B4
www.ullapool.co.uk/rogie.html
2 miles (3km) west of Strathpeffer. The word Rogie comes from the Norse language and means splashing foaming river. From the suspension bridge which spans the falls, leaping salmon may be viewed.

Rossal Interpretive Trail 134 C5
1 mile (1.5km) from the car park at Syre, on the B873 Altnaharra to Bettyhill road, Sutherland. A pre-clearance village of great historic interest. Several displays and explanations.

Rosslyn Chapel 79 D4
0131 440 2159   www.rosslynchapel.org.uk
In Roslin, 7 miles (11km) south west of Edinburgh. A 15th century chapel with unique carving throughout, including the legendary Apprentice Pillar, many references to Freemasonry and the Knights Templar. The only medieval church in Scotland used by the Scottish Episcopal Church. Featured in the book The Da Vinci Code.

Rothesay Castle 75 D4
01700 502691   www.historic-scotland.gov.uk
Castlehill Street, Rothesay, Isle of Bute. By ferry from Wemyss Bay on the A78. A remarkable 13th century castle of enclosure, circular in plan, with 16th century forework. Breaches made by Norsemen in 1240 are evident. A favourite residence of the Stewart kings.

Rothiemurchus Estate 109 F4
01479 812345   www.rothiemurchus.net
Rothiemurchus, on the B970, 1.5 miles (2.5km) from Aviemore. Guided walks, Landrover safari tours with countryside rangers. A range of tours for groups to see Highland cattle, deer and the fishery, Loch an Eilein. Various photographic viewpoints. Loch and river fishing, clay pigeon shooting and off-road driving can be booked at Rothiemurchus visitor centre. Fresh and smoked trout, venison and quality foods are available from the farm shop. Quality Scottish knitwear and craftwork from the Old School shop. Card shop. Visitor centre at Loch an Eilein.

Rough Castle 77 F3
www.historic-scotland.gov.uk
Off the B816, 6 miles (9.5km) west of Falkirk. The best preserved length of the Antonine Wall. Consists of a rampart and ditch, together with the earthworks of a fort. Also a short length of military way with quarry pits.

Rouken Glen Park 76 C5
0141 577 3000   www.eastrenfrewshire.gov.uk
Thornliebank, south Glasgow. One of Glasgow's most attractive parks with shaded walks and a waterfall. Children's playground, boating pond and garden centre.

Roving Eye 146 C3
01856 811360   www.orknet.co.uk/rov/rov.html
Houton Pier, mainland Orkney. Roving Eye boat trips explore the sunken German World War II ships of Scapa Flow. From abroad the vessel you can view images of wrecks and sea life relayed back to television monitors from the underwater 'roving eye'.

Roxburgh Castle 71 D2
Off the A699, 1 mile (1.5km) south west of Kelso. The earthworks are all that remain of the once mighty castle, destroyed in the 15th century, and the walled Royal Burgh which gave its name to the county. The present village of Roxburgh dates from a later period.

Royal Botanic Garden 79 D3
0131 552 7171   www.rbge.org.uk
20a Inverleith Row, Edinburgh. Established in 1670 on an area the size of a tennis court, it now comprises over 70 acres (28ha) of beautifully landscaped grounds. Spectacular features include the world-famous Rock Garden, the Pringle Chinese Collection and a magnificent arboretum. The amazing Glasshouse Experience, featuring Britain's tallest Palm House, leads you on a trail of discovery through Asia, Africa, the Mediterranean and the Southern Hemisphere.

Royal Burgh of Stirling Visitor Centre 77 E1
08707 200622   www.visitscottishheartlands.com
Located at Stirling Castle esplanade. The story of Royal Stirling, from the wars of independence and life in the medieval burgh, to the present day. Sound and light exhibition, multi-lingual audio-visual show.

Royal Highland Fusiliers Regimental Museum 16 A1
0141 332 5639   www.rhf.org.uk
518 Sauchiehall Street, Glasgow. A museum exhibiting medals, badges, uniforms and records which illustrate the histories of The Royal Scots Fusiliers, The Highland Light Infantry, the Royal Highland Fusiliers and Princess Margaret's Own Glasgow and Ayrshire Regiment.

Royal Lochnagar Distillery 111 D5
01339 742700
Crathie, Ballater. Guided tours of a traditional working distillery, with sample dram.

Royal Museum 20 B2
0131 247 4422   www.nms.ac.uk/royal
Chambers Street, in the centre of Edinburgh's Old Town. The museum houses international collections in a wonderful Victorian glass-topped building. Collections include applied arts, geology and zoology, natural history, social and technical history, jewellery and costume, Egyptian and African treasures. Lectures, concerts and activities for children.

Royal Scots Regimental Museum, The 20 D4
0131 310 5018
www.theroyalscots.co.uk/museum.html
The museum of the oldest regiment in the British Army, housed in Edinburgh Castle. Contains paintings, artefacts, silver and medals which tell the story of the regiment from its formation in 1633 to the present day.

Royal Scottish Academy 20 B2
0131 225 6671   www.royalscottishacademy.org
Princes Street, Edinburgh. The Royal Scottish Academy, established in 1826, is Scotland's oldest art gallery which specialises in showing contemporary art, ranging from works by Academicians and Associates of the Academy to works from students.

Royal Troon 66 B3
01292 311555   www.royaltroon.co.uk
Craigend Road, Troon. Links course created in 1878 and host of several dramatic Open Championships since 1923.

Royal Yacht Britannia, The 79 D3
0131 555 5566   www.tryb.co.uk
Ocean Drive, Leith. Visitors can view the royal family picture gallery, learn about life on board for officers and yachtsmen and see the royal barge. An audio tour takes visitors around the four main decks. See photo on the next page.

Royal Yacht Britannia

Rozelle House Galleries 66 B4
01292 445447
Rozelle Park, Monument Road, 2.5 miles (4km) from Ayr. Built in 1760 by Robert Hamilton, in the style of Robert Adam. Rebuilt in 1830 by David Bryce. Now a gallery for art and museum exhibitions.

Rumbling Bridge 78 B1
The River Devon is spanned here by two bridges one above the other. A footpath from the north side gives good access to spectacular gorges and falls, one of which is known as the Devil's Mill. Another, Cauldron Linn, is a mile downstream, whilst Vicar's Bridge is a beauty spot a mile beyond this.

Ruthven Barracks 109 E4
01667 460232   www.historic-scotland.gov.uk
On the B970, 0.5 mile (2km) south of Kingussie. The ruins of an infantry barracks erected in 1719 with two ranges of quarters and a stable block. Captured and burned by Bonnie Prince Charlie's army in 1746.

Ruthwell Cross 62 B3
01387 870249   www.historic-scotland.gov.uk
In Ruthwell Church on the B724, 8.5 miles (13.5km) south east of Dumfries. An Anglian Cross, sculptured in high relief and dating from the end of the 7th century. Considered to be one of the major monuments of Dark Age Europe. Carved with Runic characters.

Saddell Abbey 64 B2
On the B842, 9 miles (14.5km) north north-west of Campbeltown. The abbey was built in the 12th century by Somerled, Lord of the Isles, or his son Reginald. Only the walls of the original building are left, with sculptured carved tombstones.

St Abb's Head National Nature Reserve 81 E5
018907 71443   www.nts.org.uk
Off the A1107, 2 miles (3km) north of Coldingham. The most important location for cliff-nesting sea birds in south east Scotland. Remote camera link to the centre provides glimpses of nesting birds. Spectacular walks around the headland, above 300 ft (91m) cliffs. Exhibition on wildlife.

St Andrews Aquarium 91 E4
01334 474786   www.standrewsaquarium.co.uk
The Scores, St Andrews. Over 30 dramatic displays of native sea creatures. Everything from shrimps and starfish to sharks and conger eels. Graceful rays nose the surface of their display to watch you watching them. Visitors can see the resident seals and diving ducks.

St Andrews Botanic Garden 91 D4
01334 476452   www.st-andrews-botanic.org
The Canongate, St Andrews. Eighteen acres (7ha) of impressively landscaped gardens and glasshouses. Peat, rock, heath and water gardens bounded by the Kinness Burn.

St Andrews Castle 91 E4
01334 477196
www.historic-scotland.gov.uk
The Scores, St Andrews. The ruins of the castle of the Archbishops of St Andrews, dating in part from the 13th century. Notable features include a bottle dungeon and mine, and counter-mine tunnelling made during the siege that followed the murder of Cardinal Beaton in 1546. An exhibition shows the history of the castle and the cathedral.

St Andrew's Cathedral 37 C2
01224 640290
28 King Street, Aberdeen. Birthplace of the Anglican Communion overseas. The first Anglican Bishop outside of the UK was consecrated here in 1784.

St Andrews Cathedral & St Rule's Tower 91 D4
01334 472563   www.historic-scotland.gov.uk
The Scores, St Andrews. The remains of one of the largest cathedrals in Scotland and the associated domestic ranges of the priory. A museum houses an outstanding collection of early Christian and medieval monuments and other objets trouvés. St Rule's Tower in the precinct is part of the first church of the Augustinian canons at St Andrews, built early in the 12th century.

St Andrew's Church & the Glasite Hall 31 C2
King Street, Dundee. St Andrew's Church was designed by Samuel Bell and completed in 1772. It was built and paid for entirely by the Nine Trades' Guild of Dundee and there are fine stained glass windows depicting the trades emblems.

St Andrews Guided Walks 91 D4
01334 850638
Walks depart from St Andrews Pottery Shop, St Andrews. Guided walks of St Andrews cover the area around the cathedral, castle, university and golf course.

St Andrews Museum 91 D4
01334 412690
Kinburn Park, Doubledykes Road, St Andrews. Opened in 1991 in Kinburn House, a Victorian mansion set in pleasant parkland. The museum traces the development of the city as a pilgrimage shrine to St Andrew and a power centre for medieval kings and bishops, with Scotland's largest cathedral and first university.

St Andrew's Preservation Trust Museum & Garden 91 E4
01334 477629
www.standrewspreservationtrust.co.uk
12 North Street, St Andrews. A charming 16th century building with a beautiful sheltered garden. Displays include old shops and businesses in the town and some of Scotland's earliest photographs. Changing exhibitions.

St Blane's Church 75 D5
www.historic-scotland.gov.uk
At the south end of the Isle of Bute, 8.5 miles (13.5km) south of Rothesay. By ferry from Wemyss Bay on the A78. The ruins of a 12th century Romanesque chapel set within the foundations of a Celtic Monastery.

St Bride's Church
68 A2
01555 851657 www.historic-scotland.gov.uk
In Douglas, 12 miles (19km) south-west of Lanark.
The restored choir and south side of the nave of a
late 14th century parish church. The choir contains
three canopied monuments to the Douglas family.

St Bridget's Kirk, Dalgety
78 C2
www.historic-scotland.gov.uk
Off the A92 at Dalgety Bay. The shell of a medieval
church much altered in the 17th century for
Protestant worship. At the west end of the building
is a burial vault, with a laird's loft above, built for the
Earl of Dunfermline.

St Clement's Church
142 B5
www.historic-scotland.gov.uk
At Rodel, at the south end of the Isle of Harris. A fine
16th century church built by Alexander MacLeod of
Dunvegan and Harris. Contains his richly-carved
tomb.

St Columba Centre
82 B3
01681 700640 www.historic-scotland.gov.uk
Fionnphort. Exhibition on St Columba, Iona and
Celtic heritage of interest to all visitors.
Opportunities to practice script writing.

St Columba's Cave
74 A3
On the west shore of Loch Killisport (Caolisport), 10
miles (16km) south west of Ardrishaig. Traditionally
associated with St Columba's arrival in Scotland, the
cave contains a rock-shelf with an altar, above which
are carved crosses. A large basin, perhaps a Stone
Age mortar, may have been used as a font. The cave
was occupied from the Middle Stone Age. In front are
traces of houses and the ruins of a chapel (possibly
13th century). Another cave is nearby.

St Cormac's Chapel
73 F3
www.historic-scotland.gov.uk
On Eilean Mor, a small island off the coast of
Knapdale in the Sound of Jura. A chapel with a
vaulted chancel containing the effigy of an
ecclesiastical figure. Probably 12th century.

St Duthus's Chapel
119 E1
Tain. Built in the 11th or 12th century and now in
ruins. Robert the Bruce's wife and daughter were
captured here in 1306. James IV made an annual
pilgrimage to this chapel.

St Fergus Art Gallery
137 E5
01955 603489
Wick, Caithness. The gallery is situated in an
attractive 19th century building that also houses
the town's library and county archives. Exhibitions
change regularly and include a touring exhibition
and work by artists in the Highlands. All mediums
are catered for, from sculpture, painting and
ceramics to jewellery and
handmade paper.

St Fillan's Cave
91 E5
Cove Wynd, Pittenweem. A cave
associated with St Fillan, a 7th
century missionary to the Picts,
who lived in the area.

St Giles' Cathedral
20 D4
0131 225 9442
www.stgilescathedral.org.uk
On the Royal Mile in Edinburgh.
Founded in the 1100s, a triumph
of 14th and 15th century
architecture with a crown spire
that has dominated the
Edinburgh skyline for 500 years.
Contains memorials to many
great Scots, including the great
Covenanting leaders Montrose
and Argyll, Robert Louis

Stevenson and Robert Burns. Fine Victorian and 20th
century stained glass. The Thistle Chapel was
designed by Lorimer and is a jewel of Scottish
craftsmanship.

St John's
20 A2
0131 229 7565 www.stjohns-edinburgh.org.uk
Princes Street, Edinburgh. The Church of St John the
Evangelist is one of architect William Burn's early
19th century buildings. Collections of stained glass,
modern paintings and sculptures. Outside are the
graves of many famous Scots such as Sir Henry
Raeburn, Scotland's finest portrait painter, and
James Donaldson, the founder of the School for the
Deaf.

St John's Church
75 E3
Argyll Street, Dunoon. A magnificent nave and aisles
church by R. A. Bryden (1877) with Gothic spired
tower. Galleried concert hall interior, raised choir
behind central pulpit, organ 1895. Interesting
stained glass windows, including Lauder Memorial.

St John's Kirk
28 C2
01738 638482 www.st-johns-kirk.co.uk
St John's Place, Perth. Consecrated in 1242, this fine
cruciform church largely dates from the 15th
century and was restored 1923 - 26. Here in 1559
John Knox preached his momentous sermon urging
the 'purging of the churches from idolatry'.

St Kilda National Nature Reserve
144 A1
01463 232034 www.kilda.org.uk
41 miles (66km) west of Benbecula. Evacuated in
1930, these remote islands are now a World
Heritage Site, unrivalled for their sea bird colonies
and rich in archaeological remains. Each year NTS
work parties carry out conservation work. For details
of access contact NTS Regional Office on telephone
number below.

St Magnus Cathedral
147 D2
01856 874894
Broad Street, Kirkwall, Orkney. Founded by Jarl
Rognvald and dedicated to his uncle, St Magnus. The
remains of both men are in the massive east choir
piers. The original building dates from 1137-1200,
but sporadic additional work went on until the late
14th century. It contains some of the finest
examples of Norman architecture in Scotland, with
small additions in transitional styles and some early
Gothic work.

St Magnus Centre
147 D3
01856 878326
Kirkwall, Orkney. A source of information on St
Magnus and his cathedral. A 15 minute video, Saga
of Saint Magnus, tells the story of St Magnus in six
languages. Study library. Spectacular views of the
east end of St Magnus Cathedral.

Razorbill, St. Abb's Head

St Magnus Church — 148 B4
01856 841815 www.historic-scotland.gov.uk
On the Isle of Egilsay, Orkney. The complete, but roofless, ruin of a 12th century church with a remarkable round tower of the Irish type. Dramatically sited.

St Margaret's Cave — 78 B2
01383 313838
Bruce Street, Dunfermline. A site of Catholic pilgrimage where Margaret, 11th century queen and saint, sought refuge for meditation and prayer.

St Martin's Kirk — 80 A3
www.historic-scotland.gov.uk
On the eastern outskirts of Haddington. The ruined nave of a Romanesque church, altered in the 13th century.

St Mary's Cathedral — 79 D3
0131 225 6293 www.cathedral.net
Palmerston Place, in the West End of Edinburgh, near Haymarket. An Episcopal cathedral built in 1879, with the western towers added in 1917. The central spire is 276ft (84m) high. Impressive interior. Nearby is the charming Old Coates House, built in the late 17th century and now the Episcopal Church's Theological Institute.

St Mary's Chapel — 75 D4
www.historic-scotland.gov.uk
On the A845, 0.5 mile (1km) south of Rothesay on the Isle of Bute. The late-medieval remains of the chancel of the parish church of St Mary, with fine tombs.

St Mary's Chapel — 136 B3
01667 460232 www.historic-scotland.gov.uk
Off the A836, 6 miles (9.5km) west of Thurso. A simple dry-stone chapel, probably 12th century.

St Mary's Church, Grand Tully — 99 F4
www.historic-scotland.gov.uk
Off the A827 at Pitcairn Farm, 3 miles (5km) east north-east of Aberfeldy. A simple 16th century parish church with a finely painted wooden ceiling illustrating heraldic and symbolic subjects.

St Mary's Church, St Andrews — 91 E4
www.historic-scotland.gov.uk
Kirkheugh, St Andrews. The foundations of a cruciform church on the edge of a cliff. Destoyed in the Reformation this was the earliest collegiate church in Scotland.

St Mary's Collegiate Church — 80 A3
01620 823109
Sidegate, Haddington. A 14th century cruciform church, East Lothian's Cathedral. Destroyed during the Siege of Haddington in 1548, but completely restored 1971 - 3. Features Burne Jones and Sax Shaw windows; Lammermuir pipe organ. The Lauderdale Chapel is a focus for ecumenical unity.

St Mary's Episcopal Church — 79 E4
www.stmarysdalkeith.co.uk
Dalkeith Country Park. Built as a chapel for Dalkeith Palace in 1843 by William Burn and David Bryce. Early English style with many splendid features - double hammerbeam roof, glorious stained glass, heraldic floor tiles by Minton and the only working water-powered Hamilton organ in Scotland (recently restored).

St Mary's Kirk — 111 F2
01667 460232 www.historic-scotland.gov.uk
Near Lumsden, 3 miles (5km) north of Kildrummy. One of the finest medieval parish churches in Scotland, roofless, but otherwise complete. There is a rich early Romanesque doorway and a beautiful early 14th century sacrament house.

St Mary's Loch — 69 E3
Off the A708, 14 miles (22.5km) east south-east of Selkirk. Beautifully set among smooth green hills, this 3 mile (4.5km) long loch is used for sailing and fishing. On the neck of land separating it from Loch of the Lowes, at the south end, stands Tibbie Shiel's Inn. The inn was kept by Tibbie Shiel (Elizabeth Richardson, 1783 - 1878) from 1823, and was a meeting place for many 19th-century writers. Beside the road towards the north end of the loch is a seated statue of James Hogg, the Ettrick Shepherd, author of Confessions of a Justified Sinner and a friend of Scott, who farmed in this district. On the route of the Southern Upland Way.

St Mary's Medieval Church — 148 B3
01856 677777
At Pierowall on the island of Westray, Orkney. The ruins of a medieval church with some finely lettered tombstones.

St Michael's Parish Church — 78 A3
01506 842188 www.stmichaelsparish.org.uk
Kirkgate, Linlithgow. A medieval parish church consecrated in 1242 on the site of an earlier church. Close association with the royal house of Stewart - Mary, Queen of Scots was baptized here. A contemporary aluminium crown on the tower replaced the medieval stone crown removed in 1820.

St Monans Windmill — 91 E5
1 mile (2km) west of Pittenweem. A late 18th century windmill.

St Mungo Museum of Religious Life & Art — 17 C2
0141 553 2557 www.glasgowmuseums.com
2 Castle Street, next to Glasgow Cathedral. A unique museum exploring the universal themes of life, death and the hereafter through beautiful and evocative art objects associated with different religious faiths. Includes Britain's only authentic Japanese Zen garden.

St Ninian's — 75 D4
South west of Rothesay along the B878 for 2.5 miles, joining the A844 at Milton, then unclassified road to Straad. The foundations of St Ninian's chapel, dating back to the 6th century, together with its surrounding garth wall, are still clearly visible on this remote peninsula.

St Ninian's Cathedral — 60 A6
01738 632053 www.perthcathedral.co.uk
North Methven Street, Perth. St Ninian's was consecrated in 1850 as the first cathedral in Britain to be built after the Reformation.

St Ninian's Cave — 28 B1
0131 668 8600 www.historic-scotland.gov.uk
At Physgill, on the shore 4 miles (6.5km) south west of Whithorn. A cave traditionally associated with the saint. Early crosses found here are housed at Whithorn Museum. The crosses carved on the walls of the cave are now weathered.

St Ninian's Chapel — 60 A6
01542 832196
3 miles (5km) east of Fochabers. Built in 1755 ostensibly as a sheepcote, but secretly as a Catholic chapel. The oldest post-Reformation Catholic church still in use.

St Ninian's Chapel — 122 C3
0131 668 8600 www.historic-scotland.gov.uk
At Isle of Whithorn, 3 miles (5km) south east of Whithorn. The restored ruins of a 13th century chapel, probably used by pilgrims on their way to Whithorn.

St. Mary's Loch

St Orland's Stone 90 C1
www.historic-scotland.gov.uk
Near Cossans Farm, 4.5 miles (7km) west of Forfar. An early Christian sculptured slab with a cross on one side and Pictish symbols and figures on the other.

St Peter's Kirk & Parish Cross 122 A3
01896 460232 www.historic-scotland.gov.uk
Duffus. The roofless remains of the church include the base of a 14th century western tower, a 16th century vaulted porch and some interesting tombstones.

St Ronan's Wells Interpretive Centre 69 F2
01896 833583
Wells Brae, Innerleithen, on the A72, 6 miles (9.5km) from Peebles. A site associated with a novel by Sir Walter Scott. Memorabilia of Scott, information and photographs of local festival. The well water can be tasted.

St Serf's Church & Dupplin Cross 89 D4
01764 684497 www.historic-scotland.gov.uk
The parish church of Dunning, with a square Romanesque tower and tower arch. The rest of the church was rebuilt in 1810 but contains some of the original fabric.

St Triduana's Chapel 79 D3
0131 554 7400 www.historic-scotland.gov.uk
At Restalrig Church, off Restalrig Road South, 1.5 miles (2.5km) east of Edinburgh city centre. The lower part of the chapel built by James III, housing the shrine of St Triduana, a Pictish saint. The hexagonal vaulted chamber is unique.

St Vigeans Sculptured Stones 91 F1
01241 878756 www.historic-scotland.gov.uk
0.5 mile (1km) north of Arbroath. A fine collection of 32 early Christian and Pictish stones set into cottages in the village of St Vigeans. Access must be arranged in advance.

Samye Ling Tibetan Centre 69 E6
01387 373232 www.samyeling.org
Eskdalemuir, on the B709, 16 miles (25.5km) from Lockerbie. A magnificent Tibetan temple in traditional Buddhist style, in beautiful surroundings. Also guest house for visitors who attend courses on meditation, therapy, and arts and crafts. Gardens and riverside walk.

Sandaig Island Life Museum 92 A4
www.hebrideantrust.org
The Thatched Cottage Museum, Sandaig, western Tiree. Located in a terrace of traditional thatched buildings, the museum houses a unique collection of items illustrating life in a late 19th century cottar's home. The adjoining byre and barn display elements of agricultural work at the croft, a testimony to the Hebridean islanders' self-sufficiency.

Sandhaven Meal Mill 125 D3
01771 622807 www.aberdeenshire.gov.uk
Sandhaven, on the B9031, 2.5 miles (4km) west of Fraserburgh. Visitors can see how oatmeal used to be ground in this typical 19th century Scottish meal mill.

Sandwood Bay 133 D3
4 miles (6.5km) walk north from Kinlochbervie, north west Sutherland. A relatively undisturbed bay with great views. The beach is said to be haunted by a bearded mariner and is also witness to Britain's most recent recorded sighting of a mermaid.

Sanquhar Tolbooth Museum 67 F5
01659 50186
High Street, Sanquhar. Located in a fine 18th century tolbooth. Tells the story of Upper Nithsdale. Features world famous Sanquhar knitting, mines and miners of Sanquhar and Kirkconnel, history and customs of the Royal Burgh of Sanquhar, three centuries of local literature, life in Sanquhar jail, the earliest inhabitants, and the people of Upper Nithsdale, at home and at work.

Satrosphere 37 C2
01224 640340 www.satrosphere.net
Located on Constitution Street, this interactive science centre with more than 70 exciting exhibits covers all aspects of science and technology.

Savings Banks Museum 62 B3
01387 870640 www.savingsbanksmuseum.co.uk
Ruthwell, off the B724, 10 miles (16km) east of Dumfries. Housed in the original 1800 village meeting place, the museum traces the savings bank movement from its founding here in 1810 by the Rev Henry Duncan, to its growth and spread worldwide. Also displays the work of the Ruthwell Friendly Society from 1795, an early insurance scheme providing sick pay, widows' pensions, funeral grants and the chance to buy staple foods at cost price. Features restoration of the 8th century runic Ruthwell Cross.

Scalloway Castle   151 D3
01856 841815   www.historic-scotland.gov.uk
In Scalloway, 6 miles (9.5km) west of Lerwick,
Shetland. A fine castellated mansion built in 1600 in
medieval style by Patrick Stewart, Earl of Orkney.
Fell into disuse in 1615.

Scalloway Museum   150 C3
01595 880666
Main Street, Scalloway, 7 miles (11km) west of
Lerwick. Artefacts and photographs cover the history
of Scalloway over the past 100 years. A major
section is devoted to Scalloway's unique role in
World War II, when it was a secret base for
Norwegian freedom fighters. 16 Norwegian fishing
boats ran a shuttle service to Norway carrying in
weapons, ammunition and radio sets, returning with
refugees. Realising the importance of this operation,
the US Government donated three submarine
chasers which operated between 1942 and 1945.

Scott Monument

Scapa Flow   146 C3
www.scapaflow.co.uk
Sea area, enclosed by the mainland of Orkney and
the islands of Burray, South Ronaldsay, Flotta and
Hoy. Major naval anchorage in both wars and the
scene of the scuttling of the German High Seas Fleet
in 1919. Today a centre of marine activity as Flotta
is a pipeline landfall and tanker terminal for North
Sea Oil.

Scone Palace   89 E3
01738 552300   www.scone-palace.co.uk
On the A93, 2 miles (3km) north east of Perth. A
castellated palace, enlarged and embellished in
1803, incorporating the 16th century and earlier
palaces. Notable grounds and a pinetum.
Magnificent collection of porcelain, furniture, ivories,
18th century clocks and 16th century needlework.
The Moot Hill at Scone, known in the 8th century
and earlier, was the site of the famous Coronation
Stone of Scone (the Stone of Destiny), brought there
in the 9th century by Kenneth MacAlpine, King of
Scots. In 1296 the Stone was seized by the English
and taken to Westminster Abbey. In 1997 the Stone

was returned to Scotland and is now in Edinburgh
Castle.

Scotch Whisky Heritage Centre   20 D4
0131 2200441   www.whisky-heritage.co.uk
354 Castlehill, at the top of the Royal Mile. The
mystery of Scotch whisky revealed - learn about
malt, grain and blended whisky, take a barrel ride
through whisky history and meet the resident ghost.
Also free taste of whisky for adults. Whisky Bond Bar
selling over 250 different whiskies.

Scotland Street School Museum   76 C4
0141 2870500   www.glasgowmuseums.com
225 Scotland Street, 1 mile (2km) south of Glasgow
city centre. A magnificent building with twin leaded
towers and Glasgow style stone carving designed by
Charles Rennie Mackintosh in 1904. Now housing a
permanent exhibition on the history of education.
There are Victorian, World War II, 1950s and 1960s
classrooms, a drill hall and an Edwardian cookery
room.

Scotland's Secret Bunker   91 E5
01333 310301   www.secretbunker.co.uk
Crown Buildings, Troywood, on the B9131, 5 miles
(8km) from St Andrews. The amazing labyrinth built
100ft (30.5m) underground where central
government and the military commanders would
have run the country in the event of nuclear war.
Visitors can see the nuclear command centre with its
original equipment. Three cinemas show authentic
cold war films. There is a display of vehicles in the
grounds.

Scots Dyke   63 D2
Off the A7, 7 miles (11km) south of Langholm. The
remains of a wall made of clods of earth and stones,
which marked part of the border between England
and Scotland.

Scotstarvit Tower   90 C4
01334 653127   www.historic-scotland.gov.uk
Off the A916, 3 miles (5km) south of Cupar. A
handsome and well-built 15th century tower house
remodelled in the mid 16th century. Renowned as
the home of Sir John Scot.

Scott Monument   20 B2
0131 529 4068   www.cac.org.uk
East Princes Street Gardens. This imposing Gothic
structure is one of Edinburgh's most famous
landmarks. It was designed by George Meikle Kemp
to commemorate the life and work of the great
Scottish writer, Sir Walter Scott (1771 - 1832) and
was completed in 1844. It is 200ft (61m) high and
inside there are 287 steps to the top rewarding the
visitor with superb views of Edinburgh and its
surroundings. The monument is decorated with
figures from Scott's novels and the statue of Sir
Walter Scott at its base was sculpted by Sir John
Steell in Carrara marble.

Scottish Crannog Centre   88 B1
01887 830583   www.crannog.co.uk
Kenmore, 6 miles (10km) west of Aberfeldy on the
A827. A unique recreation of an Iron Age loch
dwelling, authentically built from evidence obtained
from underwater archaeological excavations of
crannogs in the loch. Visitors can walk back in time
and experience the life of crannog-dwellers.

Scottish Deer Centre   90 C4
01337 810391   www.thedeercentre.co.uk
Bow of Fife, on the A91, 3 miles (5km) west of
Cupar. Fifty-five acres (22ha) of parkland with more
than 160 deer.

Scottish Exhibition &
Conference Centre (SECC)   76 C4
0141 248 3000   www.secc.co.uk
Glasgow. Scotland's national venue for public events

and the UK's largest integrated exhibition and conference centre. The Clyde Auditorium or 'Armadillo' forms part of the complex and is an architectural landmark on the riverside.

Scottish Fisheries Museum 91 E5
01333 310628   www.scotfishmuseum.org
Anstruther. Housed in 16th to 19th century buildings, the museum displays fishing and ships' gear, model and actual fishing boats. Interior of a fisherman's cottage and extended reference library.

Scottish Football Museum 76 C4
0141 616 6139
www.scottishfootballmuseum.org.uk
Hampden Park, in the Mount Pleasant area in the south of Glasgow. Glasgow was the site of the world's first football international in 1872, when Scotland and England drew 0-0. The museum features the origins and history of the game, women's football, junior football and football fans. Visitors can see the reconstructed changing rooms and press box. Also memorabilia of Scottish football players.

Scottish Hydro-Electric Visitor Centre 100 B4
01796 473152
Pitlochry Power Station. An exhibition shows how Scottish Hydro-Electric power stations are controlled and operated. Visitors can also observe salmon coming upstream in the fish ladder and see into the station's turbine hall.

Scottish Kiltmaker Visitor Centre 42 B2
01463 222781
Hector Russell Kiltmaker, 4 - 9 Huntly Street, Inverness. Scotland's only visitor attraction devoted to the kilt. You can learn all about its history and development, its tradition and culture, as well as how it is worn today. Audio-visual, costume and tartan displays create a colourful, authentic and memorable experience. You can also see kilts being made in the world's largest kiltmaking workshop.

Scottish Liqueur Centre 89 D2
01738 787044
www.scottish-liqueur-centre.co.uk
Hilton, 7 miles (11km) north of Perth at the Bankfoot exit of the A9. The family-run company produces original Scottish liqueurs.

Scottish Maritime Museum 66 B2
01294 278283
www.scottishmaritimemuseum.org
Harbourside, Irvine. The museum reflects all aspects of Scottish maritime history. Vessels can be seen afloat in the harbour and under cover. Visitors can experience life in a 1910 shipyard worker's flat and visit the Linthouse Engine Shop, originally built in 1872, under reconstruction.

Scottish Mining Museum 79 E4
0131 663 7519
www.scottishminingmuseum.com
Lady Victoria Colliery, Newtongrange. On the A7, 10 miles (16km) south of Edinburgh. The finest surviving Victorian colliery with Scotland's largest steam engine in the winding house. Visitors can follow a miner's day in the late

19th century and learn about his work. The visitor centre contains interactive displays and exhibits, and a virtual coalface.

Scottish National Gallery of Modern Art 79 D3
0131 624 6200   www.natgalscot.ac.uk
Belford Road, 20 minute walk from west end of Edinburgh city centre. The building was designed in the 1820s by Sir William Burn and was formerly a school. It has bright spacious rooms and extensive grounds providing the perfect setting for sculptures by Barbara Hepworth, Eduardo Paolozzi, Henry Moore and others. The bulk of the collection, which amounts to almost 4000 works of art, has been amassed since 1960. There are examples of work by Matisse, Kirchner, Picasso, Magritte, Miró, Dali and Ernst. The gallery houses an unrivalled collection of 20th century Scottish art including work by Charles Rennie Mackintosh, Peploe, Fergusson and Cadell. The greatest strengths of the gallery's modern international collection are works by surrealist, German expressionist and French artists.

Scottish National Portrait Gallery 20 B1
0131 624 6200   www.natgalscot.ac.uk
1 Queen Street, in the city centre, five minute walk from Princes Street in Edinburgh. The gallery, built in the 1880s and designed by Sir Robert Rowland Anderson, provides a unique visual history of Scotland, told through the portraits of the figures who shaped it - royalty, poets, philosophers, heroes and rebels. All the portraits are of Scots but not all are by Scots. The collection holds works by great English, European and American masters such as Van Dyck, Gainsborough, Copley, Rodin, Kokoschka and Thorvaldsen. The gallery also houses the National Photography Collection.

Scottish National Portrait Gallery

Scottish Off-Road Driving Centre 90 B4
01337 860528   www.scotoffroad.co.uk
Strathmiglo, Fife. An off-road driving range covering a 100 acre (40ha) site.

Scottish Parliament, Holyrood

Scottish Parliament, Holyrood 21 C2
0131 348 5200 www.scottish.parliament.uk
Horse Wynd, Edinburgh. The Scottish parliament
moved to its home of Holyrood in 2004 and the
buildings are a striking addition to Edinburgh's
Royal Mile. There's an exhibition about the
parliament and guided tours take place on non-
business days. On business days there is public
access to see the parliament in action in the
chamber or committee room.

Scottish Sea Life Sanctuary 84 C1
01631 720386 www.sealsanctuary.co.uk
Barcaldine, Connel, on the A828, 10 miles (16km)
north of Oban. Visitors can explore over 30
fascinating natural marine habitats, including a
unique Herring Ring, and have close encounters with
many sea creatures, including seals. In a picturesque
setting among pine trees on the shore of Loch
Creran.

Scottish Seabird Centre 80 A2
01620 890202 www.seabird.org
The Harbour, North Berwick. Visitors can discover
the secret and fascinating world of Scotland's sea
birds by studying the birds close up, in their natural
environment - without disturbing them. Remote
cameras and the latest technology provide amazing
live pictures of puffins, gannets and many other sea
birds. Breathtaking views across the Firth of Forth to
the Bass Rock and Fife.

Scottish Tartans Museum 123 D3
01542 888419
The Institute, Mid Street, Keith. The museum
contains accounts of famous Scotsmen and explains
the developments of tartans and the kilt.

Scottish Vintage Bus Museum 78 B1
01383 623380 www.busweb.co.uk/svbm
M90 Commerce Park, Lathalmond, 2 miles (3km)
north of Dunfermline. A collection of over 150
historic buses from the 1920s, mostly of Scottish
origin, which can be seen in all stages of restoration.
Also many artefacts depicting Scottish bus history.
Visitors can observe restoration work or travel in a
vintage bus around the site.

Scottish Wool Centre 86 C5
01877 382850 www.scottishwoolcentre.co.uk
Off Main Street in Aberfoyle. Visitor centre and
theatre telling the story of Scottish Wool, with a live
show with live sheep. Children's farm. Traditional
spinners in action. Wide range of woollens, knitwear,
gifts and souvenirs.

Scott's View 70 B2
B6356, 4 miles east of Melrose. A view over the
Tweed to the Eildon Hills, beloved by Scott. Here the
horses taking his remains to Dryburgh for burial
stopped, as they had so often before for Sir Walter to
enjoy this panorama.

Sea Eagle Viewing 115 D5
01478 613649 www.rspb.org.uk
Portree, Isle of Skye. Located in the Aros Experience.
Displays and camera footage of sea eagle and grey
heron nest sites. RSPB staff are present between
May and September.

Seabegs Wood 77 F3
www.historic-scotland.gov.uk
1 mile (2km) west of Bonnybridge. A stretch of
rampart and ditch of the Antonine Wall with military
way behind.

Seafood Cruise 106 A2
01599 534813
8 Forestry Houses, Achmore, by Kyle. Scenic boat
tours offering marvellous views of the local scenery
and wildlife, and a delicious meal of freshly caught
fish and seafood, prepared by the seafood restaurant
based in the railway building at Kyle of Lochalsh. A
unique and enjoyable experience.

Seal Island Cruises 97 D2
01397 700714 www.oceanandoak.com
Town Pier in Fort William, next to the Crannog
Restaurant. Sail to seal island on a 90 minute cruise
aboard Souters Lass. Seal Island is home to a colony
of grey and common seals. Also view a working
salmon farm, admire the spectacular scenery,
including views of Ben Nevis, and spot other wildlife
along the coastline.

Seallam! Visitor Centre 141 E1
01859 520258 www.seallam.com
Seallam! Northton, Isle of Harris. 17 miles (27km)
south of Tarbert on the A859. A major exhibition on
the people and landscape of the Hebrides. Seallam!
is also the location for Co Leis Thu?, the genealogy
research centre for the Western Isles.

Seaprobe Atlantis 116 A6
0800 980 4846 www.seaprobe.freeserve.co.uk
Kyle of Lochalsh pier. Trips aboard the UK's only
semi-submersible passenger vessel to explore the
diverse marine life of the Kyle of Lochalsh. The
vessel has an outdoor observation deck, indoor
viewing saloon and an underwater viewing gallery.
There is a programme of frequent and varied
sailings, including otter watching, exploring
underwater kelp forests, trips to the seal and bird
colonies of Seal Island and a visit to the remains of a
World War II shipwreck.

Selkirk Glass Visitor Centre 70 A2
01750 20954
Dunsdale Haugh, on the A7 to the north of Selkirk.
Visitors can view the complete glassmaking process
and can purchase quality seconds and other gifts in
the shop.

Sensation 30 A3
01382 228800 www.sensation.org.uk
Greenmarket, Dundee. An innovative science centre,
housed in a striking building on part of a former rail
yard site. Sensation brings science to life with over
65 fun, interactive exhibits, based around the senses
and designed for people of all ages.

Seton Collegiate Church 79 F3
01875 813334 www.historic-scotland.gov.uk
Longniddry, off the A198, 1 mile (2km) south east of
Cockenzie. The chancel and apse of a fine 15th
century church. Transept and steeple added in 1513.

Shambellie House
Museum of Costume 61 F3
01387 850375 www.nms.ac.uk
New Abbey, on the A710, 7 miles (11km) south of
Dumfries. A museum housed in a mid-Victorian
country house designed by David Bryce. Costume
displays in period room settings from the National
Museums Collection.

Shawbost (Siabost) School Museum 144 C3
01851 710212
Shawbost (Siabost), 19 miles (31km) north west of
Stornoway, Isle of Lewis. Created under the Highland
Village Competition of 1970, the museum illustrates
the old way of life in Lewis.

Shetland Crofthouse Museum 151 F3
01595 695057
www.shetland-museum.org.uk/crofthouse
South Voe, Boddam. On an unclassified road, east of
the A970, 25 miles (40km) south of Lerwick. A 19th
century drystone and thatched croft, consisting of
inter-connected house, barn, byre, kiln and stable
with watermill nearby. Furnished throughout with
period implements, fixtures and furniture.

Shetland Museum 151 D2
01595 695057 www.shetland-museum.org.uk
Hay's Dock, Lerwick. A museum and archive built on
one of the last remaining sections of Lerwick's
historic dockyard. Displays cover all aspects of
Shetland's history and prehistory. Archaeology from
Neolithic to medieval times including early Christian
sculpture, Viking grave finds, medieval domestic and
fishing items. Maritime section covering fisheries,
merchant marine and shipwrecks. Agriculture and
domestic life collection, including basketwork, peat
cutting, 19th century social history. Costume
display and textiles.

Shetland Textile Working Museum 150 C1
01595 830419
Weisdale Mill, Weisdale. 8 miles (13km) north-west
of Lerwick, take the A971 and turn right on the
B9075 for 0.6 mile (1km). A unique collection of
Shetland textiles illustrating the history of spinning,
knitting and weaving in the islands from their
earliest development to the present day. Workshops
in spinning and knitting arranged and visitors have
the opportunity to see demonstrations of local craft
skills.

Shetland Wildlife Tours 150 C4
01950 422483 www.shetlandwildlife.co.uk
Longhill, Maywick. Half-day to seven-day wildlife
tours throughout the Shetland Islands with expert
naturalist guides.

Shieldaig Island 116 B4
01445 791221 www.nts.org.uk
Situated in Loch Torridon, off Shieldaig village. This
32 acre (13ha) island is almost entirely covered in
Scots pine, thought to have been planted in the mid
19th century.

Shilasdair - The Skye Yarn Company 114 B4
01470 592297 www.shilasdair-yarns.co.uk
Carnach, Waternish, Isle of Skye. 22 miles (35km)
north west of Portree on the A850, then the B886.
Fleece from the owner's flock of fine woolled sheep is
dyed in the traditional Hebridean manner with
natural dyes augmented by indigo, logwood and
cochineal. A unique range of yarns are available in
kits and finished garments. Dye garden, spinning
workshop and dyehouse open to visitors.

Shotts Heritage Centre 77 F4
01698 251000 www.northlan.gov.uk
Shotts Library, Benhar Road, Shotts. Displays three
life-size exhibits - Covenanters, a coal mine and
1940s shop front scene. Photographs and
illustrations of local history and heritage.

Silverburn Estate 90 C5
01333 427568
On the A915 Largo Road to the east of Leven.
Beautiful gardens and mature woodland, with a
variety of wildlife. Includes several paddocks used for
summer grazing for domestic animals, including
Shetland ponies. The mini farm has a collection of
farm animals and farm implements.

Sinclair & Girnigoe Castle 137 E4
www.castle-sg.org
Noss Head, near Wick. Built by Earl William Sinclair
in the 1470s. The older part of the castle, Girnigoe,
dates from between 1476 and 1486. The new wing,
locally known as Castle Sinclair, was built in 1607.
The castle was largely destroyed during a siege in
1690. It is now undergoing restoration and will be
opened to the public in stages.

Sir Hector MacDonald Monument 118 C4
Overlooking the town of Dingwall from the Mitchell
Hill Cemetery. This monument was erected in
memory of General Sir Hector MacDonald (1853 -
1903) who became an outstanding soldier, starting
his career in the Gordon Highlanders. Known as
Fighting Mac, he was born in the nearby Parish of
Ferintosh.

Sir Walter Scott's Courtroom 70 A3
01750 20096
Market Place in Selkirk, 25 miles (40km) south of
Edinburgh. The bench and chair from which Sir
Walter Scott, as Sheriff of Selkirk, administered
justice for 30 years are displayed, as are portraits of
Scott, James Hogg, Mungo Park. Watercolours by
Tom Scott RSA. Audio-visual display.

Skaill House 146 B2
01856 841501 www.skaillhouse.com
Breckness Estate, Sandwick. Beside Skara Brae, 5 miles (8km) north of Stromness. The most complete 17th century mansion house in Orkney. Built for Bishop George Graham in the 1620s, it has been inhabited by successive lairds, who have added to the house over the centuries. On show - Captain Cook's dinner service from his ship the Resolution, and gunroom with sporting and military memorabilia.

Skara Brae Prehistoric Village 146 B2
01856 841815 www.historic-scotland.gov.uk
On the B9056, 19 miles (30km) north west of Kirkwall. The best preserved group of Stone Age houses in Western Europe. Ten one-roomed houses from a former fishing village are joined by covered passages and contain stone furniture, hearths and drains. They give a remarkable picture of life in Neolithic times. There is a full scale replica of a complete house.

Skelbo Castle 129 E5
Located north of Dornoch at Skelbo. This site was probably chosen by invading Norsemen for the protection of the ships, beached on the shores of Loch Fleet, in the 9th century. The ruins can be seen from the roadside.

Skipness Castle & Chapel 74 C5
www.historic-scotland.gov.uk
On the coast at Skipness on the B8001, 10 miles (16km) south of Tarbert, Argyll. Bus from Tarbert to Skipness, then 0.5 mile (1km) walk. A fine 13th century castle with a 16th century tower house in one corner. Nearby is an early 14th century chapel with fine grave slabs.

Skye Museum of Island Life 114 C2
01470 552206 www.skyemuseum.co.uk
Kilmuir, on the A855, 5 miles (8km) north of Uig. An interesting museum of rural life housed within a group of thatched cottages. It depicts the lifestyle of the crofting community of the island a century or so ago and displays a wide range of agricultural tools and implements. One house is furnished with period furniture.

Skye Serpentarium 105 F2
01471 822209 www.skyeserpentarium.org.uk
The Old Mill, Harrapool, Broadford. On the A87, 8 miles (13km) north west of Kyleakin. A unique award-winning reptile exhibition and breeding centre in a converted water mill. Visitors can watch a world of snakes, lizards, frogs and tortoises in bright natural surroundings. Also a refuge for neglected and illegally imported reptiles. Frequent informative snake handling sessions.

Skyeskyns 114 B4
01470 592237 www.skyeskyns.co.uk
Waternish, on the B886, 4.5 miles (7km) from the A850, 19 miles (30km) north of Portree. Showroom visitors are offered guided tours of the tanning workshop, the only one of its kind in Scotland. They can see the traditional tools of the trade in use - the beam, paddles, drum, buffing wheel, combs and iron.

Sma' Shot Cottages 68 A3
0141 889 1708 www.smashot.co.uk
11-17 George Place, Paisley. A former 18th century weaver's cottage, with domestic accommodation and loom shop, linked by a garden to a 19th century artisan's house, both fully furnished. Exhibition of historic photographs and a fine collection of china and linen. Run by the Old Paisley Society.

Smailholm Tower 70 C2
01573 460365 www.historic-scotland.gov.uk
Off the B6404, 6 miles (9.5km) north west of Kelso. A small rectangular 15th century Border peel tower sited on a rocky outcrop within a stone barmkin wall. Well-preserved and containing an exhibition of costume figures and tapestries relating to Sir Walter Scott's Minstrelsy of the Scottish Borders. Scott spent some of his childhood at nearby Sandyknowe Farm.

Smithy Heritage Centre 116 C5
01520 722246
On the A896, 1 mile (2km) east of Lochcarron. A restored smithy with information on the history of the building, the business and the blacksmith who worked in it. Walk through a plantation of native trees. Speakers, demonstrations and crafts at advertised times.

Smoo Caves 133 F3
www.smoocave.org
In Durness, Sutherland. This impressive limestone cave has formed at the head of a narrow coastal inlet. An easy and safe access path has been made from the road above leading into the cave. With its entrance at least 100ft (30m) wide this is arguably one of the largest cave entrances in Britain. A wooden pathway extends into the cave and allows viewing of the second inner chamber where the Allt Smoo falls from an opening in the roof above. In the outer cave there is an ancient midden which would

Skara Brae Prehistoric Village

Smoo Cave

indicate that Stone Age man once lived here. Boat tours are available to the inner cave and waterfall in the summer.

Sorn Castle 67 D3
01290 551555
Sorn, by Mauchline, Ayrshire. A 14th century castle built on a cliff above the River Ayr. The castle was substantially added to in the 17th and 19th centuries. The interior is mainly Victorian, with many fine paintings by Scottish artists. The grounds are laid out along the riverside with handsome trees and shrubs.

Souter Johnnie's Cottage 66 A5
01655 760603   www.nts.org.uk
On the A77 Main Road in Kirkoswald, 4 miles (6.5km) south west of Maybole. Thatched cottage, home of the souter (cobbler) who inspired the character Souter Johnnie in Robert Burns' poem Tam O'Shanter. Burns memorabilia and reconstructed workshop. Restored alehouse with life-size stone figures of Burns' characters.

South Lissens Pottery 89 E5
01577 865642
22 Church Street, Milnathort. A pottery workshop located in an old Presbyterian church built in 1769. Traditional country pottery and contemporary pots decorated with unusual lustre effects.

South Rannoch Forest 99 D4
                    www.forestry.gov.uk
On the south shore of Loch Rannoch, 3 miles (4.8km) west of Kinloch Rannoch. There are fine forest walks offering panoramic views of the loch and distant hills.

Soutra Aisle 79 F4
01875 833248
Soutrahill, 0.5 miles (1km) south of the A68 or 7 miles (11km) north of the A7 on the B6368, near Gilston. From the 12th century to the 17th century, midway between Edinburgh and the magnificent Borders abbeys, stood Soutra medieval hospital - a refuge for wayfarers and the needy, high on the Royal Road, the main Anglo-Scottish highway. Visitors can see the site of the great hospital, the memorial Aisle and the unique archaeo-medical investigations and enjoy the spectacular views.

Spey Valley Smokehouse 110 B2
01479 873078
                    www.speyvalleysmokedsalmon.com
Achnagonalin, on the outskirts of Grantown-on-Spey on the B970. With a history of salmon smoking since 1888, the Spey Valley Smokehouse offers visitors the opportunity to experience the traditional smoking process in the most modern facilities. Gourmet salmon products available for purchase.

Speyside Cooperage
Visitor Centre 122 B5
01340 871108   www.speysidecooperage.co.uk
Craigellachie. Visitors can watch coopers and apprentices repairing oak casks for the whisky industry. An exhibition traces cooperage history and development.

Speyside Heather Centre 110 A2
01479 851359   www.heathercentre.com
Skye of Curr, Dulnain Bridge. Off the A95, 9 miles (14.5km) from Aviemore, 6 miles (9.5km) from Grantown-on-Spey. An exhibition, craft shop, garden centre and show garden, with heather as a speciality.

Spinningdale Cotton Mill 129 D5
In Spinningdale, between Dornoch and Bonar Bridge. The ruins of an 18th century cotton mill destroyed by fire in 1808.

Split Stone 135 E3
1 mile (1.5km) east of Melvich in the north of Sutherland. Local history says that an old woman was returning from a shopping trip and was chased by the devil. She ran round and round the stone and the devil in his temper split it. The woman escaped.

Springbank Distillery 64 B4
01586 552085   www.springbankdistillers.com
In the centre of Campbeltown. Founded in 1828, the distillery remains under the control of the great-great grandson of the original founder. Springbank Distillery is the only distillery in Scotland to carry out the entire distilling process, from traditional malting through to bottling.

Spynie Palace 122 B3
01343 546358 www.historic-scotland.gov.uk
Off the A941, 2 miles (3km) north of Elgin. The
residence of the bishops of Moray from the 14th
century to 1686. Dominated by the massive 15th
century tower.

Staffa 82 B2
www.nts.org.uk
Island 6 miles (10km) north east of Iona and 7 miles
(11km) west of Mull. Romantic uninhabited island
famed for its extraordinary basaltic column
formations. The best known of these is Fingal's Cave,
inspiration for Mendelssohn's Hebrides overture.
Visitors can view the cave from a boat, or land on
the island if weather conditions permit. A colony of
puffins nests on the island.

Staneydale Temple 150 B1
01806 841815 www.historic-scotland.gov.uk
3.5 miles (5.5km) east north-east of Walls, Shetland.
A Neolithic hall, heel-shaped externally and
containing a large oval chamber. Surrounded by the
ruins of houses, walls and cairns of the same period.

Statesman Cruises 127 F1
01971 502345
www.geocities.com/statesmancruises
Kylesku, on the A894 between Ullapool and Cape
Wrath. Cruises along a sheltered sea loch to Britain's
highest waterfall, seeing seals and cubs during
season. Commentary explains sights seen during the
cruise.

Steinacleit Cairn & Stone Circle 145 D2
01851 710395 www.historic-scotland.gov.uk
At the south end of Loch an Duin, Shader, 12 miles
(19km) north of Stornoway, Isle of Lewis. The
remains of an enigmatic building of early prehistoric
date.

Stenton Gallery 80 B3
01368 850256 www.stentongallery.com
On the B6370 (Hillfoots Trail), 3 miles (5km) from
the A1 at East Linton. Shows the best of
contemporary art throughout Scotland. Regularly
changing programme of exhibitions.

Stéphane Jaeger Knitwear 147 D4
01856 731228
Littlequoy, Burray, Orkney. Near Echnaloch, off the
A961, 12 miles (19km) south of Kirkwall. A knitwear
workshop in a traditional Orkney building. Garments
are made from wool spun and knitted from the
undyed natural fibres of the workshop's own sheep
and cashmere goats. Hand-spinning demonstrations
on request. Also collector's pieces incorporating
coloured pure cashmere, merino and silk yarns.

Stewartry Museum 60 C4
01557 331643
St Mary Street, Kirkcudbright. A wide range of
exhibits reflecting the social and natural history of
the Stewartry of Kirkcudbright. Features illustrations,
pottery and jewellery by Jessie M. King and the work
of her husband, E. A. Taylor, Phyllis Bone and other
Kirkcudbright artists. Special temporary exhibitions,
family and local history information services.

Stills Gallery 20 D4
0131 622 6200 www.stills.org
23 Cockburn Street, in Edinburgh Old Town just off
the High Street. A contemporary art gallery,
bookshop and café. Open access photography and
digital imaging labs open to visitors.

Stirling Castle 77 E1
01786 450000 www.historic-scotland.gov.uk
Castle Wynd, at the head of Stirling old town, off the
M9. Considered by many as Scotland's grandest
castle, it is certainly one of the most important. The
castle architecture is outstanding and the Great Hall
and Chapel Royal are amongst the highlights. Mary,
Queen of Scots was crowned here and narrowly
escaped death by fire in 1561. Medieval kitchen
display and exhibition on life in the royal palace.

Stirling Old Bridge 77 E1
www.historic-scotland.gov.uk
In Stirling just beside the Customs Roundabout off
the A9. A handsome bridge built in the 15th or early
16th century. The southern arch was rebuilt in 1749
after it had been blown up during the '45 rebellion
to prevent the Stuart army entering the town.

Stirling Old Town Jail 77 E1
01786 450050 www.oldtownjail.com
St John Street, at the top of the Old Town in Stirling.
A 150-year-old Victorian Gothic jail, once a military
and a civil establishment. Living history
performances detail crime and punishment through
the ages.

Stirling Smith Art Gallery & Museum 77 E1
01786 471917 www.smithartgallery.demon.co.uk
Dumbarton Road, Stirling. Displays and exhibitions

Stirling Castle

on the history of Stirling. Fine art, natural history. Educational programme (telephone for details).

Stocks, Stones & Stories 88 B3
01764 652578
Crieff. A fascinating exhibition in the basement of Crieff Town Hall, housing three of the town's conserved historical monuments: the Crieff Burgh cross; the Drummond or Mercat cross; and the town stocks - unique in design.

Stones of Stenness 146 C2
01856 841815   www.historic-scotland.gov.uk
Between Loch of Harray and Loch of Stenness, about 5 miles (8km) north east of Stromness, Orkney. The remains of a stone circle surrounded by traces of a circular earthwork.

Storehouse of Foulis 119 D3
01349 830000   www.storehouseoffoulis.co.uk
Foulis Ferry, Evanton. 16 miles (26km) north of Inverness on the A9, 1 mile (1.5km) north of Cromarty Bridge. Discover the secret of the Munro clan and explore the stories of seven centuries of land and people brought to life in the rogue's gallery. Son et lumière shows. Also information on the behaviour of seals, which visitors might see from the shore.

Storr 115 D4
Two miles (3km) from the A855, 8 miles (12.5km) north of Portree, Isle of Skye. A series of pinnacles and crags rising to 2360ft (719m). No access, but can be seen from the road. The Old Man of Storr, at the east end of the mountain, is a black obelisk, (160ft/49m) high, first climbed in 1955. Visitors can see Storr from the main road; due to erosion it is now closed to walkers.

Story of Skerryvore 92 A5
01865 311468
At Hynish village, western Tiree. Located in the old signal tower, the museum tells the story of the construction of the Skerryvore Lighthouse. Completed in 1844, by a team led by Alan Stevenson (uncle of Robert Louis Stevenson), the lighthouse is built on a remote rock over 10 miles (16km) out at sea and is the tallest in Britain.

Storybook Glen 113 D5
01224 732941   www.storybookglenaberdeen.co.uk
Maryculter, 6 miles (9.5km) west of Aberdeen. A 28 acre (11.5ha) spectacular theme park with over 100 models of nursery rhymes set in beautiful scenic gardens.

Strachur Smiddy Museum 85 E5
01369 860508
   www.scotlandwalking.co.uk/strachursmiddy/
The Clachan, Strachur, on the A815 beside Loch Fyne, 20 miles (32km) north of Dunoon and 20 miles (32km) east of Inveraray. Dating from before 1790, now restored to working order. On display are bellows, anvil, boring beam, hammers, tongs and other tools of the blacksmith and the farrier. Occasional demonstrations. Also a craft shop with a selection of modern craftwork.

Stranraer Museum 58 B3
01776 705088
Old Town Hall, George Street, Stranraer. Permanent

display on local history, archaeology, farming and polar exploration. Temporary exhibition programme throughout the year with supporting educational and family activities. Enquiry and identification service available.

Strathclyde Country Park 77 E5
01698 266155   www.northlan.gov.uk
366 Hamilton Road, Motherwell. 10 miles (16km) south of Glasgow. A 1000 acre (404ha) countryside park set in the Clyde valley. Artificial lake, mixed parkland and woodlands, and a variety of recreational facilities, including watersports. Woodland trails, countryside walks, sports pitches, sandy beaches, a caravan site, a hotel, an inn and Scotland's first theme park. The visitor centre depicts the history and wildlife of the park. Also remains of a Roman bathhouse.

Strathclyde Counrty Park

Strathearn Gallery 88 B3
01764 656100   www.strathearn-gallery.com
Crieff. Regular exhibitions of paintings and applied art by Scottish based artists and craftspeople are held throughout the year.

Strathisla Distillery 123 D3
01542 783044
Seafield Avenue, Keith. The oldest working distillery in the Highlands, established in 1786, and home to Chivas Regal blended Scotch whisky. Self-guided tour of the distillery and guided tour of the fitting store and warehouses. Whisky tasting.

Strathnaver Museum 135 D3
01641 521418   www.strathnavermuseum.org.uk
Clachan, Bettyhill, 12 miles (19km) east of Tongue. A local museum housed in the former parish church of Farr. Shows the story of the Strathnaver Clearances and the Clan Mackay. Collection of local artefacts, including prehistoric and Pictish items.

Strathspey Steam Railway   110 A3
01479 810725   www.strathspeyrailway.co.uk
Aviemore Station, Dalfaber Road, Aviemore. A steam
railway running between Aviemore and Boat of
Garten (5 miles/8km) to allow visitors to experience
a railway of the 1950s / 60s.

Stromness Museum   146 B3
01856 850025
52 Alfred Street, Stromness, Orkney. A museum of
Orkney maritime history and natural history - birds,
eggs, fossils, butterflies and moths, fishing, whaling,
Hudson's Bay Company, the German fleet in Scapa
Flow. Changing exhibitions.

Struie Viewpoint   119 D1
South of Dornoch Firth on the B9176. Overlooking
the picturesque Dornoch Firth. The Sutherland
mountains are marked on an indicator board.

Studio Jewellery Workshop, The   117 E4
01445 720227   www.studiojewellery.com
At the railway station in Achnasheen. Craft centre
incorporating jewellery/silversmithing workshop.
Viewing windows allow visitors to watch work going
on, but demonstrations are not given. Silver and gold
jewellery and small silverware are on sale, together
with other craft items. The cafe has fine views in 3
directions.

Sueno's Stone   121 E4
01667 460232   www.historic-scotland.gov.uk
At the east end of Forres. The most remarkable
Pictish sculptured monument in Britain, standing
over 20ft (6m) high (now enclosed in glass).

Sulwath Brewery   61 D3
01556 504525   www.sulwathbrewers.co.uk
Castle Douglas. Located in an old steam bakery, this
is a family-run brewery producing handcrafted beer -
two ales, a lager and a stout. Visitors can see the
production process and sample the beer.

Summer Isles Smokehouse   126 C3
01854 622353   www.summerislesfoods.com
The Smokehouse is situated at Altandhu, 5 miles
(8km) north west of Achiltibuie village, 25 miles
(40km) north west of Ullapool. A smokehouse where
visitors can view the work areas and see fish being
prepared for smoking and other processes.

Summer Queen Cruises   127 E5
01854 612472   www.summerqueen.co.uk
1 Royal Park, Ullapool, 55 miles (88km) north west
of Inverness on the A835. Boat trips to the Summer
Isles, an attractive group of islands, the largest of
which is Tanera Mhor. Pleasure cruises give views of
seals, birdlife and extraordinary rock formations. A
four-hour cruise takes in all the Summer Isles and
lands on Tanera Mhor where visitors can purchase
the unique Summer Isles stamp.

Suntrap Garden   78 C3
0131 339 7283   www.suntrap-garden.org.uk
43 Gogarbank, Edinburgh. Between the A8 and A71,
1 mile (2km) west of the city centre. A 3 acre (1.2ha)
site with several gardens in one - Italian, rock, rose,
peat and woodland. Started in 1957 by
philanthropist and keen amateur gardener George
Boyd Anderson, bequeathed to the National Trust
for Scotland and Lothian region as a centre for
gardening advice and horticultural excellence. Now
run by Oatridge Agricultural College, with excellent
demonstration facilities.

Sweeney's Cruises   76 A2
01389 752376   www.sweeny.uk.com
Balloch, Loch Lomond. Cruises at the southern end
of Loch Lomond. Private charters available.

Sweetheart Abbey   61 F3
01387 850397   www.historic-scotland.gov.uk
New Abbey, 7 miles (11km) south of Dumfries.

Splendid ruin of a late 13th century and early 14th
century Cistercian abbey founded by Devorgilla,
Lady of Galloway, in memory of her husband John
Balliol. Apart from the abbey, the principal feature is
the well-preserved precinct wall, enclosing 30 acres
(12ha).

Taigh Chearsabhagh Museum &
Arts Centre   141 E3
01876 500293   www.taigh-chearsabhagh.org
Lochmaddy, North Uist, Western Isles. Local
museum and art gallery with over 2000 archive
photos of North Uist from the 1950s and 1960s.

Tain Through Time   119 E1
01862 894089   www.tainmuseum.org.uk
Tower Street, Tain, 1 mile (2km) off the A9.
Comprises St Duthus's Chapel and Collegiate Church,
which was an important medieval pilgrimage site;
the Pilgrimage visitor centre with an audio-visual
interpretation of the history of Tain; and Tain and
District Museum offering an insight into the local
history.

Tait & Style   146 B3
01856 851186   www.taitandstyle.co.uk
Brae Studio, Stromness. A showroom where visitors
can see a collection of pure wool fashion and
furnishing accessories hand-crafted from a specially
developed felting technique.

Talbot Rice Gallery   20 B2
0131 650 2210   www.trg.ed.ac.uk
Old College, South Bridge, in the Old Town, 0.25 mile
(0.5km) from the east end of Princes Street and
Waverley station. The Red Gallery shows the
University of Edinburgh's Torrie Collection. The
White Gallery shows seven contemporary exhibitions
each year, mainly by mid-career Scottish artists, but
also artists from further afield, and occasional
historical exhibitions.

Talisker Distillery Visitor Centre   114 C6
01478 614308
Carbost, Isle of Skye. On the B8009, just off the
A863 where it joins the A87 at Sligachan. The only
distillery on Skye. An exhibition tells the history of
the distillery and its place in the community.

Tall Ship at Glasgow Harbour, The   76 C4
0141 222 2513   www.thetallship.com
100 Stobcross Road, Glasgow. West off Clydeside
Expressway. Glasgow's maritime heritage is brought
to life at the Tall Ship at Glasgow Harbour, home to
the Glenlee (1896). Exhibitions and children's
activities.

Tam O' Shanter Experience   66 B4
01292 443700   www.burnsheritagepark.com
Murdochs Lane, Alloway, 2 miles (3km) south of Ayr.
Walk your way through history, and experience the
Burns mystery and magic with two audio-visual
presentations. The first tells the story of Burns and
leads you on to the second presentation which is the
poem Tam O'Shanter in the words of Burns, using
the latest technology. See also Burns National
Heritage Park.

Tangwick Haa Museum   152 B5
01806 503389
Eshaness, Shetland. About 40 miles (64km) north of
Lerwick via the A970 and the B9078. Museum in a
restored 17th century house built by the Cheyne
family. Shows various aspects of life (agriculture,
fishing, spinning and knitting) in Northmavine
through the ages, using photographs and artefacts.
Exhibition changes annually.

Tantallon Castle   80 A2
01620 892727   www.historic-scotland.gov.uk
Off the A198, 3 miles (5km) east of North Berwick.

Sweetheart Abbey

Set on the edge of the cliffs looking out to the Bass Rock, this formidable castle was a stronghold of the Douglas family. It features earthwork defences and a massive 50ft (15m) high curtain wall. Display includes replica gun.

Tarbat Discovery Centre — 121 D1
01862 871351   www.tarbat-discovery.co.uk
Portmahomack. Housed in a beautifully restored 18th century church, records show that this site had a church on it as early as the 13th century. Recent archaeology has revealed the remains of a wealthy 8th century Pictish monastic community, the finds from which are displayed in the treasury. A recreated archaeological pit explains how the valuable artefacts were uncovered. St Coleman's Gallery describes how the local community has developed over the ages.

Tarves Heritage Centre — 124 C6
01651 851883   www.tarves.org.uk/heritage/
The Old School, Tarves. A small centre housing a recreated Victorian schoolroom and the Corbett Room which houses changing displays on local life, history and trade.

Tarves Medieval Tomb — 124 C6
01667 460232   www.historic-scotland.gov.uk
In Tarves churchyard, 15 miles (24km) north west of Aberdeen. The fine altar tomb of William Forbes, the laird who enlarged Tolquhon Castle. Remarkable carving.

Taversoe Tuick Chambered Cairn — 147 D1
01856 841815   www.historic-scotland.gov.uk
On the island of Rousay, Orkney. A Neolithic chambered mound with two burial chambers, one above the other.

Tay Rail Bridge — 90 C3
Dundee. The present bridge, carrying the main railway line from London to Aberdeen, was completed in 1887. It replaced the first Tay Rail Bridge which was blown down by a storm in 1879 with the loss of 75 lives.

Tealing Dovecot & Earth House — 91 D2
www.historic-scotland.gov.uk
0.5 mile (1km) down an unclassified road to Tealing, off the A929 5 miles (8km) north of Dundee. The dovecot dates from the late 16th century and is an elegant little building. The earth house, of Iron Age date, comprises an underground passage now uncovered.

Teampull na Trionaid — 141 D4
Cairinis (Carinish), close to the A865, North Uist. Ruined remains of an important ecclesiastical site, founded by Beatrice, daughter of Somerled, Lord of the Isles, in about 1203 on the foundations of an earlier place of worship. A major centre of learning in medieval times.

Temple Wood Stone Circles — 74 B1
www.historic-scotland.gov.uk
0.25 mile (0.5km) south west of Nether Largie, Argyll. A circle of upright stones about 3000 years old, and the remains of an earlier circle.

Tenement House, The — 16 A1
0141 3330183   www.nts.org.uk
145 Buccleuch Street, Glasgow. A typical late Victorian Glasgow tenement flat, retaining many original features. The furniture and possessions of the woman who lived here for 50 years give a fascinating glimpse of life in the early 20th century.

Teviot Water Gardens — 71 D3
01835 850253   www.teviotwatergardens.co.uk
Kirkbank House, midway between Kelso and Jedburgh on A698. The water gardens are on four levels, set amidst scenic Borders countryside. The lowest garden flows down to the River Teviot.

Thirlestane Castle — 80 A6
01578 722430   www.thirlestanecastle.co.uk
Off the A68 at Lauder. One of the seven great houses of Scotland, Thirlestane Castle was rebuilt in the 16th century as the home of the Maitland family. It became the seat of the Earls of Lauderdale and was enlarged in the 17th century by the Duke of Lauderdale, who commissioned the magnificent plasterwork ceilings in the state rooms. Still a family home, Thirlestane houses a large collection of early toys in the nursery wing, and the Border Country Life Exhibition. The old servants' hall serves as the café, and there are picnic tables alongside the adventure playground and woodland walk.

Thomas Carlyle's Birthplace — 62 B2
01576 300666   www.nts.org.uk
The Arched House, on the A74 in Ecclefechan, 5.5 miles (9km) south east of Lockerbie. Birthplace of writer Thomas Carlyle (born 1795). Furnished to reflect domestic life in his time, with an important collection of family portraits and belongings.

Threave Castle
07711 223101   www.historic-scotland.gov.uk
61 D3

North of the A75, 3 miles (5km) west of Castle Douglas. A massive tower built in the late 14th century by Archibald the Grim, Lord of Galloway. Round its base is an artillery fortification built before 1455, when the castle was besieged by James II. The castle is on an island, approached by boat.

Threave Garden & Estate
01556 502575   www.nts.org.uk
61 D3

Off A75, 1 mile (2km) west of Castle Douglas. Threave Garden has a spectacular springtime display of daffodils, colourful herbaceous beds in summer, and striking trees and heathers in autumn. The visitor centre has an exhibition and delightful terraced restaurant. Threave Estate is a wildfowl refuge, with bird hides and waymarked trails.

Three Follies at Auckengill
137 D3

Auckengill, on the A99 6 miles (9.5km) south of John o' Groats. The first folly on the left was a boats lantern; the second held a barometer, a log book and weather information; the third is known as Mervin's tower, built for a small boy who spent all his time with the workmen. The motto means hasten slowly.

Three Hills Roman Heritage Centre, The (Trimontium Museum)
01896 822651   www.trimontium.net
70 B2

The Square, Melrose. An exhibition illustrating daily life on the Roman frontier at Trimontium fortress, the remains of which can be seen on the tour. Museum contains objets trouvés.

Tighnabruaich Viewpoint
www.nts.org.uk
74 C3

North east of Tighnabruaich on the A8003. A high vantage point, with explanatory indicators identifying surrounding sites. Spectacular views over the Kyles of Bute and the islands of the Firth of Clyde.

Time Capsule
01236 449572   www.northlan.gov.uk
77 E4

100 Buchanan Street, Coatbridge. Swim through primeval swamps, ride the rapids, skate with a 14ft (4m) woolly mammoth and slide down the time tunnel. Also tiny tots play zone, ideal for toddlers.

Timespan Heritage Centre & Art Gallery
01431 821327   www.timespan.org.uk
131 D3

Dunrobin Street, Helmsdale, 70 miles (112.5km) north of Inverness, on the A9 to John o' Groats. Award-winning Timespan features the dramatic story of the Highlands, including Picts and Vikings, murder at Helmsdale Castle, the last burning of a witch, the Highland Clearances, the Kildonan Goldrush, and the North Sea oilfields. Scenes from the past are re-created with life-size sets and sound effects. Audio-visual presentation. Herb garden, beside Telford's bridge over the River Helmsdale. Art gallery with changing programme of exhibitions by leading contemporary artists.

Tobermory Distillery
01688 302645   www.burnstewartdistillers.com
95 D4

Tobermory, Isle of Mull. Malt whisky is distilled using traditional methods. Guided tours and a video presentation reveal the ingredients and distilling process.

Tolbooth Art Centre
01557 331556
60 C4

High Street, Kirkcudbright. An interpretive centre located in the 17th century tolbooth. Exhibition about the town's history as an artists' colony, including paintings by important Kirkcudbright artists. Audio-visual presentation. Temporary exhibitions programme.

Tolbooth Museum
01771 622807   www.aberdeenshire.gov.uk/heritage
113 D6

The Harbour, Stonehaven. Stonehaven's oldest building, the Earl Marischal's 16th century storehouse which served as Kincardineshire's Tolbooth from 1600 - 1767.

Tollpark & Garnhall
0131 668 8600   www.historic-scotland.gov
77 E3

West of Castlecary, this is a well-preserved section of the ditch of the Antonine Wall.

Tolquhon Castle
01651 851286   www.historic-scotland.gov.uk
113 D2

Tarves. Built for the Forbes family, the castle has an early 15th century tower with a large mansion around a courtyard. Noted for its highly ornamented gatehouse.

Tom Davidson Gallery
01896 848898   www.tomdavidson.co.uk
70 B2

High Street, Earlston, Berwickshire. On the A68, 14 miles (22km) north of Jedburgh, 38 miles (61km) south of Edinburgh. A gallery featuring mostly landscape paintings, etchings and linocuts. Davidson is known as one of Scotland's leading exponents of the linocut and he can be seen at work either cutting or printing the block.

Tomatin Distillery
01808 511444   www.tomatin.com
109 E2

Tomatin, just off the A9, 15 miles (24km) south of Inverness. Take a tour of one of Scotland's largest malt whisky distilleries.

Tomb of the Eagles
01856 831339   www.tomboftheeagles.co.uk
147 D5

Liddle, on South Ronaldsay, 20 miles (32km) south of Kirkwall. Tour starts at museum and proceeds to 5000-year-old tomb. Also a Bronze Age house. Wildlife to see en route.

Tomintoul Museum
01309 673701
110 C3

Features a reconstructed crofter's kitchen, smiddy and displays on local wildlife.

Tomnaverie Stone Circle
01667 460232   www.historic-scotland.gov.uk
111 F4

3 miles (5km) north west of Aboyne. A 4000 year old recumbent stone circle.

Torhouse Stone Circle
0131 668 8600
59 E4

Off the B733, 4 miles (6.5km) west of Wigtown. A Bronze Age recumbent circle of 19 boulders on the edge of a low mound.

Tormiston Mill
01856 761606   www.historic-scotland.gov.uk
146 C2

On the A965 about 9 miles (14.5km) west of Kirkwall, Orkney. An excellent late example of a Scottish water mill, probably built in the 1880s. The water wheel and most of the machinery have been retained. Now forms a reception centre for visitors to Maes Howe.

Torosay Castle & Gardens
01680 812421   www.torosay.com
83 F2

1 mile (2km) south east of Craignure, Isle of Mull. This Victorian family home contains furniture, pictures and scrapbooks dating from Edwardian times. Torosay is surrounded by 12 acres (5ha) of gardens, including formal terraces and a statue walk, set amidst fuchsia hedges. Woodland and water gardens, eucalyptus walk and rockery all contain many and varied plants. The gardens offer extensive views past Duart Castle and the Sound of Mull to the mountains of Arran and Lorne.

Torphichen Preceptory 78 A3
01506 653733 www.historic-scotland.gov.uk
In Torphichen village on the B792, 5 miles (8km) south south-west of Linlithgow. The tower and transepts of a church built by the Knights Hospitaller of the Order of St John of Jerusalem in the 13th century, but much altered.

Torr a'Chaisteal Fort 65 D3
0131 668 8600 www.historic-scotland.gov.uk
4 miles (6.5km) south of Blackwaterfoot, Isle of Arran. A circular Iron Age fort on a ridge.

Torridon Visitor Centre 116 C4
01445 791368 www.nts.org.uk
Off the A896, 9 miles (14.5km) south west of Kinlochewe. Around 16,000 acres (6475ha) of some of Scotland's finest mountain scenery whose peaks rise over 3000ft (914m). Of major interest to geologists, Liathach and Beinn Alligin are of red sandstone, some 750 million years old. The visitor centre at the junction of the A896 and Diabaig road has an audio-visual presentation on the local wildlife. Deer museum (unmanned) and deer park open all year. Ranger led walks in season.

Torrieston Forest Walks 122 A4
01343 820223 www.forestry.gov.uk
2 miles (3.5km) beyond Pluscarden. Three varied walks on the forested hillside.

Torrisdale Castle Organic Tannery 64 B2
01583 431233 www.torrisdalecastle.com
Torrisdale Castle on the B842, 1 mile (1.5km) south of Carradale on the east coast of Kintyre. A small rural tannery using an ancient method of tanning skins to make leather. The only organic tannery in the country. Visitors can see skins being processed by hand. Finished sheepskins for sale, as well as cushions, slippers, and gloves.

Torrylin Cairn 65 D3
0131 668 8600 www.historic-scotland.gov.uk
0.25 miles (0.5km) south east of Lagg on the south coast of the Isle of Arran. A Neolithic chambered cairn with its compartments visible.

Touchstone Maze 118 B4
Strathpeffer, west of Dingwall. A large-scale labyrinth pathway amongst standing stones and turf walls. The maze has been built to incorporate alignments with sun and moon positions.

Toward Castle 75 E4
2 miles south of Innellan on the A815. Ruins of the seat of the Clan Lamont, destroyed by the Campbells in 1646.

Townhill Country Park 78 B2
01383 725596
Town Loch, Townhill, by Dunfermline. A country park with informal recreation in lochside and woodland setting.

Traprain Law 80 A3
Off the A1, 5 miles (7.5km) west of Dunbar. A whale-backed hill, 734ft (224m) high, with Iron Age fortified site, probably continuing in use as a defended Celtic township until the 11th century. A treasure of 4th century Christian and pagan silver excavated here in 1919 is now in the Museum of Antiquities, Queen Street, Edinburgh.

Traquair House 69 F2
01896 830323 www.traquair.co.uk
Innerleithen, 6 miles (10km) south east of Peebles. Dating back to the 12th century, this is said to be the oldest continuously inhabited house in Scotland. Twenty-seven Scottish and English monarchs have visited the house, including Mary, Queen of Scots, of whom there are relics. William the Lion held court here in 1175. The well-known Bear Gates were closed in 1745, not to be reopened until the Stuarts should ascend the throne. Ale is regularly produced at the 18th century brewhouse. Exhibitions and special events are held twice during the summer months. Craft workshops, brewery with ale tasting, woodland and River Tweed walks and maze.

Treasures of the Earth 96 C2
01397 772283
Corpach, 4 miles (6.5km) from Fort William, on the A830. This is a large collection of gemstones and crystals, displayed in recreated caverns and mines, just as they were found beneath the earth. Nuggets of gold and silver, aquamarines, red garnets, rubies, opals and diamonds are amongst many other gemstones and crystals on display, some weighing hundreds of kilos.

Tron Kirk 20 D4
At the junction of High Street and South Bridge, Edinburgh. A finely proportioned building that takes its name from the public weighing beam, or tron, which once stood close by. Built between 1636 and 1647 and in use as a church until 1952. Now serves as the Old Town Information Centre with an exhibition on Old Town history.

Tropic House 60 A3
01671 404050 www.tropichouse.co.uk
Langford Nurseries, Carty Port, 2 miles (3km) south of Newton Stewart on the A714. An extensive display of carnivorous plants, including the insects which they eat. In Victorian times, explorers feared that such plants would eat humans. Exotic butterflies fly amongst the tropical plants.

Trossachs Discovery Centre 86 C5
08707 200604
Aberfoyle, Stirling. The Discovery Centre contains interactive touch screens and interpretive displays describing local geography, geology and famous local characters. Also shop selling local maps, guides and gifts.

Trossachs Pier Complex 86 B5
01877 376316
Loch Katrine, 8 miles (13km) west of Callander on the A821. Set in the heart of the Trossachs, the complex has extensive lochside walks and cycle routes, and cruises on Loch Katrine on a steam ship first launched in 1899.

Trotternish Artist Studio & Gallery 115 D2
01470 552302
Kilmaluag, Duntulm, Isle of Skye. 25 miles (40km) north of Portree on the A855. Working landscape gallery set in a beautiful part of Skye with magnificent and spectacular pinnacles and cliffs. Wide selection of originals, and mounted photographic work. All artwork exclusive to gallery.

Tullibardine Chapel 88 C4
www.historic-scotland.gov.uk
Off the A823, 6 miles (9.5km) south of Crieff. One of the most complete and unaltered small medieval churches in Scotland. Founded in 1446 and largely rebuilt circa 1500. Good architectural detail.

Tullibardine Distillery 88 C5
01764 682 252 www.tullibardine.com
Blackford, on the A9 between Perth and Stirling. The distillery is on the site of Scotland's first public brewery, operating since the 12th century, and was converted for whisky production in 1949. Closed for nine years the distillery began producing whisky again in 2004 and since then short, informative tours of the distillery with a whisky tasting have been available. Adjacent shops and café.

Turnberry Castle   65 F5
Off the A719, 6 miles (9.5km) north of Girvan. The
scant remains of the castle where Robert the Bruce
was probably born in 1274.

Turnberry Hotel Golf Courses   66 A5
01655 331000   www.turnberry.co.uk
Turnberry. Two famous world class links courses,
Ailsa and Kintyre (formerly Arran), overlooking the
isles of Arran and Ailsa Craig, which have hosted
many amateur and professional championships.
Ailsa was the venue for the Open in 1977, 1986 and
1994.

Tweed Bridge   81 D6
A698 at Coldstream, 9 miles (14.5km) east north-
east of Kelso. The 300ft (91m) long bridge was built
in 1766 by Smeaton. In the past the bridge was a
crossing into Scotland for eloping couples taking
advantage of Scotland's easier marriage laws.

Tweeddale Museum & Gallery   69 E2
01721 724820
Chambers Institute, High Street, Peebles. A 19th
century building housing a museum and gallery.
Temporary exhibitions of art and craftwork. Gallery
of local history and ornamental plasterwork.

Twelve Apostles   61 F2
Off the B729 towards Dunscore, north of Dumfries.
The largest stone circle on mainland Scotland.

Tyrebagger Forest   113 D3
01330 844537   www.forestry.gov.uk
On the A96 of Aberdeen. Waymarked walks and
sculpture trail.

Udale Bay RSPB Nature Reserve   119 E3
01463 715000   www.rspb.org.uk
0.5 mile (1km) west of Jemimaville, Black Isle. Part
of the vast spread of sand and mud deposits of Nigg
and Udale Bays National Nature Reserve. Udale Bay
is a mecca for birdwatchers. Herons, greylag geese,
widgeon, teal, mallard, goldeneye and shelduck can
all be found here in good numbers. The hide has full
disabled access and can comfortably accommodate
ten people. Colourful display panels tell visitors
about the varied birdlife.

Ugie Salmon Fish House   125 F5
01779 476209   www.ugie-salmon.co.uk
Golf Road, Peterhead. The Fish House has been used
by salmon fishermen for over 100 years. Visitors can
see the ancient art of smoking salmon and buy the
products.

Ui Church   145 E4
At Aiginis, off the A866, 2 miles (3km) east of
Stornoway, Isle of Lewis. Ruined church (pronounced
eye) containing some finely carved ancient tombs of
the Macleods of Lewis.

Uig Heritage Centre   144 A4
01851 672456
Crowlista (Cradhlastadh), Uig, 33 miles (53km) west
of Stornoway on B8011. The centre contains an
exhibition of local artefacts from the early to mid
20th century. Also photographs, croft histories, a
turn of the century replica thatched house interior
and displays of shoemaker's tools, blacksmith,
fishing, weaving and agricultural implements.

Uig Pottery   115 D3
01470 542421   www.uigpottery.co.uk
Uig, Isle of Skye. A pottery making unique and
functional pieces inspired by the surrounding area.

Ullapool Museum & Visitor Centre   127 E5
01854 612987
7 - 8 West Argyle Street, Ullapool. Housed in an A
listed historic building, a former Telford
Parliamentary Church. The award-winning museum

interprets the natural and human history of the
Lochbroom and Coigach area. This includes the
establishment of Ullapool by the British Fisheries
Society in 1788 and the voyage of the Hector in
1773, the first emigrant ship to sail direct from
Scotland to Nova Scotia. The museum displays
objects, photographs, community tapestries and
quilts, and uses audio-visual and computer
technology. Maps and records are available for
study. There is also a tape tour of the town.

Union Canal   77 F3
01324 671217
               www.waterscape.com/union_canal/
From the south of Falkirk to the centre of Edinburgh
via Linlithgow, Broxburn and Ratho. The Forth and
Clyde and the Union Canals formed an important
commercial transport corridor across central
Scotland for nearly two centuries. They fell victim to
the roads culture of the 1960s when they were
blocked at more than 30 sites and broken up into
short sections. One of the biggest canal restoration
projects in Europe, the Millennium Link has brought
the 69 miles (110km) of canal, from Glasgow and
Edinburgh and the Forth to the Clyde, back to life.

Union Suspension Bridge   81 E5
Spans the River Tweed, 2 miles (3km) south of
Paxton on an unclassified road. This suspension
bridge, the first of its type in Britain, was built by
Samuel Brown in 1820, and links England and
Scotland.

Unst Heritage Centre &
Boat Haven   153 F1
01957 711528
Haroldswick, Unst, Shetland. Local history and
family trees of Unst.

Unstan Chambered Cairn   146 B2
01856 841815   www.historic-scotland.gov.uk
About 3.5 miles (5.5km) north east of Stromness,
Orkney. A mound covering a Neolithic stone burial
chamber, divided by slabs into five compartments.

Up Helly Aa Exhibition   151 D2
St Sunniva Street, Lerwick, Shetland. An exhibition of
artefacts, photographs, costumes and a replica
galley from the annual fire festival of Up Helly Aa.
Audio-visual show.

Urquhart Bay Wood   118 C6
               www.woodland-trust.org.uk
On the north shore of Loch Ness, 1 mile (1.6km) east
of Drumnadrochit. Under restoration by the
Woodland Trust. The wood lies between the Rivers
Enrick and Coiltie and is one of the best surviving
examples of ancient wet woodland in Europe. It is a
habitat full of birds, mammals, fish and insects.
Waymarked walks.

Urquhart Castle   108 C2
01456 450551   www.historic-scotland.gov.uk
On the A82 beside Loch Ness, 2 miles (3km) south
east of Drumnadrochit. The ruins of one of the
largest castles in Scotland, which fell into decay
after 1689 and was blown up in 1692 to prevent it
being occupied by Jacobites. Most of the existing
remains date from the 16th century and include a
tower. Built on the site of a vitrified fort.

Valleyfield Wood   78 B2
On the north side of the A985, High Valleyfield, near
Culross. Beautiful woodland walks landscaped by Sir
Humphrey Repton.

Vane Farm RSPB Nature Reserve   78 C1
01577 862355   www.rspb.org.uk
Kinross, 1 mile (2km) along the B9097 east of
junction 5 off the M90. Vane Farm Visitor Centre
overlooks Loch Leven where thousands of geese and
ducks spend the winter. Two trails take visitors to

hides overlooking the wetlands and loch and through woodlands to Vane Hill.

Vennel Gallery 66 B2
01294 275059
10 Glasgow Vennel, Irvine. Gallery with a programme of changing exhibitions of contemporary art and crafts. The gallery includes the Heckling Shop, where Robert Burns worked, and the Lodging House where he lived in 1781.

Verdant Works 30 A2
01382 225282 www.verdantworks.com
West Hendersons Wynd, Dundee. A restored 19th century jute works surrounding a cobbled courtyard. Visitors can view the period office (unchanged since the last century), discover why Dundee became the jute capital of the world and see working machinery processing jute to woven cloth.

Vertical Descents 96 C3
01855 821593 www.verticaldescents.com
Inchree, Onich, 8 miles (13km) south of Fort William on the A82. Adventure activities for all levels from beginners to extremists, for groups and individuals. Canyoning, whitewater rafting, rock climbing, abseiling, raft building, mountain biking and much more.

Victoria Falls 116 B2
Off the A832, 12 miles (19km) north west of Kinlochewe, near Slattadale. Waterfall named after Queen Victoria who visited Loch Maree and the surrounding area in 1877.

Viewpark Gardens 77 E4
01698 818269 www.northlan.gov.uk
New Edinburgh Road, Viewpark, Uddingston. Off the M74 at Bellshill exit. With its ornamental gardens and colourful displays, Viewpark Gardens comprises glasshouse displays, plant collections, horticultural demonstrations, and various themed gardens including Highland, Japanese, Sustainable and Demonstration.

Vikingar! 75 F4
01475 689777 www.naleisure.co.uk
Greenock Road, Largs, 25 miles (40km) from Glasgow on the A78. The history of the Vikings in Scotland, including the Battle of Largs in 1263, is told here using multimedia. Other facilities include a swimming pool, sauna and health suite, as well as a 500 seat cinema. There is a Winter Garden café, children's play area and an activity room.

Vogrie Country Park 79 E4
01875 821990
2 miles (3km) east of Gorebridge on the B6372.

There are over 5 miles (8km) of woodland and riverside walks giving visitors year round interest and variety. Nature trails, interpretation and guided walks. Historic house open to visitors, a Garden centre, model railway, golf course and adventure play area. Events field for hire.

Wade's Bridge 88 B1
On the B846, north of Aberfeldy. The bridge across the River Tay was begun in 1733 by General Wade. It is considered to be the finest of all Wade's bridges.

Wallace's Statue 70 B2
5 miles (8km) from Melrose. A 23ft (7m) high sandstone statue commissioned in 1814 by the Earl of Buchan as a monument to Sir William Wallace.

Waltzing Waters 109 E5
01540 673752 www.waltzingwaters.co.uk
On the main street in the village of Newtonmore. Indoor water, light and music spectacular in theatrical setting.

Wanlockhead Beam Engine 68 A4
0131 668 8600 www.historic-scotland.gov.uk
In Wanlockhead, Dumfries and Galloway, on the A797. An early 19th century wooden water-balance pump for draining a lead mine, with the track of a horse engine beside it. Nearby is the privately-operated Museum of Lead Mining.

Wardlaw Mausoleum 118 C5
Kirkhill, 7 miles (11km) west of Inverness on the A862. This grade A listed burial mausoleum was built in 1634 onto the east gable of the 13th century church. The mausoleum was altered in 1722 at which time a most exceptional bartran tower was added and the interior was recast to allow the incorporation of a very elaborate memorial to Thomas Fraser, the 12th Baron Lovat.

Water of Leith Visitor Centre 79 D3
0131 455 7367 www.waterofleith.org.uk
24 Lanark Road, Edinburgh.The Water of Leith Conservation Trust operates a visitor centre with working models and explanatory displays and provides a central point for information about the river, guided walks and talks.

Waterlines 137 D6
01593 721520
Lybster, Caithness. The visitor centre explains the natural heritage of the east Caithness coast and the history of Lybster harbour, once the third most important herring port in Scotland. Live CCTV on bird cliffs, also wooden boatbuilding display.

Dolphins in the Moray Firth, see entry for WDCS Wildlife Centre on page 252

Watling Lodge 77 F2

www.historic-scotland.gov.uk
In Falkirk, signposted from the A9. The best section of the ditch of the Antonine Wall.

Waverley Paddle Steamer 16 A3

0845 130 4647   www.waverleyexcursions.co.uk
Science Centre, Glasgow. Historically one of the most interesting vessels still in operation in the country, the Waverley is the last paddle steamer to be built for service on the Clyde, and is now the last sea-going paddle steamer in the world. A variety of cruises from Glasgow and Ayr along the Clyde coast.

WDCS Wildlife Centre 122 C3

01343 820339   www.wdcs.org/mfwc
At the end of the B9104, 5 miles (8km) north of Fochabers on the A96. Housed in a former salmon fishing station built in 1768 and providing an ideal place to watch ospreys hunting, seals, dolphins, otters and many birds. Now run by the Whale and Dolphin Conservation Society (WDCS). An exhibition describes the Moray Firth dolphins and the marine environment. Hands-on activities for children.

Weavers Cottage 76 B4

01505 705588   www.nts.org.uk
The Cross, Kilbarchan, 5 miles (8km) west of Paisley. This typical cottage of an 18th century handloom weaver contains looms, weaving equipment and domestic utensils. Displays of local, historical and weaving items.

Weem Wood 99 F4

01350 727284   www.forestry.gov.uk
1.5 miles west of Aberfeldy, on the B846. A circular path takes walkers across ancient woodland-covered crags to St David's Well, a natural spring named after a 15th century local laird who lived as a hermit in one of the caves on the hillside.

Well of Seven Heads 108 A4

Off the A82 on the west shore of Loch Oich. A curious monument inscribed in English, Gaelic, French and Latin and surmounted by seven men's heads. It stands above a spring and recalls the grim story of the execution of seven brothers for the murder of the two sons of a 17th century chief of Keppoch.

West Affric 118 A6

01599 511231   www.nts.org.uk
22 miles (35.5km) east of Kyle of Lochalsh, off the A87. Stretching over 9000 acres (3642ha), this important wild and rugged landscape adjoins the NTS property at Kintail. West Affric is magnificent and challenging walking country, and includes one of the most popular east-west Highland paths. This was once the old drove road taking cattle across Scotland from the Isle of Skye to market at Dingwall.

West Highland Museum 97 D2

01397 702169   www.westhighlandmuseum.org.uk
Cameron Square, Fort William. The museum was founded in 1922 and its collections cover all aspects of Highland life. The museum is world renowned for its Jacobite memorabilia including a secret portrait of Bonnie Prince Charlie.

West Port 91 E4

www.historic-scotland.gov.uk
In South Street, St Andrews. One of the few surviving city gates in Scotland, built in 1589 and renovated in 1843.

Westquarter Dovecot 78 A3

www.historic-scotland.gov.uk
At Westquarter, near Lauriston, 2 miles (3km) east of Falkirk. A handsome rectangular dovecot with a heraldic panel dated 1647 over the entrance doorway.

Westray Heritage Centre 148 B3

01857 677414   www.westrayheritage.co.uk
7 miles (11km) from ferry terminal, minibus to Pierowall village during summer. A display on the natural heritage of Westray. Many children's hands-on activities. Large collection of black and white photos. Information on local cemeteries. Local memories of wartime, schooldays, Noup Head lighthouse, sports, kirks and sea transport.

White Horse Close

Westside Church
148 B3
01856 841815   www.historic-scotland.gov.uk
At Bay of Tuquoy on the south coast of the island of Westray, Orkney. A roofless 12th century Romanesque church. Remains of a Norse settlement to the west.

Whalebone Arch
144 C3
Bragar, on the western side of the Isle of Lewis. This arch is made from the huge jawbone of a blue whale that came ashore in 1920.

Whaligoe Steps
137 E5
At Ulbster. Three hundred flagstone steps descend the steep cliffs to a small quay below, built in the 18th century during the herring boom. Care should be taken in wet or windy conditions - the steps are not suitable for the young or infirm.

White Horse Close
20 D4
Off Canongate, Royal Mile, Edinburgh. A restored group of 17th century buildings off the High Street. The coaches to London left from White Horse Inn (named after Queen Mary's Palfrey), and there are Jacobite links.

Whiteash & Ordiequish Cycle Trails
122 C4
01343 820223   www.forestry.gov.uk
Fochabers. Three medium grade mountain bike trails through mixed forest.

Whithorn Priory & Museum
60 A5
01988 500700   www.historic-scotland.gov.uk
6 Bruce Street, Whithorn, Newton Stewart. The cradle of Christianity in Scotland, founded in the 5th century. The priory for Premonstratensian canons was built in the 12th century and became the cathedral church of Galloway. In the museum is a fine collection of early Christian stone, including the Latinus stone, the earliest Christian memorial in Scotland, and the Monreith Cross, the finest of the Whithorn school of crosses.

Whithorn Story Visitor Centre
60 A5
01988 500508
45-47 George Street, Whithorn. Since 1986 archaeologists have been investigating the site of an abandoned town. One thousand years ago the Anglo-Saxons called it Hwiterne; earlier it was called Candida Casa, the Shining House. Fifteen hundred years ago St Ninian, Scotland's first saint, built a church here. Guided tour of original dig site, priory, museum and crypts, discovery centre with archaeology puzzle. Audio-visual show, exhibitions.

Wideford Hill Chambered Cairn
147 D2
01856 841815   www.historic-scotland.gov.uk
On the west slope of Wideford Hill, 2 miles (3km) west of Kirkwall, Orkney. A fine Neolithic chambered cairn with three concentric walls and a burial chamber with three large cells.

Wigtown Martyrs' Monument
60 A4
Wigtown. Hilltop monument to the 17th century Covenanters who died for their beliefs. Their gravestones are in the churchyard and a stone shaft on the shore marks the spot where two women were drowned at the stake in 1685.

William Lamb Memorial Studio
103 E4
01674 673232
Trades Close, High Street, Montrose. The working studio of the famous Montrose sculptor includes displays of his sculptures, etchings, paintings and drawings. Also featured are his workroom and living room with self-styled furniture.

Willow Tea Rooms
16 A1
0141 3320521   www.willowtearooms.co.uk
217 Sauchiehall Street, Glasgow. The Willow Tea Rooms are housed in an original Charles Rennie Mackintosh building, designed for Miss Cranston 1904-28. Re-opened in 1983, the tearoom has the original glass and mirror work and doors, and functions as a restaurant serving light meals, teas and coffees.

Wilton Lodge Park
70 B4
01450 378023
Wilton Park Road, Hawick. 0.5 mile (1km) from the town centre. Comprises 107 acres (43 ha) of park and gardens alongside the River Teviot. Extensive shrubberies, tree-lined walks, waterfall, glasshouses and walled gardens.

Witch's Stone
119 F1
In the Littletown area of Dornoch. An upright slab bearing the date 1722, marking the place where the last witch in Scotland was burned.

Wolfstone
130 C3
Situated in a lay-by, 6 miles (9.5km) south of Helmsdale at Loth. The stone marks the spot where, in 1700, the last wolf in Scotland was killed.

Wool Stone
80 B3
In Stenton, B6370, 5 miles (7.5km) south west of Dunbar. The medieval Wool Stone, used formerly for the weighing of wool at Stenton Fair, stands on the green. See also the 14th century Rood Well, topped by a cardinal's hat, and the old doocot.

Working Sheepdogs
109 F4
01540 651310
Leault Farm, Kincraig, Kingussie. 6 miles (10km) south of Aviemore on B9152. Displays of up to eight border collies and their skilful handlers. Traditional hand-shearing displays - visitors can participate. Visitors can learn about the working day of a Highland shepherd.

Wright's of Trowmill
70 B4
01450 372555
Trowmill, on the A698, 2.5 miles (4km) north east of Hawick. A woollen weaving mill where visitors can tour the weaving unit and view the varied processes in cloth manufacture.

Writers' Museum, The
20 D4
0131 529 4901   www.cac.org.uk
Lady Stair's Close, Lawnmarket, Edinburgh. Treasure house of portraits, relics and manuscripts relating to Scotland's three great writers - Robert Burns, Sir Walter Scott and Robert Louis Stevenson. Temporary exhibitions on other writers and literary organisations.

Yarrow
69 F3
A708, west from Selkirk. A lovely valley praised by many writers including Scott, Wordsworth and Hogg. Little Yarrow Kirk dates from 1640, Scott's great-great-grandfather was minister there. Deuchar Bridge dates from the 17th century. On the surrounding hills are the remains of ancient Border keeps.

The following is a comprehensive listing of all named places and places of tourist interest which appear in this atlas. The places of tourist interest are in purple type and they are also listed and described in the separate Places of Interest section.

Administrative area abbreviations

Aber.	Aberdeenshire	*E.Renf.*	East Renfrewshire	*N.Lan.*	North Lanarkshire	*Stir.*	Stirling
Arg. & B.	Argyll & Bute	*Edin.*	Edinburgh	*Ork.*	Orkney	*W.Dun.*	West
D. & G.	Dumfries &	*Falk.*	Falkirk	*P. & K.*	Perth & Kinross		Dunbartonshire
	Galloway	*Glas.*	Glasgow	*Renf.*	Renfrewshire	*W.Isles*	Western Isles
E.Ayr.	East Ayrshire	*High.*	Highland	*S.Ayr.*	South Ayrshire		(Na h-Eileanan
E.Dun.	East	*Inclyde*	Inverclyde	*S.Lan.*	South Lanarkshire		an Iar)
	Dunbartonshire	*Midlth.*	Midlothian	*Sc.Bord.*	Scottish Borders	*W.Loth.*	West Lothian
E.Loth.	East Lothian	*N.Ayr.*	North Ayrshire	*Shet.*	Shetland		

286 Ferry information

Ferry operators

Argyll & Bute Council
01631 562125
www.argyll-bute.gov.uk

Caledonian MacBrayne
08705 650000
www.calmac.co.uk

Cromarty Ferry Company
01381 610269

Highland Council
01855 841243
www.highland.gov.uk

North Link Ferries
0845 6000 449
www.northlinkferries.co.uk

Orkney Ferries
01856 872044
www.orkneyferries.co.uk

P&O Irish Ferries
0870 24 24 777
www.poirishsea.com

Pentland Ferries
01856 831226
www.pentlandferries.co.uk

Shetland Islands Council
01426 986763
www.shetland.gov.uk/
ferries

Skye Ferry
01599 511302
www.skyeferry.gov.uk

Smyril Line
00298 34 5900
www.smyril-line.com

Stena Line
08705 707070
www.stenaline.co.uk

Super Fast Ferry Scotland
0870 234 0870
www.superfast.com

Western Ferries
01369 704452
www.western-ferries.co.uk

Ferry routes

Aberdeen to Kirkwall
6 hrs 30 mins
North Link Ferries

Aberdeen to Lerwick
12 - 14 hrs
North Link Ferries

Ardrossan to Brodick
55 mins
Caledonian MacBrayne

Ardgour to Nether
Lochaber (Corran ferry)
5 mins
Highland Council

Barra to Eriskay
40 mins
Caledonian MacBrayne

Cairnryan to Larne
1 hr - 1hr 45 mins
P&O Irish Sea

Castlebay to Lochboisdale
1 hr 50 mins
Caledonian MacBrayne

Claonaig to Lochranza
30 mins
  Summer Only
Caledonian MacBrayne

Colintraive to Rhubodach
5 mins
Caledonian MacBrayne

Coll to Tiree
1 hr 10 mins
Caledonian MacBrayne

Cromarty to Nigg
5 mins
  Summer Only
Cromarty Ferry Company

Eday to Sanday
20 mins
Orkney Ferries

Eday to Stronsay
35 mins
Orkney Ferries

Egilsay to Rousay
20 mins
Orkney Ferries

Egilsay to Wyre
20 mins
Orkney Ferries

Gills Bay to
  St Margaret's Hope
1 hr
Pentland Ferries

Glenelg to Kylerhea
5 mins
  Summer Only
Skye Ferry

Gourock to Dunoon
20 mins
Caledonian MacBrayne

Gourock to Dunoon
20 mins
Western Ferries

Houton to Flotta
15 mins
Orkney Ferries

Houton to Lyness
35 mins
Orkney Ferries

Kennacraig to Colonsay
2 hrs
Caledonian MacBrayne

Kennacraig to Port Askaig
2 hrs 5 mins
Caledonian MacBrayne

Kennacraig to Port Ellen
2 hrs 20 mins
Caledonian MacBrayne

Kirkwall to Eday
1 hr 15 mins
Orkney Ferries

Kirkwall to North
  Ronaldsay
3 hrs
Orkney Ferries

Kirkwall to Papa Westray
1 hr 50 mins
Orkney Ferries

Kirkwall to Sanday
1 hr 25 mins
Orkney Ferries

Kirkwall to Shapinsay
25 mins
Orkney Ferries

Kirkwall to Stronsay
1 hr 35 mins
Orkney Ferries

Kirkwall to Westray
1 hr 25 mins
Orkney Ferries

Largs to Cumbrae Slip
10 mins
Caledonian MacBrayne

Laxo to Whalsay
30 mins
Shetland Islands Council

Lerwick to Bergen
12 hrs 30 mins
   Summer Only
Smyril Line

Lerwick to Bressay
5 mins
Shetland Islands Council

Lerwick to Kirkwall
5 hrs 30 mins
North Link Ferries

Lerwick to Seydisfjordur
31 hrs
   Summer Only
Smyril Line

Lerwick to Skerries
2 hrs 30 mins
Shetland Islands Council

Lerwick to Torshavn
13 hrs
   Summer Only
Smyril Line

Leverburgh to Berneray
1 hr 10 mins
Caledonian MacBrayne

Lochaline to Fishnish
15 mins
Caledonian MacBrayne

Longhope to Flotta
25 mins
Orkney Ferries

Longhope to Lyness
25 mins
Orkney Ferries

Lyness to Flotta
25 mins
Orkney Ferries

Oban to Castlebay
5 hrs 10 mins
Caledonian MacBrayne

Oban to Coll
2 hrs 45 mins
Caledonian MacBrayne

Oban to Colonsay
2 hrs 20 mins
Caledonian MacBrayne

Oban to Craignure
45 mins
Caledonian MacBrayne

Oban to Lismore
50 mins
Caledonian MacBrayne

Oban to Lochboisdale
5-7 hrs
Caledonian MacBrayne

Oban to Tiree
*3 hrs 30 mins - 4 hrs
   15 mins*
Caledonian MacBrayne

Port Askaig to Colonsay
1 hr 20 mins
   Summer Only
Caledonian MacBrayne

Port Askaig to Feolin
5 mins
Western Ferries

Rosyth to Zeebrugge
17 hrs 30 mins
Superfast Ferry Scotland

Rousay to Wyre
5 mins
Orkney Ferries

Sconser to Raasay
15 mins
Caledonian MacBrayne

Scrabster to Stromness
1 hr 30 mins
North Link Ferries

Seil to Luing
5 mins
Argyll & Bute Council

Stranraer to Belfast
*1 hr 45 mins - 3 hrs
   15mins*
Stena Line

Stromness to Graemsay
15 mins
Orkney Ferries

Tarbert to Lochranza
1 hr 25 mins
   Winter Only
Caledonian MacBrayne

Tarbert to Portavadie
25 mins
Caledonian MacBrayne

Tayinloan to Gigha
20 mins
Caledonian MacBrayne

Tingwall to Rousay
25 mins
Orkney Ferries

Tingwall to Wyre
25 mins
Orkney Ferries

Tobermory to Kilchoan
35 mins
   Summer Only
Caledonian MacBrayne

Toft to Ulsta
20 mins
Shetland Islands Council

Troon to Larne
1 hr 49 mins
   Summer Only
P&O Irish Sea

Uig to Lochmaddy
1 hr 45 mins
Caledonian MacBrayne

Uig to Tarbert
1 hr 40 mins
Caledonian MacBrayne

Ullapool to Stornoway
2 hrs 45 mins
Caledonian MacBrayne

Unst to Fetlar
25 mins
Shetland Islands Council

Vidlin to Skerries
1 hr 30 mins
Shetland Islands Council

Vidlin to Whalsay
40 mins
Shetland Islands Council

Wemyss Bay to Rothesay
35 mins
Caledonian MacBrayne

Westray to Papa Westray
40 mins
Orkney Ferries

Yell to Fetlar
30 mins
Shetland Islands Council

Yell to Unst
10 mins
Shetland Islands Council

Airport information

Aberdeen Airport (ABZ)
0870 040 0006
www.baa.co.uk/main/airports/aberdeen

Barra Airport (BRR)
01871 890212
www.hial.co.uk/barra-airport.html

Benbecula Aerodrome (BEB)
01870 602310
www.hial.co.uk/benbecula-airport.html

Campbeltown (Machrihanish)
Airport (CAL)
01586 553797
www.hial.co.uk/campbeltown-airport.html

Dundee Airport (DND)
01382 662200
www.dundeecity.gov.uk/airport

Edinburgh Airport (EDI)
0870 040 0007
www.baa.co.uk/main/airports/edinburgh

Glasgow Airport (GLA)
0870 040 0008
www.baa.co.uk/main/airports/glasgow

Glasgow Prestwick International
Airport (PIK)
0871 223 0700
www.gpia.co.uk

Inverness Airport (INV)
01667 464000
www.hial.co.uk/inverness-airport.html

Islay Airport (ILY)
01496 302361
www.hial.co.uk/islay-airport.html

Kirkwall Airport(KOI)
01856 872421
www.hial.co.uk/kirkwall-airport.html

Stornoway Airport (SYY)
01851 702256
www.hial.co.uk/stornoway-airport.html

Sumburgh Airport (KOI)
01950 461000
www.hial.co.uk/sumburgh-airport.html

Tiree Airport (TRE)
01879 220456
www.hial.co.uk/tiree-airport.html

Wick Airport (WIC)
01955 602215
www.hial.co.uk/wick-airport.html

Distance chart

Distances are based on the shortest routes by classified roads.

kilometres

ABERDEEN	AYR	CARLISLE	DUMFRIES	EDINBURGH	FORT WILLIAM	GLASGOW	INVERNESS	LONDON	NEWCASTLE	PERTH	STIRLING	STRANRAER	THURSO	ULLAPOOL
282	342	337	192	246	224	165	793	362	131	184	362	308	252	
	147	93	119	217	58	322	638	235	156	99	79	504	415	
		54	148	316	150	400	491	93	213	176	160	573	482	
			117	283	119	364	545	141	182	146	107	538	451	
				211	71	248	598	167	67	57	195	421	335	
					165	105	808	378	164	155	295	282	195	
						270	642	228	92	41	135	444	357	
							850	419	180	231	399	177	91	
								439	665	668	653	1023	933	
									249	223	262	604	502	
										53	228	354	268	
											176	404	318	
												582	492	
													191	

miles (lower triangle, rows by origin)

ABERDEEN	AYR	CARLISLE	DUMFRIES	EDINBURGH	FORT WILLIAM	GLASGOW	INVERNESS	LONDON	NEWCASTLE	PERTH	STIRLING	STRANRAER	THURSO	ULLAPOOL
175														
213	91													
209	58	33												
119	74	92	73											
153	135	196	176	131										
139	36	93	74	44	102									
103	200	248	226	154	348	168								
493	397	305	339	372	502	399	528							
225	146	58	88	104	235	142	260	273						
81	97	133	113	42	102	57	112	413	155					
115	62	110	91	35	96	25	143	415	139	33				
225	49	99	66	121	183	84	248	406	163	141	109			
191	313	356	334	262	175	276	110	636	376	220	251	362		
157	258	300	280	208	121	222	56	580	312	166	198	306	119	

miles